CAMBRIDGE TEX
HISTORY OF PHILOSOPHY

—

Classic and Romantic German Aesthetics

CAMBRIDGE TEXTS IN THE
HISTORY OF PHILOSOPHY

Series editors

KARL AMERIKS
Professor of Philosophy at the University of Notre Dame

DESMOND M. CLARKE
Professor of Philosophy at University College Cork

The main objective of Cambridge Texts in the History of Philosophy is to expand the range, variety and quality of texts in the history of philosophy which are available in English. The series includes texts by familiar names (such as Descartes and Kant) and also by less well-known authors. Wherever possible, texts are published in complete and unabridged form, and translations are specially commissioned for the series. Each volume contains a critical introduction together with a guide to further reading and any necessary glossaries and textual apparatus. The volumes are designed for student use at undergraduate and postgraduate level and will be of interest not only to students of philosophy, but also to a wider audience of readers in the history of science, the history of theology and the history of ideas.

For a list of titles published in the series, please see end of book.

Classic and Romantic German Aesthetics

EDITED BY

J. M. BERNSTEIN

New School University, New York

CAMBRIDGE
UNIVERSITY PRESS

CAMBRIDGE UNIVERSITY PRESS
Cambridge, New York, Melbourne, Madrid, Cape Town, Singapore,
São Paulo, Delhi, Dubai, Tokyo

Cambridge University Press
The Edinburgh Building, Cambridge CB2 8RU, UK

Published in the United States of America by Cambridge University Press, New York

www.cambridge.org
Information on this title: www.cambridge.org/9780521001113

© Cambridge University Press 2003

First published 2003
Reprinted 2006

A catalogue record for this publication is available from the British Library

ISBN 978-0-521-80639-8 Hardback
ISBN 978-0-521-00111-3 Paperback

Transferred to digital printing 2009

Contents

Contents

Introduction

... words without spirit, method without inner illumination,
figures of speech without feeling ...

Moses Mendelssohn

Almost from the moment that modern aesthetics took on a distinctive shape in the middle of the eighteenth century there arose claims that sought to privilege aesthetic reason or experience. In the writings collected in this volume we are offered the possibility of tracing the emergence and fate of this privilege. These writings are remarkably diverse in form, ranging from Lessing's subtle mixing of art theory with art criticism, Hamann's 'rhapsody in cabbalistic prose', the manifesto for a future aesthetic philosophy entitled 'The Oldest Programme for a System of German Idealism', through Schiller's letters to his friend, Körner, Hölderlin's to Hegel, and finally to the strange fragments, neither quite philosophy nor art, of Novalis and Friedrich Schlegel. This diversity in literary form has provided reason for philosophers to keep a cautious distance from these writings, comforting themselves with the more familiar articulations of aesthetic reason found in Kant's *Critique of Judgement* and Hegel's *Aesthetics: Lectures on Fine Art*, especially Hegel's

It was Karl Ameriks who seduced me into taking on the project of editing this volume. He has been a good deal more than a commissioning editor; he has been a true collaborator. His advice at every stage along the way has been invaluable. In particular, Stefan Bird-Pollan, I, and the reader all have reason to be grateful for his patient efforts in making the translations new to this volume (the Schiller, Moritz, and Hölderlin) more philosophically accurate and more readable than at first seemed possible.

long Introduction. While these works deserve the attention that has been paid to them, so too, I want to urge, do the writings collected herein. Their philosophical weightiness has been insufficiently appreciated.[1] In a brief introduction, I thought the most helpful entrée into the world of these texts could be had through providing a theoretical framework that would characterize the main philosophical stakes running through them.

In the course of the attempt to explicate the specificity of the aesthetic there arose a simultaneous attempt to secure for it a privilege. While we are most familiar with this attempt as it appears in Nietzsche, this is not quite the form it takes in eighteenth-century aesthetics, although there are family resemblances between the two accounts. Rather, I want to argue, the most plausible account of the privilege turns upon a conception of artworks as fusing the disparate and metaphysically incommensurable domains of autonomous subjectivity and material nature, and hence, by inference, upon a conception of artistic mediums as stand-ins or plenipotentiaries for nature as (still) a source for meaningful claims. My argument has five parts: the setting up of the thesis against the background of a perceived crisis in Enlightenment reason brought on by the disenchantment of nature; the elaboration of the idea of artistic mediums in Lessing; Schiller's posing of beauty as the commensuration of freedom and sensible nature; and then the contrasting emphases of Hölderlin's tragic conception of the loss of nature with the effacement of this loss in the aesthetics of freedom of the Jena romantics, especially Friedrich Schlegel. The moment when aesthetic rationality takes on its most robust, self-authorizing articulation in romantic philosophy is equally the moment when the true claim of art becomes lost. If we watch carefully, the path that runs from Lessing to Jena romanticism looks uncannily like the path that runs from artistic modernism to the postmodern art scene of the present. So uncanny is the anticipation that we may feel it tells us more about our artistic and aesthetic present than the present can say for itself.

A crisis of reason and the aesthetic response

'I am now convinced that the highest act of reason, which embraces all Ideas, is an aesthetic act, and that *truth and goodness* are brothers *only in*

---

[1] Insufficiency does not entail absence: the suggestions for further reading on pp. xxxvi–xxxix document some high points of appreciation.

beauty.' With these infamous words the so-called 'Oldest Programme for a System of German Idealism' crystallizes the rogue moment in idealist thought when philosophical rationality in its role as mimic and defender of scientific reason is displaced by the claims of aesthetics. Aesthetic reason is a reason aestheticized, drawn out of its logical shell where the rules of deductive reason are constitutive to become, in its reformed disposition, imbued with spirit, feeling, sensuousness, life. Hence the author(s) of the 'System Programme' continues: 'The philosopher must possess just as much aesthetic power as the poet [*Dichter*] . . . The philosophy of the spirit is an aesthetic philosophy.'

The claim for aesthetic reason is best interpreted as a claim for the sort of reasoning expressed in art works as repositories for the forms of activity through which they are produced and/or consumed; hence, the claim for aesthetic reason must be, minimally, a claim about why works of art have a special claim on us which can suspend or displace the competing claims of scientific knowing and moral cognition. What kind of claim could works of art (and what is formally like them) be making that could be seen in this way? Works of art might be seen as making a peculiarly compelling claim if they could be seen as answering a *problem* given by scientific knowing and moral experience. The problem is systematically addressed in Kant's *Critique of Judgement*.

The crisis has two sides. On the one hand, it concerns the dematerialization of nature, the reduction of circumambient nature to a mechanical system whose lineaments are provided by the immaterial forms of mathematical physics. The paradigmatic allegory of the disappearance of sensuous nature and its replacement by an immaterial, mechanical system is given in the second *Meditation* by Descartes' dissolution of the sensuously resplendent piece of wax into properties (extension and malleability) graspable by the mind's eye alone. This dematerialization denies that there might be a unique, irreducible language of nature, and this is equivalent to the delegitimation of the authority of nature in favour of the authority of abstract, scientific reason. Thus the disenchantment of nature, which includes the human body, its pains and pleasures, leaves it dispossessed of voice or meaning, since all meaning is given *to* nature by (mathematical) reason. To say that reason delegitimates the authority of nature means at least that the promptings of the body come to lack *normative* authority, that they no longer operate as *reasons*, and so cannot be thought of as raising claims or demands that should (or should not) be heeded.

Such items become causal facts no different in kind than those of dead nature.

The flipside of the disenchantment of nature relates to a crisis of the subject. This crisis also involves dematerialization, the self losing its substantiality, its worldliness. Once nature is figured as a mechanical system, the self is divorced from the natural world as such. Again, it is easiest to begin with Descartes: only after he submits the whole of the natural world and his immediate experience of it to doubt does he discover what he cannot doubt: that he is thinking, and hence that he is by nature a thinking thing. Descartes' *cogito*, the sole survivor of methodical doubt, appears as utterly worldless. Kant thought Descartes still assumed too much by regarding the self as a substance of some kind. The 'I think', Kant argued, must be viewed solely through the activities which we must ascribe to it for a coherent experience of the world to be possible. So, as knower, the self becomes the active locus of the categorial forms, which shape and organize the sensory given so that it can be experienced as object related. Cognitively, the 'I think' is exhausted in executing this organizing, articulating role. Analogously in the moral domain, the self is identified with its subjective willings, the free will, and the rules, the hypothetical and categorical imperatives, that provide coherence for willing. The self is not identified with its bodily actions because as *worldly* events they stand outside the ambit of immaterial subjectivity. Only what is *fully* within our power belongs to subjectivity.

Nature dematerialized and human subjectivity deprived of worldly substantiality in their interaction and re-enforcement form the two struts supporting the various rationality crises of modernity to which it is proposed that art works and the reason they exemplify might somehow be a response. Now if art works are a response to this crisis, if they promise or exemplify a resolution, then they must suspend the dematerialization of nature and the delegitimation of its voice, on the one hand, and reveal the possibility of human meaningfulness as materially saturated and so embodied on the other. My hypothesis is that the core of art's rationality potential relates to its capacity to engender a compelling synthesis of freedom and materiality, reason and nature, with artistic mediums playing the key mediating role. By mediums I mean, minimally, the material conditions of a practice as they appear within an artistic community at a given time. So the medium(s) of sculpture at a given time includes not only the raw materials acceptable for sculpting (wood, marble, etc.), but what *kinds* of things are required to transform these materials into works. Working in a medium is working with a material conceived as a potential for sense-making in a manner that is material-specific. Hence the medium is not a neutral vehicle for the expression of an otherwise immaterial meaning, but rather the very condition for sense-making. Artistic sense-making is making sense in a medium. So mediums are a potential for sense-making. However, since mediums are at least certain types of materials, then mediums are matter conceived as a potential for sense-making. Since art is a sense-making that is medium-dependent, and mediums are aspects of nature conceived as potentials for sense-making, then art, its reason, is minimally the reason of nature as a potential for sense-making at a certain time. If art works make a claim at a particular time, then at that time nature is experienced as possessing a material-specific potentiality for sense-making. Hence, to experience a work as making a claim at a particular time is to experience the dematerialization and delegitimation of nature as suspended. The idea of an artistic medium is perhaps the last idea of material nature as possessing potentialities for meaning.

Working from the other side: in modern works of art freedom, the human capacity for autonomous sense-making, *appears*, that is, art works are *unique objects*, and as unique sources of normatively compelling claims, they are experienced as products of freedom, as creations; their uniqueness and irreducibility are understood as the material expression of an autonomous subjectivity. In autonomous works of art human autonomy appears. Beauty, Schiller tells us, is freedom in appearance. But the material bearer of appearing freedom cannot be neutral or indifferent, for then freedom would not be *embodied*, realized in sensible form, but simply carried or conveyed materially. So nature as truly amenable to human sense-making implies the notion of an artistic medium as, precisely, a potential for sense-making. Some such conception of freedom materialized and of artistic mediums as nature re-enchanted underlies the hopes for aesthetic reason. For reasons that will become apparent, giving shape to and sustaining these hopes is not easy, and for an urgent reason: modernity really is marked by the emergence of freedom and autonomy (from nature) as the distinguishing mark of subjectivity. Lessing's struggles with the problem of freedom and nature are exemplary, and hence an ideal place to begin.

Artistic mediums and the space of mortification

Suppose one believes the aim of art is to produce beautiful representations of particular objects or events, then one might equally suppose that different art practices are ideally translatable into one another: 'painting is mute poetry and poetry a speaking painting' (L, I).[2] For this theory the systematic differences between Virgil's representation of Laocoön and his sons being killed by sea serpents and that of the Laocoön group present a puzzle, if not a direct refutation. In Virgil the serpents are wound around Laocoön's back and throat, their heads towering over him, and all the while he is lifting to the stars 'horrifying shrieks; / Such bellowing as when a wounded bull has fled the altar'. However, in the sculpture one serpent is at Laocoön's waist, another in his upraised hand (neither serpent is coiled around him), and from his grimaced facial expression, his mouth half-closed, we imagine him uttering an intense, anguished groan – for Winckelmann, following Sadolet, not even that, only an 'oppressed and weary sigh' (L, I). Once extrinsic explanations for the divergence are eliminated, the best explanation for the differences between the poem and sculpture is aesthetic: by making Laocoön naked, by removing his priestly, blood-soaked fillet, by changing the position of the serpents, and, above all, by transforming the terrible scream into an anguished sigh, the sculptor is heeding the demands of his specific medium.

In a poem Lessing writes, 'A cloak is not a cloak; it conceals nothing; our imagination sees through it at all times' (L, v); hence, in the poem Laocoön's cloak neither hides the anguish of his body nor is his brow hidden by the priestly fillet. This is not the case in the plastic arts where the set of spatial relations between real things operates as a syntactic constraint on representability. If in the real world a cloak hides a body, then it also must do so in the plastic arts. Medium is syntax. Minimally, and palpably in the case of sculpture, it constrains the semantic contents that are possible. The choice, say, between priestly garb or naked body, is determined by the ends of beauty, but that one must choose is determined by the medium itself.

The transformation of the agonized howl into the muted groan is more complex. This is Lessing's dominant line of argument: Works of plastic art are made to be contemplated 'at length and repeatedly', to be capable

---

[2] *Laocoön or On the Limits of Painting and Poetry*, trans. W. A. Steel. References in the body of the text, L, are to the chapter number.

of sustaining continuous visual attention. This demand yields a medium-specific, formal content-constraint: 'The single moment of time to which [plastic] art must confine itself in virtue of its material limitations' entails that an artist never present an action or emotion at its climax (L, III). This is the rule of the pregnant moment. In the plastic arts, only a single moment is directly represented. In the representation of an emotionally charged event, the least suitable moment to depict is the climax, since that is when the action stops. In contemplating a climax the eye is riveted, and the imagination is thus *bound* to what the eye sees. Freezing imaginative engagement blocks both ongoing visual attention, depriving it of reason, and human significance. To incite imaginative response requires a moment of potentiality, full of the past which produced it and full of the future to come, so that the more we see, the more we are able to imagine. Only a moment big with past and future is suitable for material portrayal.

> Thus, if Laocoön sighs, the imagination can hear him shriek; but if he shrieks, it can neither go one step higher nor one step lower than this representation without seeing him in a more tolerable and consequently more uninteresting condition. One either hears him only groan or else sees him already dead. (L, III)

In accordance with the logic of the imagination, the *perception* of Laocoön shrieking presents him as if dead: the shriek as climax fixes the whole in *the moment*, an 'utmost' excluding past and future as affectively, aesthetically interesting. The constriction of the imagination to a moment, or the constraining of the imagination to the sheer spatial display before the eye, and thereby to the uniquely spatially given, is the freezing of time. This makes a climax, any climax, equivalent to death. Material nature, the order of things in space, is the mortification of the (temporal) life of the imagination; hence, the materialization of ideas and concepts, the work of painting and sculpture, involves their increasing mortification. Matter is death. As an underlying premise, this does not bode well for a theory of artistic mediums. One can quickly justify the complaint that Lessing's survey of the limits of painting and poetry amounts to the slaughter of painting.[3] This is the knot we need to untie.

In the opening paragraphs of chapter 16 of *Laocoön*, Lessing offers the basics for a deduction of the limits of painting and poetry 'from first

---

[3] E. H. Gombrich, 'Lessing', *Proceedings of the British Academy*, 42 (1957), pp. 133–56.

principles'. Imitations in painting use different signs than poetry, namely figures and colours in space rather than articulated sounds in time. Figures and colours are natural signs (where properties of the sign itself account (in part) for its relation to the signified), whereas words are arbitrary signs. Lessing then introduces a medium-specific constraint thesis: *signs must have a suitable or appropriate relation to what they signify*. Signs only spatially related appropriately signify items whose wholes or parts coexist; while signs following one another best express items whose wholes or parts are consecutive. Wholes or parts of wholes coexisting in space are called bodies; hence bodies with visible properties are the proper objects of painting. Items succeeding one another in time are actions; hence actions are the proper objects of poetry.

This is clearly too restrictive because too abstract; or rather, leaving the domains of mind and matter, time and space (visibility), action and object utterly distinct from one another projects an almost inhuman art, maybe a non-art: the temporally frozen depiction of visible bodies, or the disembodied depiction of human action (which is not action but its antecedents). If Lessing had stopped here, letting the transcendental distinction between space and time, visible bodies represented by natural signs and free actions by arbitrary signs, bear *all* the weight, then the result would have been inhuman extremes: painting as perfected in, literally, the still life, *nature morte*; literature wholly cerebral, all but indistinguishable from non-literary prose. So for Lessing the ultimate threat to art comes from a hypostatized differentiation of painting and poetry, sensuous materiality and imaginative freedom; one might say that the ultimate threat comes from what occurs when art is reduced to its medium. Although Lessing inscribes aesthetic limits in a medium-specific way, the purpose of the inscription is to *resist* the claim that mediums provide the normative intelligibility of the practices dependent on them, which makes sense if the mediums are understood initially in terms of the duality of a disenchanted nature and de-worlded subjectivity. Pure painting and pure poetry stand for this dualism, and thus require overcoming, where the demand for overcoming is something like the demand of art as such. Painting and poetry must, for conceptual and aesthetic reasons, be brought closer together.

Bodies persist through time, possessing a differing relation of parts to whole, or offering different combinations of wholes and parts at each moment. Each (humanly significant) moment is the causal consequence of its predecessor moment, and the cause of its successor. So what is technically a single moment can fall at the centre of an action, so to speak; hence paintings can imply actions through the disposition of a body, that is, by revealing it as such a 'centre'. Conversely, actions must be embodied. Hence, poetry can partake of the domain of bodies through the way it depicts action. These principles and inferences generate the practice-specific rules for painting and poetry. The fundamental rule for painting is the pregnant moment; *the rule of the pregnant moment is the sublation of painting by poetry*, a poeticizing of painting where the material object becomes the source for revealing, for bringing to mind its *imaginary* counterpart: the complete, temporally extended action. The opposing rule for poetry is clumsier: because it can access only a single property of the body to coordinate with a given action, poetry must choose the most sensate image of the body, the sensuous image most suggestive with respect to the action being described.

The best explanation for Lessing's suppression of painting in favour of poetry is thus evaluative: it serves the end of imaginative vision, of art as enabling the intense imaginative experience of an object, which is the value orientation of freedom with respect to nature as determined by modern experience. This value orientation opens chapter 3: we modern, Enlightened folk have determined that truth and expression are art's first law. Hence, the tendential dematerialization of painting in its sublation by poetry is premised upon the thesis that poetry is a higher art than painting because human (imaginative) freedom is higher, more intrinsically valuable, than material nature. The surprising consequence of this value orientation is the restriction of the plastic arts to the norm of beauty (L, IX), the restriction of beauty as beauty to the plastic arts, thus a general neutralizing of the value significance of material beauty. The plastic artist cannot ignore its demands because an object's beauty is the harmonious effect of its various parts absorbed by the eye at a glance, but since the syntax of the plastic arts is one of part to whole, then the material syntax of painting directly converges or overlaps with the logic of beauty. For Lessing, Winckelmann's defence of the 'stillness' of the beautiful in Greek sculpture is, finally, a praise of material deadliness.[4] We can thus construe Lessing's defence of poetry over painting, his poetic sublation of painting

---

[4] David E. Wellbery, *Lessing's Laocoön: Semiotics and Aesthetics in the Age of Reason* (Cambridge: Cambridge University Press, 1984), p. 164.

as a defence of modern freedom, against the beauty of the ancient Greeks. Deflating physical beauty and subsuming it under the higher demands of freedom breaks the grip of classicism in aesthetic thought. The rule of the pregnant moment thus transfigures the goodness of ancient beauty into the demands of modern freedom, making modern (poetic) freedom the measure.

Lessing's defence of poetry's universality is over-determined. At its core, however, and what explains poetry's limitlessness, its ability to go where painting cannot follow, is its dependence upon *arbitrary* signs succeeding one another in time. Signs meaningful by convention are the medium of poetry and the source of its power. Because these signs are arbitrary, no content is in principle unavailable to them. Because the signs are immaterial, the existential absence of the object necessary for artistic illusion is already accomplished. By absenting themselves in the representation of objects, the immateriality of arbitrary signs allows for maximal imaginative engagement. Because arbitrary signs are temporally organized, then even for an object at a particular moment in time, they can ignore physical limitations (things hiding one another) and present multiple views of the same. Because linguistic signs occur in succession, no one sign aesthetically dominates, thus allowing the ugly and terrible to be represented without ruining the aesthetic unity of the whole. Finally, the arbitrary sign's systematic distance from materiality converges with the freedom of the imagination in a way that is the inverse of the convergence of the syntactical constraints of materiality with the holistic logic of physical beauty, beauty as beauty. If Lessing had said no more, his hierarchical ranking of poetry above painting would be tantamount to an anti-aesthetic – precisely what the dematerialization of subject and object portends. On pages xxvii–xxx, I argue that it is precisely this poetic universality, including poetry's sublation of the plastic arts, which is the cornerstone of Jena romanticism's claim that romantic poetry is a progressive, universal poetry.

There is, however, a countervailing pressure in *Laocoön* to the claims of modern freedom, the poetic sublation of painting, since the universality argument relates only to pure poetry, prior to the qualification that makes poetry art. The countervailing logic requires that the linguistic presentation is maximally sensuous or sensate, *sinnlich*. The issue for Lessing: in virtue of what features of poetic discourse does a poem make its object palpable, vividly present to the imagination?

> A poetic picture is not necessarily one that can be transformed into a material painting; but every feature, and every combination of features by means of which the poet makes his object so sensate that we are more clearly conscious of this subject than of his words, is called painterly (*mahlerisch*), is styled a painting (*ein Gemählde*), because it brings us closer to that degree of illusion of which the material painting is specially capable and which can most readily and most easily be conceptualized in terms of a material painting.
>
> (L, XIV)

If poetry is different from prose, different from the ordinary language demands of communication, if it attains an imaginative vitality that is worldly, then it deploys its arbitrary signs so that they are forgotten for the sake of the object represented; hence, what is wanted from poetry is the production of the illusion of the immediacy of perceptual experience, the model for which is painting. Since what is at stake is not the production of pictures, but arbitrary signs becoming sensate, nature-like, with the power and on the model we associate with painting, then poetry requires *the idea of painting*.[5]

The *idea* of painting is the remnant of painting in the absence of painting, referring to a visual fullness, intuitive immediacy, or presentness. The idea of painting replaces painting in part because painting is eclipsed by poetry, so that aesthetically what remains of painting is its idea as a demand upon poetic production. Even so qualified, the demand that poetry live up to the idea of painting is equivalent to the demand that poetry give its representations a sensible worldliness, or, more accurately, a sense of possessing a sensateness that signifies worldliness. But to give representations the immediacy of a saturated (dense, replete) visual perception, where it is the 'at once' of a visual perception being held in place by the idea of painting, is to *recall* the medium-specific syntactical demands of painting, or, differently, to think, for the first time, of the syntax of painting provided by its medium as a *productive condition* of possibility rather than a mere limitation. Hence, the idea of painting stands in for a productive notion of artistic medium that is everywhere and nowhere in Lessing, the notion of medium that was displaced and/or cancelled by the pressures of dematerialization, including the poetic sublation of painting. Medium as productive means, minimally, material nature as conducive to human

---

[5] Ibid., p. 183.

meaningfulness. Or, to state this in terms of Lessing's semiotic theory: the idea of painting is the idea of natural signs in their naturalness as conducive to human meaningfulness, and by extension, arbitrary signs taking on the appearance of naturalness as a corrective to the abstractness of poetry in its moment of limitless universality. The idea of painting thus becomes a corrective to the idea of abstract, rationalized modernity, its agonies of dematerialization.

Lessing suggests three mechanisms by which arbitrary signs can take on the character, or immediacy, of natural signs. First, signs are relieved of their arbitrariness if their succession mimics the succession of things. Second, the unity of action provided by narrative provides an experience of oneness formally akin to wholeness of a single visual perception in the idea of painting. Finally, one offers to arbitrary signs a sense of naturalness through metaphor and simile. By likening the object of an arbitrary sign with the object of another sign, the use of the first sign brings to mind the latter's object, thus tying word and world together in a manner analogous to the way in which a natural sign brings to mind what it signifies; similarity, conceived as a natural or quasi-natural relation, thus relieves arbitrariness in the direction of naturalness.

Of freedom in appearance

Throughout the eighteenth century the power of the idea of art as fundamentally mimetic is only slowly displaced as the claim of freedom (imagination, creativity) asserts itself. In Karl Phillipp Moritz's 'On the Artistic Imitation of the Beautiful' (1788), we sense the notion of imitation being stretched to breaking. After splicing the concepts of the beautiful, the noble, the good and the useful – and preparing the way for Kant's notion that the beautiful and the useless (what is without external purpose) overlap, as well as connecting the good and the beautiful – Moritz notes how natural beauties are metaphors for the beauty of nature as a whole, which cannot be grasped by the senses or imagination. We might say the artist imitates natural beauty, not nature. This leads immediately to Moritz's conclusions: first, the artist imitates not things but nature's creating, which forms the core of the idea of artistic genius; and second, since the beautiful is connected to the *power* of human action, the capacity to create, it must exceed the power of cognition to grasp it. Hence, the beautiful must be *felt*.

Despite the fact that Schiller's 'Kallias or Concerning Beauty: Letters to Gottfried Körner' (1793) were written to reveal the connection between freedom and beauty, the grip of the notion of imitation on Schiller is palpable in his concluding account of the role of artistic mediums. One might be forgiven for thinking that Schiller was transcribing passages directly from Lessing. Schiller provides an imitative conception of fine art where an object is 'freely depicted' only if its presentation does not suffer from interference by the nature of the depicting matter: 'The nature of the medium or the matter must thus be completely vanquished by the nature of the imitated . . . In an artwork, the matter (the nature of the imitating [object]) must lose itself in the *form* (the imitated [object]), the *body* in the *idea*, the *reality* in the *appearance*.'[6] This is not just a manner of speaking; after pressing the point that the representing medium must shed and deny its own nature, he stipulates that the 'nature of the marble, which is hard and brittle, must disappear into the nature of flesh which is flexible and soft, and neither feeling nor the eye may be reminded of its disappearance'.

Turning to poetic depiction, Schiller generates the familiar problem concerning the arbitrariness of linguistic signs and their tendency, given the connection between language and conceptual understanding, towards universality and abstractness. The specific poetic application of language enables it to 'subjugate itself under the form', thereby enabling the linguistic 'body' to lose itself in the 'idea'; the beauty of poetic diction is thus the 'free self-activity of nature in the chains of language'. Although obscure, the orientation of the argument leads us naturally to construe the poetic subjugation of conceptual language as occurring through poetic figuration. However, if we study the logic of Schiller's thesis we detect in the invocation of poetic figuration a decisive swerve away from an emphasis on mimetic ends and towards a conception of art that is more explicitly autonomous, more imbued with the experience of subjectivity reaching expression in objective (linguistic, material) form. The "chains of language" are the material upon which poetic form works; nature is the object represented. Poetic form makes the object appear autonomous. The strange twist which leads the utterly inhuman to *appear* self-active, where self-activity represents both the idea of aesthetic *form* and the subjectivity of the subject, is the signature of Schiller's aesthetic theory.

---

[6] 'Kallias or Concerning Beauty: Letters to Gottfried Körner', trans. Stefan Bird-Pollan. All quotes in this section are from the 'Kallias Letters.'

The 'Kallias Letters' are a reformulation of Kant's aesthetic theory that reaches its apotheosis in *On the Aesthetic Education of Man in a Series of Letters*. While the approach of the former letters is systematic and constructive, they nonetheless have a visible philosophical spring: to reconstruct Kant's aesthetics in accordance with the thesis that nature is beautiful only when it looks like art, and art is beautiful only when it looks like nature, while replacing the role of the understanding with reason in aesthetic judgement. For Kant the beautiful pleases without a concept, and judgements of taste are not subsumptive and determinative like standard empirical judgements. Schiller finds strange, first, Kant's aligning beauty with the understanding, whose task is to judge mechanical nature, rather than with reason and freedom; second, Kant's urging the isolation of pure from dependent beauties, making arabesques and the like paradigm beauties – as if the perfection of beauty is reached once emptied of human meaning. Third, converging with this criticism, Schiller contends that by making disinterestedness the condition by which things are seen for their form, Kant makes inexplicable why some objects are beautiful and others not. The idea of disinterestedness as forwarding a notion of the aesthetic as our *stance* towards objects, and the idea that paradigmatic pure beauties are without human meaning, converge to make formalism a recipe for emptiness. Still, Schiller wants to deepen Kant's formalism, not overturn it.

The specifically aesthetic appearing of an object, the experience of an object as beautiful, is the experience of it as possessing an excess of form, and in virtue of this excess soliciting an aesthetic rather than an explanatory response. The excess of form is the objective quality that solicits the judgement of beauty. An object's excess of form is its appearing in a manner that 'we are neither able nor inclined to search for its ground outside it', its form appearing to explain itself, to be self-sufficient or self-contained. So a form is beautiful 'if it demands no explanation, or it explains itself without a concept'. Schiller uses this criterion in explicating our judgements of both nature and works of art.

When considered in accordance with the principle of causality and the laws of nature, all objects, their states and dispositions, have their true explanation outside themselves. For aesthetics, however, the issue is not what explains an object, but how it *appears* to us. What is explicitly antithetic to beauty is the experience of something as needing causal explanation, as evidently subject to mechanical law, as palpably overwhelmed by external forces, like gravity, hence as being an explicit display of dead matter, mass. To experience a haphazard, irregular thread of paint as a frozen accidental drip yields a sense that its pattern and movement is explained not by itself but externally, by the force of gravity; the irregularity of the thread's shape directly insinuates the force producing it, and thereby makes the appearing thread unavailable for aesthetic appreciation. Schiller's way of understanding the miracle of a Pollock would be that the operation of the force of gravity displayed by the threaded lines of paint is at every moment overcome, interrupted, so that the experience of the drip continually becomes the optical experience of its pattern, of loops, sashays, webbing and tangles whose patterning and interaction *appear* self-sufficient, or self-explanatory. So the experience of a Pollock is the experience of mechanical nature as a form of resistance that is sublated at each moment by intrinsic material (visual) meaningfulness, the illusion of self-sufficiency. All Schiller's examples turn upon the difference between the appearance of self-sufficiency and the interruptive look of mass requiring causal explanation: in nature, the contrast between the clumsiness of the work horse and the elegance of the light Spanish palfrey; in art we are offended by didactic literature because the author's external intention intrudes upon the movement of the narrative, the characters appearing like puppets moved by obvious strings, not self-moving. When the nature of the medium (paint as subject to gravity) or the will of the artist appears distinct, it dashes the aesthetic meaning of the work by turning internal form into external manipulation, intrinsic meaningfulness into meaning only as a means for an external end, self-movement collapsing into external compulsion.

Such judgements are hardly novel; what is new with Schiller is that the explanation of what constitutes aesthetic appearance, semblance and beauty, concerns not harmony, proportion, or perfection in their classical or rationalist sense, but autonomy as opposed to heteronomy, where finally these terms relate strictly to the will's autonomy in opposition to mechanical causality. Schiller unpacks the claim this way: what does not (experientially) insist upon its determination from without engenders the idea that it is determined from within, or is self-determining. The *form* of the object invites us to regard it as determined from within. When objects possess form we suppose there is a rule doing the self-determining. Our model here is artworks, which is to say, our model is the sort of purposiveness engendered through the kind of intentional activity exemplified in the making of works of art. A *technical rule*, or simply *technique*, is at work in producing the complex unity of an artwork. Form points to a rule that is art-like or technical. When this rule appears intrinsic, self-explanatory, we consider the form to be self-determining, which leads us to associate objects possessing technical form with freedom. Hence, this argument concludes with the claim: beauty in nature is art-likeness. Schiller states the thesis in anticipation: 'This great idea of self-determination resonates back at us from certain appearances of nature, and we call it beauty.'

Much goes awry here, above all that all purposiveness is presumed to be intentional, leaving out the possibility of living, biological systems. By ignoring the possibility of purposive life, Schiller overdoes the idea of rational freedom finding an image of itself in sensible nature; this makes the account implausibly fix upon the idea of practical reason projecting itself on to appearing nature, making natural beauty a debilitating example of anthropomorphism. But this does not mean that the governing thought, that beauty is freedom in appearance, is not required for art beauty. In fact, part of the curiosity of the 'Kallias Letters' is that its account of natural beauty keeps sounding as if it concerned art beauty, which is unsurprising since for Schiller art beauty is the model for natural beauty. But this embedded account of art beauty, prior to the explicit one concluding the letters, has the distinctive advantage of sustaining an integral connection between how material nature can appear and the will – which finally is the driving topic of the letters. In the 'Kallias Letters' the social problems of the disenchantment of nature and the de-worlding of freedom – and their overcoming in beauty – are implicit everywhere, but explicit nowhere; hence the force of the primary thesis, that beauty is freedom in appearance, possesses only formal significance. It did not take long for Schiller to see the issue more fully.

Tragedy and the loss of nature

Both Lessing and Schiller view art as a unique locale where the duality of worldless freedom and dumb nature is overcome. Subjectivity is given sensible presence in natural beauty and the work of art; and in manifesting an image of a fit between the extremes of freedom and nature, the artwork appears as a solution to the problem of their metaphysical separation, of how human meaning can become a worldly reality. Artworks have depth because they project a unification of the claims of reason and sense, freedom and nature, which is a necessary condition for the possibility of human meaningfulness.

One might consider the programmes of Hölderlin and Jena romanticism as forming opposing sides of the fragile Schillerian synthesis, and hence as underlining the crisis of reason as a whole: Hölderlin's tragic thought is premised upon and attempts to articulate the loss of (the authority of) nature, while Schlegel's aesthetics radicalizes poetry as the discourse proper to human freedom. Hölderlin intended to entitle his first contribution to Niethammer's *Philosophical Journal* 'New Letters on the Aesthetic Education of Man'. If we read Hölderlin's fragments in this light, then they can be interpreted as drawing out the dark side of Schiller's programme for re-uniting what modern history has sundered: the *need* for aesthetic education entails a tragic or elegiac modernism.

Hölderlin's fundamental philosophical achievement derives from his criticism of Fichte. The cornerstone of this criticism appears perspicuously in his letter to Hegel of 26 January 1795. Hölderlin begins by conceding to Fichte his controlling assumption that the 'I' (or the 'I think') is absolute, which means that it can have nothing outside it: if absolute, then unconditioned, if unconditioned, then without an exterior. But this raises a problem: since all consciousness is necessarily consciousness *of* something, then consciousness must have an object. So all consciousness is a relation between subject and object, even if I am the object of thought. Even minimal self-consciousness is conditioned, yielding a sense of the I as restricted, at least, Hölderlin supposes, by time. If the absolute I is unconditioned, as originally assumed, then it cannot be conscious of itself. Insofar as I am not conscious of myself, then for myself I am nothing; so the absolute I is necessarily for itself nothing. One might complain that Hölderlin is unfair to Fichte in not distinguishing between empirical and transcendental self-consciousness, and for not acknowledging Fichte's original insight: 'self-awareness is not identical to self-reflection; to make any judgement about our mental state, we must already have an immediate, non-reflective acquaintance with ourselves'.[7] Even so, as long as Fichte considers the 'I think' as origin and absolute, then this criticism is going to have force.

---

[7] Charles Larmore, 'Hölderlin and Novalis', in Karl Ameriks (ed.), *The Cambridge Companion to German Idealism* (Cambridge: Cambridge University Press, 2000), p. 146.

As is evident in 'Being Judgement Possibility', however, there is a Fichtean moment which Hölderlin accepts, namely, the idea of the unconditioned, a fundamental *unity* of subject and object, as ground. Of course, even in Kant the unconditioned is the governing idea of reason, the regulative idea orienting our explanatory and inferential activities: every conditioned ultimately presupposes an unconditioned, which is the central idea generating the Antinomies. However, the critical notion of the unconditioned is not Hölderlin's. Hölderlin thinks it is necessary for something to have a status not unlike Spinoza's notion of substance, that is, there is a necessary unity of subject and object as – well what? If this unity is not a first principle, as it is for Fichte, then what is its role? Perhaps it is the goal of striving to achieve a unity of subject and object? But what does this mean? Hölderlin's unification philosophy is a unification of what? Subject and object sounds opaque. To begin reading 'Being Judgement Possibility', I think we need the Schillerian background, the sense that the absolute unity of subject and object points to a *re*-conciliation of freedom and nature, which in turn presupposes their original unity.

In the preface to *Hyperion* we find: ' "The blessed unity of being, in the unique sense of the word, is lost to us." We have torn ourselves loose from it in order to reach it. But "neither our knowledge nor our action reaches, at any period of our existence, a point where all strife ceases". The peace of all peace is irretrievably lost. Yet we would not even seek after it if that infinite unification, that being in the only sense of the word, were not present to us. It is present – as beauty.'[8] What is lost to us is nature as home, peace figuring 'our lost childhood'.[9] There is thus the sense that there is something from which we have been separated, that we experience our relation to nature as being forever beyond it (because we live in self-consciousness, language, culture and history), where being separated and beyond are jointly experienced as loss. The experience of loss tempers and orients what we count as progress, what requires unification. In the penultimate version of the Preface to *Hyperion*, Hölderlin states: 'We all travel an eccentric path . . . we have been dislocated from nature, and what appears to have once been *one* is now at odds with itself . . . Often it is as

---

[8] Dieter Henrich, *The Course of Remembrance and Other Essays on Hölderlin*, edited by Eckart Förster (Stanford: Stanford University Press, 1997), p. 84. The phrases in double quotation marks are from the preface to *Hyperion*.

[9] Friedrich Schiller, 'On Naive and Sentimental Poetry' (1795–6), trans. Daniel Dahlstrom in *Friedrich Schiller, Essays* (New York: Continuum, 1993), p. 181.

though the world were *everything* and we *nothing*, but often too it is as though we were *everything* and the world *nothing*.'[10]

We need thus to track two moments in Hölderlin's thought. The first is the construction of the aporetic duality of judgement and being. When thinking about this first moment, something obvious becomes striking, namely, if being is not a self-evident first principle, then being is not self-evident, or available to judgement, hence not available to philosophy. So we need a second moment, which is the emergence of, let us call it beauty or poetry, or what it is for Hölderlin, namely, tragedy, as the narrative that makes manifest our separation from an origin to which we remain bound.

At one level, 'Being Judgement Possibility' proceeds in a Kantian way: judgement is original separation (this is the bad, speculative etymology: *Urteil* becomes *Ur-Teilung*, primordial division) in virtue of which there is subject and object. Subject and object are not natural existences, but internal correlatives of judgement. Hölderlin's stinging rebuke to Fichte follows: because the 'I am I' reveals an identity of the I *with* itself, then 'I am I' shows, at the theoretical level, the truth of separation. Being, in contrast, requires a unity of subject and object that cannot be violated or conjured into being as a completed synthesis. In 'Being Judgement Possibility', Hölderlin gets at the depth of this idea by distinguishing unity from identity. I am I is identity of the self with its self, not unity. Identity is the work of reflection and judgement. I am I requires separation, at least the separation of time. Judging is separating and unifying; hence any awareness of myself enables me to distinguish my acting/seeing self from my seen self; my present from my past self; my transcendental ego from my empirical ego. Identity then is other than absolute being, which we possess as something lost to us. At a stroke, Hölderlin has removed being from judgement and hence from philosophy.[11] Whatever else happens in philosophy during this period, clearly this wrenching of being from the grip of philosophy enables a general revaluation of the significance of beauty or art. We now have the more radical claim that being, or unity, has no other way of being manifest except through art. So art either replaces first philosophy or stands in for its absence.

Hölderlin states that the tragic is idealist in its significance; it is the metaphor of intellectual intuition 'which cannot be other than the unity

---

[10] Following Larmore, 'Hölderlin and Novalis', p. 149.
[11] More accurately, Hölderlin re-inscribes Kant's removal of being from philosophy.

with everything living which ... can be recognized by the spirit'.[12] In tragedy we experience nature as the (lost) ground of order. Nature in its original power or unity cannot appear directly. We know from 'Being Judgement Possibility' that this means that nature as the ground of the human cannot appear because it would have to be judged, but if judged, then it is already in a state of dispersion. So nature as the unitary ground from which we are separated can appear only in its weakness, as broken or dependent upon the human for its appearance. Art is the weakness that allows the strength of nature to appear (albeit improperly, not *eigentlich*). In tragedy nature is mediated by the sign, which is the suffering hero. As Peter Szondi states it:

> Unable to prevail against the power of nature, which ultimately destroys him, he is 'insignificant' and 'without effect'. But, in the downfall of the tragic hero, when the sign = 0, nature shows itself as conqueror 'in its strongest gift', and 'the original is openly revealed'. Hölderlin thus interprets tragedy as the sacrifice man offers to nature so that it can appear in an adequate manner. Herein lies the tragic aspect of man's situation: this service, which gives his existence meaning, is one he can perform only in death, when he becomes a sign that is 'in itself insignificant = 0'.[13]

Although pointed, this is excessive with respect to the claim that in tragedy nature appears in 'an adequate manner', which makes tragedy a stand-in for philosophical knowing rather than the rehearsal of its impossibility. As in Moritz, the whole is felt in response to a part, but the part here is the hero, not natural beauty, and the feeling is heroic suffering.[14] This explicates the dark side of Schiller: self-consciousness is grounded in an originary unity from which it is necessarily separated. Tragedy thus reveals *the necessity and impossibility* of the unity of freedom with nature.

---

[12] Hölderlin, 'On the Difference of Poetic Modes' in Friedrich Hölderlin, *Essays and Letters on Theory*, trans. Thomas Pfau (Albany: SUNY Press, 1988), p. 85.

[13] Peter Szondi, 'The Notion of the Tragic in Schelling, Hölderlin, and Hegel' in his *On Textual Understanding and Other Essays*, trans. Harvey Mendelsohn (Minneapolis: University of Minnesota Press, 1986), p. 47. The moment when the sign equals zero appears in 'Remarks on Oedipus' as the tragic transport, the poetic logic of which is given in the account of the caesura as the counter-rhythmic interruption. Broadly speaking, Oedipus' 'savage search', the 'insane questioning' for full consciousness, is the stand-in for the ambition of philosophy, an ambition that is tragically satisfied only through his destruction.

[14] I am here relying on Hölderlin's 'On the Difference of Poetic Modes'.

Freedom and universal poesy

In a manner continuous with Lessing's conception of poetry as the expression of the freedom of imagination, Friedrich Schlegel comes to think of modern, romantic poetry as the exemplary instance of human freedom, its fullest expression and articulation. The cost of so conceiving of poetry is that the connection between freedom and nature which was the dominant leitmotif of eighteenth-century aesthetics is severed. The seeds of Schlegel's conception of poesy are planted in *On the Study of Greek Poetry* (1795),[15] where the characteristic comprehension of the relation between ancient and modern literature is first laid down. Equally, Schlegel develops a conception of poetry in relation to the other arts that explicitly elaborates upon Lessing's. Schlegel contends that classical art stands to modern art as natural *Bildung* stands to artificial *Bildung*, which is here given in its multiple senses: development, culture, education, formation, maturation. In the Greek world, ideal and actual are joined. In the modern world, in light of the emergence of subjectivity and the experience of freedom as belonging to the individual, as its essence, the ideal is removed from the domain of empirical actuality: 'with greater intellectual development [*Bildung*], the goal of modern poetry naturally becomes *individuality* that is *original and interesting*. The simple imitation of the particular is, however, a mere skill of the *copyist*, not a free art. Only by means of an *arrangement* that is *ideal* does the characteristic of an individual become a philosophical work of art.'[16] Individuality emerges when self-realization no longer occurs through identification with established social roles. Individuality is expressed through originality and the interesting; they are what individualize an individual. The interesting for Schlegel is a provisional aesthetic totalization manifesting the disappearance of taken-for-granted universality. Sophocles wrote objective tragedies, Shakespeare interesting ones. Sophocles summoned the fate of a culture as a whole, while Shakespeare narrated the experience of individuals etched by the absence of a governing culture. Modern works

---

[15] Translated by Stuart Barnett (Albany: SUNY Press, 2001). Although written wholly independently, this essay contains a conception of the relation of ancient to modern that is quite similar to that found in Schiller's *On Naïve and Sentimental Poetry*, published just months before Schlegel's essay, forcing him to write a Preface taking into account Schiller's work. *On the Study of Greek Poetry* thus can be regarded as triangulating romanticism with Schiller's modernism and Lessing's defence of poetry.

[16] *On the Study of Greek Poetry*, p. 32.

stand in relation to an ideal separate from the work; the gap between the ideal and actual, the infinite and finite, is what makes the modern an incomplete striving. The modern age is an artificial formation because self-realization is something striven for in accordance with *proposed ideals*, hence without determinately objective ends or criteria, which is why our perfectibility and corruptibility go together, why our world lacks cultural cohesion. Schlegel deems the modern work of literature philosophical because its arrangement occurs by means of a *concept* whose ideality, again, both informs and stands apart from the work. So modern artworks are riven with a critical self-consciousness of themselves as works of art in relation to indeterminate ideals from which they remain forever separate.

Schlegel's direct borrowings from Lessing begin in a discussion of the universality of the arts. It may be the case, Schlegel concedes, that not all circumstances, cultural and/or geographical, are propitious for the production of the plastic arts; but this is not the case with respect to poetry, which is a 'universal art' because 'its organ, *fantasy*, is already incomparably more closely related to freedom, and more independent from external influence. Poetry and poetic taste is thus far more corruptible than plastic taste, but also *infinitely more perfectible*.'[17] Poetry's reliance upon the imagination, or fantasy, makes it proximate to pure freedom and hence independent from the constraints of external circumstance, which is the ground of poetry's anthropological universality, in comparison to the other arts, and its infinite perfectibility. When Schlegel raises this issue again later, poetry's relative universality has become absolute: poetry is the 'single actual *pure art* without borrowed vitality and external assistance'.[18] The other arts, Schlegel contends, are 'hybrids that fall between pure nature and pure art'.[19] The vitality and particularity of music and the plastic arts are not intrinsic to these arts as arts, but are borrowed from nature. An appeal to the senses was thought by Lessing to distinguish art-meanings from non-art-meanings; it here becomes the remnant of nature *intruding* upon art, making any art so dependent a 'hybrid', human and inhuman at the same time. Hence, nature, even as a principle of sensible vitality, is conceived as essentially extrinsic to *pure art*; only poetry, 'whose tool, an arbitrary sign-language, is the work of man, and is endlessly perfectible and corruptible'.[20] So an argument that begins by asserting poetry's 'unrestricted compass', giving it an advantage over

---

[17] Ibid., p. 42.   [18] Ibid., p. 59.   [19] Ibid.   [20] Ibid.

the other arts, concludes by making the other arts hybrids between nature and art, and poetry alone pure art. Pure art, the meaning of art, is thus aligned directly with freedom and universality, which are our capacities for infinite perfectibility, in opposition to the limiting character of what belongs to intuition and sensibility.

The Lessing influence of this defence of poetry as the only pure art is underlined in the following paragraph where Schlegel compares the kinds of unities achievable by the different arts. Because an action is only completed in time, then sculpture cannot truly represent an action. Equally, the most fully determined sculptural character presupposes the world in which it belongs, a world that sculpture itself cannot provide. Hence, 'the most perfect statue is still only a sundered, incomplete fragment, not a whole perfect unto itself. The most that images can attain is an *analogon of unity*.'[21] Poetry, conversely, offers the perfection of artistic integration since it can present a complete action, which, Schlegel contends, 'is the sole unconditioned whole in the realm of appearance'.[22] Action, however, is not what works represent, but the work of representing: 'An entirely accomplished act, a completely realized objective yields the fullest satisfaction. A completed poetic action is a whole unto itself, a *technical world*.'[23] The integration of the work *as poetic action* enables the poetic work to be an actual unity, and it is the model of the poetic action itself, the model of the work as act, that offers the notion of completion and fulfilment to action.

This is Lessing's poetry without the complement of the idea of painting, and Schiller's defence of reason and freedom without the concern for *sensible* presentation. For Schlegel, only by escaping the constraint of materiality, a *resistant medium*, does the unity of action appear – the infinite perfectibility which 'arbitrary sign-language' provides to poetry derives from its indefinite plasticity. So the linguistic medium ideally is not a specifically artistic medium at all, which is its strength. The *arbitrariness* of the sign-language, having no causal or material reasons for relating *this* sign to *that* object or meaning, is the profound source of its universal power. That power, so understood, is the mainspring of 'romantic poetry' as 'progressive, universal poetry', uniting all the separate species of poetry

---

[21] Ibid., p. 60.   [22] Ibid.

[23] Ibid. It is certainly plausible to think that this notion of technique refers back to Schiller's in the 'Kallias Letters'.

in itself, and, significantly, poetry with philosophy; romantic poetry is to be the self-consciousness of modernity.

Athenaeum fragment (hereafter: AF) 216 sets the terms aligning modernity and romanticism: 'The French revolution, Fichte's philosophy, Goethe's *Meister* are the greatest tendencies of the age.' The mutual references of these three items form the constellation composing Jena romanticism. They share: the experience of the collapse and overturning of traditional authority; the premising of all forms – social, political, theoretical, literary – on freedom and autonomy; the necessity for including within forming action a reflective account of it ('the new version of the theory knowledge is simultaneously philosophy and the philosophy of philosophy' (AF, 281) – Fichte's philosophy and Goethe's *Meister* providing the self-consciousness of the Revolution; the removal of hierarchy (the levelling out and mixing of classes and genders in society, and genres in literature); the affirmation of becoming and history (hence the infinite perfectibility of literature as paradigmatic for the infinite perfectibility of the self); and the accounting of history through a process of self-creation (self-positing), self-destruction (positing the other as not self), and self-restriction.[24]

In Schlegel's 'On Goethe's *Meister*' (1798), the exegesis of the third element of his constellation, he argues, 'This book is absolutely new and unique. We can learn to understand it only on its own terms. To judge it according to an idea of genre drawn from custom and belief... is as if a child tried to clutch the stars and the moon in his hand and pack them in his satchel.' The novel as 'new and unique' is constitutive of what it is to be a novel; it must exceed genre requirements – as emblems of traditional authority – as a condition for it being an artwork. To fail in this regard would make the work a mere imitation, a copy. The absence of pre-established standards entails that the idea of what it is for something *to be* a novel, and by inference to be a work *überhaupt*, is only given through the work itself. Hence the work inscribes and projects its own account of what it is to be a work. To judge a work on the basis of genre considerations, say the ideals of the classical, would miss the true nature of the work entirely. It requires understanding on its own terms, which is to say that a romantic work 'spares the critic his labour' since 'it carries its own judgement within itself... not only does it judge itself, it also

[24] *Critical Fragments*, number 37.

describes itself'. A romantic work is both itself and the Idea of itself. Thus, if an artwork is new and unique, it implicitly proposes a new Idea of what it is to be a work, which is a philosophical task. Hence, a romantic work is both a work and a philosophy of itself, which is historical because the Idea being proposed is historically novel, a progress beyond where literature (poesy, art) has been.

'On Goethe's *Meister*' offers a prescient account of artistic modernism; not waiting upon Flaubert, James, Joyce, Proust, or Mann, it unnervingly anticipates some of the burdens the novel would be required to undertake. But it also overburdens the novel, pushing it in a direction where it ceases being a work of art, where the 'beautiful self-mirroring' of Pindar or the lyric fragments of the Greeks are eclipsed by the demands of transcendental reflection. If Schlegel goes awry in these demands, he does so with reason; his error is subtle, not crude. The precise *conceptual* difficulty Schlegel attempts to solve, what he thinks a truly modern philosophy of art must explicate, is how it is possible to have a conception of art which shows how works are *normatively compelling without following any antecedent norms*. Schlegel is clear that the notion of poetry is normative; a definition of poetry does not establish a natural kind, but an ideal to be realized (AF, 114). However, with the end of classicism, this ideal cannot timelessly be stated. The famous closing sentences of *Athenaeum* fragment 116 assert this thought:

> The romantic kind of poetry is still in the state of becoming; that, in fact, is its real essence: that it should forever be becoming and never be perfected. It can be exhausted by no theory and only a divinatory criticism would dare try to characterize its ideal. It alone is infinite, just as it alone is free; and it recognizes as its first commandment that the will of the poet can tolerate no law above itself. The romantic kind of poetry is the only one that is more than a kind, that is, as it were, poetry itself: for in a certain sense all poetry is or should be romantic.

If there is no systematic account of how judgements of taste or works of art are possible, no purely theoretical account of the intelligibility of art and taste, then there is no separate philosophy of art, no determination of the meaning of art apart from works. Only works reveal how they are normatively possible, from which it follows that authentic artworks satisfy what we might call 'a transcendental function', that is, each authentic work of art, necessarily and minimally, *exemplifies* what it is to be a work of art. In this respect, there is something 'philosophical' about the modern, autonomous work of art. But here a slippage occurs: Schlegel conflates the legitimate insight that, with the coming-to-be of art as a fully autonomous domain, philosophy can no longer legislate for art, and hence that authentic artworks themselves satisfy a transcendental function, with the untoward claim that what satisfies a transcendental function must be conceived as *explicitly* offering a reflective, transcendental account of its object: art must explicitly become philosophy.

Once philosophy no longer extrinsically legislates, and the requirement for transcendental accounting (the representation of the producer along with product) is accepted, then philosophy becomes poetry, and all poetry is a transcendental philosophy, a poetry of poetry. I interpret Schlegel's essay 'On Incomprehensibility' (1800), a commentary on *Athenaeum* fragment 216, as a radicalization of the shift from poetry to philosophy within romantic poesy. This essay, the final item in the final issue of the *Athenaeum*, was thus the journal's summation, apologia and farewell, where the *Athenaeum* generally, and the fragments from 1798 in particular, come to displace Goethe's *Meister* as the exemplary romantic work, or: fragment and irony come to displace work and reflection. Schlegel's growing doubts about Goethe's novel can be understood as a consequence of coming to see it as more representative of Weimar classicism than Jena romanticism, and hence of coming to doubt that it could bear the weight of significance originally attributed to it. While not wrong, the real doubt about *Wilhelm Meister*, I think, is simply that it is *a work*.

The closing sentences of *Athenaeum* fragment 116 can be interpreted as stipulating that with romanticism the meaning of art is given through works and cannot be legislated a priori. But this radically underdetermines the effort of transcendental reflection Schlegel thinks an authentic work must accomplish. Jena romanticism contends that each authentic work reflectively articulates itself as a further determination of the Idea of art, but if the heart of romanticism is taken as the *philosophical thought* that the Idea of art is given through each work, then no fully self-sufficient work, no matter how self-conscious, is adequate to the Idea. Any *determinate* work is insufficient with respect to the Idea that romantic poetry 'should be forever becoming'. Hence, even exemplary works can be taken as falsifying the thesis that 'the will of the poet can tolerate no law above itself'. So the slippage from implicit to explicit came to be understood as disqualifying autonomous works as satisfying the romantic Idea of art. Schlegel thus insists that the core impulse of fragment 216 is not given through the constellation formed by the troika of the French Revolution, Fichte and Goethe, but 'lies in the word *tendencies*... And so I now let irony go to the winds and declare point blank that in the dialectic of the fragments the word means that everything now is only a tendency, that the age is the Age of Tendencies.'

The palpable collapse that occurs in the claim that since the romantic Idea of art is necessarily indeterminate, then a determinate work is incompatible with it, must be taken as a consequence of the earlier conflation of the requirement that works satisfy a transcendental function with the requirement that they provide a transcendental accounting of themselves. Without this pressure, it is not obvious why determinate works are insufficient to romanticism. If, however, only works are the reflective bearers of the Idea of art in romanticism, and this Idea entails that romanticism is forever becoming, then a self-sufficient work transparently belies the Idea. For a work to fully exemplify and reflectively articulate the Idea of poetry as infinite becoming, it would have to cancel itself as work, bracket itself as work for the sake of the indeterminate Idea, unwork its being as work, forfeit its status as material presence in favour of art's 'not yet', be itself and always beyond itself. It would be a fragment without being part of a whole, and rehearse an ironic displacement of whatever immanent claim it would make.[25] So the romantic concepts of fragment and irony emerge as the form of work and reflection required by a transcendental poetry which will sustain the Idea of art as forever becoming. As the dissolution of the autonomous work, fragment and irony are the systematic undoing of the claim of the idea of painting. The idea of painting is what romanticism emphatically disqualifies. In the midst of its presumptive pantheism, Jena romanticism cancels any synthesis, or harmonization, of materiality and the social sign. On the contrary, and doubtless despite itself, romanticism becomes the thought of their incommensurability.

[25] For a detailing of these ideas of fragment and irony see Philippe Lacoue-Labarthe and Jean-Luc Nancy, *The Literary Absolute: The Theory of Literature in German Romanticism*, trans. Philip Barnard and Cheryl Lester (Albany: State University of New York Press, 1988) and the works by Blanchot, Critchley, and de Man listed in the section in Further Reading.

Chronology

1797	Hölderlin, *Hyperion* I; Friedrich Schlegel, 'Critical Fragments' (in the Journal *Lyceum*, hence sometimes called *Lyceum Fragments*)
1798–1800	Friedrich Schlegel edits the journal *Athenaeum*
1798	Novalis, *Grains of Pollen* (or: *Miscellaneous Remarks*); 'Monologue'; 'Dialogues'; 'On Goethe'; Friedrich Schlegel (with A. W. Schlegel, Schleiermacher and Novalis), *Athenaeum fragments*; F. Schlegel, 'On Goethe's *Meister*'
1799	Hölderlin, *Hyperion* II; Novalis, 'Studies in the Visual Arts'; *Christianity or Europe*; F. Schlegel, *Lucinde*; *Dialogue on Poetry* (includes 'Letter About the Novel')
1800	Schelling, *System of Transcendental Idealism*; F. Schlegel, 'Ideas'; 'On Incomprehensibility'; Novalis, *Hymns to the Night*; Hölderlin, 'On the Process of Poetic Spirit'
1802	Novalis, *Heinrich von Ofterdingen*; Hölderlin, 'The Significance of Tragedy'
1803	Hölderlin, 'Remarks' on *Oedipus* and *Antigone*

Further reading

Translations

A more contemporary translation of Lessing's *Laocoön: An Essay on the Limits of Painting and Poetry* (Baltimore: The Johns Hopkins University Press, 1984) by Edward Allen McCormick includes a useful introduction, eighty pages of extremely valuable notes and a concluding list of biographical notes. While, so far as I am aware, Stefan Bird-Pollan's translation of the 'Kallias Letters' is the first appearance of this work in English, the remainder of the writings on aesthetics can be found in Friedrich Schiller, *Essays*, ed. Walter Hinderer and Daniel Dahlstrom (New York: Continuum Press, 1998). The translation, with facing German and English, of *On the Aesthetic Education of Man in a Series of Letters* (Oxford: Clarendon Press, 1967) by Elizabeth M. Wilkinson and L. A. Willoughby includes a monograph-length introduction, commentary, a glossary of technical terms and an extensive bibliography. Friedrich Hölderlin, *Essays and Letters on Theory*, translated and edited by Thomas Pfau (Albany: State University of New York Press, 1988) contains all of his philosophical fragments, literary theory essays, his remarks on tragedy and a selection of relevant letters. There is a translation of *Hyperion* by W. R. Trask in E. L. Santner (ed.), *Friedrich Hölderlin. Hyperion and Selected Poems* (New York: Continuum Press, 1994). Novalis, *Philosophical Writings* (Albany: State University of New York Press, 1997), translated and edited by Margaret Mahony Stoljar, presents a wide sampling of fragments and essays. It is often claimed that romantic literary theory is put into practice in Novalis' novel, *Henry von Ofterdingen* (Prospects Heights: Waveland Press, 1964). Friedrich Schlegel, *Philosophical Fragments*, translated by

Peter Firchow (Minneapolis: University of Minnesota Press, 1991) contains the 'Critical Fragments', '*Athenaeum* Fragments', and 'Ideas'; it includes a penetrating forward on the very idea of the romantic fragment, 'Ideality in Fragmentation', by Rodolphe Gasché. The now out of print 1971 edition of this volume included a translation of Schlegel's only novel, *Lucinde*. There is now a good translation by Stuart Barnett of Schlegel's *On the Study of Greek Poetry* (Albany: State University Press of New York, 2001). *Theory as Practice: A Critical Anthology of Early German Romantic Writings*, edited and translated by Jochen Schulte-Sasse, Haynes Horne, Andrew Michel *et al.* (Minneapolis: University of Minnesota Press, 1997) is a wide-ranging reader for advanced students that includes, along with standard material, selections from: the Fichte-Schelling correspondence, Novalis' 'Fichte Studies', August Schlegel's 'Theory of Art' and, from various hands (Novalis, Friedrich Schlegel, Dorothea Veit-Schlegel, Caroline Schlegel-Schelling), romantic writings on gender and the feminine. Also worth consulting is F. Beiser, trans. and ed., *Early Political Writings of the German Romantics* (Cambridge: Cambridge University Press, 1996).

Secondary sources

Useful overviews and helpful bibliographical information for all the authors in this volume can be found in Michael Kelly (ed.), *Encyclopedia of Aesthetics*, 4 vols. (New York and Oxford: Oxford University Press, 1998). For an informative philosophical survey of this period, including fine essays dealing with Hamann and Schiller by Daniel O. Dahlstrom, and Hölderlin and Novalis by Charles Larmore, with an extensive bibliography, see Karl Ameriks (ed.), *The Cambridge Companion to German Idealism* (Cambridge: Cambridge University Press, 2000). Andrew Bowie's clear and persuasive *Aesthetics and Subjectivity: From Kant to Nietzsche* (Manchester: Manchester University Press, 1990) sees the aesthetic writings of this period anticipating twentieth-century continental philosophy; the volume includes discussion of the philosophy of music. Jean-Marie Schaeffer's *Art of the Modern Age: Philosophy of Art from Kant to Heidegger*, trans. Steven Rendall (Princeton: Princeton University Press, 2000), a mirror image of Bowie's study, considers the speculative privileging of art during this period mystical and unfounded.

For a vigorous reading of Hamann see Isaiah Berlin's *The Magus of the North: J. G. Hamann and the Origins of Modern Irrationalism* (New York: Farrar, Strauss and Giroux, 1993). D. E. Wellbery's *Lessing's Laocoön: Semiotics and Aesthetics in the Age of Reason* (Cambridge: Cambridge University Press, 1984) is a superb study providing not a semiotic reading of Lessing, but, plausibly, interpreting *Laocoön* through its contrast between natural and arbitrary signs. Still valuable is Ernst Cassier's appreciation of Lessing in *The Philosophy of the Enlightenment*, trans. F. Koelln and J. P. Pettegrove (Princeton: Princeton University Press, 1951). Jane Kneller's 'Imaginative Freedom and the German Enlightenment', *Journal of the History of Ideas* (1990), elegantly defends the inner connecting of freedom and aesthetics in Lessing and Kant. Dieter Henrich, 'Beauty and Freedom: Schiller's Struggle with Kant's Aesthetics', in Ted Cohen and Paul Guyer (eds.), *Essays in Kant's Aesthetics* (Chicago: University of Chicago Press, 1982) locates the 'Kallias Letters' in the context of the development of Schiller's aesthetic theory. A wide range of useful material is to be found in L. Sharpe, *Schiller's Aesthetic Essays: Two Centuries of Criticism* (Columbia, SC: Camden House, 1995). Paul Guyer, *Kant and the Experience of Freedom: Essays on Aesthetics and Morality* (New York: Cambridge University Press, 1993) contains instructive essays tracking themes in Schiller (disinterestedness) and Moritz (autonomy) in relation to their articulation in Kant.

Dieter Henrich's *The Course of Remembrance and Other Essays on Hölderlin* (Stanford: Stanford University Press, 1997), includes invaluable essays on the early fragments, especially 'Being Judgement Possibility'. The best single essay on the tragic in Hölderlin remains Peter Szondi, 'The Notion of the Tragic in Schelling, Hölderlin, and Hegel' in his *On Textual Understanding and Other Essays*, trans. Harvey Mendelsohn (Minneapolis: University of Minnesota Press, 1986); the volume includes two seminal, idealist interpretations of Schlegel: 'Friedrich Schlegel and Romantic Irony', and 'Friedrich Schlegel's Theory of Poetical Genres'. Philippe Lacoue-Labarthe's 'The Caesura of the Speculative', trans. Robert Eisenhauer in *Typographies: Mimesis, Philosophy, Politics* (Cambridge, MA: Harvard University Press, 1989), contests Szondi's reading of Hölderlin on the tragic from a deconstructive perspective. Four recent and interesting essays on Hölderlin's tragic thought – by Jean-François Courtine, François Dastur, David Farrell Krell, and Lacoue-Labarthe – are included in Miguel de Beistegui and Simon Sparks (eds.),

Philosophy and Tragedy (London: Routledge, 2000). The chapter on Hölderlin in Dennis J. Schmidt, *On Germans and Other Greeks: Tragedy and Ethical Life* (Bloomington: Indiana University Press, 2001), contains the most lucid account of his conception of tragedy in the anglophone literature. Azade Seyhan's *Representation and its Discontents: The Critical Legacy of German Romanticism* (Berkeley: University of California Press, 1992) offers a postmodern reading of romanticism against the background of the 'Kallias Letters' and Schiller's theory of drives.

The best overview of Jena romanticism is Ernst Behler, *German Romantic Literary Theory* (Cambridge: Cambridge University Press, 1993); Behler, like Seyhan, usefully connects theory and practice. Géza von Molnár, *Romantic Vision, Ethical Context: Novalis and Artistic Autonomy* (Minneapolis: University of Minnesota Press, 1987) seeks to provide a unified account of Novalis' achievement. The issue of an open temporality raised by the French Revolution for romantic poetry is persuasively handled by Alice Kuzniar, *Delayed Endings: Nonclosure in Novalis and Hölderlin* (Athens: University of Georgia Press, 1987), while Novalis' conception of subjectivity receives appropriate defence in Jane E. Kneller, 'Romantic Conceptions of the Self in Hölderlin and Novalis', David E. Klemm and Günther Zöller (eds.), *Figuring the Self: Subject, Absolute, and Others in Classical German Philosophy*. The postmodern, deconstructive interpretation of Schlegel's Jena romanticism was first essayed by Maurice Blanchot, 'The Athenaeum', in his *The Infinite Conversation*, trans. Susan Hanson (Minneapolis: University of Minnesota Press, 1993); the core thesis of this essay is provided with a powerful defence by Philippe Lacoue-Labarthe and Jean-Luc Nancy, *The Literary Absolute: The Theory of Literature in German Romanticism*, trans. Philip Barnard and Cheryl Lester (Albany: State University of New York Press, 1988), which is, in turn, elegantly refined (right back to its origins in Blanchot) by Simon Critchley, *Very Little...Almost Nothing: Death, Philosophy, Literature* (London: Routledge, 1997). Paul de Man wrote two compelling essays on Schlegel's conception of irony, both of which contest Szondi's interpretation and relate it to Fichte's account of subjectivity: 'The Rhetoric of Temporality' reprinted in the second edition of his *Blindness and Insight: Essays in the Rhetoric of Contemporary Criticism* (Minneapolis: University of Minnesota Press, 1983) and 'The Concept of Irony' in his *Aesthetic Ideology* (Minneapolis: University of Minnesota Press, 1996).

Note on the texts

Hamann, *Aesthetica in nuce*
Translated by Joyce P. Crick from the German text in *Sämtliche Werke*, edited by Nadler (1949–57), II, 195–217.

Lessing, *Laocoön: An Essay on the Limits of Painting and Poetry*
Translated by W. A. Steel from the German text in *Sämtliche Schriften*, edited by Karl Lachmann and Franz Muncker (1886–1924), IX, 1–177.

Moritz, 'On the Artistic Imitation of the Beautiful'
Translated by Stefan Bird-Pollan from the German text in *Werke*, edited by Günthe (1981), 549–64.

Schiller, *Kallias or Concerning Beauty: Letters to Gottfried Körner*
Translated by Stefan Bird-Pollan from the German text in *Schillers Werke*, edited by Mayer, IV (1966).

Hölderlin texts
The letter to Hegel is translated by Stefan Bird-Pollan from the German text in *Sämtliche Werke und Briefe*, edited by Mieth (1970), IV. The other texts are translated by Stefan Bird-Pollan from the *Sämtliche Werke*, edited by Sattler (1975–), II, XVII, XIV and XVI respectively.

Novalis texts
Translated by Joyce P. Crick from the German text in *Novalis Schriften*, edited by Kluckhorn and Samuel (1960–75), II.

Schlegel texts
'Letter About the Novel' is translated by Ernst Behler and R. Struc (1968). The other texts are translated by P. Firchow from the German

text in the *Kritische Friedrich-Schlegel-Ausgabe*, edited by Ernst Behler, Jean-Jacques Anstett and Hans Eichner (1958–).

The Novalis and Schlegel translations previously appeared in Kathleen Wheeler (ed.), *German Aesthetic and Literary Criticism: The Romantic Ironists and Goethe* (Cambridge University Press (1984)). The Hamann and Lessing translations previously appeared in H. B. Nisbet (ed.), *German Aesthetic and Literary Criticism: Winckelmann, Lessing, Hamann, Herder, Schiller and Goethe* (Cambridge University Press, 1985).

Annotation to the new translations is by J. M. Bernstein.

J. G. HAMANN

Aesthetica in nuce[1]:
A Rhapsody in Cabbalistic Prose (1762)

Judges v, 30

A prey of divers colours in needlework, meet for the necks of them that take the spoil.

Elihu in the Book of Job, XXXII, 19–22

Behold, my belly is as wine which hath no vent; it is ready to burst like new bottles.

I will speak, that I may be refreshed: I will open my lips and answer.

Let me not, I pray you, accept any man's person, neither let me give flattering titles unto man.

For I know not to give flattering titles; in so doing my maker would soon take me away.[2]

J. G. Hamann's own notes are printed at the foot of the page, indicated by superscript letters in the text. Editorial notes, printed beneath the author's notes, are indicated by superscript numbers; these include editorial notes to the lettered notes, which are numbered in one sequence with the notes to the text.

[1] 'Aesthetics in a Nutshell'; the title is probably modelled on that of Christoph Otto von Schönaich's (1725–1809) Complete Aesthetics in a Nutshell (Die ganze Ästhetik in einer Nuß, 1754), a satirical work against Klopstock.

[2] This, and the previous quotation from Judges, are given by Hamann in the original Hebrew.

I

Horace

The uninitiate crowd I ban and spurn!
Come ye, but guard your tongues! A song that's new
    I, priest of the Muses, sing for you
      Fair maids and youths to learn!

Kings o'er their several flocks bear sway. O'er kings
Like sway hath Jove, famed to have overthrown
    The Giants, by his nod alone
      Guiding created things.[3]

Not a lyre! Nor a painter's brush! A winnowing-fan for my Muse, to clear the threshing-floor of holy literature! Praise to the Archangel on the remains of Cannan's tongue![4] – on white asses[a] he is victorious in the contest, but the wise idiot of Greece[5] borrows Euthyphro's[b] proud stallions for the philological dispute.

Poetry is the mother-tongue of the human race; even as the garden is older than the ploughed field, painting than script; as song is more ancient than declamation; parables older than reasoning;[c] barter than trade. A deep sleep was the repose of our farthest ancestors; and their movement a frenzied dance. Seven days they would sit in the silence of deep thought or wonder; – and would open their mouths to utter winged sentences.

---

[a] Judges, v, 10.

[b] See Plato's *Cratylus*: '*Hermogenes* Indeed, Socrates, you do seem to me to be uttering oracles, exactly like an inspired prophet.

    Socrates Yes, Hermogenes, and I am convinced that the inspiration came to me from Euthyphro the Prospaltian [Hamann's text: the son of Pantios]. For I was with him and listening to him for a long time early this morning. So he must have been inspired, and he not only filled my ears but took possession of my soul with his superhuman wisdom. So I think this is our duty: we ought today to make use of this wisdom . . . but tomorrow, if the rest of you agree, we will conjure it away and purify ourselves, when we have found someone, whether priest or sophist, who is skilled in that kind of purifying . . . But ask me about any others [i.e. other names] you please, "that you may see what" Euthyphro's "horses are".' [Plato, *Cratylus*, translated by H. N. Fowler, Loeb Classical Library (London, 1926), 396d–397a and 407d; the quotation at the end is from Homer, *Iliad*, v, 221 f.].

[c] '. . . as hieroglyphs are older than letters, so are parables older than arguments', says Bacon, my Euthyphro.

[3] Hamann quotes Horace in the original Latin (as he does with subsequent Latin authors). The translation is by John Marshall (1908).

[4] The 'Archangel' (Michael) is an allusion to Johann David Michaelis (1717–91), theologian and philologist, whose rationalistic approach to the poetic language of the Old Testament aroused Hamann's strong opposition.

[5] The 'wise idiot' is Socrates – and Hamann himself.

The senses and passions speak and understand nothing but images. The entire store of human knowledge and happiness consists in images. The first outburst of Creation, and the first impression of its recording scribe; – the first manifestation and the first enjoyment of Nature are united in the words: Let there be Light! Here beginneth the feeling for the presence of things.[d]

Finally GOD crowned the revelation of His splendour to the senses with His masterpiece – with man. He created man in divine form – in the image of God created He him. This decision of our prime originator unravels the most complex knots of human nature and its destiny. Blind heathens have recognized the invisibility which man has in common with GOD. The veiled figure of the body, the countenance of the head, and the extremities of the arms are the visible schematic form in which we wander the earth; but in truth they are nothing but a finger pointing to the hidden man within us.

> Each man is a counterpart of God in miniature.[e]

The first nourishment came from the realm of plants; wine – the milk of the ancients; the oldest poetry was called botanical[f] by its learned commentator[6] (to judge from the tales of Jotham and of Joash);[g] and man's first apparel was a rhapsody of fig-leaves.

But the LORD GOD made coats of skins and clothed them – our ancestors, whom the knowledge of good and evil had taught shame. If necessity is the mother of invention, and made the arts and conveniences, then we have good cause to wonder with Goguet first how the fashion of clothing ourselves could have arisen in Eastern lands, and second why it should

---

[d] Ephesians, v, 13: 'for whatsoever doth make manifest is light'.

[e] Manilius Astron. Lib. IV. [Marcus Manilius, *Astronomica*, IV, 895].

[f] 'for being as a plant which comes from the lust of the earth without a formal seed, poetry has sprung up and spread abroad more than any other kind of learning' (Bacon, *de Augm. Scient.* Lib. II Cap. 13). See Councillor Johann David Michaelis' observations on Robert Lowth, *de sacra poesi Praelectionibus Academicis Oxonii habitis*, p. 100 (18).

[g] Judges, IX; II Chronicles, xxv, 18.

[6] The allusion is again to Michaelis. The latter's work on Lowth, referred to in Hamann's footnote (f), is his annotated edition of Robert Lowth's (1710–87) lectures on Hebrew poetry, *Praelectiones de Sacra Poesi Hebraeorum* (originally published in England in 1753). The quotation from Bacon in the same footnote is from *De Augmentis Scientiarum*, Book II, chapter 13. Translations of this and subsequent Latin quotations from Bacon's works are from the English versions in vols. IV and V of Francis Bacon, *Works*, edited by James Spedding, Robert Leslie Ellis and Douglas Denon Heath, 14 vols. (London, 1857–74); the present quotation is from IV, 318.

have been in the skins of beasts.[7] Let me risk a conjecture which seems to me at least ingenious. I place the origin of this costume in the universal constancy of animal characters,[8] familiar to Adam from consorting with the ancient poet (known as Abaddon in the language of Canaan, but called Apollyon in the Hellenistic tongue).[9] This moved primal man to hand on to posterity beneath this borrowed skin an intuitive knowledge of past and future events . . .

Speak, that I may see Thee! This wish was answered by the Creation, which is an utterance to created things through created things, for day speaketh unto day, and night proclaimeth unto night. Its word traverses every clime to the ends of the earth, and its voice can be heard in every dialect. The fault may lie where it will (outside us or within us): all we have left in nature for our use is fragmentary verse and *disjecta membra poetae*.[10] To collect these together is the scholar's modest part; the philosopher's to interpret them; to imitate them,[h] or – bolder still – to adapt them, the poet's.

To speak is to translate – from the tongue of angels into the tongue of men, that is, to translate thoughts into words – things into names – images into signs; which can be poetic or cyriological,[i] historic or symbolic or hieroglyphic – and philosophical or characteristic.[j] This kind of

h   You learn to compose verses with a divided name;
      Thus you will become an imitator of the singer Lucilius.
          Ausonius *Epist.* v. [Ausonius, *Epistolae*, XVI, 37–8]
i For an explanation, consult Wachter's *Naturae et Scripturae Concordia. Commentatio de literis ac numeris primaevis aliisque rebus memorabilibus cum ortu literarum coniunctis.* Lips. et Hafn. 1752, in the first section.[11]
j The following passage in Petronius is to be understood as being of this kind of sign. I am obliged to quote it in its context, even if it has to be read as a satire on the philologist himself and his contemporaries:[12] 'Your flatulent and formless flow of words is a modern immigrant from Asia to Athens. Its breath fell upon the mind of ambitious youth like the influence of a baleful planet, and when the old tradition was once broken, eloquence halted and grew dumb. In a word, who after this came to equal the splendour of Thucydides? (He is called the Pindar of historians.) [Hamann's parenthesis] Or of Hyperides? (who bared Phryne's bosom to convince the judges of his good cause) [Hamann's parenthesis] Even poetry did not glow with the colour of health, but the whole of art, nourished on one universal diet, lacked the vigour to reach the grey hairs of old age. The decadence in painting was the same, as soon as Egyptian charlatans had found a short cut to this high calling.' [Petronius, *Satyricon*, 2; translated by Michael Heseltine, Loeb Classical Library (London, 1913).] Compare this with the profound prophecy which Socrates put into the mouth of the Egyptian King Thamus about the inventions of Thoth, such that Phaedrus was moved to cry: 'Socrates, you easily make up stories of Egypt or any country you please.' [Plato, *Phaedrus*, 275b.]
7 The reference is to Antoine Yves Goguet (1716–58), *De l'origine des loix, des arts et des sciences et leur progrès chez les anciens peuples* (1758), I, 114 f. Goguet maintained that the original purpose of clothing cannot have been to protect man from the elements, since it was worn in countries whose climate made such protection unnecessary.

translation (I mean, speech) resembles more than ought else the wrong side of a tapestry:

And shows the stuff, but not the workman's skill;[13]

or it can be compared with an eclipse of the sun, which can be looked at in a vessel of water.[k]

Moses' torch illumines even the intellectual world, which also has its heaven and its earth. Hence Bacon compares the sciences with the waters above and below the vault of our vaporous globe.[17] The former are a glassy sea,[18] like unto crystal with fire; the latter, by contrast, are clouds from the ocean, no bigger than a man's hand.[19]

But the creation of the setting bears the same relation to the creation of man as epic to dramatic poetry. The one takes place by means of the word, the other by means of action. Heart, be like unto a tranquil sea! Hear this counsel: let us make men in our image, after our likeness, and let them have dominion! – Behold the deed: and the LORD GOD formed man of the dust of the ground – Compare word and deed: worship the mighty speaker with the Psalmist;[l] adore the supposed gardener[m] with

---

[k] The one metaphor comes from the Earl of Roscommon's *Essay on Translated Verse* and Howel's *Letters*.[14] Both, if I am not mistaken, borrowed the comparison from Saavedra.[15] The other is borrowed from one of the most excellent weekly journals, *The Adventurer*.[16] But there they are used *ad illustrationem* (to adorn the garment), here they are used *ad involucrum* (as a covering for the naked body), as Euthyphro's muse would distinguish.

[l] Psalms, XXXIII, 9.   [m] John, XX, 15–17.

[8] A satirical reference to Lessing, whose essay *On the Use of Animals in Fables* (1759) argues that the writers of fables employed animals rather than men because of the 'universally known constancy of animal characters'; see G. E. Lessing, *Werke*, edited by Herbert G. Göpfert, 8 vols. (Munich, 1970–9), V, 398. Hamann, of course, finds Lessing's rationalistic explanation unacceptable.

[9] Abaddon . . . Apollyon: see Revelation, IX, II.

[10] 'the limbs of the dismembered poet' (Horace, *Satires*, I, 4, line 62).

[11] The philologist Johann Georg Wachter (1673–1757), in the work referred to, distinguished three phases in the development of writing (cyriological, symbolic or hieroglyphic, and characteristic) from pictorial representation to abstract signs. Hamann adds the terms 'poetic', 'historic' and 'philosophical' to indicate parallel phases in the development of human thought.

[12] Hamann's satirical reference and quotation are aimed at the rationalistic philology of Michaelis (and its prolix expression).

[13] See the Earl of Roscommon, *Poems* (London, 1717), p. 9 (on a prose translation of Horace).

[14] James Howell (*c.* 1594–1666), *Familiar Letters* (1645–55).

[15] That is, Cervantes (Miguel Cervantes de Saavedra).

[16] *The Adventurer*, no. 49, 24 April 1753.

[17] The reference is to Bacon's distinction between two types of knowledge: divine revelation, and the empirical data of the senses (Bacon, *Works*, I, 520).

[18] See Revelation, IV, 6.   [19] See I Kings, XVIII, 44.

her who bore the news to the disciples; honour the free potter[n] with the Apostle to the Hellenistic scribes and philosophers of the Talmud![20]

The hieroglyphic Adam is the history of the entire race in the symbolic wheel: the character of Eve is the original of Nature's beauty and of systematic economy, which is not flaunted as a sacred method, but is formed beneath the earth and lies hidden in the bowels, in the very reins of things.

Virtuosos of the present aeon, cast by the LORD GOD into a deep trance of sleep! Ye noble few! Take advantage of this sleep, and make from this Endymion's rib[21] the newest version of the human soul, which the bard of midnight songs[22] beheld in his morning dream[o] – but not from close at hand. The next aeon will awake like a giant from a drunken sleep to embrace your muse and rejoice and bear witness: Yea, that is bone of my bone and flesh of my flesh!

If some modern literary Levite[24] were to take passing note of this rhapsody, I know in advance that he will bless himself like Saint Peter[p] at the vision of the great sheet knit at the four corners, upon which he fastened his eyes and saw four-footed beasts of the earth, and wild beasts, and creeping things, and fowls of the air . . . 'Oh no, thou one possessed, thou Samaritan' – (that is how he will scold the philologist in his heart) – 'for readers of orthodox tastes, low expressions and unclean vessels[25] are not proper' – *Impossibilissimum est, communia proprie dicere*[26] – Behold, that is why an author whose taste is but eight days old, but who is circumcised,[27] will foul his swaddling clothes with white gentian[28] – to the honour of

---

[n] Romans, IX, 21.

[o] See Dr Young's *Letter to the Author of Grandison on Original Composition.*[23]

[p] Acts, x, II.

[20] The reference is to St Paul, as Apostle to the Gentiles and a scholar learned in the Scriptures.

[21] A combined reference to the creation of woman from Adam's rib (Genesis, II, 21–3) and to Endymion, the beautiful youth whom the moon-goddess Selene visited while he slept.

[22] A reference to Edward Young's (1683–1765) poem *Night Thoughts* (1742–4).

[23] A reference to Edward Young's *Conjectures on Original Composition, in a Letter to the Author of Sir Charles Grandison* (1759).

[24] A reference to the Jewish philosopher and critic Moses Mendelssohn (1729–86), friend of Lessing and contributor, with Lessing and Nicolai, to the *Letters concerning Recent Literature* (1759–65); the 'passing Levite' alludes to Luke, x, 32 (the parable of the Good Samaritan).

[25] See Mark, VII, 4 and 8.

[26] Horace, *Ars poetica*, 127 (*Difficile est proprie communia dicere*): 'It is difficult to deal adequately with familiar subjects'; or, in Hamann's context, 'It is utterly impossible to call vulgar things by their proper name.'

[27] See Genesis, XVII, 12.

[28] According to Adelung's dictionary 'white gentian' was a vulgar expression in German for the white excrement of dogs.

human excrement! The old Phrygian's fabled ugliness[29] was never so dazzling as the aesthetic beauty of Aesop the younger.[30] Today, Horace's typical ode to Aristus[q] is fulfilled, that the poet who sings the praises of sweet-smiling Lalage, whose kiss is still sweeter than her laughter, has made dandies out of Sabine, Apuline and Mauretanian monsters.[31] True, one can be a man without finding it necessary to become an author. But whoever expects his good friends to think of the writer apart from the man, is more inclined to poetic than to philosophical abstractions.[32] Therefore do not venture into the metaphysics of the fine arts without being initiated into the orgies[r] and Eleusinian mysteries. But the senses belong to Ceres, and to Bacchus the passions, the ancient foster-parents of Nature the beautiful:

> Come to us, Bacchus, with the sweet grape cluster hanging
> From thy horns, and, Ceres, wreathe thy temples with the corn ears![s]

If this rhapsody might even be honoured by the judgement of a Master in Israel,[34] then let us go to meet him in holy prosopopoeia,[t] which is as welcome in the realm of the dead as it is in the realm of the living[35] (. . . si NUX modo ponor in illis):[36]

Most Worthy and Learned Rabbi!

'The postilion of the Holy Roman Empire, who bears the motto *Relata refero* on the shield of his escutcheon,[37] has made me desirous of the

---

[q] Lib. I, Od. 22. [Horace, *Odes*, I, 22; ode on Lalage to Aristius Fuscus.]
[r] 'Orgia nec Pentheum nec Orpheum tolerant.' Bacon, *de Augm. Scient.* Lib. II, Cap. 13.[33]
[s] Tibullus Libr. II, Eleg. I. [Tibullus, *Elegies*, II, I.]
[t] 'L' art de personifier ouvre un champ bien moins borné et plus fertile que l'ancienne Mythologie.' Fontenelle sur la poésie en général. Tom. VIII.
[29] A reference to the proverbial ugliness of Aesop.
[30] A reference to Lessing, whose *Fables* were published in 1759.
[31] The geographical names are taken from Horace's ode (I, 22) to Aristius; the target of satire is again Lessing, who wrote frivolous Anacreontic poetry in his early years.
[32] A reference to Lessing's contention, in the *Letters concerning Recent Literature*, that the private life of an author is irrelevant to his writing (see Lessing, *Werke*, ed. Göpfert, V, 43).
[33] 'Orgies cannot endure either Pentheus or Orpheus' (that is, both were torn to pieces by frenzied Maenads); see Bacon, *Works*, IV, 335.
[34] Another reference to Michaelis; also to John, III, 10.
[35] Personification (prosopopoeia) was employed in ancient rhetoric not only as an everyday figure of speech, but also as a means of introducing deceased personages as spokesmen in dialogues. (Hamann himself is about to address an ironic dialogue to the 'Rabbi' Michaelis.)
[36] 'if as a NUT I count as one of them' (Ovid, *Nux*, 19); an allusion to the title of Hamann's essay.
[37] A reference to the weekly newspaper *Ordentliche Wöchentliche Kayserliche Reichs-Postzeitung*, published in the Imperial city of Frankfurt; its motto was *Relata refero* ('I report reports').

second half of the homilies *da sacra poesi*.³⁸ I yearn for them, and have waited in vain until this day, even as the mother of the Hazorite captain looked out of a window for her son's chariot and cried through the lattice³⁹ – so do not think ill of me if I speak to you like the ghost in *Hamlet*, with signs and beckonings, until I have a proper occasion to declare myself in *sermones fideles*.ᵘ⁴⁰ Will you believe without proof that *Orbis pictus*,⁴¹ the book by that renowned fanatic, school-master, and philologist Amos Comenius,ᵛ and the *Exercitia* of Muzelius⁴² are both far too learned for children still pract-is-ing their spell-ing, and verily, verily, we must become even as little children if we are to receive the spirit of truth which passeth the world's understanding, for it seeth it not, and (even if it were to see it)

ᵘ John, III, II. The following passage from Bacon, *de Augm.* Lib. IX may help to guard against the crude and ignorant idea of pronouncing the present imitation of cabbalistic style to be good or bad: 'in the free way of interpreting Scripture, there occur two excesses. The one presupposes such perfection in Scripture, that all philosophy likewise should be derived from its sources; as if all other philosophy were something profane and heathen. This distemper has principally grown up in the school of Paracelsus and some others; but the beginnings thereof came from the Rabbis and Cabalists. But these men do not gain their object; and instead of giving honour to the Scriptures as they suppose, they rather embase and pollute them ... and as to seek divinity in philosophy is to seek the living among the dead, so to seek philosophy in divinity is to seek the dead among the living. The other method of interpretation which I set down as an excess, appears at the first glance sober and modest, yet in reality it both dishonours the Scriptures themselves, and is very injurious to the Church. This is, (in a word), when the divinely inspired Scriptures are explained in the same way as human writings. But we ought to remember that there are two things which are known to God the author of the Scriptures, but unknown to man; namely, the secrets of the heart, and the successions of time. And therefore as the dictates of Scripture are written to the hearts of men, and comprehend the vicissitudes of all ages; with an eternal and certain foreknowledge of all heresies, contradictions and differing and changing estates of the Church, as well in general as of the individual elect, they are not to be interpreted only according to the latitude and obvious sense of the place; or with respect to the occasion whereon the words were uttered; or in precise context with the words before or after; or in contemplation of the principal scope of the passage; but we must consider them to have in themselves, not only totally or collectively, but distributively also in clauses and words, infinite springs and streams of doctrines, to water every part of the Church and the souls of the faithful. For it has been well observed that the answers of our Saviour to many of the questions which were propounded to Him do not appear to the point, but as it were impertinent thereto. The reason whereof is twofold; the one, that knowing the thoughts of his questioners not as we men do by their words, but immediately and of himself, he answered their thoughts and not their words; the other, that He did not speak only to the persons then present, but to us also now living, and to men of every age and nation to whom the Gospel was to be preached. And this also holds good in other passages of Scripture.' [Bacon, *Works*, IV, 116–18].

ᵛ See Kortholt's collection of letters by Leibniz, vol. III, Ep. 29.

³⁸ Hamann refers to the newspaper announcement of the publication of the second part of Michaelis' edition of Lowth's work on Hebrew poetry (see note 6 above), which appeared in 1761.

³⁹ See Judges, v, 28.

⁴⁰ *sermones fideles*: true expressions (as distinct from the 'cabbalistic' style of the present work).

⁴¹ *Orbis pictus sensualium* (1657) by the Czech scholar and educationalist Johann Amos Comenius (1592–1671), an illustrated textbook designed to teach children by concrete, visual methods.

⁴² Friedrich Muzelius (1684–1753), philologist and author of school textbooks.

knoweth it not – Ascribe the fault to the foolishness of my way of writing, which accords so ill with the original mathematical sin of your oldest writing, and still less with the witty rebirth of your most recent works, if I borrow an example from the spelling-book which doubtless may be older than the Bible. Do the elements of the ABC lose their natural meaning, if in their infinite combinations into arbitrary signs they remind us of ideas which dwell, if not in heaven, then in our brains? But if we raise up the whole deserving righteousness of a scribe upon the dead body of the letter, what sayeth the spirit to that? Shall he be but a groom of the chamber to the dead letter, or perhaps a mere esquire to the deadening letter? God forbid! According to your copious insight into physical things,[43] you know better than I can remind you that the wind bloweth where it listeth – regardless of whether one hears it blowing; so one looks to the fickle weather-cock to find out where it comes from, or rather, whither it is going.'

> O outrageous crime! Shall the precious work be destroyed?
> Rather let the venerable power of the laws be infringed.
> Bacchus and sweet Ceres, come to our aid! . . . [w][44]

---

[w] See the poetic edict of the Emperor Octavius Augustus, according to which Virgil's last will *de abolenda Aeneide* [i.e. that the *Aeneid* should be destroyed] is said to have been nullified. One can concede whole-heartedly what Dr George Benson[45] has to say about the unity of sense, though he has scarcely developed his ideas, rather pulled them together with little thought, selection or smoothness. If he had tried to convey some earthly propositions about the unity of reading, his thoroughness would strike us more strongly. One cannot leaf through the four volumes of this paraphrastic explanation without a sly smile, nor miss the frequent passages where Dr Benson, the beam of popery in his own eye, inveighs against the mote in the Roman Church's, passages where he imitates our own official theologians when they applaud any blind and over-hasty bright idea honouring the creature more than the creator. First I would want to ask Dr Benson whether unity cannot exist without multiplicity? A lover of Homer is exposed to the same danger of losing his unity of sense by French paraphrasts like de la Motte or thoughtful dogmatists like Samuel Clarke. The literal or grammatical sense, the corporeal or dialectical sense, the Capernaitic[46] or historical sense are all profoundly mystical, and they are determined by minor circumstances of such a fleeting, arbitrary, spiritual nature that without ascending to heaven we cannot find the key to their understanding. We must not shrink from any journey across the seas or to the regions of such shadows as have believed, spoken, suffered for a day, for two, for a hundred or a thousand years – oh mysteries! –. The general history of the world can tell us hardly as much about them as can be writ on the narrowest tombstone, or as can be retained by Echo, that nymph of the laconic memory. The thinker who wants to intimate to us the schemes which thoughtful writers in a critical place devise in order to convert their unbelieving brethren must have the keys to heaven and hell. Because Moses placed life in the blood,[47] all the baptized rabbis are afraid of the spirit and life of the prophets, which make a sacrifice of the literal understanding, the child of their heart (ἐν παραβολῇ)[48] and turn the streams of Eastern wisdom to blood. A dainty stomach will have no use for these stifled thoughts. – *Abstracta initiis occultis; Concreta maturitati conveniunt*, according to Bengel's *Sonnenweiser*.[49] (*plane pollex, non index*.[50])

[43] A reference to Michaelis' emphasis on geographical and climatic factors in his rationalistic exegesis of the Scriptures.

The opinions of the philosophers are variant readings of Nature, and the precepts of the theologians variants of the Scriptures. The author is the best interpreter of his own words. He may speak through created things and through events – or through blood and fire and vapour of smoke,[x] for these constitute the sacramental language.

The Book of Creation contains examples of general concepts which GOD wished to reveal to His creatures through His Creation. The Books of the Covenant contain examples of secret articles which GOD wished to reveal to man through man. The unity of the great Author is mirrored even in the dialect of his works – in all of them a tone of immeasurable height and depth! A proof of the most splendid majesty and of total self-divesting! A miracle of such infinite stillness that makes GOD resemble Nothingness, so that in all conscience one would have to deny His existence, or else be a beast.[y] But at the same time a miracle of such infinite power, which fulfils all in all, that we cannot escape the intensity of His affection!

If it is a question of the good taste of the devotions, which are constituted by the philosophical spirit and poetic truth, and if it is a matter of the statecraft[z] of the versification, can we present a more credible witness than the immortal Voltaire, who virtually declares religion to be the cornerstone of epic poetry and whose greatest lament is that his religion[aa] is the reverse of mythology?

---

[x] Acts, II, 19. [y] Psalms, LXXIII, 21, 22.

[z] 'La seule politique dans un Poème doit être de faire de bons vers', says M. Voltaire in his credo on the epic [Voltaire's *Idée de la Henriade*].

[aa] Whatever M. Voltaire understands by religion, *Grammatici certant et adhuc sub Judice lis est;*[51] the philologist has as little to worry about here as his readers. We may look for it in the liberties of the Gallican Church, or in the flowers of sulphur of refined Naturalism, but neither explanation will do any harm to the unity of the sense.

44 Quoted by Hamann in Latin from *Anthologia Latina*, 672, lines 4, 20, and 8. The quotation expresses Hamann's unease at the violence done to Scripture by such interpreters as Michaelis.

45 George Benson (1699–1762), liberal theologian and author of various paraphrases, with commentaries, of books of the New Testament. (Michaelis had translated some of Benson's work.) Benson rejected the notion of the multiple sense of Scriptural passages, arguing for the unity of sense (that is, every passage has only a single meaning). Antoine Houdart de la Motte (1672–1731) and Samuel Clarke (1675–1729) applied the same thesis to Homer; for further details, see Sven-Aage Jørgensen's notes to his edition of Hamann's *Sokratische Denkwürdigkeiten* and *Aesthetica in nuce* (Stuttgart, 1968), pp. 102–4.

46 Capernaitic: pertaining to the doctrine of transubstantiation.

47 See Leviticus, XVII, II. 48 'as an example'.

49 'The abstract is appropriate to dark beginnings, the concrete to maturity': inaccurate quotation from Johann Albrecht Bengel's (1687–1752) *Gnomon* [= German *Sonnenweiser*] *Novi Testamenti* (1742). Hamann wishes to suggest by this quotation that the true prophetic sense of the Scriptures, denied by the literalist Benson, will come to light in the fullness of time.

Bacon represented mythology as a winged boy of Aeolus, the sun at his back, and with clouds for his footstool, fleeting away the time piping on a Grecian flute.[bb]

But Voltaire, High Priest in the Temple of Taste, can draw conclusions as compellingly as Caiaphas,[cc] and thinks more fruitfully than Herod.[dd] For if our theology is not worth as much as mythology, then it is simply impossible for us to match the poetry of the Heathens, let alone excel it[54] – which would be most appropriate to our duty and to our vanity. But if our poetry is worthless, our history will look leaner than Pharaoh's kine; but fairy-tales and court gazettes will take the place of our historians. And it is not worth the trouble of thinking of philosophy; all the more systematic calendars instead! – more than spider-webs in a ruined castle. Every idle fellow who can just about manage dog-Latin or Switzer-German, but whose name is stamped by the whole number M or half the number of the academic beast[55] is a blatant liar, and the benches and the clods sitting on them would have to cry 'outrage!' if the former only had ears, and the latter, ironically called listeners, only exercised their ears to listen with –

> Where is Euthyphro's whip, timid jade?
> So that my cart does not get stuck . . .

[bb] 'I take mythological fables to be a kind of breath from the traditions of more ancient nations, which fell into the pipes of the Greeks.' *De Augm. Scient.* Lib. II, Cap. 13 [Bacon, *Works*, IV, 317].

[cc] 'Qu'un homme ait du jugement ou non, il profite également de vos ouvrages: il ne lui faut que de la MÉMOIRE', is what a writer who utters prophecy has said to M. Voltaire's face. 'The rhapsodist should not forget this': Socrates in Plato's *Ion* [*Ion*, 539e].

[dd] Photius (in his *Amphilochiis Quaest.* CXX, which Johann Christoph Wolf has added to his cornucopia of critical and philological whimsies)[52] looks for a prophecy in the words of Herod to the Wise Men of the East – 'that I may come and worship him also' – and compares them with Caiaphas's statement in John XI, 49–52. He observes: 'There are perhaps other remarks of this kind, spoken by one of evil intention and murderous heart, which are ultimately prophetic.' Photius conceives Herod as a Janus bifrons,[53] who represented the Gentiles by his race and the Jews by his office. Many malicious and empty utterances (on which both master and servant pride themselves) might appear in a wholly different light if we were to ask ourselves from time to time whether they are speaking of their own accord or whether they should be understood as prophetic.

[50] 'Plainly a thumb, not an index finger': pun from Cicero, *Epistles to Atticus*, XIII, 46, as a humorous indication (*index*) of the importance of the preceding quotation.

[51] Horace, *Ars poetica*, line 78: 'scholars argue, and the case is so far undecided'. Hamann now transfers his satire to Voltaire as a leader of the rationalistic Enlightenment.

[52] Johann Christoph Wolf (1683–1739) quotes the passage from Photius (820–91) in his *Curae philologicae et criticae*, IV (Hamburg, 1735).

[53] Janus bifrons: the Roman god of doorways, with two faces looking in opposite directions.

[54] A reference to the *querelle des anciens et des modernes*.

[55] Typically oblique reference to the academic degrees of Master (M) and Doctor (D, the Roman numeral for 500, and half of M or 1,000).

Mythology here, mythology there![ee] Poetry is an imitation of Nature the beautiful – and the revelations of Nieuwentyt,[56] Newton and Buffon will surely be able to replace a tasteless mythology? Indeed they should, and they would too, if they could. So why does it not happen? – Because it is impossible, say your poets.

Nature works through the senses and the passions. But whoso maims these instruments, how can he feel? Are crippled sinews fit for movement?

Your lying, murderous philosophy has cleared Nature out of the way, and why do you demand that we should imitate her? – So that you can renew the pleasure by murdering the young students of Nature too.

Verily, you delicate critics of art, go on asking what is truth, and make for the door, because you cannot wait for an answer to this question. Your hands are always washed, whether you are about to eat bread, or whether you have just pronounced a death-sentence. Do you not also ask: what means did you employ to clear Nature out of the way? Bacon accuses you of flaying her with your abstractions. If Bacon is a witness to the truth, well then, stone him – and cast clods of earth or snowballs at his shade – If one single truth, like the sun, prevaileth, it is day. But if you behold instead of this One truth, as many as the sands of the seashore; and here close by, a little light[ff] which excels in brightness[gg] a whole host of suns; that is a night beloved of poets and thieves. The poet[hh] at the beginning of days is the same as the thief[ii] at the end of days.

All the colours of the most beautiful world grow pale if once you extinguish that light, the firstborn of Creation. If the belly is your god, then even the hairs on your head are under his guardianship. Every created thing becomes alternately your sacrifice and your idol. Cast down against its will, but hoping still, it groans beneath your yoke, or at your vanity; it

---

[ee] Fontenelle sur la Poésie en général. 'Quand on saura employer d'une manière nouvelle les images fabuleuses, il est sûr qu'elles feront un grand effet.'

[ff] '...et notho...–...lumine...' Catull. *Carm Sec. ad Dian.* ['and with borrowed light', Catullus, *Hymn to Diana*, II. 15 f.]

[gg]   '...And yet more bright
       Shines out the Julian star, as moon outglows
       Each lesser light'
                [Horace, Odes, I, 12, lines 46–8;
                        translation by John Marshall]

[hh] II Corinthians, IV, 6.   [ii] Revelation, XVI, 15.

[56] Bernhard Nieuwentyt (1654–1720), Dutch scientist and physico-theologian; he, Newton and Buffon are named simply as representatives of modern science, the Enlightenment's faith in which Hamann did not share.

does its best to escape your tyranny, and longs even in the most passionate embrace for that freedom with which the beasts paid Adam homage, when GOD brought them unto man to see what he would call them; for whatsoever man would call them, that was the name thereof.

This analogy of man to the Creator endows all creatures with their imprint and their stamp, on which faithfulness and faith in all Nature depends. The more vividly this idea of the image of the invisible GOD[jj] dwells in our heart, the more able we are to perceive his loving-kindness in his creatures; and to taste, and see it and grasp it with our hands. Every impression of Nature in man is not only a memorial, but also a warrant of fundamental truth: who is the LORD. Every counter-effect of man in GOD's created world is charter and seal that we partake of the divine nature,[kk] and that we are his offspring.[ll]

Oh for a muse like a refiner's fire, and like a fuller's soap![mm] – She will dare to purify the natural use of the senses from the unnatural use of abstractions,[nn] which distorts our concepts of things, even as it suppresses the name of the Creator and blasphemes against Him. I speak with you, o ye Greeks, for you deem yourselves wiser than the chamberlains with the gnostic key; go on and try to read the *Iliad* if you have first, with your abstractions, sifted out the two vowels alpha and omega, and then give me your opinion of the poet's sense and sound!

> Sing, -G-ddess, the wr-th -f Peleus's s-n -chilles[57]

Behold, the scribes of worldly wisdom, great and small, have overwhelmed the text of Nature, like the Great Flood. Were not all its beauties and riches

---

[jj] 'the image of the invisible God', Colossians, I, 15.

[kk] 'partakers of the divine nature', II Peter, I, 4; 'to be conformed to the image of his Son', Romans, VIII, 29.

[ll] Acts, XVII, 27, etc.   [mm] Malachi, III, 2.

[nn] Bacon, *de interpretatione Naturae et regno Hominis*, Aphorism. CXXIV: 'But I say that those foolish and apish images of worlds which the fancies of men have created in philosophical systems must be utterly scattered to the winds, Be it known then how vast a difference there is between the Idols of the human mind and the Ideas of the divine. The former are nothing more than arbitrary abstractions; the latter are the creator's own stamp upon creation, impressed and defined in matter by true and exquisite lines. Truth therefore and utility are here the very same things: and the works of nature themselves are of greater value as pledges of truth than as contributing to the comforts of life' [Bacon, *Novum organum*, I, Aphorism 124, in *Works*, IV, 110]. Elsewhere Bacon repeats this reminder that we should use the works of nature not only as amenities of living but also as pledges of truth.

[57] Homer, *Iliad*, I, I; Hamann omits the alphas and omegas in quoting the Greek, producing an effect similar to that of deleting the 'a's and 'o's from the English translation 'Sing, O Goddess, the wrath of Peleus's son Achilles'.

bound to turn into water? But you perform far greater miracles than ever delighted the gods,[oo] with oak-trees[pp] and pillars of salt, with petrifactions, alchemical transformations and fables, to convince the human race. You make Nature blind, that she might be your guide! Or rather, you have with your Epicureanism[58] put out the light of your own eyes, that you might be taken for prophets who spin your inspirations and expositions out of your own heads. Oh, you would have dominion over Nature, and you bind your own hands and feet with your Stoicism,[59] that you may warble all the more movingly in your Poetic Miscellanies at the diamond fetters of fate.

If the passions are limbs of dishonour, do they therefore cease to be weapons of virility? Have you a wiser understanding of the letter of reason than that allegorical chamberlain of the Alexandrian Church had of the letter of the Scriptures when he castrated himself in order to reach heaven?[60] The prince of this aeon takes his favourites from among the greatest offenders against themselves; his court fools are the worst enemies of Nature in her beauty; true, she has Corybants and Gauls as her pot-bellied priests, but *esprits forts* as her true worshippers.[61]

A philosopher such as Saul[qq] sets up laws for celibates – passion alone gives hands, feet and wings to abstractions and hypotheses, and to pictures and signs gives spirit life, and tongue. Where will you find a swifter syllogism? Where is the rolling thunder of eloquence begotten? And where its companion, the single-syllabled lightning-flash?[rr]

[oo] 'for the gods also have a sense of humour'. Socrates in *Cratylus* [Plato, *Cratylus*, 406 c.]

[pp] Socrates to Phaedrus: 'They used to say, my friend, that the words of the oak in the holy place of Zeus at Dodona were the first prophetic utterances. The people of that time, not being so wise as you young folks, were content in their simplicity to hear an oak or a rock, provided only it spoke the truth; but to you, perhaps, it makes a difference who the speaker is and where he comes from, for you do not consider only whether his words are true or not.' [Plato, *Phaedrus*, 275 b–c; translated by H. N. Fowler, Loeb Classical Library (London, 1914)]

[qq] I Samuel, XIV, 24.

[rr]   'Brief as the lightning in the collied night,
        That (in a spleen) unfolds heav'n and earth
        And ere man has power to say: Behold!
        The jaws of darkness do devour it up.'
        Shakespeare, *A Midsummer Night's Dream*

[58] A reference to such secular philosophers and freethinkers of the Enlightenment as Gassendi, La Mettrie, and Frederick the Great (who much admired the Epicurean philosophy of Lucretius).

[59] A reference to modern scientific determinism, as a counterpart to the determinism of the ancient Stoics.

[60] An allusion to Matthew, XIX, 12 and to the Church Father Origen (c. 185–c. 254), who castrated himself for the sake of religion.

Why should I paraphrase *one* word for you with an infinity of them, you readers whose estate, honour and dignity make you so ignorant? For they can observe for themselves the phenomena of passion everywhere in human society; even as everything, however remote, can touch our hearts in a particular direction; even as each individual feeling extends over the range of all external objects;[ss] even as we can make the most general instances our own by applying them to ourselves personally, and expand any private circumstance into the public spectacle of heaven and earth. Each individual truth grows into the foundation of a design more miraculously than the fabled cow-hide grew into the extent of a state, and a plan greater than the hemisphere comes together in the focus of perception. In short, the perfection of the design, the strength of the execution – the conception and birth of new ideas and new expressions – the labour and the rest of the wise man, the consolation and the loathing he finds in them, lie hidden from our senses in the fruitful womb of the passions.

'The philologist's public, his world of readers, seems to resemble that lecture-hall which Plato filled by himself.'[tt] Antimachus continued confidently, as it is written:

like the leech which does not drop off the skin until it is sated.[63]

Just as if our learning were a mere remembering, our attention is constantly being drawn to the monuments of the ancients, to shape our minds through memory. But why stop at the fountain of the Greeks, all riddled with holes as it is, and abandon the most living sources of antiquity? Perhaps we do not really know ourselves what it is in the Greeks and Romans that we admire even to idolatry.[64] This is where that accursed lying[uu] in our symbolic textbooks comes from, for to this day they are daintily bound in

---

[ss] 'C'est l'effet ordinaire de notre ignorance de nous peindre tout semblable à nous et de repandre nos portraits dans toute la nature', says Fontenelle in his *Histoire du Théâtre Franc*. 'Une grande passion est une espèce d'Ame, immortelle à sa manière et presque indépendante des Organes', Fontenelle in *Eloge de M. du Verney*.

[tt] 'for Plato alone is worth all of them to me'. Cicero, *Brutus*.[62]   [uu] Psalms, LIX, 12.

[61] The 'prince of this aeon' is Frederick the Great; the 'court fools', 'Gauls', and *esprits forts* are the French freethinkers (La Mettrie, Voltaire, etc.) with whom Frederick associated.

[62] Antimachus, in the anecdote alluded to, was reading a long poem, and all of his audience except Plato left the lecture room. He then made the remark quoted by Hamann (Cicero, *Brutus*, LI, 191).

[63] Horace, *Ars poetica*, line 476 (the final line of the poem).

[64] An allusion to Winckelmann, and an example of Hamann's hostility towards neo-classicism.

sheep's parchment, but within, verily, within they are whited sepulchres and full of hypocritical wickedness.^{vv}

We treat the ancients like a man who gazes on his visible face in a looking-glass, but who, having looked upon it, straightway goes and forgets how he was formed. A painter sits for his self-portrait in a wholly different spirit. Narcissus (the bulbous plant of *beaux esprits*) loves his picture more than his life.^{ww}

Salvation comes from the Jews.[66] I had not yet seen their philosophical writings, but I was certain of finding sounder concepts in them – to your shame, Christians! Yet you feel the sting of that worthy name by which ye are called^{xx} as little as you feel the honour GOD did himself in taking the vile name of Son of Man.

Nature and Scripture then are the materials of the beautiful spirit which creates and imitates – Bacon compares matter with Penelope. Her importunate suitors are the scribes and philosophers.[67] The tale of the beggar who appeared at the court of Ithaca you know, for has not Homer translated it into Greek, and Pope into English verse?

But how are we to raise the defunct language of Nature from the dead? By making pilgrimages to the fortunate lands of Arabia,[68] and by going on crusades to the East, and by restoring their magic art. To steal it, we must employ old women's cunning, for that is the best sort. Cast your eyes down, ye idle bellies, and read what Bacon has to say about the magic art.^{yy} Silken feet in dancing shoes will not bear you on such a weary journey, so be ready to accept guidance from this hyperbole.^{zz}

^{vv} See Part II of the *Letters concerning Recent Literature* (*Briefe, die neueste Literatur betreffend*) passim, a little here, a little there, but mainly p. 131.[65]

^{ww} Ovid, *Metamorph.*, Lib. III. [Hamann, in this footnote, goes on to quote Ovid's version of the myth of Narcissus at length, from *Metamorphoses*, III, 415–510.]

^{xx} James, II, 7.

^{yy} 'But indeed the chief business of magic was to note the correspondences between the architectures and fabrics of things natural and things civil. Neither are these only similitudes (as men of narrow observation may perhaps conceive them to be), but plainly the same footsteps of nature treading or printing upon different subjects and matters.' So Bacon in the third book of *De augmentis scientiarum*, in which he claims to explain the magic art also by means of a 'science of the universal consents of things', and in the light of this, the appearance of the Wise Men at Bethlehem. [Bacon, *Works*, IV, 339 and 366.]

^{zz} I Corinthians, XII, 31: 'and yet I show unto you a more excellent way'.

[65] The reference is to an (anonymous) attack by Nicolai, in the *Letters* referred to, on a volume of poems which had impressed Hamann favourably. Hamann throws back at the anonymous critic some of the abuse the latter had directed at the poems. For further details, see Hans-Martin Lumpp, *Philologia crucis. Zu Johann Georg Hamanns Auffassung von der Dichtkunst* (Tübingen, 1970), pp. 87–9.

[66] See John, IV, 22.

O Thou who tearest the heavens and camest down from them, before whose arrival the mountains melt as hot water boils on a bright fire, that Thy name shall be proclaimed among its enemies, who nevertheless call themselves by it; and that anointed heathens may learn to tremble before the wonders that Thou doest, which are beyond their understanding. Let new false lights rise in the Orient! Let the pert cleverness of their magi be roused by new stars into bearing their treasures in person to our country. Myrrh, frankincense and their gold, which mean more to us than their magic art! Let kings be gulled by it, and their philosophical muse rage at children and children's lore;[69] but let not Rachel weep in vain! -

Why should we swallow death from the pots,[70] to make the garnish palatable for the children of the prophets? And how shall we appease the vexed spirit[71] of the Scripture: 'Will I eat the flesh of bulls, or drink the blood of goats?'[72] Neither the dogmatic thoroughness of the orthodox Pharisees nor the poetic extravagance of the free-thinking Sadducees will renew the mission of the spirit which inspired GOD's holy men (in season or out of season) to speak and write. That dearly loved disciple of GOD's only-begotten Son, which is in the bosom of the Father, has declared it to us:[73] that the spirit of prophecy liveth in the testimony of the name of the ONE GOD, who alone maketh us blessed and through whom alone we may inherit the promise of this and the next life; the name which no one knows except he who receives it, the name which is above all names, that all things which dwell in Heaven and upon the earth and beneath the earth should bow their knee in the name of JESUS; and that all tongues should confess that JESUS CHRIST is the LORD to the glory of GOD the creator, to whom be praise in all eternity, Amen!

Thus the testimony of JESUS is the spirit of prophecy,[aaa] and the first sign by which He reveals the majesty of His humble figure transforms

---

[aaa] Revelation, XIX, 10.

[67] See Bacon, *Works*, IV, 319–20: Pan (Nature) is the son of Penelope (formless matter) and her suitors (the Platonic Ideas or Forms), according to one myth discussed by Bacon, who himself suggests that Nature is rather the son of matter and Mercury (the Logos or Word of God). Hamann's following sentence presents Odysseus, the true master, as a typological forerunner of Christ, appearing in lowly form (as a beggar).

[68] Allusion to a Danish scientific expedition (1761–7) to 'Arabia felix' (Southern Arabia) under Carstens Niebuhr (1733–1815), which was mounted at the suggestion of Michaelis, who remains the chief target of Hamann's satire.

[69] Another allusion to Frederick the Great and his circle of *philosophes*.

[70] See II Kings, IV, 38–42.   [71] See Isaiah, LXIII, 10.   [72] Psalms, L. 13.

[73] See John, I, 18 and XIII, 23–5.

the holy books of the convenant into fine old wine, which deceives the steward's judgement[74] and strengthens the weak stomach of the critics. 'If you read the prophetic books without understanding Christ', says the Punic[bbb] Father of the Church, 'what insipidity and foolishness you will find! If you understand Christ in them, then what you read will not only be to your taste, but will also intoxicate you.'[80] – 'But to put a curb on the proud and wicked spirits here, Adam must surely have been dead before he would suffer this thing and drink the strong wine. Therefore have a care that you drink no wine while you are still a suckling child; every doctrine has its measure, time and age.'[ccc]

[bbb] See pp. 66 and 67 of the *Answer to the Question as to the Influence of Opinions on Language and of Language on Opinions* which received the prize awarded by the Royal Academy of Sciences in 1759.[75] Also to be consulted in this connection: *Ars Punica sive Flos Linguarum: The Art of Punning, or the Flower of Languages in seventy-nine Rules for the farther Improvement of Conversation and Help of Memory*. By the Labour and Industry of TUM PUN-SIBI.[76]

'Bons-mots promoted by an equivocation are deemed the very wittiest, though not always concerned with jesting, but often even with what is important ... for the power to divert the force of a word into a sense quite different from that in which other folk understand it seems to indicate a man of talent' (Cicero, *De Orat.*, lib. 2) [Cicero, *De Oratore*, II, 250 and 254].

See the second edition [of *Ars Punica*], 1719, octavo, The author of this learned work (of which I have, unfortunately, only a defective copy) is Swift, the glory of the priesthood ('The glory of the Priesthood and the shame!', *Essay on Criticism*).[77] It begins with definitions: logical, physical, and moral. In the logical sense, 'Punning is essentially something of which it is said that it applies to something else or is in any manner applied to something else.' According to the natural science of the extravagant and whimsical Cardanus, 'Punning is an Art of Harmonious Jingling upon Words, which passing in at the Ears and falling upon the Diaphragma, excites a titillary Motion in those Parts, and this being convey'd by the Animal Spirits into the Muscles of the Face raises the Cockles of the Heart.' But according to Casuistry, it is 'a Virtue, that most effectually promotes the End of good Fellowship'. An example of this artful virtue can be found among others of the same ilk in the answer quoted above to the Punic comparison between Mahomet the Prophet and Augustine the Church Father, which resembles a hybrid lover of poetry, with an imagination half inspirational, half scholastic, who is not nearly learned enough to appreciate the use of figurative language properly, let alone be able to scrutinize religious experience.[78] The good Bishop spoke Hebrew without knowing it, just as M. Jourdain spoke prose without knowing it, and just as even today this raising and answering of learned questions without knowing it, can reveal the barbarism of the age and the treachery of the heart, at the cost of this profound truth: that we are all sinners, and devoid of the glory that is ascribed to us, the lying prophet of Arabia as much as the good African shepherd, as well as that clever wit (whom I should have named first of all) who thought up that far-fetched comparison between the two believers in providence by putting together such ridiculous parallel passages according to the Punic theory of reason of our modern cabbalists, for whom every fig-leaf yields a sufficient reason, and every insinuation a fulfilment.[79]

[ccc] Our Luther's words (reading Augustine, it is said, spoiled his taste somewhat), taken from his famous Preface to the Epistle to the Romans,[81] which I never weary of reading, just as I never tire of his Preface to the Psalms. I have introduced this passage by means of an accommodation, as they say, because in it Luther speaks of the abyss of Divine Providence, and, after his admirable custom, rests upon his dictum: 'that one cannot without suffering the cross and the pains of death trade Providence against God without harm and secret rage'.

[74] See John, II. 8–10.

After GOD had grown weary of speaking to us through Nature and Scripture, through created things and prophets, through reasonings and figures, through poets and seers, and had grown short of breath, He spoke to us at last in the evening of days through His Son – yesterday and today! – until the promise of His coming, no longer as a servant, shall be fulfilled –

> Thou art the King of Glory, O Christ,
> Thou art the everlasting Son of the Father,
> Thou didst not abhor the Virgin's womb.[ddd] [82]

We would pass a judgement for slander if we were to call our clever sophists fools and idiots when they describe the Law-Giver of the Jews as an ass's head and when they compare the proverbs of their great singers to dove's dung.[84] But the day of the LORD, a Sabbath darker than the midnight in which indomitable armadas are but as a stubble-field – the gentlest zephyr, herald of the last Thunderstorm – as poetical as the LORD of Hosts could think and express it – will drown the blasts of even the sturdiest trumpeter – Abraham's joy shall reach its pinnacle – his cup shall run over, then with his own hand GOD shall wipe away Abraham's last tear, more precious than all the pearls wantonly wasted by the last Queen of Egypt;[85] the last tear shed over the last ashes of Sodom and the

---

[ddd] The devout reader will be able to complete the hymnic cadence of this section for himself. My memory abandons me out of sheer wilfulness; 'Ever hastening to the end . . . and what he cannot hope to accomplish . . . he omits'.[83]

[75] The prize essay referred to is by Michaelis, and the reference is to remarks by him on Augustine's Punic (Carthaginian) origin and native language. Hamann goes on to pun on the word 'Punic' in his footnote, and makes fun, at considerable length, of Michaelis' learned deliberations.

[76] Hamann, as his subsequent comments make clear, shares the belief of his contemporaries that the work was by Jonathan Swift. It is now ascribed to Thomas Sheridan (see Jørgensen *Sokratische Denkwüdig Keiten*, p. 132).

[77] Pope, *Essay on Criticism*, line 694 (on Erasmus).

[78] All of this is oblique criticism of Michaelis and his attempts to rationalize Biblical references to miracles etc. as merely figurative expressions.

[79] Satirical references to the philosophical doctrines of the Enlightenment such as the Leibnizian principle of sufficient reason.

[80] The quotation is from St Augustine's commentary (IX, 3) on St John: see J. P. Migne, *Patrologia Latina*, XXXV, 1379 f.

[81] See Martin Luther, *Vorreden zur Heiligen Schrift* (Munich, 1934), pp. 78–93. Luther warns, in the passage referred to, against philosophical speculation on the mysteries of predestination and divine grace.

[82] The quotation is from Luther's translation of the *Te Deum*.

[83] Fragmentary quotation from Horace, *Ars poetica*, lines 148 ff.   [84] See II Kings, VI, 25.

[85] The reference is to Cleopatra, who dissolved a pearl to drink Antony's health.

fate of the last martyr[eee] GOD will wipe from the eye of Abraham, from the father of the faithful.

That day of the LORD, which gives the Christian courage to preach the LORD's death, will publish and make known the most stupid village idiots among all the angels for whom the fires of hell are waiting. The devils believe and tremble! But your senses, crazed by the cunning of reason, tremble not. You laugh when Adam the sinner chokes on the apple, and Anacreon the wise man on the grape-pip. Do ye not laugh when the geese fill the Capitol with alarm, and the ravens feed the lover of his country, whose spirit was Israel's artillery and cavalry? You congratulate yourselves secretly on your blindness when GOD on the cross is numbered among the criminals, and when some outrage in Geneva or Rome, in the opera or the mosque,[86] reaches its apotheosis or purgation.

> Paint two snakes! Consecrated ground, my lads:
> Not the place for a piss! I take my leave ... [87]
> (Persius)

The birth of a genius will be celebrated, as usual, to the accompanying martyrdom of innocents – I take the liberty of comparing rhyme and metre to innocent children, for our most recent poetry seems to put them in mortal danger.

If rhyme belongs to the same genus as paronomasia and word-play,[fff] then its origins must be almost as old as the nature of language and our sense-impressions. The poet who finds the yoke of rhyme too heavy to bear is not therefore justified in denigrating its talents.[ggg] The failed rhyme might otherwise have given this frivolous pen as much occasion for a satire as Plato may have had to immortalize Aristophanes's hiccups in *The Symposium*, or Scarron his own hiccups in a sonnet.[90]

[eee] II Peter, II, 8.

[fff] See note 76 of the editor, Lowth's *Praelect.*, xv; Algarotti, vol. III.[88]

[ggg] Gently rhyme creepeth into the heart, if 'tis not under compulsion; Harmony's staff and adornment, speech in our mem'ry it fixes. *Elegien und Briefe*, Strasburg, 1760.[89]

[86] That is, in the Catholic mass (Rome) or the austere Calvinist church (Geneva).

[87] Persius, Satires, I, 113; snakes, sacred to the house, were used as a sign to warn against desecration. Here, the satirist responds ironically to protests by influential persons against his attacks.

[88] Michaelis, in his edition of Lowth, discusses wordplay at length, and considers it of little aesthetic merit; the second reference is to Francesco Algarotti's (1712–64) *Oeuvres*, III, 76 (*Essai sur la rime*).

[89] The collection of poems quoted is by Ludwig Heinrich von Nicolay (1737–1820).

[90] Plato, *Symposium*, 185c-e; Paul Scarron (1610–60), French poet.

The free structure which that great restorer of lyric song, Klopstock, has allowed himself is, I would guess, an archaism, a happy imitation of the mysterious workings of sacred poetry among the ancient Hebrews.[91] And, as the most thorough critics of our time[hhh] shrewdly observe, what we apprehend in it is nothing but 'an artificial prose whose periods have been broken down into their elements, each one of which can be read as a single line in a particular metre; and the reflections and feelings of the most ancient and holy poets seem of their own accord' (perhaps just as randomly as Epicurus' cosmic atoms) 'to have arranged themselves into symmetrical lines which are full of harmony, although they have no (prescribed or mandatory) metre'.[92]

Homer's monotonous metre ought to seem at least as paradoxical to us as the free rhythms of our German Pindar.[iii] My admiration or ignorance of the causes for the Greek poet's use of the same metre throughout was modified when I made a journey through Courland and Lithuania. In certain parts of these regions, you can hear the Lettish or non-German people at work, singing only a single cadence of a few notes, which greatly resembles a poetic metre.[96] If a poet were to emerge among them, it would

---

[hhh] See the editor's fourth note to Lowth's third lecture, p. 149, and the fifty-first letter in the third part of the *Letters concerning Recent Literature*.

[iii] Wouldn't it be funny if Herr Klopstock were to specify to his printer or to some Margot la Ravaudeuse,[93] as the philologist's muse, the reasons why he had his poetic feelings printed in separate lines, when the vulgar think they are concerned with *qualitatibus occultis* and the language of dalliance calls them feelings par excellence. Despite the gibberish of my dialect, I would willingly acknowledge Herr Klopstock's prosaic manner to be a model of classical perfection. From having read a few small specimens, I would credit this writer with a profound knowledge of his mother tongue, particularly of its prosody. Indeed, his musical metre would seem highly appropriate as a lyrical garb for a poet who seeks to shun the commonplace. I distinguish the original compositions of our Asaph[94] from his transformations of old church hymns, indeed even from his epic,[95] whose story is well-known, and resembles Milton's in profile at least, if not entirely.

[91] Friedrich Gottlieb Klopstock (1724–1803), the most acclaimed lyric poet in Germany in the 1760s and 1770s, established the use of free rhythms and rhymeless verse in German.

[92] The 'thorough critics' are Michaelis (as editor of Lowth's lecture) and Lessing, whose comments (in the *Letters concerning Recent Literature*) Hamann here quotes. The praise of the 'thorough critics' is, of course, ironic. Hamann valued Klopstock for his piety and Biblical language as well as for his verse.

[93] According to Jørgensen, Sokratische Denkwürdig Keiten, p. 142, the title of a novel by Fougeret de Monbron.

[94] Asaph: psalmist (see Psalms, L and LXXIII-LXXXIII); circumlocution for Klopstock as a singer of sacred songs.

[95] References to Klopstock's *Geistliche Lieder* (1758) and his epic poem *The Messiah*, of which only part had been published when Hamann wrote.

[96] Note Hamann's interest in folk poetry, which Herder was soon to echo more fully in his essay on Ossian (see pp. 154–61).

be quite natural for him to tailor all his lines to this measure initiated by their voices. To place this small detail in the appropriate light ('perhaps to please the foolish – who wish to burn it with their curling irons'),[97] compare it with several other phenomena, trace their causes and develop their fruitful consequences would take too much time.

> Surely enough of snow and icy showers
> From the stern north Jove hath in vengeance called,
> Striking with red right hand his sacred towers,
> And Rome appalled –
>
> Ay, the whole earth – lest should return the time
> Of Pyrrha's blank amaze at sights most strange,
> When Proteus drove his finny herd to climb
> The mountain range.[98]
>
> (Horace)

Gloss

As the oldest reader of this Rhapsody in cabbalistic prose, I feel obliged by the right of primogeniture to bequeath to my younger brethren who will come after, one more example of a merciful judgement, as follows:

Everything in this aesthetic nutshell tastes of vanity, vanity! The Rhapsodist[iii] has read, observed, reflected, sought and found agreeable words, quoted faithfully, gone round about like a merchant ship and brought his far-fetched cargo home. He has calculated sentence for sentence as arrows are counted on a battle-field;[kkk] and circumscribed his figures as stakes are measured for a tent. Instead of stakes and arrows he has, with the amateurs and pedants of his time, . . . written obelisks and asterisks.[lll]

[iii] 'the rhapsodists – interpreters of the interpreters' (Socrates in Plato's *Ion*).[99]

[kkk] Procopius, *De bello persico*, 1, 18.

[lll] 'An asterisk | = little star | makes a light shine out, an obelisk | = little dagger | stabs and pierces' (Jerome's preface to the Pentateuch, cf. Diogenes Laertius on Plato). In skilful hands, these masoretic signs could equally well be used to rejuvenate the writings of Solomon, as one of the most recent commentators has interpreted two Epistles of St Paul by the method of paragraphs and tables.

[97] Cicero, *Brutus*, LXXV, 262; that is, 'who will merely use my writings as wastepaper'.

[98] Horace, *Odes*, 1, 2, lines 1–8 (translation by John Marshall); the reference in the poem to Deucalion's flood and the return of ancient chaos is for Hamann a figure for the coming Day of Judgement.

[99] Plato, *Ion*, 535a; compare p. 144 above: 'The opinions of the philosophers are variant readings of Nature, and the precepts of the theologians variants of the Scriptures. The author is the best interpreter of his own words.'

Let us now hear the sum total of his newest aesthetic, which is the oldest:

Fear GOD, and give glory to Him; for the time of His judgement is come; and worship Him that made heaven, and earth, and the sea, and the fountains of waters![100]

[100] Revelation, XIV, 7.

GOTTHOLD EPHRAIM LESSING

Laocoön:
An Essay on the Limits of Painting and Poetry[1] (1766)

Preface

The first who likened painting and poetry to each other must have been a man of delicate perception, who found that both arts affected him in a similar manner. Both, he realized, present to us appearance as reality, absent things as present; both deceive, and the deceit of either is pleasing.

A second sought to penetrate to the essence of the pleasure and discovered that in both it flows from one source. Beauty, the conception of which we at first derive from bodily objects, has general rules which can be applied to various things: to actions, to thoughts, as well as to forms.

A third, who reflected on the value and the application of these general rules, observed that some of them were predominant rather in painting, others rather in poetry; that, therefore, in the latter poetry could help out painting, in the former painting help out poetry, with illustrations and examples.

The first was the amateur; the second the philosopher; the third the critic.

[1] There is a useful commentary on the *Laocoön* in Lessing's *Werke*, edited by Herbert G. Göpfert, 8 vols. (Munich, 1970–9), VI, 861–917. The fullest collection of drafts, variants and background materials is still that in Hugo Blümner's edition of Lessing's *Laokoon*, second edition (Berlin, 1880). In the present translation, those of Lessing's long and learned footnotes which are now of only antiquarian interest are omitted. Where his footnotes contain material essential to his argument or to an understanding of the text, their substance is incorporated in the notes which follow here.

The two former could not easily make a false use either of their feeling or of their conclusions. But in the remarks of the critic, on the other hand, almost everything depends on the justice of their application to the individual case; and, where there have been fifty witty to one clear-eyed critic, it would have been a miracle if this application had at all times been made with the circumspection needful to hold the balance true between the two arts.

Supposing that Apelles and Protogenes[2] in their lost treatises upon painting confirmed and illustrated the rules of the same by the already settled rules of poetry, then one can certainly believe it must have been done with the moderation and exactitude with which we still find Aristotle, Cicero, Horace, Quintilian, in their writings, applying the principles and practice of painting to eloquence and poetry. It is the prerogative of the ancients, in everything to do neither too much nor too little.

But we moderns in several things have considered ourselves their betters, when we transformed their pleasant little byeways to highroads, even if the shorter and safer highroads shrink again to footpaths as they lead us through the wilds.

The startling antithesis of the Greek Voltaire,[3] that painting is a dumb poetry, and poetry a vocal painting, certainly was not to be found in any manual. It was a sudden inspiration, such as Simonides had more than once; the true element in it is so illuminating that we are inclined to ignore what in it is false or doubtful.

Nevertheless, the ancients did not ignore it. Rather, whilst they confined the claim of Simonides solely to the effect of the two arts, they did not omit to point out that, notwithstanding the complete similarity of this effect, they were yet distinct, both in their subjects and in the manner of their imitation (ὕλη καὶ τρόποις μιμήσεως).[4]

But entirely as if no such difference existed, many of our most recent critics have drawn from that correspondence between painting and poetry the crudest conclusions in the world. Now they force poetry into the narrower bounds of painting; and again, they propose to painting to fill

---

[2] Greek painters of the fourth century BC.

[3] The Greek lyric poet Simonides of Ceos, 556–467 BC.

[4] 'They differ in their objects and mode of imitation.' The quotation, used by Lessing as a motto on the title page of his work, is from Plutarch, 'Whether the Athenians were more Famous for their Martial Accomplishments or for their Knowledge', chapter 3.

the whole wide sphere of poetry. Everything that is right for the one is to be granted to the other also; everything which in the one pleases or displeases is necessarily to please or displease in the other; and, obsessed by this notion, they utter in the most confident tone the shallowest judgements; and we see them, in dealing with the works of poets and painters beyond reproach, making it a fault if they deviate from one another, and casting blame now on this side and now on that, according as they themselves have a taste for poetry or for painting.

Indeed, this newer criticism has in part seduced the virtuosos themselves. It has engendered in poetry the rage for description, and in painting the rage for allegorizing, in the effort to turn the former into a speaking picture without really knowing what she can and should paint, and to turn the latter into a silent poem without considering in what measure she can express general concepts and not at the same time depart from her vocation and become a freakish kind of writing.

To counteract this false taste and these ill-founded judgements is the primary object of the pages that follow. They have come together incidentally, according to the order of my reading, instead of being built up by a methodical development of general principles.[5] They are, therefore, rather unordered *collectanea* for a book than themselves a book.

Yet I flatter myself that even as such they are not wholly to be despised. Of systematic books there is no lack amongst us Germans. Out of a few assumed definitions to deduce most logically whatever we will – this we can manage as well as any nation in the world.

Baumgarten[6] confessed that for a great part of the examples in his *Æsthetics* he was indebted to Gesner's Dictionary.[7] If my argument is not as conclusive as Baumgarten's, at all events my examples will taste more of the original sources.

As I started, as it were, from Laocoön and return to him several times, I have desired to give him a share in the superscription. Some other little digressions concerning various points in the history of ancient art contribute less to my purpose, and they only stand here because I cannot hope ever to find for them a more suitable place.

---

[5] This claim is not strictly true.

[6] Alexander Gottlieb Baumgarten (1714–62), the founder of aesthetics as a philosophical discipline (*Aesthetica*, 1750).

[7] Johann Matthias Gesner (1691–1761), humanist and antiquary; the work referred to is his *Novus linguae et eruditionis romanae Thesaurus*.

I would further remind the reader that under the name of Painting I include the plastic arts in general, and am not prepared to maintain that under the name of Poetry I may not have had some regard also to the other arts whose method of imitation is progressive.

I

The general distinguishing excellence of the Greek masterpieces in painting and sculpture Herr Winckelmann places in a noble simplicity and quiet greatness, both in arrangement and in expression. 'Just as the depths of the sea', he says,

> always remain quiet, however the surface may rage, in like manner the expression in the figures of the Greek artists shows under all passions a great and steadfast soul.
>
> This soul is depicted in the countenance of the Laocoön, and not in the countenance alone, under the most violent sufferings. The pain which discovers itself in every muscle and sinew of the body, and which, without regarding the face and other parts, one seems almost oneself to feel from the painfully contracted abdomen alone – this pain, I say, yet expresses itself in the countenance and in the entire attitude without passion. He raises no agonizing cry, as Virgil sings of his Laocoön; the opening of the mouth does not permit it: much rather is it an oppressed and weary sigh, as Sadoleto[8] describes it. The pain of the body and the greatness of the soul are by the whole build of the figure distributed and, as it were, weighed out in equal parts. Laocoön suffers, but he suffers like the Philoctetes of Sophocles: his misery touches us to the soul; but we should like to be able to endure misery as this great man endures it.
>
> The expression of so great a soul goes far beyond the fashioning which beautiful Nature gives. The artist must have felt in himself the strength of spirit which he impressed upon the marble. Greece had artist and philosopher in one person, and more than one Metrodorus.[9] Wisdom stretched out her hand to Art and breathed more than common souls into the figures that she wrought, etc., etc.

[8] Jacopo Sadoleto (1477–1547), Italian cardinal and author of a Latin poem on the Laocoön group.
[9] Metrodorus of Athens, a philosopher and painter of the second century BC. On his dual accomplishment cf. Pliny's *Natural History*, XXV, 135.

The remark which is fundamental here – that the pain does not show itself in the countenance of Laocoön with the passion which one would expect from its violence – is perfectly just. This, too, is incontestable, that even in this very point in which a sciolist might judge the artist to have come short of Nature and not to have reached the true pathos of the pain: that just here, I say, his wisdom has shone out with especial brightness.

Only in the reason which Winckelmann gives for this wisdom, and in the universality of the rule which he deduces from this reason, I venture to be of a different opinion.

I confess that the disapproving side-glance which he casts on Virgil at first took me rather aback; and, next to that, the comparison with Philoctetes. I will make this my starting-point, and write down my thoughts just in the order in which they come.

'Laocoön suffers like the Philoctetes of Sophocles.' How, then, does the latter suffer? It is singular that his suffering has left with us such different impressions – the complaints, the outcry, the wild curses, with which his pain filled the camp and disturbed the sacrifices and all the sacred functions, resounded no less terribly through the desert island, as it was in part they that banished him thither. What sounds of anger, of lamentation, of despair, by which even the poet in his imitation made the theatre resound! People have found the third act of this drama disproportionately short compared with the rest. From this one gathers, say the critics, that the ancient dramatists considered an equal length of acts as of small consequence. That, indeed, I believe; but in this question I should prefer to base myself upon another example than this. The piteous outcries, the whimpering, the broken ἄ, ἄ, φεῦ, ἀτταταῖ, ὢ μοι, μοι![10] the whole long lines full of παπα, παπα,[11] of which this act consists and which must have been declaimed with quite other hesitations and drawings-out of utterance than are needful in a connected speech, doubtless made this act last pretty well as long in the presentation as the others. On paper it appears to the reader far shorter than it would to the listeners.

To cry out is the natural expression of bodily pain. Homer's wounded warriors not seldom fall to the ground with cries. Venus scratched screams loudly; not in order that she may be shown as the soft goddess of pleasure, but rather that suffering Nature may have her rights. For even the iron

---

[10] Exclamations of pain.   [11] See note 10.

Mars, when he feels the spear of Diomedes, screams so horribly, like ten thousand raging warriors at once, that both hosts are terrified.

However high in other respects Homer raises his heroes above Nature, they yet ever remain faithful to her when it comes to the point of feeling pain and injury, and to the utterance of this feeling by cries, or tears, or abusive language. By their deeds they are creatures of a superior order, by their sensibilities mere men.

I am well aware that we Europeans of a wiser posterity know better how to control our mouth and our eyes. Politeness and dignity forbid cries and tears. The active fortitude of the first rude ages has with us been transformed into the fortitude of endurance. Yet even our own ancestors were greater in the latter than in the former. Our ancestors, however, were barbarians. To conceal all pains, to face the stroke of death with unaltered eye, to die smiling under the teeth of vipers, to bewail neither his sin nor the loss of his dearest friend, are the marks of the ancient Northern hero. Palnatoko[12] gave his Jomsburgers the command to fear nothing nor once to utter the word fear.

Not so the Greek! He both felt and feared; he uttered his pain and his trouble; he was ashamed of no human weaknesses; but none must hold him back on the way to honour or from the fulfilment of duty. What with the barbarian sprang from savagery and hardness, was wrought in him by principle. With him heroism was like the hidden sparks in the flint, which sleep quietly so long as no outward force awakes them, and take from the stone neither its clearness nor its coldness. With the barbarian, heroism was a bright devouring flame, which raged continually and consumed, or at least darkened, every other good quality in him. When Homer leads out the Trojans to battle with wild outcries, and the Greeks, on the other hand, in resolute silence, the commentators remark with justice that the poet in this wishes to depict those as barbarians and these as civilized people. I am surprised that they have not remarked in another passage a similar characteristic contrast. The opposing hosts have concluded a truce; they are busy with the burning of their dead, which on neither side takes place without hot tears: δάκρυα θερμὰ χέοντες.[13] But Priam forbids his Trojans to weep; οὐδ᾽ εἴα κλαίειν Πρίαμος μέγας.[14] He forbids them to

---

[12] Danish hero and legendary founder of the town of Jomsburg.
[13] 'shedding hot tears'.   [14] 'but the great Priam forbade them to weep'.

weep, says Dacier,[15] because he dreads that they will weaken themselves too much and return to battle on the morrow with less courage. Good! But I ask, Why must Priam dread this? Why does not Agamemnon, too, give his Greeks the same command? The sense of the poet goes deeper. He would teach us that only the civilized Greek can at the same time weep and be brave, whilst the uncivilized Trojan in order to be so must first stifle all human feeling. Νεμεσσῶμαί γε μὲν οὐδὲν κλαίειν,[16] in another place, he puts in the mouth of the understanding son of wise Nestor.

It is worthy of remark that amongst the few tragedies that have come down to us from antiquity two pieces are to be found in which bodily pain is not the smallest part of the calamity that befalls the suffering hero: there is, besides the Philoctetes, the dying Hercules.[17] And even the latter Sophocles represents complaining, whining, weeping and crying aloud. Thanks to our polite neighbours, those masters of the becoming,[18] today a whimpering Philoctetes, a screaming Hercules, would be the most laughable, the most unendurable persons on the stage. It is true one of their latest dramatists has ventured on Philoctetes.[19] But would he venture to show them the true Philoctetes?

Amongst the lost dramas of Sophocles is numbered even a 'Laocoön'. Would that Fate had only granted us this Laocoön also! From the slight references made to it by some ancient grammarians it is not easy to gather how the theme was handled. Of one thing I feel sure: that the poet will not have depicted Laocoön as more of a stoic than Philoctetes and Hercules. All stoicism is untheatrical, and our pity is always proportionate to the suffering which the interesting subject expresses. If we see him bear his misery with greatness of soul, then indeed this greatness of soul will excite our admiration, but admiration is a cold emotion, whose passive wonder excludes every other warmer passion as well as every other more significant representation.

And now I come to the inference I wish to draw. If it is true that outcries on the feeling of bodily pain, especially according to the ancient Greek way of thinking, can quite well consist with a great soul; then the expression of such a soul cannot be the reason why, nevertheless, the artist in his

---

[15] Anne Lefèvre Dacier (1654–1720), philologist and translator of classical texts, including the *Iliad* (Paris, 1711).
[16] 'I in no way condemn weeping.'   [17] In the *Trachiniae* of Sophocles.   [18] The French.
[19] Jean Baptiste Vivien de Chateaubrun (1686–1775), author of the drama *Philoctète* (1775).

marble refuses to imitate this crying: there must be other grounds why he deviates here from his rival, the poet, who expresses this crying with obvious intention.

II

Whether it be fable or history that Love prompted the first attempt in the plastic arts,[20] it is at least certain that she was never weary of lending her guiding hand to the ancient masters. For if painting, as the art which imitates bodies on plane surfaces, is now generally practised with an unlimited range of subject, certainly the wise Greek set her much straiter bounds, and confined her solely to the imitation of beautiful bodies. His artist portrayed nothing but the beautiful; even the ordinary beautiful, beauty of inferior kinds, was for him only an occasional theme, an exercise, a recreation. In his work the perfection of the subject itself must give delight; he was too great to demand of those who beheld it that they should content themselves with the bare, cold pleasure arising from a well-caught likeness or from the daring of a clever effort; in his art nothing was dearer to him, and to his thinking nothing nobler, than the ultimate purpose of art.

'Who will wish to paint you, when no one wishes to see you?' says an old epigrammatist concerning an extremely misshapen man. Many a more modern artist would say, 'Be you as misshapen as is possible, I will paint you nevertheless. Though, indeed, no one may wish to see you, people will still wish to see my picture; not in so far as it represents you, but in so far as it is a demonstration of my art, which knows how to make so good a likeness of such a monster.'

To be sure, with pitiful dexterities that are not ennobled by the worth of their subjects, the propensity to such rank boasting is too natural for the Greeks to have escaped without their Pauson, their Pyreicus.[21] They had them; but they did strict justice upon them. Pauson, who confined himself entirely to the beauty of vulgar things and whose lower taste delighted most in the faulty and ugly in human shape, lived in the most sordid poverty. And Pyreicus, who painted, with all the diligence of a Dutch artist, nothing but barbers' shops, filthy factories, donkeys and cabbages,

---

[20] This legend is reported by Pliny, *Natural History*, XXXV, 151.
[21] Greek genre painters of the fifth century BC and the Hellenistic period respectively.

as if that kind of thing had so much charm in Nature and were so rarely to be seen, got the nickname of the rhyparograph, the dirt-painter, although the luxurious rich weighed his works against gold, to help out their merit by this imaginary value.

The magistrates themselves considered it not unworthy of their attention to keep the artist by force in his proper sphere. The law of the Thebans, which commanded him in his imitation to add to beauty, and forbade under penalties the exaggeration of the ugly, is well known. It was no law against the bungler, as it is usually, and even by Junius,[22] considered. It condemned the Greek Ghezzis;[23] the unworthy artifice of achieving likeness by exaggeration of the uglier parts of the original: in a word, caricature.

Indeed, it was direct from the spirit of the Beautiful that the law of the Hellanodiken[24] proceeded. Every Olympian victor received a statue; but only to the three-times victor was an Iconian statue[25] awarded. Of mediocre portraits there ought not to be too many amongst works of art. For although even a portrait admits of an ideal, still the likeness must be the first consideration; it is the ideal of a certain man, not the ideal of a man.

We laugh when we hear that with the ancients even the arts were subject to municipal laws. But we are not always right when we laugh. Unquestionably the laws must not usurp power over the sciences, for the ultimate purpose of the sciences is truth. Truth is a necessity of the soul; and it is nothing but tyranny to offer her the slightest violence in satisfying this essential need. The ultimate purpose of the arts, on the other hand, is pleasure, and pleasure can be dispensed with. So, of course, it may depend on the law-giver what kind of pleasure, and in what measure any kind of it, he will permit. The plastic arts in particular, beyond the unfailing influence they exert on the character of a nation, are capable of an effect that demands the close supervision of the law. When beautiful men fashioned beautiful statues, these in their turn affected them, and the State had beautiful statues in part to thank for beautiful citizens. With us the tender, imaginative power of mothers appears to express itself only in monsters.[26]

---

[22] Franciscus Junius (1589–1677), French antiquarian and author of *De pictura veterum* (1637).
[23] Pier Leone Ghezzi (1674–1755), historical painter and caricaturist.
[24] Judges at the ancient Olympic games.   [25] That is, a portrait likeness.
[26] An allusion to the popular superstition that pregnant mothers exposed to frightening impressions produced malformed offspring.

From this point of view I believe that in certain ancient legends, which men cast aside without hesitation as lies, something of truth may be recognized. The mothers of Aristomenes, of Aristodamas,[27] of Alexander the Great, of Scipio, of Augustus, of Galerius, all dreamed in their pregnancy that they had to do with a serpent. The serpent was a symbol of deity, and the beautiful statues and pictures of a Bacchus, an Apollo, a Mercury and a Hercules were seldom without a serpent. The honest women had by day feasted their eyes on the god, and the bewildering dream called up the image of the reptile. Thus I save the dream, and surrender the interpretation which the pride of their sons and the shamelessness of flatterers gave it. For there must certainly be a reason why the adulterous phantasy was never anything but a serpent.

Here, however, I am going off the line. I merely wished to establish the fact that with the ancients beauty was the supreme law of the plastic arts. And this being established, it necessarily follows that all else after which also the plastic arts might strive, if it were inconsistent with beauty must wholly yield to her, and if it were consistent with beauty must at least be subordinate.

I will dwell a little longer on *expression*. There are passions and degrees of passion which express themselves in the countenance by the most hideous grimaces, and put the whole frame into such violent postures that all the beautiful lines are lost which define it in a quieter condition. From these, therefore, the ancient artists either abstained wholly or reduced them to lower degrees in which they were capable of a measure of beauty. Rage and despair disfigured none of their works. I dare maintain that they never depicted a Fury.[28]

Wrath they reduced to sternness: with the poet it was an angry Jupiter who sent forth his lightnings; with the artist the god was calmly grave.

Lamentation was toned down to sadness. And where this softening could not take place, where lamentation would have been just as deforming as belittling – what then did Timanthes?[29] His picture of Iphigenia's sacrifice, in which he imparted to all the company the peculiar degree of sadness befitting them individually, but veiled the father's face, which

---

[27] An error of Lessing's; intended is perhaps Aratus of Sicyon, 271–213 BC, whose mother's name was Aristodama, or Aristodemus, a hero of the first Messenian War (c. 735–715 BC).

[28] Lessing adds a learned footnote, in which he tries to prove that supposed representations of the Furies in ancient art are in fact of other mythological figures.

[29] Greek painter (c. 420–380 BC).

should have shown the supreme degree, is well known, and many nice things have been said about it. He had, says one, so exhausted himself in sorrowful countenances that he despaired of being able to give the father one yet more grief-stricken. He confessed thereby, says another, that the pain of a father in such events is beyond all expression. I, for my part, see here neither the impotence of the artist nor the impotence of art. With the degree of emotion the traces of it are correspondingly heightened in the countenance; the highest degree is accompanied by the most decided traces of all, and nothing is easier for the artist than to exhibit them. But Timanthes knew the limits which the Graces set to his art. He knew that such misery as fell to Agamemnon's lot as a father expresses itself by distortions which are at all times ugly. So far as beauty and dignity could be united with the expression of sorrow, so far he carried it. He might have been willing to omit the ugliness had he been willing to mitigate the sorrow; but as his composition did not admit of both, what else remained to him but to veil it? What he dared not paint he left to be guessed. In a word, this veiling was a sacrifice which the artist offered to Beauty. It is an example, not how one should force expression beyond the bounds of art, but rather how one must subject it to the first law of art, the law of Beauty.

And if we refer this to the Laocoön, the motive for which I am looking becomes evident. The master was striving after the highest beauty, under the given circumstances of bodily pain. This, in its full deforming violence, it was not possible to unite with that. He was obliged, therefore, to abate, to lower it, to tone down cries to sighing; not because cries betrayed an ignoble soul, but because they disfigure the face in an unpleasing manner. Let one only, in imagination, open wide the mouth in Laocoön, and judge! Let him shriek, and see! It was a form that inspired pity because it showed beauty and pain together; now it has become an ugly, a loathsome form, from which one gladly turns away one's face, because the aspect of pain excites discomfort without the beauty of the suffering subject changing this discomfort into the sweet feeling of compassion.

The mere wide opening of the mouth – apart from the fact that the other parts of the face are thereby violently and unpleasantly distorted – is a blot in painting and a fault in sculpture which has the most untoward effect possible. Montfaucon[30] showed little taste when he passed off an old,

---

[30] Bernard de Montfaucon (1655–1741), *L'antiquité expliquée et représentée en figures*, 5 vols. (Paris, 1719–24), I, 50.

bearded head with widespread mouth for an oracle-pronouncing Jupiter. Must a god shriek when he unveils the future? Would a pleasing contour of the mouth make his speech suspicious? I do not even believe Valerius,[31] that Ajax in the imaginary picture of Timanthes should have cried aloud. Far inferior artists, in times when art was already degraded, never once allow the wildest barbarians, when, under the victor's sword, terror and mortal anguish seize them, to open the mouth to shrieking-point.

Certain it is that this reduction of extremest physical pain to a lower degree of feeling is apparent in several works of ancient art. The suffering Hercules in the poisoned garment, from the hand of an unknown ancient master, was not the Sophoclean who shrieked so horribly that the Locrian cliffs and the Euboean headlands resounded. It was more sad than wild. The Philoctetes of Pythagoras Leontinus[32] appeared to impart this pain to the beholder, an effect which the slightest trace of the horrible would have prevented. Some may ask where I have learnt that this master made a statue of Philoctetes? From a passage of Pliny which ought not to have awaited my emendation, so manifestly forged or garbled is it.

III

But, as we have already seen, Art in these later days has been assigned far wider boundaries. Let her imitative hand, folks say, stretch out to the whole of visible Nature, of which the Beautiful is only a small part. Let fidelity and truth of expression be her first law, and as Nature herself at all times sacrifices beauty to higher purposes, so also must the artist subordinate it to his general aim and yield to it no further than fidelity of expression permits. Enough, if by truth and faithful expression an ugliness of Nature be transformed into a beauty of Art.

Granted that one would willingly, to begin with, leave these conceptions uncontested in their worth or worthlessness, ought not other considerations quite independent of them to be examined – namely, why the artist is obliged to set bounds to expression and never to choose for it the supreme moment of an action?

The fact that the material limits of Art confine her imitative effort to one single moment will, I believe, lead us to similar conclusions.

[31] Valerius Maximus, Roman historian of the first century AD, and author of *De factis dictisque memorabilibus libri IX*.

[32] Greek sculptor of Rhegium, fifth century BC.

If the artist can never, in presence of ever-changing Nature, choose and use more than one single moment, and the painter in particular can use this single moment only from one point of vision; if, again, their works are made not merely to be seen, but to be considered, to be long and repeatedly contemplated, then it is certain that that single moment, and the single viewpoint of that moment, can never be chosen too significantly. Now that alone is significant and fruitful which gives free play to the imagination. The more we see, the more must we be able to add by thinking. The more we add thereto by thinking, so much the more can we believe ourselves to see. In the whole gamut of an emotion, however, there is no moment less advantageous than its topmost note. Beyond it there is nothing further, and to show us the uttermost is to tie the wings of fancy and compel her, as she cannot rise above the sensuous impression, to busy herself with weaker pictures below it, the visible fullness of expression acting as a frontier which she dare not transgress. When, therefore, Laocoön sighs, the imagination can hear him shriek; but if he shrieks, then she cannot mount a step higher from this representation, nor, again, descend a step lower without seeing him in a more tolerable and consequently more uninteresting condition. She hears him only groan, or she sees him already dead.

Further. As this single moment receives from Art an unchangeable continuance, it must not express anything which thought is obliged to consider transitory. All phenomena of whose very essence, according to our conceptions, it is that they break out suddenly and as suddenly vanish, that what they are they can be only for a moment – all such phenomena, whether agreeable or terrible, do, by the permanence which Art bestows, put on an aspect so abhorrent to Nature that at every repeated view of them the impression becomes weaker, until at last the whole thing inspires us with horror or loathing. La Mettrie, who had himself painted and engraved as a second Democritus, laughs only the first time that one sees him.[33] View him often, and from a philosopher he becomes a fool, and the laugh becomes a grin. So, too, with cries. The violent pain which presses out the cry either speedily relaxes or it destroys the sufferer. If, again, the most patient and resolute man cries aloud, still he does not cry out without intermission. And just this unintermitting aspect in the

---

[33] Julien Offray de La Mettrie (1709–51), materialistic philosopher and author of *L'homme machine* (1748); Democritus of Abdera (*c*. 460–370 BC), 'the laughing philosopher', traditionally opposed in iconography to the mournful Heracleitus.

material imitations of Art it is which would make his cries an effeminate or a childish weakness. This at least the artist of the Laocoön had to avoid, if cries had not been themselves damaging to beauty, and if even it had been permitted to his art to depict suffering without beauty.

Among the ancient painters Timomachus[34] seems to have chosen by preference themes of the extremest emotion. His Frenzied Ajax, his Medea the child-murderess, were famous pictures. But from the descriptions we have of them it clearly appears that he understood excellently well, and knew how to combine, that point where the beholder does not so much see the uttermost as reach it by added thought, and that appearance with which we do not join the idea of the transitory so necessarily that the prolongation of the same in Art must displease us. Medea he had not taken at the moment in which she actually murders the children, but some moments earlier, when motherly love still battles with jealousy. We foresee the end of the fight. We tremble beforehand, about to see Medea at her cruel deed, and our imagination goes out far beyond everything that the painter could show us in this terrible moment. But for this very reason we are so little troubled by the continued indecision of Medea, as Art presents it, that rather we devoutly wish it had so continued in Nature itself, that the struggle of passions had never been decided, or had at least endured long enough for time and reflection to weaken rage and assure the victory to motherly feeling. To Timomachus, moreover, this wisdom of his brought great and manifold tributes, and raised him far above another unknown painter who had been misguided enough to represent Medea in the height of her rage, and thus to give to this transient extreme of frenzy a permanence that revolts all Nature. The poet who blames him on this account remarks, very sensibly, addressing the picture itself: 'Dost thou, then, thirst perpetually for the blood of thy children? Is there constantly a new Jason, always a new Creusa here, to embitter thee for evermore? To the devil with thee, even in the painting!' he adds, with angry disgust.

Of the Frenzied Ajax of Timomachus we can judge by Philostratus' account.[35] Ajax appeared not as he rages amongst the herds and binds and slays oxen and goats for his enemies. Rather, the master showed him when, after these mad-heroic deeds, he sits exhausted and is meditating self-destruction. And that is actually the Frenzied Ajax; not because just

---

[34] Greek painter of the Hellenistic period.
[35] Flavius Philostratus, second to third century AD, author of the *Life of Apollonius of Tyana*; Lessing's reference is to Book II, chapter 22 of this work.

then he rages, but because one sees that he has raged, because one perceives the greatness of his frenzy most vividly by the despair and shame which he himself now feels over it. One sees the storm in the wreckage and corpses it has cast upon the shore.

IV

Glancing at the reasons adduced why the artist of the Laocoön was obliged to observe restraint in the expression of physical pain, I find that they are entirely drawn from the peculiar nature of Art and its necessary limits and requirements. Hardly, therefore, could any one of them be made applicable to poetry.

Without inquiring here how far the poet can succeed in depicting physical beauty, so much at least is undeniable, that, as the whole immeasurable realm of perfection lies open to his imitative skill, this visible veil, under which perfection becomes beauty, can be only one of the smallest means by which he undertakes to interest us in his subject. Often he neglects this means entirely, being assured that if his hero has won our goodwill, then his nobler qualities either so engage us that we do not think at all of the bodily form, or, if we think of it, so prepossess us that we do, on their very account, attribute to him, if not a beautiful one, yet at any rate one that is not uncomely. At least, with every single line which is not expressly intended for the eye he will still take this sense into consideration. When Virgil's Laocoön cries aloud, to whom does it occur then that a wide mouth is needful for a cry, and that this must be ugly? Enough, that *clamores horrendos ad sidera tollit*[36] is an excellent feature for the hearing, whatever it might be for the vision. Whosoever demands here a beautiful picture, for him the poet has entirely failed of his intention.

In the next place, nothing requires the poet to concentrate his picture on one single moment. He takes up each of his actions, as he likes, from its very origin and conducts it through all possible modifications to its final close. Every one of these modifications, which would cost the artist an entire separate canvas or marble-block, costs the poet a single line; and if this line, taken in itself, would have misled the hearer's imagination, it was either so prepared for by what preceded, or so modified and supplemented by what followed, that it loses its separate impression, and in its proper

---

[36] 'He raises terrible shouts to the stars above' (*Aeneid*, II, 222).

connection produces the most admirable effect in the world. Were it therefore actually unbecoming to a man to cry out in the extremity of pain, what damage can this trifling and transient impropriety do in our eyes to one whose other virtues have already taken us captive? Virgil's Laocoön shrieks aloud, but this shrieking Laocoön we already know and love as the wisest of patriots and the most affectionate of fathers. We refer his cries not to his character but purely to his unendurable suffering. It is this alone we hear in his cries, and the poet could make it sensible to us only through them. Who shall blame him then, and not much rather confess that, if the artist does well not to permit Laocoön to cry aloud, the poet does equally well in permitting him?

But Virgil here is merely a narrative poet. Can the dramatic poet be included with him in this justification? It is a different impression which is made by the narration of any man's cries from that which is made by the cries themselves. The drama, which is intended for the living artistry of the actor, might on this very ground be held more strictly to the laws of material painting. In him we do not merely suppose that we see and hear a shrieking Philoctetes; we hear and see him actually shriek. The closer the actor comes to Nature in this, the more sensibly must our eyes and ears be offended; for it is undeniable that they are so in Nature when we hear such loud and violent utterances of pain. Besides, physical pain does not generally excite that degree of sympathy which other evils awaken. Our imagination is not able to distinguish enough in it for the mere sight of it to call out something like an equivalent feeling in ourselves. Sophocles could, therefore, easily have overstepped a propriety not merely capricious, but founded in the very essence of our feelings, if he allowed Philoctetes and Hercules thus to whine and weep, thus to shriek and bellow. The bystanders could not possibly take so much share in their suffering as these unmeasured outbursts seem to demand. They will appear to us spectators comparatively cold, and yet we cannot well regard their sympathy otherwise than as the measure of our own. Let us add that the actor can only with difficulty, if at all, carry the representation of physical pain to the point of illusion; and who knows whether the later dramatic poets are not rather to be commended than to be blamed, in that they have either avoided this rock entirely or only sailed round it with the lightest of skiffs?

How many a thing would appear irrefragable in theory if genius had not succeeded in proving the contrary by actual achievement! None of these considerations is unfounded, and yet Philoctetes remains one of the masterpieces of the stage. For some of them do not really touch Sophocles, and by treating the rest with contempt he has attained beauties of which the timid critic without this example would never dream. The following notes deal with this point in fuller detail.

1. How wonderfully has the poet known how to strengthen and enlarge the idea of the physical pain! He chose a wound – for even the circumstances of the story one can contemplate as if they had depended on choice, in so far, that is to say, as he chose the whole story just because of the advantages the circumstances of it afforded him – he chose, I say, a wound and not an inward malady, because a more vivid representation can be made of the former than of the latter, however painful this may be. The mysterious inward burning which consumed Meleager[37] when his mother sacrificed him in mortal fire to her sisterly rage would therefore be less theatrical than a wound. And this wound was a divine judgement. A supernatural venom raged within without ceasing, and only an unusually severe attack of pain had its set time, after which the unhappy man fell ever into a narcotic sleep in which his exhausted nature must recover itself to be able to enter anew on the selfsame way of suffering. Chateaubrun[38] represents him merely as wounded by the poisoned arrow of a Trojan. What of extraordinary can so commonplace an accident promise? To such every warrior in the ancient battles was exposed; how did it come about that only with Philoctetes had it such terrible consequences? A natural poison that works nine whole years without killing is, besides, more improbable by far than all the mythical miraculous with which the Greek has furnished it.

2. But however great and terrible he made the bodily pains of his hero, he yet was in no doubt that they were insufficient in themselves to excite any notable degree of sympathy. He combined them, therefore, with other evils, which likewise, regarded in themselves, could not particularly move us, but which by this combination received just as melancholy a tinge as in their turn they imparted to the bodily pains. These evils were – a total deprivation of human society, hunger, and all the inconveniences of life to which in such deprivations one is exposed under an

---

[37] Figure of Greek mythology, whose life depended on a piece of wood rescued from the fire by his mother. His mother, when Meleager slew her brothers, cast the wood upon the fire and Meleager was himself consumed.

[38] See note 19 above.

inclement sky. Let us conceive of a man in these circumstances, but give him health, and capacities and industry, and we have a Robinson Crusoe who makes little demand upon our compassion, although otherwise his fate is not exactly a matter of indifference. For we are rarely so satisfied with human society that the repose which we enjoy when wanting it might not appear very charming, particularly under the representation which flatters every individual, that he can learn gradually to dispense with outside assistance. On the other hand, give a man the most painful, incurable malady, but at the same time conceive him surrounded by agreeable friends who let him want for nothing, who soften his affliction as far as lies in their power, and to whom he may unreservedly wail and lament; unquestionably we shall have pity for him, but this pity does not last, in the end we shrug our shoulders and recommend him patience. Only when both cases come together, when the lonely man has an enfeebled body, when others help the sick man just as little as he can help himself, and his complainings fly away in the desert air; then, indeed, we behold all the misery that can afflict human nature close over the unfortunate one, and every fleeting thought in which we conceive ourselves in his place awakens shuddering and horror. We perceive nothing before us but despair in its most dreadful form, and no pity is stronger, none more melts the whole soul than that which is mingled with representations of despair. Of this kind is the pity which we feel for Philoctetes, and feel most strongly at that moment when we see him deprived of his bow, the one thing that might preserve him his wretched life. Oh, the Frenchman, who had neither the understanding to reflect on this nor the heart to feel it! Or, if he had, was small enough to sacrifice all this to the pitiful taste of his countrymen. Chateaubrun gives Philoctetes society. He lets a young Princess come to him in the desert island. Nor is she alone, for she has her governess with her; a thing of which I know not whether the Princess or the poet had the greater need. The whole excellent play with the bow he set quite aside. Instead of it he gives us the play of beautiful eyes. Certainly to young French heroes bow and arrow would have appeared a great joke. On the other hand, nothing is more serious than the anger of beautiful eyes. The Greek torments us with the dreadful apprehension that poor Philoctetes must remain on the desert island without his bow, and perish miserably. The Frenchman knows a surer way to our hearts: he makes us fear the son of Achilles must retire without his Princess. At the time the Parisian critics proclaimed this a triumphing over the ancients, and one of them proposed to call Chateaubrun's piece *La Difficulté vaincue*.[39]

3. After the general effect let us consider the individual scenes, in which Philoctetes is no longer the forsaken invalid; in which he has hope of speedily leaving the comfortless wilderness behind and of once more reaching his own kingdom; in which, therefore, the painful wound is his sole calamity. He whimpers, he cries aloud, he goes through the most frightful convulsions. To this behaviour it is that the reproach of offended propriety is particularly addressed. It is an Englishman who utters this reproach;[40] a man, therefore, whom we should not easily suspect of a false delicacy. As we have already hinted, he gives a very good reason for the reproach. All feelings and passions, he says, with which others can only slightly sympathize, are offensive when they are expressed too violently.

> For this reason there is nothing more unbecoming and more unworthy of a man than when he cannot bear pain, even the most violent, with patience, but weeps and cries aloud. Of course we may feel sympathy with bodily pain. When we see that any one is about to get a blow on the arm or the shin-bone, and when the blow actually falls, in a certain measure we feel it as truly as he whom it strikes. At the same time, however, it is certain that the trouble we thus experience amounts to very little; if the person struck, therefore, sets up a violent outcry, we do not fail to despise him, because we are not at all in the mind to cry out with so much violence.
>
> (Adam Smith, *Theory of the Moral Sentiments*, Part I, sect. 2, ch. i, p. 41, London, 1761)

Nothing is more fallacious than general laws for human feelings. The web of them is so fine-spun and so intricate that it is hardly possible for the most careful speculation to take up a single thread by itself and follow it through all the threads that cross it. And supposing it possible, what is the use of it? There does not exist in Nature a single unmixed feeling; along with every one of them there arise a thousand others simultaneously, the very smallest of which completely alters the first, so that exceptions on exceptions spring up which reduce at last the supposed general law itself to the mere experience of a few individual cases. We despise him, says the Englishman, whom we hear shriek aloud under bodily pain. No; not

---

[39] Lessing's footnote refers to the *Mercure de France*, April 1755, p. 177.
[40] Or rather, a Scotsman: Adam Smith (1723–90), *The Theory of Moral Sentiments* (London, 1761).

always, nor at first; not when we see that the sufferer makes every effort to suppress it; not when we know him otherwise as a man of fortitude; still less when we see him even in his suffering give proof of his fortitude, when we see that the pain can indeed force cries from him, but can compel him to nothing further – that he will rather submit to the longer endurance of this pain than change his opinions or his resolves in the slightest, even if he might hope by such a change to end his agony. And all this we find in Philoctetes. With the ancient Greeks moral greatness consisted in just as unchanging a love to friends as an unalterable hatred to enemies. This greatness Philoctetes maintains in all his torments. His pain has not so dried his eyes that they can spare no tears for the fate of his old friends. His pain has not made him so pliable that, to be rid of it, he will forgive his enemies and allow himself willingly to be used for their selfish purposes. And this rock of a man ought the Athenians to have despised because the surges that could not shake him made him give forth a cry? I confess that in the philosophy of Cicero, generally speaking, I find little taste; and least of all in that second book of his *Tusculan Disputations*, where he pours out his notions about the endurance of bodily pain. One might almost think he wanted to train a gladiator, he declaims so passionately against the outward expression of pain. In this alone does he seem to find a want of fortitude, without considering that it is frequently anything but voluntary, whilst true bravery can only be shown in voluntary actions. In Sophocles he hears Philoctetes merely complain and cry aloud, and overlooks utterly his otherwise steadfast bearing. Where save here could he have found the opportunity for his rhetorical outburst against the poets? 'They would make us weaklings, showing us as they do the bravest of men lamenting and bewailing themselves.' They must bewail themselves, for a theatre is not an arena. The condemned or venal gladiator it behoved to do and suffer everything with decorum. No complaining word must be heard from him, nor painful grimace be seen. For as his wounds and his death were to delight the spectators, Art must learn to conceal all feeling. The least utterance of it would have aroused compassion, and compassion often excited would have speedily brought an end to these icily gruesome spectacles. But what here it was not desired to excite is the one object of the tragic stage, and demands therefore an exactly opposite demeanour. Its heroes must show feeling, must utter their pain, and let Nature work in them undisguisedly. If they betray restraint and training, they leave our hearts cold, and pugilists in the cothurnus could at best only excite admiration. This designation would befit all the persons of the so-called Seneca tragedies,[41] and I firmly believe that the gladiatorial plays were the principal reason why the Romans in tragedy remained so far below the mediocre. To disown human nature was the lesson the spectators learned in the bloody amphitheatre, where certainly a Ctesias[42] might study his art, but never a Sophocles. The tragic genius, accustomed to these artistic death scenes, necessarily sank into bombast and rodomontade. But just as little as such rodomontade could inspire true heroism, could the laments of Philoctetes make men weak. The complaints are those of a man, but the actions those of a hero. Both together make the human hero, who is neither soft nor hardened, but appears now the one and now the other, according as Nature at one time, and duty and principle at another, demand. He is the highest that Wisdom can produce and Art imitate.

4. It is not enough that Sophocles has secured his sensitive Philoctetes against contempt; he has also wisely taken precautions against all else that might, according to the Englishman's remark, be urged against him. For if we certainly do not always despise him who cries aloud in bodily pain, still it is indisputable that we do not feel so much sympathy for him as these outcries seem to demand. How, then, shall all those comport themselves who have to do with the shrieking Philoctetes? Shall they affect to be deeply moved? That is against nature. Shall they show themselves as cold and as disconcerted as we are really accustomed to be in such cases? That would produce for the spectator the most unpleasant dissonance. But, as we have said, against this Sophocles has taken precautions. In this way, namely, that the secondary persons have an interest of their own; that the impression which the cries of Philoctetes make on them is not the one thing that occupies them, and the spectator's attention is not so much drawn to the disproportion of their sympathy with these cries, but rather to the change which arises or should arise in their disposition and attitude from sympathy, be it as weak or as strong as it may. Neoptolemus and his company have deceived the unhappy Philoctetes; they recognize into what despair their betrayal will plunge him; and now, before their eyes, a terrible accident befalls him. If this accident is not enough to arouse any particular feeling of sympathy within them, it still will move them to repent, to have regard to a misery so great, and indispose them to add to it

---

[41] In Lessing's day, Seneca's authorship of the tragedies traditionally attributed to him was doubted.

[42] Lessing's error; intended is probably Cresilas, an artist of the first century AD to whom Pliny (XXXVI, 77) attributes a statue of a dying gladiator.

by treachery. This is what the spectator expects, and his expectations are not disappointed by the noble-minded Neoptolemus. Philoctetes mastering his pain would have maintained Neoptolemus in his dissimulation. Philoctetes, whom his pain renders incapable of dissimulation, however imperatively necessary it may seem to him, so that his future fellow-travellers may not too soon regret their promise to take him with them; Philoctetes, who is nature itself, brings Neoptolemus, too, back to his own nature. This conversion is admirable, and so much the more touching as it is entirely wrought by humane feeling. With the Frenchman,[43] on the contrary, beautiful eyes have their share in it. But I will say no more of this burlesque. Of the same artifice – namely, to join to the pity which bodily pain should arouse another emotion in the onlookers – Sophocles availed himself on another occasion: in the *Trachiniae*. The agony of Hercules is no enfeebling agony, it drives him to frenzy in which he pants for nothing but revenge. He had already, in his rage, seized Lichas and dashed him to pieces upon the rocks. The chorus is of women; so much the more naturally must fear and horror overwhelm them. This, and the expectant doubt whether yet a god will hasten to the help of Hercules, or Hercules succumb to the calamity, form here the real general interest, mingled merely with a slight tinge of sympathy. As soon as the issue is determined by the oracle, Hercules becomes quiet, and admiration of his final steadfast resolution takes the place of all other feelings. But in comparing the suffering Hercules with the suffering Philoctetes, one must never forget that the former is a demigod and the latter only a man. The man is not for a moment ashamed of his lamentations; but the demigod is ashamed that his mortal part has prevailed so far over the immortal that he must weep and whimper like a girl. We moderns do not believe in demigods, but our smallest hero we expect to feel and act as a demigod.

Whether an actor can bring the cries and grimaces of pain to the point of illusion I will not venture either to assert or to deny. If I found that our actors could not, then I should first like to know whether it would be impossible also to a Garrick;[44] and if even he did not succeed, I should still be able to suppose a perfection in the stage-business and declamation of the ancients of which we today have no conception.

---

[43] Chateaubrun; see note 19 above.
[44] The actor David Garrick (1717–79) was revered in Germany, where he had appeared on tour in 1763, no less than in England.

V

There are some learned students of antiquity who regard the Laocoön group as indeed a work of Greek masters, but of the time of the Emperors, because they believe that the Laocoön of Virgil served as its model.[45] Of the older scholars who are of this opinion I will name only Bartholomew Marliani,[46] and of the modern, Montfaucon.[47] They doubtless found so close an agreement between the work of art and the poet's description that they thought it impossible that the two should have lighted by chance upon identical details such as are far from offering themselves unsought. At the same time their presumption is that if it be a question of the honour of the invention and first conception, the probability is incomparably greater that it belongs rather to the poet than to the artist.

Only they appear to have forgotten that a third case is possible. For it may be that the poet has as little imitated the artist as the artist has the poet, and that both have drawn from an identical source older than either. According to Macrobius,[48] this more ancient source might have been Pisander.[49] For when the works of this Greek poet were still extant, it was a matter of common knowledge, *pueris decantatum*,[50] that the Roman had not so much imitated as faithfully translated from him the whole of the Capture and Destruction of Ilium, his entire Second Book. Now, therefore, if Pisander had been Virgil's predecessor also in the story of Laocoön, then the Greek artists needed not to learn their lesson from a Latin poet, and the surmise as to their era is based upon nothing.

All the same, were I obliged to maintain the opinion of Marliani and Montfaucon, I should suggest to them the following way out. Pisander's

---

[45] This and the following chapter deal with the dating of the Laocoön group, a question which archaeologists still debate. For recent arguments, see Margarete Bieber, *Laocoön: The Influence of the Group since its Rediscovery*, revised edition (Detroit, 1967), pp. 37–41; Gisela M. A. Richter, *The Sculpture and Sculptors of the Greeks*, fourth edition (New Haven and London, 1970), pp. 237 ff.; and A. F. Stewart, 'To Entertain an Emperor: Sperlonga, Laokoon and Tiberius at the Dinner Table', *Journal of Roman Studies*, 67 (1977), 76–94. According to Stewart, the latest evidence suggests that the group was executed in the reign of Augustus or even Tiberius, not up to a century earlier, as was until recently believed. If this is indeed the case, Lessing's conjecture that the group post-dates Virgil's *Aeneid* (*c*. 26–19 BC) could well be correct.

[46] Bartolomeo Marliani (died *c*. 1560), author of *Topographia urbis Romae* (1544); Lessing's reference is to Book IV, chapter 14 of this work.

[47] See note 30 above; Lessing's reference is to the supplement to *L'antiquité expliquée*, Part I, p. 242.

[48] Aurelius Ambrosius Theodosius Macrobius (*c*. 400 AD), author of *Saturnalia sive conviviorum libri VII*; Lessing's reference is to Book V, chapter 2.

[49] Pisander, Greek epic poet of the seventh century BC, of whose work only fragments survive.

[50] 'Recited by schoolchildren' (the phrase is quoted from Macrobius).

poems are lost; how the story of Laocoön was told by him no one can say with certainty; but it is probable that it was with the same details of which we still find traces in the Greek writers. Now, these do not agree in the least with Virgil's narrative, and the Roman poet must have recast the Greek legend as he thought best. His manner of telling the tale of Laocoön is his own invention; consequently, if the artists in their representation are in harmony with him, it is almost a certainty that they followed him and wrought according to his pattern.

In Quintus Calaber,[51] indeed, Laocoön displays a similar suspicion of the Wooden Horse as in Virgil; but the wrath of Minerva which he thereby draws upon himself expresses itself quite differently. The earth trembles under the warning Trojan; horror and dread seize him; a burning pain rages in his eyes; his brain reels; he raves; he goes blind. Only when, though blind, he ceases not to urge the burning of the Wooden Horse, does Minerva send two terrible dragons, and these attack only the children of Laocoön. In vain they stretch out their hands to their father; the poor blind man cannot help them; they are torn in pieces, and the serpents glide away into the earth. To Laocoön himself they do nothing; and that this account was not peculiar to Quintus, but must rather have been universally accepted, is proved by a passage in Lycophron,[52] where these serpents bear the epithet 'child-eaters'.

If, however, this account had been universally received amongst the Greeks, the Greek artists in that case would hardly have been bold enough to deviate from it, and it would hardly have happened that they should deviate from it in precisely the same way as a Roman poet did if they had not known this poet, if perhaps they had not actually had the express commission to follow his lead. On this point, I think, we must insist if we would defend Marliani and Montfaucon. Virgil is the first and only one who describes the father as well as the children destroyed by the serpents;[53] the sculptors do this likewise, while yet as Greeks they ought not: therefore it is probable that they did it at the prompting of Virgil.

I quite understand how far this probability falls short of historical certainty. But as I do not intend to draw any historical conclusions from it, I yet believe at least that it can stand as a hypothesis which the critic

---

[51] Quintus Calaber or Smyrnaeus (third to fourth century AD), author of *Posthomerica*, a continuation of Homer's *Iliad*.
[52] Lycophron, grammarian and poet (third century BC), author of the monodrama *Cassandra*.
[53] Virgil's account of Laocoön's death is in Book II of the *Aeneid*, lines 199–224.

in forming his views may take into account. Proven or not proven, that the sculptors followed Virgil in their works, I will assume it merely to see how in that case they did follow him. Concerning the outcries, I have already explained my opinion. Perhaps a further comparison may lead us to observations not less instructive.

The idea of binding the father with his two sons into one group by the deadly serpents is unquestionably a very happy one, evincing an uncommonly graphic imagination. To whom is it to be assigned? The poet, or the artist? Montfaucon refuses to find it in the poet. But Montfaucon, as I think, has not read him with sufficient attention.

> ... Illi agmine certo
> Laocoönta petunt, et primum parva duorum
> Corpora natorum serpens amplexus uterque
> Implicat et miseros morsu depascitur artus.
> Post ipsum, auxilio subeuntem ac tela ferentem,
> Corripiunt, spirisque ligant ingentibus ... [54]

The poet has depicted the serpents as of a marvellous length. They have enfolded the boys, and when the father comes to their aid, seize him also (*corripiunt*). From their size they could not at once uncoil themselves from the boys; there must therefore be a moment in which they had attacked the father with their heads and foreparts, while they still with their other parts enveloped the children. This moment is required in the development of the poetic picture; the poet makes it sufficiently felt; only the time had not yet been reached for finishing the picture. That the ancient commentators actually realized this appears to be shown by a passage in Donatus.[55] How much less would it escape the artists in whose understanding eyes everything that can advantage them stands out so quickly and so plainly.

In the coils themselves with which the poet's fancy sees the serpents entwine Laocoön, he very carefully avoids the arms, in order to leave the hands their freedom.

---

[54] *Aeneid*, II, 212–17: 'they forged on, straight at Laocoön. First each snake took one of his little sons, twined round him, tightening, and bit, and devoured the tiny limbs. Next they seized Laocoön, who had armed himself and was hastening to the rescue; they bound him in the giant spirals of their scaly length' (*The Aeneid*, translated by W. F. Jackson Knight (Harmondsworth, 1956)).

[55] Tiberius Claudius Donatus (fourth century AD), author of *Interpretationes Vergilianae*, a commentary on Virgil. Lessing's footnote quotes Donatus' comment on *Aeneid*, II, 227, which confirms his own reconstruction of the serpents' attack on Laocoön as described by Virgil.

Ille simul manibus tendit divellere nodos.[56]

In this the artists must necessarily follow him. Nothing gives more life and expression than the movement of the hands; in emotion especially the most speaking countenance without it is insignificant. Arms fast bound to the body by the coils of the serpents would have spread frost and death over the whole group. For this reason we see them, in the chief figure as well as in the secondary figures, in full activity, and busiest there where for the moment there is the most violent anguish.

Further, too, the artists, in view of the convolutions of the serpents, found nothing that could be more advantageously borrowed from the poet than this movement of the arms. Virgil makes the serpents wind themselves doubly about the body and doubly about the neck of Laocoön, with their heads elevated above him.

Bis medium amplexi, bis collo squamea circum
Terga dati, superant capite et cervicibus altis.[57]

This picture satisfies the imagination completely; the noblest parts are compressed to suffocation, and the poison goes straight to the face. Nevertheless, it was not a picture for artists, who want to exhibit the effects of the pain and the poison in the bodily frame. For in order to make these visible the chief parts must be as free as possible, and no external pressure whatever must be exercised upon them which could alter and weaken the play of the suffering nerves and straining muscles. The double coil of the serpents would have concealed the whole body, so that the painful contraction of the abdomen, which is so expressive, would have remained invisible. What one would still have perceived of the body, over, or under, or between the coils would have appeared under pressures and swellings caused not by the inward pain, but by the external burden. The neck so many times encircled would have spoiled completely the pyramidal tapering of the group which is so agreeable to the eye; and the pointed serpent heads standing out into the air from this swollen bulk would have made so abrupt a break in proportion that the form of the whole would have been repulsive in the extreme. There are doubtless draughtsmen who would nevertheless have been unintelligent enough to

---

[56] *Aeneid*, II, 220: 'His hands strove frantically to wrench the knots apart.'
[57] *Aeneid*, II, 218–19: 'twice round his middle, twice round his throat; and still their heads and necks towered above him'.

follow the poet slavishly. But what would have come of that, we can, to name no other instances, understand from a drawing of Franz Cleyn,[58] which can be looked on only with disgust. (This occurs in the splendid edition of Dryden's English Virgil.[59]) The ancient sculptors perceived at a glance that their art demanded an entire modification. They removed all the serpent coils from neck and body to thighs and feet. Here these coils, without injuring the expression, could cover and press as much as was needful. Here they aroused at once the idea of retarded flight and of a kind of immobility which is exceedingly advantageous to the artistic permanence of a single posture.

I know not how it has come about that the critics have passed over in perfect silence this distinction, which is exhibited so plainly in the coilings of the serpents, between the work of art and the poet's description. It exalts the artistic wisdom of the work just as much as the other which they mention, which, however, they do not venture to praise, but rather seek to excuse. I mean the difference in the draping of the subject. Virgil's Laocoön is in his priestly vestments, but in the group appears, with both his sons, completely naked. I am told there are people who find something preposterous in representing a prince, a priest, unclothed, at the altar of sacrifice. And to these people connoisseurs of art reply, in all seriousness, that certainly it is an offence against custom, but that the artists were compelled to it, because they could not give their figures any suitable attire. Sculpture, say they, cannot imitate any kind of cloth; thick folds would make a bad effect. Of two embarrassments, therefore, they had chosen the smaller, and were willing rather to offend against truth than to incur the risk of blame for their draperies. If the ancient artists would laugh at the objection, I really cannot tell what they would have said about the answer. One cannot degrade Art further than by such a defence. For, granted that sculpture could imitate the different materials just as well as painting, should then Laocoön necessarily have been clothed? Should we lose nothing by this draping? Has a costume, the work of slavish hands, just as much beauty as the work of the Eternal Wisdom, an organized body? Does it demand the same faculties, is it equally meritorious, does it bring the same honour, to imitate the former as to imitate the latter? Do our eyes only

---

[58] Franz Cleyn (1590–1658), Dutch painter and engraver who died in London.
[59] (London, 1697).

wish to be deceived, and is it all the same to them with what they are deceived?

With the poet a cloak is no cloak; it conceals nothing; our imagination sees through it at all times. Let Laocoön in Virgil have it or lack it, his suffering in every part of his body is, to the imagination, an evil equally visible. The brow is bound about for her with the priestly fillet, but it is not veiled. Indeed, it does not only not hinder, this fillet, it even strengthens yet more the conception that we form of the sufferer's misfortunes.

> Perfusus sanie vittas atroque veneno.[60]

His priestly dignity helps him not a whit; the very symbol which secures him everywhere respect and veneration is soaked and defiled by the deadly venom.

But this accessory idea the artist had to sacrifice if the main work were not to suffer damage. Besides, had he left to Laocoön only this fillet, the expression would in consequence have been much weakened. The brow would have been partly covered, and the brow is the seat of expression. So, just as in that other particular, the shriek, he sacrificed expression to beauty, in the same way here he sacrificed custom to expression. Generally speaking, custom, in the view of the ancients, was a matter of little consequence. They felt that the highest aim of Art pointed to dispensing with the customary altogether. Beauty is this highest aim; necessity invented clothing, and what has Art to do with necessity? I grant you there is also a beauty of drapery; but what is it compared with the beauty of the human form? And will he who is able to reach the higher content himself with the lower? I am much afraid that the most finished master in draperies shows by that very dexterity in what it is he is lacking.

VI

My hypothesis – that the artists imitated the poet – does not redound to their disparagement. On the contrary, this imitation sets their wisdom in the fairest light. They followed the poet without allowing themselves to be misled by him in the slightest. They had a pattern, but as they had to transpose this pattern from one art into another, they found opportunity enough to think for themselves. And these thoughts of theirs, which are

---

[60] *Aeneid*, II, 221: 'Filth and black venom drenched his priestly hands.'

manifest in their deviation from their model, prove that they were just as great in their art as he in his own.

And now I will reverse the hypothesis and suppose the poet to have imitated the artists. There are scholars who maintain this supposition to be the truth. Whether they had historical grounds for that, I do not know. But when they found the work of art so superlatively beautiful, they could not persuade themselves that it might belong to a late period. It must be of the age when Art was in its perfect flower, because it deserved to be of that age.

It has been shown that, admirable as Virgil's picture is, there are yet various features of it which the artists could not use. The statement thus admits of being reduced to this, that a good poetic description must also yield a good actual painting, and that the poet has only so far described well when the artist can follow him in every feature. One is inclined to presume this restricted sense, even before seeing it confirmed by examples; merely from consideration of the wider sphere of poetry, from the boundless field of our imagination, and from the spiritual nature of the pictures, which can stand side by side in the greatest multitude and variety without one obscuring or damaging another, just as the things themselves would do or the natural signs of the same within the narrow bounds of space and time.

But if the less cannot include the greater, the greater can contain the less. This is my point – if not, every feature which the descriptive poet uses can be used with like effect on the canvas or in the marble. Might perhaps every feature of which the artist avails himself prove equally effective in the work of the poet? Unquestionably; for what we find beautiful in a work of art is not found beautiful by the eye, but by our imagination through the eye. The picture in question may therefore be called up again in our imagination by arbitrary or natural signs,[61] and thus also may arise at any time the corresponding pleasure, although not in corresponding degree.

This, however, being admitted, I must confess that to my mind the hypothesis that Virgil imitated the artists is far less conceivable than the contrary supposition. If the artists followed the poet, I can account for their deviations. They were obliged to deviate, because the selfsame features as the poet delineated would have occasioned them difficulties such as do not embarrass the poet. But what should make the poet deviate? If he had followed the group in every detail would he not, all the same,

---

[61] On 'arbitrary' and 'natural' signs, see Lessing's explanations in chapter 16 below.

have presented to us an admirable picture? I can conceive quite well how his fancy, working on its own account, might suggest one feature and another; but the reasons why his imagination should think that beautiful features, already before his eyes, ought to be transformed into those other features – such reasons, I confess, never dawn upon me.

It even seems to me that if Virgil had had the group as his pattern he could scarcely have refrained from permitting the union together, as it were in a knot, of the three bodies to be at least conjectured. It was too vivid not to catch his eye, and he would have appreciated its excellent effect too keenly not to give it yet more prominence in his description. As I have said, the time was not yet arrived to finish this picture of the entwined group. No; but a single word more would perhaps have given to it, in the shadow where the poet had to leave it, a very obvious impression. What the artist was able to discover without this word, the poet, if he had seen it in the artist's work, would not have left unspoken.

The artist had the most compelling reasons not to let the suffering of Laocoön break out into a cry. But if the poet had had before him the so touching union of pain and beauty in the work of art, what could have so imperatively obliged him to leave completely unsuggested the idea of manly dignity and great-hearted endurance which arises from this union of pain and beauty, and all at once to shock us with the terrible outcries of Laocoön? Richardson says, 'Virgil's Laocoön must shriek, because the poet desires to arouse not so much pity for him as terror and horror in the ranks of the Trojans.'[62] I grant, although Richardson seems not to have considered it, that the poet does not make the description in his own person, but lets Aeneas make it, and this, too, in the presence of Dido, to whose compassion Aeneas could never enough appeal. It is not, however, the shriek that surprises me, but the absence of any gradation leading up to the cry, a gradation that the work of art would naturally have shown the poet to be needful, if, as we have supposed, he had had it for a pattern. Richardson adds, 'The story of Laocoön should lead up merely to the pathetic description of the final ruin; the poet, therefore, has not thought fit to make it more interesting, in order not to waste upon the misfortune of a single citizen the attention which should be wholly fixed on Troy's last dreadful night.' Only, this sets out the affair as one to be regarded

---

[62] Jonathan Richardson (1665–1745), author of *The Theory of Painting* (1715), which Lessing's footnote cites in a French translation of 1728.

from a painter's point of view, from which it cannot be contemplated at all. The calamity of Laocoön and the Destruction of the City are not with the poet pictures set side by side; the two together do not make a great whole which the eye either should or could take in at a glance; and only in such a case would it be needful to arrange that our eyes should fall rather upon Laocoön than upon the burning city. The two descriptions follow each other successively, and I do not see what disadvantage it could bring to the second, how greatly soever the preceding one had moved us. That could only be, if the second in itself were not sufficiently touching.

Still less reason would the poet have had to alter the coiling of the serpents. In the work of art they leave the hands busy and bind the feet. This disposition pleases the eye, and it is a living picture that is left by it in the imagination. It is so clear and pure that it can be presented almost as effectively by words as by actual material means.

> Micat alter, et ipsum
> Laocoönta petit, totumque infraque supraque
> Implicat et rabido tandem ferit ilia morsu
>
> . . . .
>
> At serpens lapsu crebro redeunte subintrat
> Lubricus, intortoque ligat genua infima nodo.[63]

These are the lines of Sadoleto,[64] which would, no doubt, have come from Virgil with a more picturesque power if a visible pattern had fired his fancy, and which would in that case certainly have been better than what he now gives us in their place:

> Bis medium amplexi, bis collo squamea circum
> Terga dati, superant capite et cervicibus altis.[65]

These details, certainly, fill the imagination; but it must not rest in them, it must not endeavour to make an end here; it must see now only the serpents and now only Laocoön, it must try to represent to itself what kind of figure is made by the two together. As soon as it sinks to this the

---

[63] 'The one snake darts upwards and seizes Laocoön, winds round him from top to bottom and wounds him in the side with a furious bite . . . But the slippery serpent turns downward in repeated circles and binds his knees in a tight knot.'

[64] Jacopo Sadoleto (1477–1547), cardinal and poet, author of the poem *De Laocoontis statua* from which the quotation here is taken.

[65] See note 57 above.

Virgilian picture begins to dissatisfy, and it finds it in the highest degree unpictorial.

If, however, the changes which Virgil had made in the pattern set before him had not been unsuccessful, they would yet be merely arbitrary. One imitates in order to resemble. Can resemblance be preserved when alterations are made needlessly? Rather, when this is done, the design obviously is – not to be like, and therefore not to imitate.

Not the whole, some may object, but perhaps this part and that. Good! But what, then, are these single parts that agree in the description and in the work of art so exactly that the poet might seem to have borrowed them from the latter? The father, the children, the serpents – all these the story furnished to the poet as well as to the artists. Excepting the story itself, they agree in nothing beyond the one point that they bind father and children in a single serpent-knot. But the suggestion of this arose from the altered detail, that the selfsame calamity overtook the father and the children. This alteration, as has already been pointed out, Virgil appears to have introduced; for the Greek legend says something quite different. Consequently, when, in view of that common binding by the serpent coils, there certainly was imitation on one side or the other, it is easier to suppose it on the artist's side than on that of the poet. In all else the one deviates from the other; only with the distinction that, if it is the artist who has made these deviations, the design of imitating the poet can still persist, the aim and the limitations of his art obliging him thereto; if, on the other hand, it is the poet who is supposed to have imitated the artist, then all the deviations referred to are an evidence against the supposed imitation, and those who, notwithstanding, maintain it, can mean nothing further by it than that the work of art is older than the poetic description.

VII

When one says that the artist imitates the poet, or that the poet imitates the artist, this is capable of two interpretations. Either the one makes the work of the other the actual subject of his imitation, or they have both the same subject and the one borrows from the other the style and fashion of the imitation. When Virgil describes the shield of Aeneas, it is in the first of these senses that he imitates the artist who made it. The work of art itself, not that which is represented upon it, is the subject of his imitation, and although certainly he describes at the same time what one sees represented thereon, yet he describes it only as a part of the shield, and not the thing itself. If Virgil, on the other hand, had imitated the Laocoön group, this would be an imitation of the second kind. For he would not have imitated the group, but what the group represents, and only the characteristics of his imitation would have been borrowed from it. In the first imitation the poet is original, in the second he is a copyist. The former is a part of the general imitation which constitutes the essence of his art, and he works as genius, whether his subject be a work of other arts or of Nature. The latter, on the contrary, degrades him wholly from his dignity; instead of the things themselves, he imitates the imitations of them, and gives us cold recollections of features from another's genius in place of original features of his own.

When, however, poet and artist, as not seldom happens, view the subjects that they have in common from an identical standpoint, it can hardly fail that there should be agreement in many particulars without implying the slightest degree of imitation or common aim between them. These agreements in contemporaneous artists and poets, concerning things that are no longer extant, may contribute to reciprocal illustration; but to attempt to establish such illustration by finding design in what was mere accident, and especially to attribute to the poet in every trifle a reference to this statue or that painting, is to render him a very equivocal service. And not to him alone, but to the reader also, for whom the most beautiful passage is thereby made, if God will, very intelligible, but at the same time admirably frigid.

This is the purpose, and the error, of a famous English work. Spence wrote his *Polymetis*[66] with much classical erudition and a very intimate acquaintance with the surviving works of ancient art. His design of explaining by these the Roman poets, and, on the other hand, of deriving from the poets elucidations for ancient works of art hitherto unexplained, he often accomplished very happily. But nevertheless I contend that his book is altogether intolerable to any reader of taste.

---

[66] Joseph Spence (1699–1768), historian and antiquary, author of *Polymetis: or, An Enquiry concerning the Agreement between the Works of the Roman Poets and the Remains of the Antient Artists* (London, 1747). Characteristically, Lessing develops his own views by attacking those of another, just as he subsequently does with Caylus in chapter XII. That he is far from fair to Spence, misrepresenting his arguments when it suits him, has been shown by Donald T. Siebert, '*Laokoon* and *Polymetis*: Lessing's Treatment of Joseph Spence', *Lessing Yearbook*, 3 (1971), 71–83.

It is natural that, when Valerius Flaccus describes the Winged Lightning upon the Roman shields –

> Nec primus radios, miles Romane, corusci
> Fulminis et rutilas scutis diffuderis alas,[67]

this description becomes to me far clearer when I perceive the representation of such a shield upon an ancient monument. It may be that Mars, hovering exactly as Addison fancied he saw him hovering, over the head of Rhea upon a coin, was also represented by the ancient armourers on shields and helmets, and that Juvenal had such a shield or helmet in mind when he alluded to it in a single word which, until Addison, remained a riddle for all the commentators.[68] For my part, I think that the passage of Ovid where the exhausted Cephalus calls to the cooling breezes:

> Aura . . . venias . . .
> Meque juves, intresque sinus, gratissima, nostros![69]

and his Procris takes this Aura for the name of a rival – that to me, I say, this passage appears more natural when I gather from the works of ancient artists that they actually personified the soft breezes and worshipped a kind of female sylphs under the name of Aurae. I grant you, that when Juvenal styles a distinguished good-for-nothing a Hermes-statue,[70] one could hardly find the likeness in the comparison without seeing such a statue, without knowing that it is a miserable pillar, which bears merely the head, or at most the torso, of the god, and, because we perceive thereon neither hands nor feet, awakens the conception of slothfulness. Illustrations of this sort are not to be despised, although, in fact, they are neither always necessary nor always adequate. The poet had the work of art in view as a thing existing for itself, and not as an imitation; or with both artist and poet certain conceptions of an identical kind were taken for granted, in consequence of which a further agreement in their

---

[67] 'And you were not the first, Roman warrior, to bear the rays of gleaming lightning nor the reddish wings on your shield'; from Valerius Flaccus (died *c.* 90 AD), author of the *Argonautica*, an unfinished poem in eight books; Lessing's reference is to Book VI, 55–6.

[68] Joseph Addison (1672–1719), *Dialogues upon the Usefulness of Ancient Medals* (1702); Lessing's lengthy footnote discusses Spence's and Addisons's comments on Juvenal, *Satires*, XI, 100–7 and related images on antique coins.

[69] Ovid, *Metamorphoses*, VII, 813 f.: 'Come, Zephyr, to my breast, a most welcome visitor, and soothe me.'

[70] Juvenal, *Satires*, VIII, 52–5.

representations must appear, from which, again, we can reason back to the generally accepted nature of these conceptions.

But when Tibullus[71] describes the form of Apollo, as he appeared to him in a dream – the most beautiful of youths, his temples bound about with the modest laurel; Syrian odours exhaling from the golden hair that flows about his neck; a gleaming white and rosy red mingled on the whole body, as on the tender cheek of the bride as she is led to her beloved – why must these features be borrowed from famous old pictures? Echion's[72] *nova nupta verecundia notabilis*[73] may have been seen in Rome, may have been copied a thousand times. Had then the bridal blush itself vanished from the world? Since the painter had seen it, was it no longer to be seen by a poet save in the painter's imitation? Or if another poet speaks of the exhausted Vulcan, or calls his face heated before the forge a red and fiery countenance, must he needs learn first from the work of a painter that labour wearies and heat reddens?[74] Or when Lucretius describes the changes of the seasons and causes them to pass before us in their natural order with the entire succession of their effects in earth and sky, was Lucretius an ephemeron?[75] Had he not lived through a whole year himself to witness all these transformations, but must depict them after a procession in which their statues were carried around? Must he first learn from these statues the old poetic artifice whereby abstract notions are turned into actual beings? Or Virgil's *pontem indignatus Araxes*, that splendid poetic picture of a stream overflowing its banks and tearing down the bridge thrown over it, does it not lose all its beauty if the poet is there alluding merely to a work of art in which this river-god is represented as actually breaking down a bridge?[76] What do we want with these commentaries which in the clearest passages supplant the poet in order to let the suggestion of an artist glimmer through?

I lament that so useful a book as *Polymetis* might otherwise have been has, by reason of this tasteless crotchet of foisting upon the ancient poets

---

[71] Albius Tibullus (*c*. 54–18 BC), author of *Elegiae*; Lessing's reference is to the fourth elegy of Book III, and to Spence's comments in *Polymetis*, Dialogue VIII, p. 84.

[72] Action (fourth century BC), famed for his pictures of the marriage of Alexander the Great.

[73] 'newly wed bride distinguished by her bashfulness'.

[74] P. Papinius Statius (*c*. 61–96 AD), author of five books of *Silvae* and other poems; Lessing's reference is to *Silvae*, I, 5, line 8, and to Spence's comments in *Polymetis*, Dialogue VIII, p. 81.

[75] Titus Lucretius Carus (95–*c*. 52 BC), *De rerum natura*, V, 736–47. Lessing's footnote contains another polemic against Spence.

[76] *Aeneid*, VIII, 725, 'Araxes enraged at the bridge'; Lessing's reference to Spence is to *Polymetis*, Dialogue XIV, p. 230.

in place of their own proper fancy an acquaintance with another's, been made so offensive and so much more damaging to the classic authors than the watery expositions of the shallowest philologist could ever have been. I regret yet more that in this matter Spence should have been preceded by Addison himself, who, from a passionate desire to exalt the works of ancient art into a means of interpretation, has just as little distinguished between the cases in which it is becoming in a poet to imitate the artist and those in which it is disparaging.[77]

VIII

Of the likeness which poetry and painting bear to each other Spence has the most singular conceptions possible. He believes the two arts in ancient times to have been so closely united that they always went hand in hand, that the poet constantly kept the painter in view, and the painter the poet. That poetry is the more comprehensive art, that beauties are at her command which painting can never attain, that she may frequently have reason to prefer unpicturesque beauties to picturesque – of this he does not appear to have a notion, and therefore the smallest difference which he detects between poets and artists of the old world puts him in a difficulty, and he resorts to the most extraordinary subterfuges to escape from his embarrassment.

The ancient poets generally endow Bacchus with horns. It is quite wonderful, then, says Spence, that we find these horns so seldom on his statues. He lights on this explanation and on that: on the uncertainty of the antiquaries, on the smallness of the horns themselves, which might have crept into concealment under the grapes and ivy-leaves, the unfailing headcovering of the god. He winds around and about the true reason without ever suspecting it. The horns of Bacchus were not natural horns, such as we see on the fauns and satyrs. They were but a garnishment of the brow, which he could assume and lay aside at will.

> Tibi, cum sine cornibus adstas,
> Virgineum caput est –[78]

---

[77] See note 68 above.

[78] Ovid, *Metamorphoses*, IV, 19 f.: 'When you stand there without horns, your head is like that of a maiden.'

so runs the solemn invocation of Bacchus in Ovid. He could thus show himself also without horns, and did so when he would appear in his virginal beauty. The artists certainly would also wish so to represent him, and would therefore avoid every less pleasing adjunct. Such an adjunct the horns would have been if attached to the diadem, as we may see them on a head in the royal cabinet at Berlin. Such an adjunct was the diadem itself, hiding the beautiful brow, and for this reason it occurs on the statues of Bacchus just as rarely as the horns, although indeed it was dispensed with just as often by the poets, both in the representations of Bacchus and in those of his great progenitor. The horns and the diadem prompted the poet's allusions to the deeds and the character of the god; to the artist, on the contrary, they were hindrances to the exhibition of greater beauties, and if Bacchus, as I believe, for that very reason had the surname *Biformis*, Δίμορφος,[79] because he could show himself in a fair and in a terrible aspect, then it was quite natural for the artists greatly to prefer that one of his forms which best answered the purpose of their art.

Minerva and Juno in the Roman poets often dart forth lightning. 'Then why not also in their images?' asks Spence.[80] He replies, 'It was an especial privilege of these two goddesses, the grounds of which were perhaps only to be learned in the Samothracian mysteries; artists, moreover, were regarded by the ancient Romans as common people, were therefore seldom admitted to those mysteries, and so doubtless knew nothing of them, and what they did not know they could not depict.' I might in return ask Spence, did these common people work out their own notions, or work at the command of more distinguished persons who might have been instructed in the mysteries? Were artists among the Greeks regarded with a like contempt? Were the Roman artists not for the greater part born Greeks? And so on.

Statius[81] and Valerius Flaccus[82] depict an angry Venus, and with features so terrible that at the moment we should rather take her for one of the Furies than for the Goddess of Love. Spence looks round in vain amongst the works of ancient art for such a Venus. And what is his conclusion? That more is permitted to the poet than to the sculptor or the painter? That is the conclusion he ought to have drawn, but he has accepted the

---

[79] 'of two shapes'. [80] Lessing's reference is to *Polymetis*, Dialogue VI, p. 63.
[81] See note 74 above. [82] See note 67 above.

principle once for all, that in a poetic description nothing is good which would be unsuitable to be represented in a painting or a statue.[83] Consequently, the poets must have erred. 'Statius and Valerius belong to an age when Roman poetry was in its decline. They show in this particular also their corrupt taste and their faulty judgement. With the poets of a better time one will not find these offences against graphic expression.'[84]

To speak in this way betrays a very poor faculty of discrimination. All the same, I do not intend to take up the cudgels for either Statius or Valerius, but will confine myself to but one general observation. The gods and sacred persons, as the artist represents them, are not entirely the same beings which the poet knows. With the artist they are personified abstractions which must constantly retain the selfsame characterization, if they are to be recognizable. With the poet, on the other hand, they are actual persons who live and act, who possess beyond their general character other qualities and emotions, which will stand out above it according to occasion and circumstances. Venus to the sculptor is nothing but Love; he must therefore endow her with the modest, blushful beauty and all the gracious charms that delight us in beloved objects and that we therefore combine in the abstract conception of Love. Deviate however slightly from this ideal, and we shall fail to recognize the picture. Beauty, but with more majesty than modesty, is at once no Venus, but a Juno. Charms, but commanding, masculine, rather than gracious charms, give us a Minerva in place of a Venus. In reality, an angry Venus, a Venus moved by revenge and rage, is to the sculptor a contradiction in terms; for Love as Love is never angry, never revengeful. To the poet, on the other hand, Venus certainly is Love, but she is more: she is the Goddess of Love, who beyond this character has an individuality of her own, and consequently must be just as capable of the impulse of aversion as of inclination. What wonder, then, that to him she blazes in rage or anger, especially when it is injured love that so transforms her?

Certainly it is true that the artist also in composition may just as well as the poet introduce Venus or any other divinity, out of her character, as a being actually living and acting. But in that case her actions must at least not contradict her character, even if they are not direct consequences of it. Venus commits to her son's charge her divine weapons; this action

[83] Lessing's footnote cites *Polymetis*, Dialogue XX, p. 311: 'Scarce any thing can be good in a poetical description, which would appear absurd, if represented in a statue or picture.'
[84] Lessing's reference is to *Polymetis*, Dialogue VII, p. 74.

the artist can represent as well as the poet. Here nothing hinders him from giving to Venus all the grace and beauty that appertain to her as the Goddess of Love; rather, indeed, will she thereby be so much the more recognizable in his work. But when Venus would avenge herself on her contemners, the men of Lemnos; when in magnified and savage form, with stained cheeks and disordered hair, she seizes the torch, throws around her a black vesture and stormily plunges down on a gloomy cloud; surely that is not a moment for the artist, because in such a moment he cannot by any means make her distinguishable. It is purely a moment for the poet, since to him the privilege is granted of so closely and exactly uniting with it another aspect, in which the goddess is wholly Venus, that we do not lose sight of her even in the Fury. This Flaccus does:

> Neque enim alma videri
> Jam tumet, aut tereti crinem subnectitur auro
> Sidereos diffusa sinus. Eadem effera et ingens
> Et maculis suffecta genas, pinumque sonantem
> Virginibus Stygiis, nigramque simillima pallam.[85]

Statius does just the same:

> Illa Paphon veterem centumque altaria linquens,
> Nec vultu nec crine prior, solvisse jugalem
> Ceston, et Idalias procul ablegasse volucres
> Fertur. Erant certe, media qui noctis in umbra
> Divam alios ignes majoraque tela gerentem,
> Tartarias inter thalamis volitasse sorores
> Vulgarent: utque implicitis arcana domorum
> Anguibus et saeva formidine cuncta replerit
> Limina. —[86]

Or we might say, to the poet alone belongs the art of depicting with negative traits, and by mixing them with positive to bring two images into

---

[85] *Argonautica* (cf. note 67), II, 102–6: 'Now she no longer wishes to appear as a lovely goddess, and her hair, no longer fastened with gold, falls down on her divine breast. Wild and terrible, her cheeks stained, bearing a blazing torch, and dressed in black, she resembles the Stygian maidens [i.e. the Eumenides].'

[86] Statius (cf. note 74), *Thebaïs* (a heroic poem in twelve books), V, 61–9: 'She [Venus] left ancient Paphos and its hundred altars, her face and hair transformed; she unloosed her girdle and sent the Idalian doves far from her. Some even say that, in the darkness of midnight, bearing other flames and larger arrows than usual, she appeared in the nuptial chambers amidst the Stygian sisters [the Eumenides], and filled the innermost part of the houses with writhing serpents and all their thresholds with holy terror.'

one. No longer the gracious Venus, no longer the hair fastened with golden clasps, floated about by no azure vesture, but without her girdle, armed with other flames, with greater arrows, companioned by like Furies. But because the artist is obliged to dispense with such an artifice, must the poet too in his turn abstain from using it? If painting will be the sister of poesy, let not the younger forbid to the elder all the garniture and bravery which she herself cannot put on.

IX

If in individual cases we wish to compare the painter and the poet with one another, the first and most important point is to observe whether both of them have had complete freedom, whether they have, in the absence of any outward compulsion, been able to aim at the highest effect of their art.

Religion was often an outward compulsion of this kind for the ancient artist. His work, designed for reverence and worship, could not always be as perfect as if he had had a single eye to the pleasure of the beholder. Superstition overloaded the gods with symbols, and the most beautiful of them were not everywhere worshipped for their beauty. In his temple at Lemnos, from which the pious Hypsipyle rescued her father under the shape of the god,[87] Bacchus stood horned, and so doubtless he appeared in all his temples, for the horns were a symbol that indicated his essential nature. Only the free artist who wrought his Bacchus for no holy shrine left this symbol out; and if amongst the statues of him still extant we find all without horns, this is perhaps a proof that they are not of the consecrated forms in which he was actually worshipped. Apart from this, it is highly probable that it was upon these last that the rage of the pious iconoclasts in the first centuries of Christianity chiefly fell, their fury sparing only here and there a work of art which had not been defiled by idolatrous worship.

As, however, works of both kinds are still found amongst antiquities in excavation, I should like the name of 'works of art' to be reserved for those alone in which the artist could show himself actually as artist, in which beauty has been his first and last object. All the rest, in which

[87] Lessing's footnote cites Valerius Flaccus, *Argonautica*, II, 263–73.

too evident traces of religious ritual appear, are unworthy of the name, because Art here has not wrought on her own account, but has been an auxiliary of religion, looking in the material representations which she made of it more to the significant than to the beautiful; although I do not mean by this that she did not often put great significance into the beauty, or, out of indulgence to the art and finer taste of the age, remitted her attention to the former so much that the latter alone might appear to predominate.

If we make no such distinction, then the connoisseur and the antiquary will be constantly at strife because they do not understand each other. If the former, with his insight into the aims of art, contends that this or that work was never made by the ancient artist – that is to say, not as artist, not voluntarily – then the latter will assert that neither religion nor any other cause lying outside the region of art has caused the artist to make it – the artist, that is to say, as workman. He will suppose that he can refute the connoisseur with the first figure that comes to hand, which the other without scruple, but to the great annoyance of the learned world, will condemn to the rubbish-heap once more from which it has been drawn.[88]

Yet, on the other hand, it is possible to exaggerate the influence of religion upon art. Spence affords a singular example of that tendency. He found that Vesta was not worshipped in her temple under any personal image, and this he deemed enough to warrant the conclusion that no statues of this goddess ever existed, and that every one so considered really represented not Vesta, but a vestal.[89] Strange inference! Did the artist, then, lose his right to personify a being to whom the poets give a distinct personality, whom they make the daughter of Saturnus and Ops, whom they expose to the danger of ill-usage at the hands of Priapus, and all else they relate of her – did he lose his right, I ask, to personify this being in his own way, because she was worshipped in one temple merely under the symbol of fire? For Spence here falls into this further error: that what Ovid[90] says only of a certain temple of Vesta – namely, of that at Rome – he extends to all temples of the goddess without distinction and to her worship in general. She was not everywhere worshipped as she was

---

[88] Lessing's adds a long footnote in which he argues that the Furies, as ugly objects, were never represented as such in ancient works of art, other than perhaps in miniature form on gems etc.
[89] Lessing's reference is to *Polymetis*, Dialogue VII, p. 81. [90] Ovid, *Fasti*, VI, 295–8.

worshipped in this temple at Rome, nor even in Italy itself before Numa[91] built it. Numa desired to see no divinity represented in human or animal form; and without doubt the reform which he introduced in the service of Vesta consisted in this, that he banished from it all personal representation. Ovid himself teaches us that before Numa's time there were statues of Vesta in her temple, which when her priestess Sylvia became a mother raised their maiden hands in shame before their eyes.[92] That even in the temples which the goddess had in the Roman provinces outside the city her worship was not wholly of the kind which Numa prescribed, various ancient inscriptions appear to prove, where mention is made of a 'Pontificus Vestae'.[93] At Corinth also there was a temple of Vesta without any statues, with a mere altar whereon offerings were made to the goddess. But had the Greeks therefore no statues of Vesta? At Athens there was one in the Prytaneum, beside the statue of Peace. The people of Iasos boasted of one, which stood in their city under the open sky, that neither snow nor rain fell upon it. Pliny mentions a sitting figure from the hand of Scopas which in his time was to be seen in the Servilian Gardens at Rome.[94] Granted that it is difficult for us now to distinguish a mere vestal from Vesta herself, does this prove that the ancients could not distinguish them, or indeed did not wish to distinguish them? Notoriously, certain characteristics indicate rather the one than the other. Only in the hands of the goddess can we expect to find the sceptre, the torch, the palladium.[95] The tympanum[96] which Codinus[97] associates with her belongs to her perhaps only as the Earth, or Codinus did not recognize very well what he saw.

X

I notice another expression of surprise in Spence which shows plainly how little he can have reflected on the limits of Poetry and Painting. 'As for what concerns the Muses in general,' he says, 'it is certainly singular

---

[91] Legendary second king of Rome.   [92] Ovid, *Fasti*, III, 45 f.   [93] 'Priest of Vesta'.

[94] Pliny, *Natural History*, XXXVI, section 4, p. 727 (Lessing's reference).

[95] Sacred image of Pallas (Athene).   [96] Cultic drum.

[97] Georgius Codinus (fifteenth century), Byzantine historian, supposed author of *De originibus Constantinopolitanis*, included in *Corpus Byzantinae historiae* (Venice, 1729); Lessing's reference is to p. 12 of this edition, and his footnote discusses the significance of the tympanum.

that the poets are so sparing in the description of them – more sparing by far than we should expect with goddesses to whom they owe such great obligations.'[98]

What is this, but to wonder that when the poets speak of them they do not use the dumb language of the painter? Urania is for the poets the Muse of Astronomy; from her name, from her functions, we recognize her office. The artist in order to make it distinguishable must exhibit her with a pointer and a celestial globe; this wand, this celestial globe, this attitude of hers are his alphabet from which he helps us to put together the name Urania. But when the poet would say that Urania had long ago foretold his death by the stars:

> Ipsa diu positis lethum praedixerat astris Uranie. –[99]

why should he, thinking of the painter, add thereto, Urania, the pointer in her hand, the celestial globe before her? Would it not be as if a man who can and may speak aloud should at the same time still make use of the signs which the mutes in the Turk's seraglio have invented for lack of utterance?

The very same surprise Spence again expresses concerning the personified moralities, or those divinities whom the ancients set over the virtues and the conduct of human life. 'It is worthy of remark,' says he, 'that the Roman poets say far less of the best of these personified moralities than we should expect. The artists in this respect are much richer, and he who would learn the particular aspect and attire of each need only consult the coins of the Roman Emperors: the poets speak of these beings frequently, indeed, as of persons; in general, however, they say very little of their attributes, their attire and the rest of their outward appearance.'[100]

When the poet personifies abstract qualities, these are sufficiently characterized by their names and by what they do. To the artist these means are wanting. He must therefore attach symbols to his personifications by which they can be distinguished. By these symbols, because they are something different and mean something different, they become allegorical figures. A woman with a bridle in her hand, another leaning on a

---

[98] Lessing's reference is to *Polymetis*, Dialogue VIII, p. 91.
[99] Statius, *Thebaïs*, (cf. note 86), VIII, 551: 'Urania had long since foretold his death from the position of the stars.' Lessing adds a reference to *Polymetis*, Dialogue X, p. 137.
[100] Lessing's reference is to *Polymetis*, Dialogue X, pp. 137–9.

pillar, are in art allegorical beings. But Temperance and Steadfastness are to the poet allegorical beings, and merely personified abstractions. The symbols, in the artist's representation, necessity has invented. For in no other way can he make plain what this or that figure signifies. But what the artist is driven to by necessity, why should the poet force on himself when no such necessity is laid upon him?

What surprises Spence so much deserves to be prescribed to the poets as a law. They must not make painting's indigence the rule of their wealth. They must not regard the means which Art has invented in order to follow poetry as if they were perfections which they have reason to envy. When the artist adorns a figure with symbols, he raises a mere figure to a superior being. But when the poet makes use of these plastic bedizenments, he makes of a superior being a mere lay-figure.

And just as this rule is authenticated by its observance amongst the ancient poets, so is its deliberate violation a favourite weakness amongst their successors. All their creatures of imagination go in masquerade, and those who understand this masquerade best generally understand least the chief thing of all, which is to let their creatures act and to distinguish and characterize them by their actions.

Yet amongst the attributes with which the artists distinguish their abstract personalities there is one sort which is more susceptible and more worthy of poetic employment. I mean those which properly have nothing allegorical in their nature, but are to be regarded as implements of which the being to whom they are assigned would or might make use when acting as real persons. The bridle in the hand of Temperance, the pillar on which Steadfastness leans, are purely allegorical, and thus of no use to the poet. The scales in the hand of Justice are certainly less purely allegorical, because the right use of the scales is really a part of justice. But the lyre or flute in the hand of a Muse, the spear in the hand of Mars, hammer and tongs in the hands of Vulcan, are not symbols at all, but mere instruments, without which these beings could not effect the achievements we ascribe to them. Of this kind are the attributes which the ancient poets did sometimes weave into their descriptions, and which I on that ground, distinguishing them from the allegorical, would call the poetic. The latter signify the thing itself, the former only some likeness of it.[101]

---

[101] Lessing adds a long footnote in which he criticizes Spence on further points of detail.

XI

Count Caylus, again, appears to require that the poet shall embellish the creatures of his imagination with allegorical attributes.[102] The Count was more at home with painting than with poetry. In the work, nevertheless, where he expresses this requirement I have found the suggestion of more important considerations, the most essential of which, for the better judging of them, I will mention here.

The artist, according to the Count's view, should make himself very thoroughly acquainted with the greatest of descriptive poets, with Homer, with this 'second Nature'. He shows him what rich and still unused material for most admirable pictures is offered by the story handled by the Greek, and how much more perfect his delineations will prove the more closely he clings to the very smallest circumstances noticed by the poet.

Now in this proposition we see a mingling of the two kinds of imitation which we have separated above. The painter is not only to imitate what the poet has imitated, but he is further to imitate it with the self-same features; he is to use the poet not as narrator only, but as poet.

This second species of imitation, however, which detracts so much from the poet's merit, why is it not equally disparaging to the artist? If before Homer such a succession of pictures as Count Caylus cites from his pages had been extant, and we were aware that the poet had based his work on them, would he not lose unspeakably in our estimation? How comes it that we withdraw from the artist no whit of our esteem even though he does nothing more than translate the words of the poet into figures and colours?

The reason appears to be this. With the artist we deem the execution more difficult than the invention; with the poet, again, it is the contrary, and we deem the execution, as compared with the invention, the lighter task. Had Virgil taken from the sculptured group the entangling of Laocoön and his children, the merit in his picture which we consider the greater and the harder of attainment would be lost, and only the smaller would remain. For to shape this entangling by the power of imagination

---

[102] Anne Claude Philippe de Tubières, Comte de Caylus (1692–1765), antiquarian and author of *Tableaux tirés de l'Iliade* (Paris, 1757), the work with which Lessing here takes issue. His greatest work, however, was the monumental *Recueil d'antiquités*, 7 vols. (Paris, 1752–67). Lessing adds a footnote in which he takes issue with Caylus on the manner in which ancient artists depicted death. He later devoted a separate treatise to this problem, entitled *How the Ancients Portrayed Death* (1769).

is far more important than to express it in words. Had, on the other hand, the artist borrowed this entangling from the poet, he would still, in our minds, retain sufficient merit, although the merit of invention is withdrawn. For expression in marble is more difficult by far than expression in words; and when we weigh invention and representation against each other we are always inclined to abate our demands on the artist for the one, in proportion to the excess we feel that we have received of the other.

There are two cases in which it is a greater merit for the artist to copy Nature through the medium of the poet's imitation than without it. The painter who represents a lovely landscape according to the description of a Thomson[103] has done more than he who copies it direct from Nature. The latter has his model before him; the former must first of all strain his imagination to the point that enables him to see it before him. The one makes a thing of beauty out of lively sensuous impressions, the other from weak and wavering descriptions of arbitrary signs.

But natural as the readiness may be to abate in our demands on the artist for the particular merit of invention, it is equally so on his part, for like reasons, to be indifferent to it. For when he sees that invention can never become his more shining merit, that his greatest praise depends on execution, it becomes all one to him whether the former is old or new, used once or times without number, and whether it belongs to himself or to another. He remains within the narrow range of a few designs, become familiar both to him and to everybody, and directs his inventive faculty merely to changes in the already known and to new combinations of old subjects. That, too, is actually the idea which the manuals of painting connect with the word *Invention*. For although certainly they divide into the pictorial and the poetic, yet the poetic is not made to consist in the production of the design itself, but purely in the arrangement or the expression. It is invention, but not invention of the whole, only of separate parts and their position in relation to each other. It is invention, but of that lower type which Horace recommended to his tragic poet:

> ... Tuque
> Rectius Iliacum carmen deducis in actus
> Quam si proferres ignota indictaque primus.[104]

---

[103] James Thomson (1700–48), author of *The Seasons*, a poem which was greatly admired and imitated in eighteenth-century Germany.

[104] Horace, *Ars Poetica*, lines 128–30: 'it is better for you to put the song of Troy [the *Iliad*] into dramatic form than to be the first to treat unknown and unsung subjects'.

Recommended, I say, but not commanded. Recommended, as easier for him, more fitting, more advantageous; but not commanded as better and nobler in itself.

In fact the poet has a great advantage who treats a well-known story and familiar characters. A hundred indifferent trifles which otherwise would be indispensable to the understanding of the whole he can pass by; and the more quickly he becomes intelligible to his hearers, the more quickly he can interest them. This advantage the painter also has if his theme is not strange to us, if we make out at the first glance the purpose and meaning of his entire composition, if we at once not merely see his characters speaking, but hear also what they speak. It is on the first glance that the main effect depends, and if this forces on us troublesome reflection and conjecture, our inclination to be moved grows cold; in order to be avenged on the unintelligible artist, we harden ourselves against the expression, and woe betide him if he has sacrificed beauty to expression! We then find nothing whatever that can charm us to tarry before his work; what we see does not please us; and what we are to think concerning it we are left uninstructed.

Now let us consider these two things together; first, that the invention or novelty of the theme is far from being the principal thing that we desire of the painter; secondly, that a well-known theme furthers and facilitates the effect of his art; and I judge that the reason why he so seldom attempts new themes we need not, with Count Caylus, seek in his convenience, his ignorance, or the difficulty of the mechanical part of art, demanding all his time and diligence; but we shall find it more deeply founded, and it may be that what at first appears to be the limitations of art and the spoiling of our pleasure we shall be inclined to praise as a restraint wise in itself and useful to ourselves. Nor am I afraid that experience will confute me. The painters will thank the Count for his goodwill, but hardly follow his counsels so generally as he expects. If they should, in another hundred years a new Caylus would be wanted who should bring again to remembrance the old themes and reconduct the artist into the field where others before him have gathered immortal laurels. Or do we desire that the public shall be as learned as the connoisseur with his books? That to the public all scenes of history or fable which might suggest a beautiful picture shall become known and familiar? I grant that the artists would have done better if since Raphael's day they had made Homer instead of Ovid their manual. But as that in fact has not happened, let us leave the public in their old rut, and not make their pleasure harder to attain than a pleasure must be in order to be what it should.

Protogenes[105] had painted the mother of Aristotle. I don't know how much the philosopher paid him for the picture. But, either instead of payment or in addition thereto, he gave him counsel that was worth more than the payment. For I cannot imagine that his counsel was a mere flattery. But chiefly because he considered the need of art – to be intelligible – he advised him to paint the achievements of Alexander, achievements of which at that time all the world was speaking, and of which he could foresee that they would be memorable also to posterity. Yet Protogenes had not discernment enough to follow this counsel; *impetus animi*, says Pliny, *et quaedam artis libido*,[106] a certain arrogance of art, a certain lust for the strange and the unknown, attracted him to quite other subjects. He preferred to paint the story of a Ialysus, of a Cydippe[107] and the like, of which today one cannot even guess what they represented.

XII

Homer treats of a twofold order of beings and actions: visible and invisible. This distinction it is not possible for painting to suggest; with it all is visible, and visible in one particular way. When, therefore, Count Caylus lets the pictures of the invisible actions run on in unbroken sequence with the visible; when in the pictures of mingled actions, in which visible and invisible things take part, he does not, and perhaps cannot, suggest how the latter, which only we who contemplate the picture should discover therein, are so to be introduced that the persons in the picture do not see them, or at least must appear not necessarily to see them; it is inevitable that the entire composition, as well as many a separate portion of it, becomes confused, inconceivable and self–contradictory.

Yet, with the book in one's hand, there might be some remedy for this error. The worst of it is simply this, that by the abrogation of the difference between the visible and invisible things all the characteristic features are at once lost by which the higher are raised above the inferior

---

[105] See note 2 above.
[106] 'an inner compulsion and a desire for artistic production'; Lessing's reference is to Pliny, *Natural History*, xxxv, Section 36, p. 700.
[107] Ialysus, a hero of Rhodes; Cydippe, mother of Ialysus.

species. For example, when at last the divided gods come to blows among themselves over the fate of the Trojans, the whole struggle passes with the poet invisibly, and this invisibility permits the imagination to enlarge the stage, and leaves it free play to conceive the persons of the gods and their actions as great, and elevated as far above common humanity as ever it pleases. But painting must assume a visible stage the various necessary parts of which become the scale for the persons acting on it, a scale which the eye has immediately before it, and whose disproportion, as regards the higher beings, turns these higher beings, who were so great in the poet's delineation, into sheer monsters on the canvas of the artist.

Minerva, on whom in this struggle Mars ventures the first assault, steps back and snatches up from the ground with powerful hand a black, rough, massive stone, which in ancient days many hands of men together had rolled thither as a landmark –

Ἡ δ' ἀναχασσαμένη λίθον εἵλετο χειρὶ παχείῃ,
Κείμενον ἐν πεδίῳ, μέλανα τρηχύν τε, μέγαν τε,
Τὸν ῥ' ἄνδρες πρότεροι θέσαν ἔμμεναι οὖρον ἀρούρης.[108]

In order to estimate adequately the size of this stone, let us bear in mind that Homer makes his heroes as strong again as the strongest men of his time, and represents these, too, as far excelled in strength by the men whom Nestor had known in his youth. Now, I ask, if Minerva flings a stone which not one man, but several men of Nestor's youth had set for a landmark, if Minerva flings such a stone at Mars, of what stature is the goddess to be? If her stature is in proportion to the size of the stone, the marvellous vanishes. A man who is three times bigger than I must naturally also be able to fling a three-times bigger stone. But if the stature of the goddess is not in keeping with the size of the stone, there is imported into the picture an obvious improbability, the offence of which is not removed by the cold reflection that a goddess must have superhuman strength. Where I see a greater effect I would also see a greater instrument. And Mars, struck down by this mighty stone –

Ἑπτὰ δ' ἔπεσχε πέλεθρα . . .

---

[108] Homer, *Iliad*, xxi, 403–5: 'But she gave ground, and seized with her stout hand a stone lay upon the plain, black and jagged and great, that men of former days had set to be the boundary mark of a field' (*The Iliad*, translated by A. T. Murray, Loeb Classical Library (London, 1925)).

'covered three hides of land'. It is impossible that the painter can give the god this monstrous bulk. Yet if he does not, then Mars does not lie upon the ground, not the Homeric Mars, but only a common warrior.

Longinus[109] remarks that it often appeared to him as if Homer wished to elevate his men to gods and to degrade his gods to men. Painting carries out this degradation. In painting everything vanishes completely which with the poet sets the gods yet higher than godlike men. Stature, strength, swiftness – of which Homer has in store a higher and more wonderful degree for his gods than he bestows on his most pre-eminent heroes – must in picture sink down to the common measure of humanity, and Jupiter and Agamemnon, Apollo and Achilles, Ajax and Mars, become the same kind of beings, to be recognized no otherwise than by stipulated outward signs.

The means of which painting makes use to indicate that in her compositions this or that must be regarded as invisible, is a thin cloud in which she covers it from the view of the persons concerned. This cloud seems to have been borrowed from Homer himself. For when in the tumult of the battle one of the greater heroes comes into danger from which only heavenly power can deliver him, the poet causes him to be enveloped by the tutelary deity in a thick cloud or in actual night, and thus to be withdrawn from the place; as Paris was by Venus, Idäus by Neptune, Hector by Apollo. And this mist, this cloud Caylus never forgets heartily to commend to the artist when he is sketching for him a picture of such events. But who does not perceive that with the poet the enveloping in mist and darkness is nothing but a poetical way of saying invisible? It has, on this account, always surprised me to find this poetical expression realized and an actual cloud introduced into the picture, behind which the hero, as behind a screen, stands hidden from his enemy. That was not the poet's intention. That is to transgress the limits of painting; for this cloud is here a true hieroglyph, a mere symbolic sign, that does not make the rescued hero invisible, but calls out to the beholder, 'You must regard him as invisible to you.' This is no better than the inscribed labels which issue from the mouths of the persons in ancient Gothic pictures.

[109] Cassius Longinus (*c*. 213–73 AD), to whom the aesthetic treatise *On the Sublime* was traditionally attributed. Lessing's reference is to chapter 9 of that work.

It is true Homer makes Achilles, when Apollo snatches away Hector from him, strike yet three times at the thick vapour with his spear: τρὶς δ' ἠέρα τύψε βαθεῖαν.[110] But even that, in the poet's language, means no more than that Achilles became so enraged that he struck yet thrice before he noticed that he no longer had his foe in front of him. An actual mist Achilles did not see, and the whole artifice by which the gods made things invisible consisted not at all in the cloud, but in the swift snatching. Only, in order to show at the same time that no human eye could follow the body thus snatched away, the poet first of all envelops it beforehand in vapour; not that instead of the body withdrawn a fog was seen, but that whatever is under fog we think of as not visible. Therefore at times he inverts the order of things, and, instead of making the object invisible, causes the subject to be struck with blindness. Thus Neptune darkens the eyes of Achilles to save Aeneas from his murderous hands, removing him in a moment from out the tumult of the rearguard. In fact, however, the eyes of Achilles are here just as little darkened as in the other case the withdrawn heroes were enveloped in fog; the poet merely adds the one thing and the other, in order thereby to make more perceptible the extreme swiftness of the withdrawal which we call the vanishing.

The Homeric mist, however, the painters have made their own not merely in the cases where Homer himself uses or would have used it – in actual invisibilities or vanishings – but everywhere when the beholder is to recognize something in the picture which the persons in it, either altogether or in part, do not recognize. Minerva became visible to Achilles alone when she held him back from assaulting Agamemnon. 'To express this,' says Caylus, 'I know no other way than to veil her in a cloud from the rest of the council.' This is quite contrary to the spirit of the poet. To be invisible is the natural condition of his gods: no blinding, no cutting-off of the light, was needed in order that they should not be seen, but an illumination, a heightening of mortal vision, was necessary if they were to be seen. It is not enough, therefore, that the cloud is an arbitrary and unnatural sign with the painters; this arbitrary sign has not at all the positive significance which it might have as such, for they use it as frequently to make the visible invisible as they do the reverse.

[110] *Iliad*, xx, 446: 'And thrice he stabbed the dense mist.'

XIII

If Homer's works were entirely lost, and nothing was left of his *Iliad* and *Odyssey* save a succession of pictures such as Caylus has suggested might be drawn from them, should we from these pictures, even from the hand of the most perfect master, be able to form the conception we now have, I do not say of the poet's whole endowment, but even of his pictorial talent alone? Let us try the experiment with the first passage that occurs to us – the picture of the pestilence.[111] What do we perceive on the canvas of the artist? Dead corpses, flaming funeral pyres, dying men busy with the dead, the angry god upon a cloud letting fly his arrows. The greatest riches of this picture are, compared with the poet, mere poverty. For if we were to replace Homer from the picture, what could we make him say? 'Then did Apollo become enraged and shot his arrows amongst the Grecian host. Many Greeks died and their corpses were burned.' Now let us turn to Homer himself:

> Βῆ δὲ κατ' Οὐλύμποιο καρήνων | χωόμενος κῆρ,|
> Τόξ' ὤμοισιν ἔχων | ἀμφηρεφέα τε φαρέτρην·
> Ἔκλαγξαν δ' ἄρ' ὀϊστοὶ ἐπ' ὤμων χωομένοιο,
> Αὐτοῦ κινηθέντος· ὁ δ' ἤϊε νυκτὶ ἐοικώς|.
> Ἕζετ' ἔπειτ' ἀπάνευθε νεῶν, μετά | δ' ἰὸν ἕηκε·
> Δεινὴ δὲ κλαγγὴ γένετ' ἀργυρέοιο βιοῖο·
> Οὐρῆας μὲν πρῶτον ἐπῴχετο | καὶ κύνας ἀργούς,
> Αὐτὰρ ἔπειτ' αὐτοῖσι | βέλος ἐχεπευκὲς ἐφιεὶς
> Βάλλ' αἰεὶ δὲ πυραὶ | νεκύων | καίοντο θαμειαί.[112]

Just as far as life is above painting, the poet here is above the painter. With his bow and quiver the enraged Apollo descends from the rocky peak of Olympus. I do not merely see him descend, I hear him. At every step the arrows rattle about the shoulders of the wrathful god. He glides along like night. And now he sits opposite the ships – fearfully twangs the silver bow – he darts the first arrow at the mules and dogs. And then, with a more poisonous shaft, he strikes the men themselves; and

---

[111] *Iliad*, 1, 44–53: Lessing adds a reference to Caylus, *Tableaux*, p. 7.
[112] *Iliad*, 1, 44–52: 'Down from the peaks of Olympus he strode, wroth at heart, bearing on his shoulders his bow and covered quiver. The arrows rattled on the shoulders of the angry god, as he moved; and his coming was like the night. Then he sate him down apart from the ships and let fly a shaft: terrible was the twang of the silver bow. The mules he assailed first and the swift dogs, but thereafter on the men themselves he let fly his stinging arrows, and smote; and ever did the pyres of the dead burn thick.'

everywhere without cessation break into flame the corpse-encumbered pyres. The musical painting which we hear in the words of the poet it is not possible to translate into another language. It is just as impossible to gather it from the material picture, although it is only a very trivial advantage which the poetic picture possesses. The chief advantage is that what the material painting drawn from him exhibits, the poet leads us up to through a whole gallery of pictures.

But, then, perhaps the pestilence is not an advantageous subject for painting. Here is another having more charms for the eye – the gods taking counsel together over their wine. A golden palace open to the sky, arbitrary groups of the most beautiful and the most worshipful forms, their cups in their hands, waited on by Hebe, the image of eternal youth. What architecture, what masses of light and shade, what contrasts, what manifold expression! Where can I begin, and where leave off, to feast my eyes? If the painter so enchants me, how much more will the poet! I turn to his pages, and find – that I am deceived. Four simple lines only, such as might serve for the inscription of a picture; the material for a picture is there, but they themselves do not make a picture:

Οἱ δὲ θεοὶ πὰρ Ζηνὶ καθήμενοι ἠγορόωντο
Χρυσέῳ ἐν δαπέδῳ, μετὰ δέ σφισι πότνια Ἥβη
Νέκταρ ἐῳνοχόει· τοὶ δὲ χρυσέοις δεπάεσσι
Δειδέχατ᾽ ἀλλήλους, Τρώων πόλιν εἰσορόωντες.[113]

This an Apollonius[114] or an even more mediocre poet would have said equally well; and Homer here stands just as far below the painter as in the former case the painter stood below him.

Yet more, Caylus finds in the whole of the Fourth Book of the *Iliad* no other picture, not one, than in these four lines. 'However much', he remarks, 'the Fourth Book is marked by manifold encouragements to the attempt, owing to the abundance of brilliant and contrasted characters and to the art with which the poet shows us the entire multitude whom he will set in action – yet it is perfectly unusable for painting.' He might have added, rich as it is otherwise in that which we call poetic picture. For

---

[113] *Iliad*, IV, 1–4: 'Now the gods, seated by the side of Zeus, were holding assembly on the golden floor, and in their midst the queenly Hebe poured them nectar, and they with golden goblets pledged one another as they looked forth upon the city of the Trojans'; Lessing adds a reference to Caylus, *Tableaux*, p. 30.

[114] Apollonius of Rhodes (third century BC), epic poet, author of the *Argonautica*.

truly these are for number and perfection as remarkable as in any other Book. Where is there a more finished or more striking picture than that of Pandarus, as, on the incitement of Minerva, he breaks the truce and lets fly his arrow at Menelaus? Or that of the approach of the Grecian host? Or that of the two-sided, simultaneous onset? Or that of Ulysses' deed by which he avenges the death of his Leucus?

What, then, follows from the fact that not a few of the finest descriptions in Homer afford no picture for the artist, and that the artist can draw pictures from him where he himself has none? That those which he has and the artist can use would be very poverty-stricken pictures if they did not show more than can be shown by the artist? What else do they, but give a negative to my former question? That from the material paintings for which the poems of Homer provide the subjects, however numerous they may be and however excellent, nothing can be concluded as to the pictorial talent of the poet.

XIV

But if it is so, and if one poem may yield very happy results for the painter yet itself be not pictorial; if, again, another in its turn may be very pictorial and yet offer nothing to the painter; this is enough to dispose of Count Caylus' notion, which would make this kind of utility the criterion or test of the poets and settle their rank by the number of pictures which they provide for the artist.[115]

Far be it from us, even if only by our silence, to allow this notion to gain the authority of a rule. Milton would fall the first innocent sacrifice to it. For it seems really that the contemptuous verdict which Caylus passes upon him was not mere national prejudice, but rather a consequence of his supposed principle. 'The loss of sight', he says, 'may well be the nearest resemblance Milton bore to Homer.' True, Milton can fill no galleries. But if, so long as I had the bodily eye, its sphere must also be the sphere

---

[115] Lessing's footnote quotes Caylus, *Tableaux*, Avertissement, p. v, as follows: 'On est toujours convenu, que plus un Poëme fournissoit d'images et d'actions, plus il avoit de supériorité en Poësie. Cette réflexion m'avoit conduit à penser que le calcul des differens Tableaux, qu'offrent les Poëmes, pouvoit servir à comparer le merite respectif des Poëmes et des Poëtes. Le nombre et le genre des Tableaux que presentent ces grands ouvrages, auroient été une espèce de pierre de touche, ou plutôt une balance certaine du mérite de ces Poëmes et du Genie de leurs Auteurs.'

of my inward eye, then would I, in order to be free of this limitation, set a great value on the loss of the former. The *Paradise Lost* is not less the first epic poem since Homer on the ground of its providing few pictures, than the story of Christ's Passion is a poem because we can hardly put the point of a needle into it without touching a passage that might have employed a multitude of the greatest artists. The Evangelists relate the facts with all the dry simplicity possible, and the artist uses the manifold parts of the story without their having shown on their side the smallest spark of pictorial genius. There are paintable and unpaintable facts, and the historian can relate the most paintable in just as unpictorial a fashion as the poet can represent the least paintable pictorially.

We are merely misled by the ambiguity of words if we take the matter otherwise. A poetic picture is not necessarily that which can be transmuted into a material painting; but every feature, every combination of features by means of which the poet makes his subject so perceptible that we are more clearly conscious of this subject than of his words is called painterly, is styled a painting, because it brings us nearer to the degree of illusion of which the material painting is specially capable and which can most readily and most easily be conceptualized in terms of a material painting.

XV

Now the poet, as experience shows, can raise to this degree of illusion the representations even of other than visible objects. Consequently the artist must necessarily be denied whole classes of pictures in which the poet has the advantage over him. Dryden's Ode on St Cecilia's Day is full of musical pictures that cannot be touched by the paint-brush. But I will not lose myself in instances of the kind, from which in the end we learn nothing more than that colours are not tones and that eyes are not ears.

I will confine myself to the pictures of purely visible objects which are common to the poet and the painter. How comes it that many poetical pictures of this kind cannot be used by the painter, and, *vice versa*, many actual pictures lose the best part of their effect in the hands of the poet?

Examples may help us. I repeat it – the picture of Pandarus in the Fourth Book of the *Iliad* is one of the most finished and most striking in all Homer. From the seizing of the bow to the very flight of the arrow every moment is depicted, and all these moments are kept so close together, and yet so distinctly separate, that if we did not know how a bow was to be managed we might learn it from this picture alone.[116] Pandarus draws forth his bow, fixes the bowstring, opens his quiver, chooses a yet unused, well-feathered shaft, sets the arrow on the string, draws back both string and arrow down to the notch, the string is brought near to his breast and the iron head of the arrow to the bow; back flies the great bent bow with a twang, the bowstring whirs, off springs the arrow flying eager for its mark.

This admirable picture Caylus cannot have overlooked. What, then, did he find in it to render it incapable of employing his artist? And for what reason did he consider fitter for this purpose the assembly of the carousing gods in council? In the one, as in the other, we find visible subjects, and what more does the painter want than visible subjects in order to fill his canvas? The solution of the problem must be this. Although both subjects, as being visible, are alike capable of actual painting, yet there exists the essential distinction between them, that the former is a visible continuous action, the different parts of which occur step by step in succession of time, the latter, on the other hand, is a visible arrested action, the different parts of which develop side by side in space. But now, if painting, in virtue of her signs or the methods of her imitation, which she can combine only in space, must wholly renounce time, then continuous actions as such cannot be reckoned amongst her subjects; but she must content herself with actions set side by side, or with mere bodies which by their attitudes can be supposed an action. Poetry, on the other hand –

XVI

But I will turn to the foundations and try to argue the matter from first principles.[117]

My conclusion is this. If it is true that painting employs in its imitations quite other means or signs than poetry employs, the former – that is to say,

---

[116] *Iliad*, IV, 105–26.

[117] The following deductive argument had in fact formed the basis of Lessing's plan for the whole work: see Introduction, pp. xiii–xv.

figures and colours in space – but the latter articulate sounds in time; as, unquestionably, the signs used must have a definite relation to the thing signified, it follows that signs arranged together side by side can express only subjects which, or the various parts of which, exist thus side by side, whilst signs which succeed each other can express only subjects which, or the various parts of which, succeed each other.

Subjects which, or the various parts of which, exist side by side, may be called *bodies*. Consequently, bodies with their visible properties form the proper subjects of painting.

Subjects which or the various parts of which succeed each other may in general be called *actions*. Consequently, actions form the proper subjects of poetry.

Yet all bodies exist not in space alone, but also in time. They continue, and may appear differently at every moment and stand in different relations. Every one of these momentary appearances and combinations is the effect of one preceding and can be the cause of one following, and accordingly be likewise the central point of an action. Consequently, painting can also imitate actions, but only by way of suggestion through bodies.

On the other hand, actions cannot subsist for themselves, but must attach to certain things or persons. Now in so far as these things are bodies or are regarded as bodies, poetry too depicts bodies, but only by way of suggestion through actions.

Painting, in her coexisting compositions, can use only one single moment of the action, and must therefore choose the most pregnant, from which what precedes and follows will be most easily apprehended.

Just in the same manner poetry also can use, in her continuous imitations, only one single property of the bodies, and must therefore choose that one which calls up the most living picture of the body on that side from which she is regarding it. Here, indeed, we find the origin of the rule which insists on the unity and consistency of descriptive epithets, and on economy in the delineations of bodily subjects.

This is a dry chain of reasoning, and I should put less trust in it if I did not find it completely confirmed by Homer's practice, or if, rather, it were not Homer's practice itself which had led me to it. Only by these principles can the great manner of the Greeks be settled and explained, and its rightness established against the opposite manner of so many modern poets, who would emulate the painter in a department where they must necessarily be outdone by him.

Homer, I find, paints nothing but continuous actions, and all bodies, all single things, he paints only by their share in those actions, and in general only by one feature. What wonder, then, that the painter, where Homer himself paints, finds little or nothing for him to do, his harvest arising only there where the story brings together a multitude of beautiful bodies, in beautiful attitudes, in a place favourable to art, the poet himself painting these bodies, attitudes, places, just as little as he chooses? Let the reader run through the whole succession of pictures piece by piece, as Caylus suggests, and he will discover in every one of them evidence for our contention.

Here, then, I leave the Count, who wishes to make the painter's palette the touchstone of the poet, that I may expound in closer detail the manner of Homer.

For one thing, I say, Homer commonly names one feature only. A ship is to him now the black ship, now the hollow ship, now the swift ship, at most the well-rowed black ship. Beyond that he does not enter on a picture of the ship. But certainly of the navigating, the putting to sea, the disembarking of the ship, he makes a detailed picture, one from which the painter must make five or six separate pictures if he would get it in its entirety upon his canvas.

If indeed special circumstances compel Homer to fix our glance for a while on some single corporeal object, in spite of this no picture is made of it which the painter could follow with his brush; for Homer knows how, by innumerable artifices, to set this object in a succession of moments, at each of which it assumes a different appearance, and in the last of which the painter must await it in order to show us, fully arisen, what in the poet we see arising. For instance, if Homer wishes to let us see the chariot of Juno, then Hebe must put it together piece by piece before our eyes. We see the wheels, the axles, the seat, the pole and straps and traces, not so much as it is when complete, but as it comes together under the hands of Hebe. On the wheels alone does the poet expend more than one feature, showing us the brazen spokes, the golden rims, the tyres of bronze, the silver hub, in fullest detail. We might suggest that as there were more wheels than one, so in the description just as much more time must be given to them as their separate putting-on would actually itself require.

Ἥβη δ' ἀμφ' ὀχέεσσι θοῶς βάλε καμπύλα κύκλα,
Χάλκεα ὀκτάκνημα, σιδηρέῳ ἄξονι ἀμφίς.
Τῶν ἤτοι χρυσέη ἴτυς ἄφθιτος, αὐτὰρ ὕπερθεν
Χάλκε' ἐπίσσωτρα προσαρηρότα, θαῦμα ἰδέσθαι.
Πλῆμναι δ' ἀργύρου εἰσὶ περίδρομοι ἀμφοτέρωθεν·
Δίφρος δὲ χρυσέοισι καὶ ἀργυρέοισιν ἱμᾶσιν
Ἐντέταται, δοιαὶ δὲ περίδρομοι ἄντυγές εἰσι.
Τοῦ δ' ἐξ ἀργύρεος ῥυμὸς πέλεν· αὐτὰρ ἐπ' ἄκρῳ
Δῆσε χρύσειον καλὸν ζυγόν, ἐν δὲ λέπαδνα
Κάλ' ἔβαλε, χρύσεια.[118]

If Homer would show us how Agamemnon was dressed, then the King must put on his whole attire piece by piece before our eyes: the soft undervest, the great mantle, the fine laced boots, the sword; and now he is ready and grasps the sceptre. We see the attire as the poet paints the action of attiring; another would have described the garments down to the smallest ribbon, and we should have seen nothing of the action.

Μαλακὸν δ' ἔνδυνε χιτῶνα,
Καλόν, νηγάτεον, περὶ δ' αὖ μέγα βάλλετο φᾶρος·
Ποσσὶ δ' ὑπαὶ λιπαροῖσιν ἐδήσατο καλὰ πέδιλα,
Ἀμφὶ δ' ἄρ' ὤμοισιν βάλετο ξίφος ἀργυρόηλον·
Εἵλετο δὲ σκῆπτρον πατρώϊον, ἄφθιτον αἰεί.[119]

And of this sceptre which here is called merely the paternal, ancestral sceptre, as in another place he calls a similar one merely χρυσείοις ἥλοισι πεπαρμένον – that is, the sceptre mounted with studs of gold – if, I say, of this mighty sceptre we are to have a fuller and exacter picture, what, then, does Homer? Does he paint for us, besides the golden nails, the wood also and the carved knob? Perhaps he might if the description were intended for a book of heraldry, so that in after times one like to it might be made precisely to pattern. And yet I am certain that many a modern poet would have made just such a heraldic description, with the naive idea that he has

[118] *Iliad*, v, 722–31: 'Hebe quickly put to the car on either side the curved wheels of bronze, eight-spoked, about the iron axle-tree. Of these the felloe verily is of gold imperishable, and thereover are tyres of bronze fitted, a marvel to behold; and the naves are of silver, revolving on this side and on that; and the body is plaited tight with gold and silver thongs, and two rims there are that run about it. From the body stood forth the pole of silver, and on the end thereof she bound the fair golden yoke, and cast thereon the fair golden breast-straps.'

[119] *Iliad*, II, 42–6: 'He put on his soft tunic, fair and glistening, and about him cast his great cloak, and beneath his shining feet he bound his fair sandals, and about his shoulders flung his silver-studded sword; and he grasped the sceptre of his fathers, imperishable ever.'

himself so painted it because the painter may possibly follow him. But what does Homer care how far he leaves the painter behind? Instead of an image he gives us the story of the sceptre: first, it is being wrought by Vulcan; then it gleams in the hands of Jupiter; again, it marks the office of Mercury; once more, it is the marshal's baton of the warlike Pelops, and yet again, the shepherd's crook of peace-loving Atreus.

> Σκῆπτρον ἔχων, τὸ μὲν Ἥφαιστος κάμε τεύχων.
> Ἥφαιστος μὲν δῶκε Διὶ Κρονίωνι ἄνακτι,
> Αὐτὰρ ἄρα Ζεὺς δῶκε διακτόρῳ Ἀργεϊφόντῃ·
> Ἑρμείας δὲ ἄναξ δῶκεν Πέλοπι πληξίππῳ,
> Αὐτὰρ ὁ αὖτε Πέλοψ δῶκ' Ἀτρέϊ, ποιμένι λαῶν·
> Ἀτρεὺς δὲ θνῄσχων ἔλιπε πολύαρνι Θυέστῃ,
> Αὐτὰρ ὁ αὖτε Θυέστ' Ἀγαμέμνονι λεῖπε φορῆναι,
> Πολλῇσι νήσοισι καὶ Ἄργεϊ παντὶ ἀνάσσειν.[120]

And so in the end I know this sceptre better than if a painter had laid it before my eyes or a second Vulcan delivered it into my hands. It would not surprise me if I found that one of the old commentators of Homer had admired this passage as the most perfect allegory of the origin, progress, establishment and hereditary succession of the royal power amongst mankind. True, I should smile if I were to read that Vulcan, the maker of this sceptre, as fire, as the most indispensable thing for the preservation of mankind, represented in general the satisfaction of those wants which moved the first men to subject themselves to the rule of an individual monarch; that the first king, a son of Time (Ζεὺς Κρονίων),[121] was an honest ancient who wished to share his power with, or wholly transfer it to, a wise and eloquent man, a Mercury (Διακτόρῳ Ἀργεϊφόντῃ);[122] that the wily orator, at the time when the infant State was threatened by foreign foes, resigned his supreme power to the bravest warrior (Πέλοπι πληξίππῳ);[123] that the brave warrior, when he had quelled the aggressors and made the realm secure, was able to hand it over to his son, who, as a peace-loving ruler, as a benevolent shepherd of his people (ποιμὴν

---

[120] *Iliad*, II, 101–8: '... bearing in his hands the sceptre which Hephaestus had wrought with toil. Hephaestus gave it to king Zeus, son of Cronos, and Zeus gave it to the messenger Argeiphontes; and Hermes, the lord, gave it to Pelops, driver of horses, and Pelops in turn gave it to Atreus, shepherd of the host; and Atreus at his death left it to Thyestes, rich in flocks, and Thyestes again left it to Agamemnon to bear, so that he might be lord of many isles and of all Argos.'

[121] 'Zeus, son of Cronos'; Lessing here accepts the false equation of the latter name with 'Chronos' (time).

[122] 'the messenger Argeiphontes'.   [123] 'Pelops, driver of horses'.

λαῶν),[124] made them acquainted with luxury and abundance, whereby after his death the wealthiest of his relations (πολύαρνι Θυέστη)[125] had the way opened to him for attracting to himself by presents and bribes that which hitherto only confidence had conferred and which merit had considered more a burden than an honour, and to secure it to his family for the future as a kind of purchased estate. I should smile, but nevertheless should be confirmed in my esteem for the poet to whom so much meaning can be attributed. – This, however, is a digression, and I am now regarding the story of the sceptre merely as an artifice to make us tarry over the one particular object without being drawn into the tedious description of its parts. Even when Achilles swears by his sceptre to avenge the contempt with which Agamemnon has treated him, Homer gives us the history of this sceptre. We see it growing green upon the mountains, the axe cutting it from the trunk, stripping it of leaves and bark and making it fit to serve the judges of the people for a symbol of their godlike dignity.

> Ναὶ μὰ τόδε σκῆπτρον, τὸ μὲν οὔποτε φύλλα καὶ ὄζους
> Φύσει, ἐπεὶ δὴ πρῶτα τομὴν ἐν ὄρεσσι λέλοιπεν,
> Οὐδ' ἀναθελήσει· περὶ γάρ ῥά ἑ χαλκὸς ἔλεψε
> Φύλλα τε καὶ φλοιόν· νῦν αὖτέ μιν υἷες Ἀχαιῶν
> Ἐν παλάνῃς φορέουσι δικασπόλοι, οἵ τε θέμιστας
> Πρὸς Διὸς εἰρύαται...[126]

It was not so much incumbent upon Homer to depict two staves of different material and shape as to furnish us with a symbol of the difference in the powers of which these staves were the sign. The former a work of Vulcan, the latter carved by an unknown hand in the mountains; the former the ancient property of a noble house, the latter intended for any fist that can grasp it; the former extended by a monarch over all Argos and many an isle besides, the latter borne by any one out of the midst of the Grecian hosts, one to whom with others the guarding of the laws had been committed. Such was actually the distance that separated Agamemnon from Achilles, a distance which Achilles himself, in all the blindness of his wrath, could not help admitting.

---

[124] 'shepherd of the host' (Atreus).   [125] 'Thyestes, rich in flocks'.
[126] *Iliad*, I, 234–9: 'Verily by this staff, that shall no more put forth leaves or shoots since at the first it left its stump among the mountains, neither shall it again grow green, for the bronze hath stripped it of leaves and bark, and now the sons of the Achaeans that give judgement bear it in their hands, even they that guard the dooms by ordinance of Zeus.'

Yet not in those cases alone where Homer combines with his descriptions this kind of ulterior purpose, but even where he has to do with nothing but the picture, he will distribute this picture in a sort of story of the object, in order to let its parts, which we see side by side in Nature, follow in his painting after each other and as it were keep step with the flow of the narrative. For instance, he would paint for us the bow of Pandarus – a bow of horn, of such and such a length, well polished, and mounted with gold plate at the extremities. How does he manage it? Does he count out before us all these properties dryly one after the other? Not at all; that would be to sketch, to make a copy of such a bow, but not to paint it. He begins with the chase of the deer, from the horns of which the bow was made; Pandarus had waylaid and killed it amongst the crags; the horns were of extraordinary length, and so he destined them for a bow; they are wrought, the maker joins them, mounts them, polishes them. And thus, as we have already said, with the poet we see arising what with the painter we can only see as already arisen.

Τόξον ἐΰξοον ἰξάλου αἰγὸς
Ἀγρίου, ὅν ῥά ποτ' αὐτὸς ὑπὸ στέρνοιο τυχήσας
Πέτρης ἐκβαίνοντα δεδεγμένος ἐν προδοκῆσι,
Βεβλήκει πρὸς στῆθος· ὁ δ' ὕπτιος ἔμπεσε πέτρη.
Τοῦ κέρα ἐκ κεφαλῆς ἐκκαιδεκάδωρα πεφύκει·
Καὶ τὰ μὲν ἀσκήσας κεραοξόος ἤραρε τέκτων,
Πᾶν δ' εὖ λειήνας χρυσέην ἐπέθηκε κορώνην.[127]

I should never have done, if I were to cite all the instances of this kind. A multitude of them will occur to everyone who knows his Homer.

XVII

But, some will object, the signs or characters which poetry employs are not solely such as succeed each other; they may be also arbitrary;[128] and, as arbitrary signs, they are certainly capable of representing bodies just

---

[127] *Iliad*, IV, 105–11: '...his polished bow of the horn of a wild ibex, that he had himself smitten beneath the breast as it came forth from a rock, he lying in wait the while in a place of ambush, and had struck it in the chest, so that it fell backward in a cleft of the rock. From its head the horns grew to a length of sixteen palms; these the worker in horn had wrought and fitted together, and smoothed all with care, and set thereon a tip of gold.'

[128] On 'natural' and 'arbitrary' signs, see Introduction pp. xiv ff.

as they exist in space. We find instances of this in Homer himself, for we have only to remember his Shield of Achilles in order to have the most decisive example in how detailed and yet poetical a manner some single thing can be depicted, with its various parts side by side.

I will reply to this twofold objection. I call it twofold, because a just conclusion must prevail even without examples, and, on the other hand, the example of Homer weighs with me even if I know not how to justify it by any argument. It is true, as the signs of speech are arbitrary, so it is perfectly possible that by it we can make the parts of a body follow each other just as truly as in actuality they are found existing side by side. Only this is a property of speech and its signs in general, but not in so far as it suits best the purposes of poetry. The poet is not concerned merely to be intelligible, his representations should not merely be clear and plain, though this may satisfy the prose writer. He desires rather to make the ideas awakened by him within us living things, so that for the moment we realise the true sensuous impressions of the objects he describes, and cease in this moment of illusion to be conscious of the means – namely, his words – which he employs for his purpose. This is the substance of what we have already said of the poetic picture. But the poet should always paint; and now let us see how far bodies with their parts set side by side are suitable for this kind of painting.

How do we arrive at the distinct representation of a thing in space? First we regard its parts singly, then the combination of these parts, and finally the whole. Our senses perform these various operations with so astonishing a swiftness that they seem to us but one, and this swiftness is imperatively necessary if we are to arrive at a conception of the whole, which is nothing more than the result of the conceptions of the parts and their combination. Provided, then, the poet leads us in the most beautiful order from one part of the object to another; provided he knows also how to make the combination of those parts equally clear – how much time does he need for that? What the eye sees at a glance, he counts out to us gradually, with a perceptible slowness, and often it happens that when we come to the last feature we have already forgotten the first. Nevertheless, we have to frame a whole from those features; to the eye the parts beheld remain constantly present, and it can run over them again and again; for the ear, on the contrary, the parts heard are lost if they do not abide in the memory. And if they so abide, what trouble, what effort it costs to renew their impressions, all of them in their due order, so vividly, to think of them together with even a moderate swiftness, and thus to arrive at an eventual conception of the whole. Let us try it by an example which may be called a masterpiece of its kind:[129]

> Dort ragt das hohe Haupt vom edeln Enziane
> Weit übern niedern Chor der Pöbelkräuter hin,
> Ein ganzes Blumenvolk dient unter seiner Fahne,
> Sein blauer Bruder selbst bückt sich und ehret ihn.
> Der Blumen helles Gold, in Strahlen umgebogen,
> Thürmt sich am Stengel auf, und krönt sein grau Gewand,
> Der Blätter glattes Weiß, mit tiefem Grün durchzogen,
> Strahlt von dem bunten Blitz von feuchtem Diamant.
> Gerechtestes Gesetz! daß Kraft sich Zier vermähle,
> In einem schönen Leib wohnt eine schönre Seele.
>
> Hier kriecht ein niedrig Kraut, gleich einem grauen Nebel,
> Dem die Natur sein Blatt im Kreuze hingelegt;
> Die holde Blume zeigt die zwei vergöldten Schnäbel,
> Die ein von Amethyst gebildter Vogel trägt.
> Dort wirft ein glänzend Blatt, in Finger ausgekerbet,
> Auf einen hellen Bach den grünen Widerschein;
> Der Blumen zarten Schnee, den matter Purpur färbet,
> Schließt ein gestreifter Stern in weiße Strahlen ein.
> Smaragd und Rosen blühn auch auf zertretner Heide,
> Und Felsen decken sich mit einem Purpurkleide.

Here are weeds and flowers which the learned poet paints with much art and fidelity to Nature. Paints, but without any illusion whatever. I

---

[129] The following quotation consists of stanzas 39 and 40 of the didactic poem *The Alps* (*Die Alpen*, 1729) by the Swiss poet and scientist Albrecht von Haller (1708–77): 'There the high head of the noble gentian towers far above the lowly chorus of the vulgar herbs. A whole nation of flowers serves under his banner, and even his blue brother [a lesser species of gentian] bows low and honours him. The bright gold of the flowers, radiating outwards [centaury], ascends the stalk and crowns its grey garment; the smooth white of the leaves, streaked with dark green, shines with the coloured sparkle of the dewy diamond. Most equitable law! That strength should join with ornament; in a beautiful body there dwells a more beautiful soul.
  Here creeps a lowly herb [antirrhinum], like a grey mist, whose leaf nature has formed in a cross; the lovely flower displays the two gilded beaks of a bird made of amethyst. There a gleaming leaf, its edges divided into fingers, casts its green reflection on a bright rivulet; the delicate snow of the flowers, dyed with crimson, surrounds a striped star with its white rays [*Astrantia major*, masterwort]. Emerald and roses bloom even on the trodden heath [wild rosemary], and rocks are clothed in a dress of purple [campion].' (Haller himself, in footnotes to the poem, elucidates the botanical references.)

will not say that out of this picture he who has never seen these weeds and flowers can make no idea of them, or as good as none. It may be that all poetic pictures require some preliminary acquaintance with their subjects. Neither will I deny that for one who possesses such an acquaintance here the poet may not have awakened a more vivid idea of some parts. I only ask him, how does it stand with the conception of the whole? If this also is to be more vivid, then no single parts must stand out, but the higher light must appear divided equally amongst them all, our imagination must be able to run over them all with equal swiftness, in order to unite in one from them that which in Nature we see united in one. Is this the case here? And if it is not the case, how could anyone maintain 'that the most perfect drawing of a painter must be entirely lifeless and dark compared with this poetic portrayal'?[130] It remains infinitely below that which lines and colours on canvas can express, and the critic who bestows on it this exaggerated praise must have regarded it from an utterly false point of view: he must have looked rather at the ornaments which the poet has woven into it, at the heightening of the subject above the mere vegetative life, at the development of the inner perfection to which the outward beauty serves merely as a shell, than at the beauty itself and at the degree of life and resemblance in the picture which the painter and which the poet can assure to us from it. Nevertheless, we are concerned here purely with the latter, and whoever says that the mere lines:

Der Blumen helles Gold, in Strahlen umgebogen,
Thürmt sich am Stengel auf, und krönt sein grün Gewand,
Der Blätter glattes Weiß, mit tiefem Grün durchzogen,
Strahlt von dem bunten Blitz von feuchtem Diamant

– that these lines in respect of their impression can compete with the imitation of a Huysum,[131] can never have interrogated his feelings, or must be deliberately denying them. They may, indeed, if we have the flower itself in our hands, be recited concerning it with excellent effect; but in themselves alone they say little or nothing. I hear in every word the toiling poet, and am far enough from seeing the thing itself.

---

[130] The praise of Haller quoted here is by his fellow Swiss, Johann Jakob Breitinger (1701–76), in his *Kritische Dichtkunst (Critical Poetics* (Zurich, 1740)), Part II, p. 407 (Lessing's reference).
[131] Jan van Huysum (1682–1749), one of the most famous Dutch flower-painters of his day.

Once more, then; I do not deny to speech in general the power of portraying a bodily whole by its parts: speech can do so, because its signs or characters, although they follow one another consecutively, are nevertheless arbitrary signs; but I do deny it to speech as the medium of poetry, because such verbal delineations of bodies fail of the illusion on which poetry particularly depends, and this illusion, I contend, must fail them for the reason that the *coexistence* of the physical object comes into collision with the *consecutiveness* of speech, and the former being resolved into the latter, the dismemberment of the whole into its parts is certainly made easier, but the final reunion of those parts into a whole is made uncommonly difficult and not seldom impossible.

Wherever, then, illusion does not come into the question, where one has only to do with the understanding of one's readers and aims only at plain and as far as possible complete concepts, those delineations of bodies (which we have excluded from poetry) may quite well find their place, and not the prose-writer alone, but the didactic poet (for where he dogmatizes he is not a poet) can employ them with much advantage. So Virgil, for instance, in his poem on agriculture, delineates a cow suitable for breeding from:

> . . . Optima torvae
> Forma bovis, cui turpe caput, cui plurima cervix,
> Et crurum tenus a mento palearia pendent;
> Tum longo nullus lateri modus: omnia magna,
> Pes etiam, et camuris hirtae sub cornibus aures.
> Nec mihi displiceat maculis insignis et albo,
> Aut juga detractans interdumque aspera cornu
> Et faciem tauro propior, quaeque ardua tota,
> Et gradiens ima verrit vestigia cauda.[132]

---

[132] Virgil, *Georgics*, III, 51–9:

> In a cow the following
> Points should be looked for – a rough appearance, a coarse head,
> Generous neck, and dewlaps hanging from jaw to leg;
> Flanks as roomy as you like; everything built on a large scale,
> Even the hoof; and shaggy ears under the crooked horns.
> I have nothing against an animal of prominent white markings,
> Or one that rejects the yoke and is hasty at times with her horn –
> More like a bull to look at,
> Tall all over, dusting the ground with her tail as she goes.

(Virgil, The *Eclogues, Georgics and Aeneid*, translated by C. Day Lewis (London, 1966)).

Or a beautiful foal:

> ... Illi ardua cervix
> Argutumque caput, brevis alvus, obesaque terga,
> Luxuriatque toris animosum pectus, etc.[133]

For who does not see that here the poet is concerned rather with the setting forth of the parts than with the whole? He wants to reckon up for us the characteristics of a fine foal and of a well-formed cow, in order to enable us, when we have more or less taken note of these, to judge of the excellence of the one or the other; whether, however, all these characteristics can be easily gathered together into one living picture or not, that might be to him a matter of indifference.

Beyond such performances as these, the detailed pictures of physical objects, barring the above-mentioned Homeric artifice of changing the Coexisting into an actual Successive, has always been recognized by the best judges as a frigid kind of sport for which little or nothing of genius is demanded. 'When the poetic dabbler', says Horace, 'can do nothing more, he begins to paint a hedge, an altar, a brook winding through pleasant meads, a brawling stream, or a rainbow:

> ... Lucus et ara Dianae
> Et properantis aquae per amoenos ambitus agros,
> Aut flumen Rhenum, aut pluvius describitur arcus.'[134]

Pope, in his manhood, looked back on the pictorial efforts of his poetic childhood with great contempt. He expressly required that whosoever would not unworthily bear the name of poet should as early as possible renounce the lust for description, and declared a merely descriptive poem to be a dinner of nothing but soup.[135] Of Herr von Kleist I can avow that he

---

[133] Virgil, *Georgics*, III, 79–81:
> He shows a proud neck,
> A finely tapering head, short barrel and fleshy back,
> And his spirited chest ripples with muscle.
> (Translated by C. Day Lewis)

[134] Horace, *Ars Poetica*, lines 16–18: 'they describe Diana's grove and altar, the meanderings of a stream through a pleasant landscape, or the River Rhine, or a rainbow'.

[135] Alexander Pope (1688–1744); Lessing's reference is to his *Epistle to Arbuthnot* (*Prologue to the Satires*), lines 148 f. and 340 f. Lessing's footnote shows that he is aware that Warburton, in his commentary on the poem, is the author of the culinary reference he cites, but he (Lessing) maintains that Warburton is merely echoing Pope's own sentiments.

was far from proud of his 'Spring': had he lived longer, he would have given it an entirely different shape.[136] He thought of putting some design into it, and mused on means by which that multitude of pictures which he seemed to have snatched haphazard, now here, now there, from the limitless field of rejuvenated Nature, might be made to arise in a natural order before his eyes and follow each other in a natural succession. He would at the same time have done what Marmontel,[137] doubtless on the occasion of his Eclogues,[138] recommended to several German poets; from a series of pictures but sparingly interspersed with sensations he would have made a succession of sensations but sparingly interspersed with pictures.

XVIII

And yet may not Homer himself sometimes have lapsed into these frigid delineations of physical objects?

I will hope that there are only a few passages to which in this case appeal can be made; and I am assured that even these few are of such a kind as rather to confirm the rule from which they seem to be exceptions. It still holds good; succession in time is the sphere of the poet, as space is that of the painter. To bring two necessarily distant points of time into one and the same picture, as Fr. Mazzuoli[139] has done with the Rape of the Sabine Women and their reconciling their husbands to their kinsfolk, or as Titian with the whole story of the Prodigal Son, his dissolute life, his misery, and his repentance, is nothing but an invasion of the poet's sphere by the painter, which good taste can never sanction. The several parts or things which in Nature I must needs take in at a glance if they are to produce a whole - to reckon these up one by one to the reader, in order to form for him a picture of the whole, is nothing but an invasion of the painter's sphere by the poet, who expends thereby a great deal of imagination to no purpose. Still, as two friendly, reasonable neighbours will not at all permit that one of them shall make too free with the most intimate concerns of the other, yet will exercise in things of less importance a mutual forbearance

---

[136] Christian Ewald von Kleist (1715–59), poet and officer in Frederick the Great's army, who died of wounds received in the Seven Years' War. His descriptive poem *Der Frühling* (*The Spring*) was greatly admired in Lessing's day. Kleist had been a close friend of Lessing's.

[137] Jean François de Marmontel (1723–99), French critic, author of a *Poétique française* (1763); Lessing's reference is to Part II, p. 501, of this work.

[138] The reference is to Kleist's (not Marmontel's) Eclogues or pastoral poems.

[139] Francesco Mazzola Parmigianino (1503–40), Italian painter.

and on either side condone trifling interferences with one's strict rights to which circumstances may give occasion, so it is with Painting and Poetry.

It is unnecessary here for my purpose to point out that in great historical pictures the single moment is almost always amplified to some extent, and that there is perhaps no single composition very rich in figures where every figure has completely the movement and posture which at the moment of the main action it ought to have; one is earlier, another later, than historical truth would require. This is a liberty which the master must make good by certain niceties of arrangement, by the position or distance of his *personae*, such as will permit them to take a greater or a smaller share in what is passing at the moment. Let me here avail myself of but one remark which Herr Mengs has made concerning the drapery of Raphael.[140] 'All folds', he says, 'have with him their reasons, it may be from their own weight or by the pulling of the limbs. We can often see from them how they have been at an earlier moment; even in this Raphael seeks significance. One sees from the folds whether a leg or an arm, before the moment depicted, has stood in front or behind, whether the limb has moved from curvature to extension, or after being stretched out is now bending.' It is undeniable that the artist in this case brings two different moments into one. For as the foot which has rested behind and now moves forward is immediately followed by the part of the dress resting upon it, unless the dress be of very stiff material and for that very reason is altogether inconvenient to paint, so there is no moment in which the dress makes a fold different in the slightest from that which the present position of the limb demands; but if we permit it to make another fold, then we have the previous moment of the dress and the present moment of the limb. Nevertheless, who will be so particular with the artist who finds his advantage in showing us these two moments together? Who will not rather praise him for having the intelligence and the courage to commit a fault so trifling in order to attain a greater perfection of expression?

The poet is entitled to equal indulgence. His progressive imitation properly allows him to touch but one single side, one single property of his physical subject at a time. But if the happy construction of his language permits him to do this with a single word, why should he not also venture now and then to add a second such word? Why not even, if it

---

[140] Anton Raphael Mengs (1728–79), painter and friend of Winckelmann in Rome, author of *Gedanken über die Schönheit und über den Geschmack in der Malerei* (Zurich, 1762); Lessing's reference is to p. 69 of that work.

is worth the trouble, a third? Or, indeed, perhaps a fourth? I have said that
to Homer a ship was either the black ship, or the hollow ship, or the swift
ship, or at most the well-rowed black ship. This is to be understood of his
manner in general. Here and there a passage occurs where he adds the
third descriptive epithet: Καμπύλα κύκλα, χάλκεα, ὀκτάκνημα, round,
brazen, eight-spoked wheels.[141] Even the fourth: ἀσπίδα πάντοσε ἴσην,
καλήν, χαλκείην, ἐξήλατον, a completely polished, beautiful, brazen,
chased shield.[142] Who will blame him for that? Who will not rather owe
him thanks for this little exuberance, when he feels what an excellent
effect it may have in a suitable place?

I am unwilling, however, to argue the poet's or the painter's proper justification from the simile I have employed, of the two friendly neighbours.
A mere simile proves and justifies nothing. But they must be justified in
this way: just as in the one case, with the painter, the two distinct moments
touch each other so closely and immediately that they may without offence count as but one, so also in the other case, with the poet, the several
strokes for the different parts and properties in space succeed each other
so quickly, in such a crowded moment, that we can believe we hear all of
them at once.

And in this, I may remark, his splendid language served Homer marvellously. It allowed him not merely all possible freedom in the combining
and heaping-up of epithets, but it had, too, for their heaped-up epithets
an order so happy as quite to remedy the disadvantage arising from the
suspension of their application. In one or several of these facilities the
modern languages are universally lacking. Those, like the French, which,
to give an example, for καμπύλα κύκλα, χάλκεα, ὀκτάκνημα, must use
the circumlocution 'the round wheels which were of brass and had eight
spokes', express the sense, but destroy the picture. The sense, moreover,
is here nothing, and the picture everything; and the former without the
latter makes the most vivid poet the most tedious babbler – a fate that has
frequently befallen our good Homer under the pen of the conscientious
Madame Dacier.[143] Our German tongue, again, can, it is true, generally
translate the Homeric epithets by epithets equivalent and just as terse,
but in the advantageous order of them it cannot match the Greek. We
say, indeed, '*Die runden, ehernen, achtspeichigten*';[144] but '*Räder*'[145] trails

---

[141] *Iliad*, v, 722 f.   [142] *Iliad*, xii, 296.   [143] See note 15 above.
[144] 'the round, brazen, eight-spoked'.   [145] 'wheels'.

behind. Who does not feel that three different predicates, before we know the subject, can make but a vague and confused picture? The Greek joins the subject and the first predicate immediately, and lets the other follow after; he says, '*Runde Räder, eherne, achtspeichigte*'. So we know at once of what he is speaking, and are made acquainted, in consonance with the natural order of thought, first with the thing and then with its accidents. This advantage our language does not possess. Or, shall I say, possesses it and can only very seldom use it without ambiguity? The two things are one. For when we would place the epithets after, they must stand in *statu absoluto*; we must say, '*Runde Räder, ehern und achtspeichigt*'. But in this *status* our adjectives are exactly like adverbs, and must, if we attach them as such to the next verb which is predicated of the thing, produce a meaning not seldom wholly false, and, at best, invariably ambiguous.

But here I am dwelling on trifles, and seem to have forgotten the Shield – Achilles' Shield, that famous picture in respect of which especially Homer was from of old regarded as a teacher of painting. A shield, people will say – that is surely a single physical object, the description of which and its parts ranged side by side is not permissible to a poet? And this particular Shield, in its material, in its form, in all the figures that covered the vast surface of it, Homer has described in more than a hundred splendid verses, with such exactness and detail that it has been easy for modern artists to make a replica of it alike in every feature.

To this special objection I reply, that I have replied to it already. Homer, that is to say, paints the Shield not as a finished and complete thing, but as a thing in process. Here once more he has availed himself of the famous artifice, turning the *coexisting* of his design into a *consecutive*, and there by making of the tedious painting of a physical object the living picture of an action. We see not the Shield, but the divine artificer at work upon it. He steps up with hammer and tongs to his anvil, and after he has forged the plates from the rough ore, the pictures which he has selected for its adornment stand out one after another before our eyes under his artistic chiselling. Nor do we lose sight of him again until all is finished. When it is complete, we are amazed at the work, but it is with the believing amazement of an eye-witness who has seen it in the making.

The same cannot be said of the Shield of Aeneas in Virgil. The Roman Poet either did not realize the subtlety of his model here, or the things that he wanted to put upon his Shield appeared to him to be of a kind that could not well admit of being shown in execution. They were prophecies, which could not have been uttered by the god in our presence as plainly as the poet afterwards expounds them. Prophecies, as such, demand an obscurer language, in which the actual names of persons yet-to-be may not fitly be pronounced. Yet these veritable names, to all appearance, were the most important things of all to the poet and courtier. If, however, this excuses him, it does not remove the unhappy effect of his deviation from the Homeric way. Readers of any delicacy of taste will justify me here. The preparations which Vulcan makes for his labour are almost the same in Virgil as in Homer. But instead of what we see in Homer – that is to say, not merely the preparations for the work, but also the work itself – Virgil after he has given us a general view of the busy god with his Cyclops:

> Ingentem clypeum informant...
> ...Alii ventosis follibus auras
> Accipiunt redduntque, alii stridentia tingunt
> Aera lacu. Gemit impositis incudibus antrum.
> Illi inter sese multa vi brachia tollunt
> In numerum, versantque tenaci forcipe massam –[146]

drops the curtain at once and transports us to another scene, bringing us gradually into the valley where Venus arrives at Aeneas' side with the armour that has meanwhile been completed. She leans the weapons against the trunk of an oak-tree, and when the hero has sufficiently gazed at, and admired, and touched and tested them, the description of the pictures on the Shield begins, and, with the everlasting: 'Here is', 'and there is', 'near by stands' and 'not far off one sees', becomes so frigid and tedious that all the poetic ornament which Virgil could give it was needed to prevent us finding it unendurable. Moreover, as this picture is not drawn by Aeneas as one who rejoices in the mere figures and knows nothing of their significance:

> ...rerumque ignarus imagine gaudet;[147]

nor even by Venus, although conceivably she must know just as much of the future fortunes of her dear grandchildren as her obliging husband;[148]

---

[146] Virgil, *Aeneid*, VIII, 447–53: 'They shape an enormous shield ... Others, with bellows full of wind, draw in and discharge the air. Others again temper the hissing bronze in a vessel of water. The cave resounds with the blows on the anvils. They powerfully raise their arms together in rhythm and turn the mass of metal with the grip of their tongs.'

[147] *Aeneid*, VIII, 730: 'he delights in the image, though ignorant of the things represented'.

[148] That is, Vulcan.

but proceeds from the poet's own mouth. The progress of the action meanwhile is obviously at a standstill. No single one of his characters takes any share in it; nor does anything represented on the Shield have any influence, even the smallest, on what is to follow; the witty courtier shines out everywhere, trimming up his matter with every kind of flattering allusion, but not the great genius, depending on the proper inner vitality of his work and despising all extraneous expedients for lending it interest. The Shield of Aeneas is consequently a sheer interpolation, simply and only intended to flatter the national pride of the Romans, a foreign tributary which the poet leads into his main stream in order to give it a livelier motion. The Shield of Achilles, on the other hand, is a rich natural outgrowth of the fertile soil from which it springs; for a Shield had to be made, and as the needful thing never comes bare and without grace from the hands of the divinity, the Shield had also to be embellished. But the art was, to treat these embellishments merely as such, to inweave them into the stuff, in order to show them to us only by means of the latter; and this could only be done by Homer's method. Homer lets Vulcan elaborate ornaments because he is to make a Shield that is worthy of himself. Virgil, on the other hand, appears to let him make the Shield for the sake of its ornaments, considering them important enough to be particularly described, after the Shield itself has long been finished.

XIX

The objections which the elder Scaliger, Perrault, Terrasson, and others make to the Shield in Homer are well known. Equally well known is the reply which Dacier, Boivin, and Pope made to them.[149] In my judgement, however, the latter go too far, and, relying on their good cause, introduce arguments that are not only indefensible, but contribute little to the poet's justification.

[149] A reference to the famous *Querelle des anciens et des modernes* of the late seventeenth and early eighteenth centuries. Perrault and Terrasson were among those who, from the perspective of modern rationalism, criticized the supposed backwardness of the classical writers; the last three, as critics or translators, adopted a more sympathetic attitude. Julius Caesar Scaliger (1484–1558), classical philologist; Charles Perrault (1628–1703), author of *Le parallèle des anciens et des modernes* (1688–98); Jean Terrasson (1670–1750), author of *Dissertations critiques sur L'Iliade de Homère* (1715); André Dacier (1651–1722), editor of *La poétique d'Aristote* (1692); Jean Boivin de Villeneuve (1649–1722), author of the *Apologie d'Homère et du bouclier d'Achille* (1715); Alexander Pope (1688–1744), whose translation of Homer included 'Observations on the Shield of Achilles'.

In order to meet the main objection – that Homer has crowded the Shield with a multitude of figures such as could not possibly find room within its circumference – Boivin undertook to have it drawn, with a note of the necessary dimensions. His notion of the various concentric circles is very ingenious, although the words of the poet give not the slightest suggestion of it, whilst, furthermore, not a trace of proof is to be found that the ancients possessed shields divided off in this manner. Seeing that Homer himself calls it σάκος πάντοσε δεδαιδαλμένον – 'a shield artfully wrought upon all sides' – I would rather, in order to reserve more room, have taken in aid the concave surface; for it is well known that the ancient artists did not leave this vacant, as the Shield of Minerva by Phidias proves.[150] Yet it was not even enough for Boivin to decline availing himself of this advantage; he further increased without necessity the representations themselves for which he was obliged to provide room in the space thus diminished by half, separating into two or three distinct pictures what in the poet is obviously a single picture only. I know very well what moved him to do so, but it ought not to have moved him; instead of troubling himself to give satisfaction to the demands of his opponents, he should have shown them that their demands were illegitimate.

I shall be able to make my meaning clearer by an example. When Homer says of the one City:

Λαοὶ δ' εἰν ἀγορῇ ἔσαν ἀθρόοι· ἔνθα δὲ νεῖκος
Ὠρώρει, δύο δ' ἄνδρες ἐνείκεον εἵνεκα ποινῆς
Ἀνδρὸς ἀποφθιμένου· ὁ μὲν εὔχετο πάντ' ἀποδοῦναι
Δήμῳ πιφαύσκων, ὁ δ' ἀναίνετο μηδὲν ἑλέσθαι·
Ἄμφω δ' ἱέσθην ἐπὶ ἵστορι πεῖραρ ἑλέσθαι.
Λαοὶ δ' ἀμφοτέροισιν ἐπήπυον, ἀμφὶς ἀρωγοί·
Κήρυκες δ' ἄρα λαὸν ἐρήτυον· οἱ δὲ γέροντες
Εἵατ' ἐπὶ ξεστοῖσι λίθοις ἱερῷ ἐνὶ κύκλῳ,
Σκῆπτρα δὲ κηρύκων ἐν χέρσ' ἔχον ἠεροφώνων·
Τοῖσιν ἔπειτ' ἤϊσσον, ἀμοιβηδὶς δὲ δίκαζον.
Κεῖτο δ' ἄρ' ἐν μέσσοισι δύω χρυσοῖο τάλαντα –[151]

---

[150] Lessing's reference is to Pliny, *Natural History*, XXXVI, section 4, p. 726.

[151] *Iliad*, XVIII, 497–507; 'But the folk were gathered in the place of assembly; for there a strife had arisen, and two men were striving about the blood-price of a man slain; the one avowed that he had paid all, declaring his cause to the people, but the other denied that he had received anything; and each was anxious to win the issue in the word of an arbitrator. Moreover, the people were cheering both, showing favour to this side and to that. And heralds held back the people, and the

he is not then, in my view, trying to sketch more than a single picture – the picture of a public lawsuit on the questionable satisfaction of a heavy fine for the striking of a death-blow. The artist who would carry out this sketch cannot in any single effort avail himself of more than a single moment of the same; either the moment of the arraignment, or of the examination of witnesses, or of the sentence, or whatever other moment, before or after, he considers the most suitable. This single moment he makes as pregnant as possible, and endows it with all the illusions which art commands (art, rather than poetry) in the representation of visible objects. Surpassed so greatly on this side, what can the poet who is to paint this very design in words, and has no wish entirely to suffer shipwreck – what can he do but in like manner avail himself of his own peculiar advantages? And what are these? The liberty to enlarge on what has preceded and what follows the single moment of the work of art, and the power thus to show us not only that which the artist has shown, but also that which he can only leave us to guess. By this liberty and this power alone the poet draws level with the artist, and their works are then likest to each other when the effect of each is equally vivid; and not when the one conveys to the soul through the ear neither more nor less than the other can represent to the eye. This is the principle that should have guided Boivin in judging this passage in Homer; he would then not so much have made distinct pictures out of it as have observed in it distinct moments of time. True, he could not well have united in a single picture all that Homer tells us; the accusation and the defence, the production of witnesses, the acclamations of the divided people, the effort of the heralds to allay the tumult, and the decisions of the judge, are things which follow each other and cannot subsist side by side. Yet what, in the language of the schools, was not *actu* contained in the picture lay in it *virtute*,[152] and the only true way of copying in words a material painting is this – to unite the latter with the actually visible, and refuse to be bound by the limits of art, within which the poet can indeed enumerate the *data* for a picture, but never produce the picture itself.

Just so is it when Boivin divides the picture of the besieged city[153] into three different tableaux. He might just as well have divided it into twelve as into three. For as he did not at all grasp the spirit of the poet,

___

elders were sitting upon polished stones in the sacred circle, holding in their hands the staves of the loud-voiced heralds. Therewith then they would spring up and give judgement, each in turn. And in the midst lay two talents of gold.'

[152] *actu . . . virtute*: in fact . . . in essence.   [153] *Iliad*, XVIII, 509–40 (Lessing's reference).

and required him to be subject to the unities of the material painting, he might have found far more violations of these unities, so that it had almost been necessary to assign to every separate stroke of the poet a separate section of the Shield. But, in my opinion, Homer has not altogether more than ten distinct pictures upon the entire Shield, every one of which he introduces with the phrases ἐν μὲν ἔτευξε, *or* ἐν δὲ ποίησε, *or* ἐν δ᾽ ἐτίθει, *or* ἐν δὲ ποίκιλλε Ἀμφιγυήεις.[154] Where these introductory words do not occur one has no right to suppose a separate picture; on the contrary, all which they unite must be regarded as a single picture to which there is merely wanting the arbitrary concentration in a single point of time – a thing the poet was in nowise constrained to indicate. Much rather, had he indicated it, had he confined himself strictly to it, had he not admitted the smallest feature which in the actual execution could not be combined with it – in a word, had he managed the matter exactly as his critics demand, it is true that then these gentlemen would have found nothing to set down against him, but indeed neither would a man of taste have found anything to admire.

Pope was not only pleased with Boivin's plan of dividing and designing, but thought of doing something else of his own, by now further showing that each of these dismembered pictures was planned according to the strictest rules of painting as it is practised today. Contrast, perspective, the three unities – all these he found observed in the best manner possible. And this, although he certainly was well aware that, according to the testimony of quite trustworthy witnesses, painting in the time of the Trojan War was still in its cradle; so that either Homer must, by virtue of his godlike genius, not so much have adhered to what painting then or in his own time could perform, as, rather, have divined what painting in general was capable of performing; or even those witnesses themselves cannot be so trustworthy that they should be preferred to the ocular demonstration of the artistic Shield itself. The former anyone may believe who will; of the latter at least no one can be persuaded who knows something more of the history of art than the mere data of historians. For, that painting in Homer's day was still in its infancy, he believes not merely because a Pliny or such another says so, but above all because he judges, from the works of art which the ancients esteemed, that many centuries later they had not got much further; he knows, for instance, that the paintings

---

[154] 'there he created', 'there he made', 'there he placed', 'there the lame one | Vulcan | fashioned'.

of Polygnotus are far from standing the test which Pope believes would be passed by the pictures on the Shield of Homer. The two great works at Delphi of the master just mentioned, of which Pausanias has left us so circumstantial a description,[155] are obviously without any perspective. This aspect of art was entirely unknown to the ancients, and what Pope adduces in order to prove that Homer had already some conception of it, proves nothing more than that Pope's own conception of it was extremely imperfect. 'That Homer', he says, 'was not a stranger to aerial perspective, appears in his expressly marking the distance of object from object: he tells us, for instance, that the two spies lay a little remote from the other figures; and that the oak, under which was spread the banquet of the reapers, stood *apart*: what he says of the valley sprinkled all over with cottages and flocks, appears to be a description of a large country in perspective. And indeed, a general argument for this may be drawn from the number of figures on the shield; which could not be all expressed in their full magnitude: and this is therefore a sort of proof that the art of lessening them according to perspective was known at that time.'[156] The mere observation of the optical experience that a thing appears smaller at a distance than close at hand, is far indeed from giving perspective to a picture. Perspective demands a single viewpoint, a definite natural field of vision, and it was this that was wanting in ancient paintings. The base in the pictures of Polygnotus was not horizontal, but towards the background raised so prodigiously that the figures which should appear to stand behind one another appeared to stand above one another. And if this arrangement of the different figures and their groups were general, as may be inferred from the ancient bas-reliefs, where the hindmost always stand higher than the foremost and look over their heads, then it is natural that we should take it for granted also in Homer's description, and not separate unnecessarily those of his pictures that can be combined in one picture. The twofold scene of the peaceful city through whose streets went the joyous crowd of a wedding-party, whilst in the market-place a great lawsuit was being decided, demands according to this no twofold picture,

---

[155] Polygnotus (fifth century BC), whose compositions at Delphi of the Sack of Troy and of the descent of Odysseus into Hades are described by the traveller and geographer Pausanias (second century AD) in his *Itinerary of Greece*; Lessing's reference is to Pausanias's description of Phocis in that work, chapters 25–31.

[156] See *The Iliad of Homer*, translated by Alexander Pope, edited by Gilbert Wakefield, new edition, 3 vols. (London, 1817), III, 93.

and Homer certainly was able to consider it a single one, representing to himself the entire city from so high a point of vision that it gave him a free and simultaneous prospect both of the streets and the market-place.

I am of the opinion that the knowledge of true perspective in painting was only arrived at incidentally in the painting of scenery,[157] and also that when this was already in its perfection, it yet cannot have been so easy to apply its rules to a single canvas, seeing that we still find in later paintings amongst the antiquities of Herculaneum many and diverse faults of perspective such as we should nowadays hardly forgive to a schoolboy.

But I absolve myself from the trouble of collecting my scattered notes concerning a point on which I may hope to receive the fullest satisfaction in Herr Winckelmann's promised history of art.[158]

XX

I rather turn gladly to my own road, if a rambler can be said to have a road.

What I have said of physical objects in general is even more pertinent to beautiful physical objects. Physical beauty arises from the harmonious effect of manifold parts that can be taken in at one view. It demands also that these parts shall subsist side by side; and as things whose parts subsist side by side are the proper subject of painting, so it, and it alone, can imitate physical beauty. The poet, who can only show the elements of beauty one after another, in succession, does on that very account forbear altogether the description of physical beauty, as beauty. He recognizes that those elements, arranged in succession, cannot possibly have the effect which they have when placed side by side; that the concentrating gaze which we would direct upon them immediately after their enumeration still affords us no harmonious picture; that it passes the human imagination to represent to itself what kind of effect this mouth, and this nose, and these eyes together have if one cannot recall from Nature or art a similar composition of such features.

Here, too, Homer is the pattern of all patterns. He says: 'Nireus was beautiful; Achilles was more beautiful still; Helen possessed a divine

---

[157] Lessing bases this conclusion on Vitruvius (first century BC), *De architectura*, preface to Book VII.
[158] Lessing's footnote to this sentence reads 'Written in the year 1763'. His *Laocoön* was not published until 1766, by which time Winckelmann's *History of the Art of Antiquity* (1764) had already appeared.

beauty.' But nowhere does he enter upon the more circumstantial delineation of those beauties. For all that, the poem is based on the beauty of
Helen. How greatly would a modern poet have luxuriated in the theme!

True, a certain Constantinus Manasses tried to adorn his bald chronicle
with a picture of Helen.[159] I must thank him for the attempt. For really I
should hardly know where else I could get hold of an example from which
it might more obviously appear how foolish it is to venture something
which Homer has so wisely forborne. When I read in him, for example:

Ἦν ἡ γυνὴ περικαλλής, εὔοφρυς, εὐχρουστάτη,
Εὐπάρειος, εὐπρόσωπος, βοῶπις, χιονόχρους,
Ἑλικοβλέφαρος, ἁβρά, χαρίτων γέμον ἄλσος,
Λευκοβραχίων, τρυφερά, κάλλος ἄντικρυς ἔμπνουν,
Τὸ πρόσωπον κατάλευκον, ἡ παρειὰ ῥοδόχρους,
Τὸ πρόσωπον ἐπίχαρι, τὸ βλέφαρον ὡραῖον,
Κάλλος ἀνεπιτήδευτον, ἀβάπτιστον, αὐτόχρουν,
Ἔβαπτε τὴν λευκότητα ῥοδόχροια πυρίνη,
Ὡς εἴ τις τὸν ἐλέφαντα βάψει λαμπρᾷ πορφύρᾳ.
Δειρὴ μακρά, κατάλευκος, ὅθεν ἐμυθουργήθη
Κυκνογενῆ τὴν εὔοπτον Ἑλένην χρηματίζειν[160]

then I imagine I see stones rolling up a mountain, from which at the top
a splendid picture is to be constructed, the stones, however, all rolling
down of themselves on the other side. What kind of picture does it leave
behind – this torrent of words? What was Helen like, then? Will not, if a
thousand men read this, every man of the thousand make for himself his
own conception of her?

Still, it is certain the political verses[161] of a monk are not poetry. Let us
therefore hear Ariosto, when he describes his enchanting Alcina:[162]

---

[159] Constantinus Manasses (twelfth century), Byzantine monk, author of a verse chronicle of the
world up to 1080 AD; Lessing quotes it from the collection *Corpus Byzantinae historiae* (Venice,
1729), p. 20.

[160] 'She was a beautiful woman, with a fair brow, fine complexion and cheeks, a lovely face, large eyes,
pale skin, curling eyelashes, her breast a seat of the graces, with white arms, in the full radiance
of beauty, her countenance very pale, her cheeks rosy, her expression delightful, her eyes bright,
with youthful charm; without artifice, in the adornment of her natural beauty, white and delicate
but tinged with a rosy glow, like ivory dyed in radiant purple; with a long, white, shining neck,
recalling the legend that the lovely Helen was born of the race of swans.'

[161] *Stichos politikos*, an epic verse-form used in medieval Greek.

[162] Ludovico Ariosto (1474–1533), *Orlando furioso*, Canto VII, verses 11–15: 'She was so beautifully
modelled, no painter, however much he applied himself, could have achieved anything more
perfect. Her long blonde tresses were gathered in a knot: pure gold itself could have no finer

Di persona era tanto ben formata,
Quanto mai finger san pittori industri:
Con bionda chioma, lunga e annodata,
Oro non è, che piu risplenda, e lustri,
Spargeasi per la guancia delicata
Misto colour di rose e di ligustri
Di terso avorio era la fronte lieta,
Che lo spazio finia con giusta meta.

Sotto due negri, e sottilissimi archi
Son due negri occhi, anzi due chiari soli,
Pietosi à riguardar, à mover parchi,
Intorno à cui par ch' Amor scherzi, e voli,
E ch' indi tutta la faretra scarchi,
E che visibilmente i cori involi.
Quindi il naso per mezo il viso scende
Che non trova l'invidia ove l'emende.

Sotto quel sta, quasi fra due valette,
La bocca sparsa di natio cinabro,
Quivi due filze son di perle elette,
Che chiude, ed apre un bello e dolce labro;
Quindi escon le cortesi parolette,
Da render molle ogni cor rozo e scabro;
Quivi si forma quel soave riso
Ch' apre a sua posta in terra il paradiso.

---

lustre. Roses and white privet blooms lent their colours to suffuse her delicate cheeks. Her serene brow was like polished ivory, and in perfect proportion. Beneath two of the thinnest black arches, two dark eyes – or rather, two bright suns; soft was their look, gentle their movement. Love seemed to flit, frolicsome, about them; indeed, Love from this vantage point would let fly his full quiver and openly steal away all hearts. Down the midst of the face, the nose – Envy herself could find no way of bettering it. Below this, the mouth, set between two dimples; it was imbued with native cinnabar. Here a beautiful soft pair of lips opened to disclose a double row of choicest pearls. Here was the course of those winning words which could not but soften every heart, however rugged and uncouth. Here was formed the melodious laughter which made a paradise on earth. Snow-white was her neck, milky her breast; the neck was round, the breast broad and full. A pair of apples, not yet ripe, fashioned in ivory, rose and fell like the sea-swell at times when a gentle breeze stirs the ocean. Argus himself could not see them entire, but you could easily judge that what lay hidden did not fall short of what was exposed to view. Her arms were justly proportioned, and her lily-white hands were often to be glimpsed: they were slender and tapering, and quite without a knot or swelling vein. A pair of small, neat, rounded feet completes the picture of this august person. Her looks were angelic, heaven-sent – no veil could have concealed them' (*Orlando furioso*, translated by Guido Waldman (Oxford, 1974), pp. 61–2).

Bianca neve è il bel collo, e'l petto latte,
Il collo è tondo, il petto colmo e largo;
Due pome acerbe, e pur d'avorio fatte,
Vengono e van, come onda al primo margo,
Quando piacevole aura il mar combatte.
Non potria l'altre parti veder Argo,
Ben si può guidicar, che corrisponde,
A quel ch' appar di fuor, quel che s'asconde.

Mostran le braccia sua misura giusta,
Et la candida man spesso si vede,
Lunghetta alquanto, e di larghezza angusta,
Dove nè nodo appar, nè vena eccede.
Si vede al fin de la persona augusta
Il breve, asciutto e ritondetto piede.
Gli angelici sembianti nati in cielo
Non si ponno celar sotto alcun velo.

Milton says of the building of Pandemonium: 'the work some praise, and some the architect'.[163] The praise of the one, then, is not always the praise of the other. A work of art may deserve all applause while nothing very special redounds from it to the credit of the artist. On the other hand, an artist may justly claim our admiration even when his work does not completely satisfy us. If we do not forget this, quite contradictory verdicts may often be reconciled. The present case is an instance. Dolce in his dialogue on Painting[164] puts in Aretino's mouth an extravagant eulogy of Ariosto on the strength of these stanzas just cited; and I, on the contrary, choose them as an example of a picture that is no picture. We are both right. Dolce admires in it the knowledge which the poet displays of physical beauty; but I look merely to the effect which this knowledge, expressed in words, produces on my imagination. Dolce argues, from that knowledge, that good poets are also good painters; and I, from the effect, that what painters can by line and colour best express can only be badly expressed by words. Dolce commends Ariosto's delineation to all painters as the most perfect model of a beautiful woman; and I commend it to all poets as the most instructive warning against attempting even

---

[163] Milton, *Paradise Lost*, I, 731 f.
[164] Lodovico Dolce (1508–66), *Dialogo della Pittura, intitolato L'Aretino* (Florence, 1735), p. 178.

more unfortunately what failed in the hands of an Ariosto. It may be that, when Ariosto says:

> Di persona era tanto ben formata,
> Quanto mai finger san pittori industri –[165]

he proves thereby that he perfectly understood the theory of proportions as only the most diligent artist can gather it from Nature and from antiquity. He may, who knows? in the mere words:

> Spargeasi per la guancia delicata
> Misto colour di rose e di ligustri –[166]

show himself the most perfect of colourists, a very Titian. One might also, from the fact that he only compares Alcina's hair with gold but does not call it golden hair, argue as cogently that he disapproves the use of actual gold in laying on the colour. One may even find in his 'descending nose':

> Quindi il naso per mezzo il viso scende –[167]

the profile of those ancient Greek noses, copied also by Roman artists from the Greeks. What good is all this erudition and insight to us his readers who want to have the picture of a beautiful woman, who want to feel something of the soft excitement of the blood which accompanies the actual sight of beauty? If the poet is aware what conditions constitute a beautiful form, do we too, therefore, share his knowledge? And if we did also know it, does he here make us aware of those conditions? Or does he in the least lighten for us the difficulty of recalling them in a vividly perceptible manner? A brow in its most graceful lines and limits:

> ... la fronte
> Che lo spazio finia con giusta meta;[168]

a rose in which envy itself can find nothing to improve:

> Che non trova l'invidia ove l'emende;[169]

a hand somewhat long and rather slender:

---

[165] 'She was so beautifully modelled, no painter, however much he applied himself, could have achieved anything more perfect.'
[166] 'Roses and white privet blooms lent their colours to suffuse her delicate cheeks.'
[167] 'Down the midst of the face, the nose –'. [168] 'Her brow was in perfect proportion.'
[169] 'Envy herself could find no way of bettering it.'

Lunghetta alquanto, e di larghezza angusta:[170]

what kind of picture do we gather from these general formulas? In the mouth of a drawing-master who is calling his pupils' attention to the beauties of the school model they might perhaps be useful; for by a glance at the model they perceive the pleasing lines of the delightful brow, the exquisite modelling of the nose, the slenderness of the dainty hand. But in the poet I see nothing, and feel with vexation how vain is my best effort to see what he is describing.

In this particular, where Virgil can best imitate Homer by forbearing action altogether, Virgil, too, has been rather happy. His Dido also is to him nothing further than *pulcherrima Dido*.[171] If indeed he describes anything of her more circumstantially, it is her rich jewellery, her splendid attire:

Tandem progreditur ...
Sidoniam picto chlamydem circumdata limbo:
Cui pharetra ex auro, crines nodantur in aurum,
Aurea purpuream subnectit fibula vestem.[172]

If we on that account would apply to him what the ancient artist said to a pupil who had painted a Helen in elaborate finery – 'As you are not able to paint her beautiful, you have painted her rich' – then Virgil would answer, 'It is no fault of mine that I cannot paint her beautiful; the blame rests on the limits of my art; be mine the praise, to have remained within those limits.'

I must not forget here the two songs of Anacreon in which he analyses for us the beauty of his beloved and of his Bathyllus.[173] The turn he gives it there makes everything right. He imagines a painter before him, and sets him to work under his eye. So, he says, fashion me the hair, so the brow, so the eyes, so the mouth, so neck and bosom, so the hips and hands! Of what the artist can put together only part by part the poet can only set a copy in the same way. His purpose is not that we shall recognize and feel in this verbal instruction of the painter the whole beauty of the beloved subject; he himself feels the insufficiency of the verbal expression, and

---

[170] 'They were slender and tapering.'   [171] 'most beautiful Dido'.

[172] *Aeneid*, IV, 136–9: 'At last she steps forth ... dressed in a Sidonian mantle with embroidered hem. Her quiver is of gold, her hair is held in a gold clasp, and a golden brooch fastens her purple tunic.'

[173] Anacreon (fifth and sixth centuries BC), Greek lyric poet; Lessing refers to his *Odes*, 15 [28] and 16 [29].

for this very reason calls to his aid the expressive power of art, the illusion of which he so greatly heightens that the whole song appears to be more a hymn to Art than to his beloved. He does not see the image, he sees herself and believes that she is just about to open her lips in speech:

'Απέχει· βλέπω γὰρ αὐτήν,
Τάχα, κηρέ, καὶ λαλήσεις.[74]

In the sketch, too, of Bathyllus the praise of the beautiful boy is so inwoven with praise of art and the artist that it is doubtful for whose honour Anacreon really intended the poem. He collects the most beautiful parts from various paintings in which the particular beauty of these parts was its characteristic feature; the neck he takes from an Adonis, breast and hands from a Mercury, the hips from a Pollux, the abdomen from a Bacchus; till he sees the whole Bathyllus in a perfect Apollo:

Μετὰ δὲ πρόσωπον ἔστω,
Τὸν 'Αδώνιδος παρελθών,
'Ελεφάντινος τράχηλος·
Μεταμάζιον δὲ ποίει
Διδύμας τε χεῖρας 'Ερμοῦ,
Πολυδεύκεος δὲ μηρούς,
Διονυσίην δὲ νηδὺν...
Τὸν 'Απόλλωνα δὲ τοῦτον
Καθελὼν ποίει Βάθυλλον.[75]

Similarly also Lucian does not know how to give us a conception of the beauty of Panthea except by reference to the finest female statues of ancient artists.[76] And what is this but to confess that language by itself is here powerless, that poetry stammers and eloquence is dumb where Art does not in some measure serve them as interpreter?

XXI

But does not Poetry lose too much if we take from her all pictures of physical beauty? Who wishes to do so? If we seek to close to her one

---

[74] Anacreon, *Odes*, 15 [28], lines 33–4: 'Enough! I see her as real. Her image is about to address me.'
[75] Anacreon, *Odes*, 16 [29], lines 27–33 and 43–4: 'Paint beneath his face an ivory neck surpassing that of Adonis. Model his breast and hands on those of Mercury, his hips on Pollux, his abdomen on Bacchus... Transform Apollo to create Bathyllus!'
[76] Lucian (second century AD) wrote the dialogue Εἰκόνες in praise of Panthea, mistress of the Emperor Lucius Aurelius Verus; Lessing's reference is to Section 3, Part II, of this dialogue.

single road, on which she hopes to achieve such pictures by following in the footsteps of a sister art, where she stumbles painfully without ever attaining the same goal, do we, then, at the same time close to her every other road, where Art in her turn can but follow at a distance?

Even Homer, who with evident intention refrains from all piecemeal delineation of physical beauties, from whom we can scarcely once learn in passing that Helen had white arms and beautiful hair – even he knows how, nevertheless, to give us such a conception of her beauty as far outpasses all that Art in this respect can offer. Let us recall the passage where Helen steps into the assembly of the Elders of the Trojan people. The venerable old men looked on her, and one said to the other:

Οὐ νέμεσις Τρῶας καὶ ἐϋκνήμιδας Ἀχαιοὺς
Τοιῆδ᾽ ἀμφὶ γυναικὶ πολὺν χρόνον ἄλγεα πάσχειν·
Αἰνῶς ἀθανάτῃσι θεῆς εἰς ὦπα ἔοικεν.[177]

What can convey a more vivid idea of Beauty than to have frigid age confessing her well worth the war that has cost so much blood and so many tears? What Homer could not describe in its component parts, he makes us feel in its working. Paint us, then, poet, the satisfaction, the affection, the love, the delight, which beauty produces, and you have painted beauty itself. Who can imagine as ill-favoured the beloved object of Sappho,[178] the very sight of whom she confesses robbed her of her senses and her reason? Who does not fancy he beholds with his own eyes the fairest, most perfect form, as soon as he sympathizes with the feeling which nothing but such a form can awaken? Not because Ovid shows us the beautiful body of his Lesbia part by part:

Quos humeros, quales vidi tetigique lacertos!
   Forma papillarum quam fuit apta premi!
Quam castigato planus sub pectore venter!
   Quantum et quale latus! quam juvenile femur! –[179]

---

[177] *Iliad*, III, 156–8: 'Small blame that Trojans and well-greaved Achaeans should for such a woman suffer woes for so long; for she is indeed like an immortal goddess to look upon.'

[178] Sappho (*c.* 600 BC), poetess of Lesbos.

[179] Ovid, *Amores*, I, 5, lines 19–22:
   What arms and shoulders did I touch and see,
   How apt her breasts were to be press'd by me!
   How smooth a belly under her waist saw I!
   How large a leg, and what a lusty thigh!
(Translation by Christopher Marlowe.) The name of Ovid's mistress was in fact Corinna; Lesbia was the mistress of Catullus.

but because he does so with the voluptuous intoxication in which it is so easy to awaken our longing, we imagine ourselves enjoying the same sight of exquisite beauty which he enjoyed.

Another way in which poetry in its turn overtakes art in delineation of physical beauty is by transmuting beauty into grace. Grace is beauty in motion, and just for that reason less suitable to the painter than to the poet. The painter can only help us to guess the motion, but in fact his figures are motionless. Consequently grace with him is turned into grimace. But in poetry it remains what it is – a transitory beauty which we want to see again and again. It comes and goes; and as we can generally recall a movement more easily and more vividly than mere forms and colours, grace can in such a case work more powerfully on us than beauty. All that still pleases and touches us in the picture of Alcina is grace. The impression her eyes make does not come from the fact that they are dark and passionate, but rather that they:

> Pietosi à riguardar, à mover parchi –

'look round her graciously and slowly turn'; that Love flutters about them and from them empties all his quiver. Her mouth delights us, not because lips tinted with cinnabar enclose two rows of choicest pearls; but because there the lovely smile is shaped which in itself seems to open up an earthly paradise; because from it the friendly words come forth that soften the most savage breast. Her bosom enchants us, less because milk and ivory and apples typify its whiteness and delicate forms than because we see it softly rise and fall, like the waves at the margin of the shore when a playful zephyr contends with the ocean:

> Due pome acerbi, e pur d'avorio fatte,
> Vengono e van, come onda al primo margo,
> Quando piacevole aura il mar combatte.[180]

I am sure such features of grace by themselves, condensed into one or two stanzas, will do more than all the five into which Ariosto has spun them out, inweaving them with frigid details of the fair form, far too erudite for our appreciation.

---

[180] Ariosto, *Orlando furioso* (see note 162 above): 'A pair of apples, not yet ripe, fashioned in ivory, rose and fell like the sea-swell at times when a gentle breeze stirs the ocean.'

Even Anacreon himself would rather fall into the apparent impropriety of demanding impossibilities from the painter than leave the picture of his beloved untouched with grace:

Τρυφεροῦ δ' ἔσω γενείου,
Περὶ λυγδίνῳ τραχήλῳ
Χάριτες πέτοιντο πᾶσαι.[181]

Her chin of softness, her neck of marble – let all the Graces hover round them, he bids the artist. And how? In the exact and literal sense? That is not capable of any pictorial realization. The painter could give the chin the most exquisite curve, the prettiest dimple, *Amoris digitulo impressum*[182] (for the ἔσω appears to me to signify a dimple); he could give the neck the most beautiful carnation; but he can do no more. The turning of this fair neck, the play of the muscles, by which that dimple is now more visible, now less, the peculiar grace, all are beyond his powers. The poet said the utmost by which his art could make beauty real to us, so that the painter also might strive for the utmost expression in his art. A fresh example of the principle already affirmed – that the poet even when he speaks of works of art is not bound in his descriptions to confine himself within the limits of art.

XXII

Zeuxis[183] painted a Helen and had the courage to set under it those famous lines of Homer in which the enchanted Elders confess their emotions. Never were painting and poetry drawn into a more equal contest. The victory remained undecided, and both deserved to be crowned. For, just as the wise poet showed beauty merely in its effect, which he felt he could not delineate in its component parts, so did the no less wise painter show us beauty by nothing else than its component parts and hold it unbecoming to his art to resort to any other method. His picture consisted in the single figure of Helen, standing in naked beauty. For it is probable that it was the very Helen which he painted for the people of Crotona.[184]

---

[181] 'In the dimple of her soft chin and round her marble neck let all the Graces play.'
[182] 'impressed by Amor's finger'.
[183] Zeuxis (fifth century BC), Greek painter of Heraclea.
[184] Town in southern Italy; the painting was for the temple of Hera there.

Let us compare with this, for wonder's sake, the painting which Caylus sketches from Homer's lines for the benefit of a modern artist:

> Helen, covered with a white veil, appears in the midst of an assemblage of old men, in whose ranks Priam also is to be found, recognizable by the signs of his royal dignity. It must be the artist's business to make evident to us the triumph of beauty in the eager gaze and in the expression of amazed admiration on the faces of the sober greybeards. The scene is by one of the gates of the city. The background of the painting thus can lose itself in the open sky or against the city's lofty walls; the former were the bolder conception, but one is as fitting as the other.

Let us imagine this picture carried out by the greatest master of our time and place it against the work of Zeuxis. Which will show the real triumph of beauty? That in which I myself feel it, or this where I must argue it from the grimaces of the susceptible greybeards? *Turpe senilis amor*;[185] a lustful look makes the most venerable countenance ridiculous; an old man who betrays youthful passions is really a loathsome object. This objection cannot be made to the Homeric elders; for the emotion they feel is a momentary spark which their wisdom extinguishes immediately; intended only to do honour to Helen, but not to disgrace themselves. They confess their feeling and forthwith add:

> Ἀλλὰ καὶ ὧς, τοίη περ ἐοῦσ᾽, ἐν νηυσὶ νεέσθω,
> Μηδ᾽ ἡμῖν τεκέεσσί τ᾽ ὀπίσσω πῆμα λίποιτο.[186]

Without this resolution they would be old coxcombs, which, indeed, they appear in the picture of Caylus. And on what, then, do they direct their greedy glances? On a masked and veiled figure! That is Helen, is it? Inconceivable to me how Caylus here can leave the veil. Homer, indeed, gives it her expressly:

> Αὐτίκα δ᾽ ἀργεννῇσι καλυψαμένη ὀθόνῃσιν
> Ὡρμᾶτ᾽ ἐκ θαλάμοιο . . . [187]

---

[185] 'Base is the lust of old men' (Ovid, *Amores*, i, 9, line 4).
[186] *Iliad*, iii, 159 f.: 'But even so, despite her attractiveness, let her depart upon the ships, and not be left here to be a bane to us and to our children after us.'
[187] *Iliad*, iii, 141 f.: 'and straightway she veiled herself with shining linen, and went forth from her chamber'.

but it is to cross the streets in it; and if indeed with Homer the elders already betray their admiration before she appears to have again taken off or thrown back the veil, it was not then the first time the old men saw her; their confession therefore might not arise from the present momentary view: they may have already often felt what on this occasion they first confessed themselves to feel. In the painting nothing like this occurs. If I see here enchanted old men, I wish at the same time to see what it is that charms them; and I am surprised in the extreme when I perceive nothing further than, as we have said, a masked and veiled figure on which they are passionately gazing. What is here of Helen? Her white veil and something of her well-proportioned outline so far as outline can become visible beneath raiment. Yet perhaps it was not the Count's intention that her face should be covered, and he names the veil merely as a part of her attire. If this is so – his words, indeed, are hardly capable of such an interpretation: '*Hélène couverte d'un voile blanc*'[188] – then another surprise awaits me; he is so particular in commending to the artist the expression on the faces of the elders, but on the beauty of Helen's face he does not expend a syllable. This modest beauty, in her eyes the dewy shimmer of a remorseful tear, approaching timidly! What! Is supreme beauty something so familiar to our artists that they do not need to be reminded of it? Or is expression more than beauty? And are we in pictures, too, accustomed, as on the stage, to let the ugliest actress pass for a charming princess, if only her prince declares warmly enough the love he bears her?

In truth, Caylus' picture would bear the same relation to that of Zeuxis as burlesque does to the loftiest poetry.

Homer was, without doubt, read in former times more diligently than today. Yet one finds ever so many pictures unmentioned which the ancient artists would have drawn from his pages. Only of the poet's hint at particular physical beauties they do appear to have made diligent use; these they did paint, and in such subjects alone, they understood well enough, it was granted them to compete with the poet. Besides Helen, Zeuxis also painted Penelope, and the Diana of Apelles was the Homeric Diana in company of her nymphs. I may here call to mind that the passage of Pliny in which the latter is mentioned requires an emendation.[189] But to paint actions from Homer simply because they offer a rich composition,

---

[188] 'Helen, covered in a white veil'.
[189] Lessing's reference is to Pliny, *Natural History*, xxxv, section 36, p. 698, and he quotes the passage: 'Fecit et Dianam sacrificantium virginum choro mixtam: quibus vicisse Homeri versus videtur

excellent contrasts, artistic lights, seemed to the ancient artists not to be their *métier*, nor could it be so long as art remained within the narrower limits of her own high vocation. Instead, they nourished themselves on the spirit of the poet; they filled their imagination with his most exalted characteristics; the fire of his enthusiasm kindled their own; they saw and felt like him; and so their works became copies of the Homeric, not in the relation of a portrait to its original, but in that of a son to his father – like, yet different. The resemblance often lies only in a single feature, the rest having amongst them all nothing alike except that they harmonize with the resembling feature in the one case as well as in the other.

As, moreover, the Homeric masterpieces in poetry were older than any masterpiece of art, as Homer had observed Nature with a painter's eye earlier than a Phidias[190] or an Apelles, it is not to be wondered at that various observations of particular use to them the artists found already made in Homer before they themselves had had the opportunity of making them in Nature. These they eagerly seized on, in order to imitate Nature through Homer. Phidias confessed that the lines:

Ἦ, καὶ κυανέῃσιν ἐπ' ὀφρύσι νεῦσε Κρονίων·
Ἀμβρόσιαι δ' ἄρα χαῖται ἐπερρώσαντο ἄνακτος
Κρατὸς ἀπ' ἀθανάτοιο· μέγαν δ' ἐλέλιξεν Ὄλυμπον[191]

served him as a model in his Olympian Jupiter, and that only by their aid did he achieve a divine countenance, *propemodum ex ipso caelo petitum.*[192] Whosoever considers this to mean nothing more than that the fancy of the artist was fired by the poet's exalted picture, and thereby became capable of representations just as exalted – he, it seems to me, overlooks the most essential point, and contents himself with something quite general where, for a far more complete satisfaction, something very special is demanded. In my view Phidias confesses here also that in this passage he first noticed

---

id ipsum describentis.' ('He also painted a Diana in a group of sacrificing virgins; he seems thereby to have surpassed the verses in which Homer describes the same scene.') Lessing finds the reading *sacrificantium* ('sacrificing') implausible, and suggests *venantium* ('hunting') or *sylvis vagantium* ('wandering in the woods') instead. He goes on to criticize Spence (see note 66 above) for accepting the reading *sacrificantium* at face value.

[190] Phidias (fifth century BC), the greatest of the Greek sculptors.

[191] *Iliad*, I, 528–30: 'The son of Cronos spake, and bowed his dark brow in assent, and the ambrosial locks waved from the king's immortal head; and he made great Olympus to quake.'

[192] 'almost as if fetched from heaven itself'.

how much expression lies in the eyebrows, *quanta pars animi*[193] is shown in them. Perhaps also it induced him to devote more attention to the hair, in order to express in some measure what Homer means by 'ambrosial' locks. For it is certain that the ancient artists before the days of Phidias little understood what was significant and speaking in the countenance, and almost invariably neglected the hair. Even Myron was faulty in both these particulars, as Pliny has remarked, and after him Pythagoras Leontinus was the first who distinguished himself by the elegance of coiffure.[194] What Phidias learned from Homer, other artists learned from the works of Phidias.

Another example of this kind I may specify which has always very much pleased me. Let us recall what Hogarth has noted concerning the Apollo Belvedere. 'This Apollo', he says,

> and the Antinous are both to be seen in the same palace at Rome. If, however, the Antinous fills the spectator with admiration, the Apollo amazes him, and, indeed, as travellers have remarked, by an aspect above humanity which usually they are not capable of describing. And this effect, they say, is all the more wonderful because when one examines it, the disproportionate in it is obvious even to a common eye. One of the best sculptors we have in England, who recently went there on purpose to see this statue, corroborated what has just been said, and in particular that the feet and legs in relation to the upper part are too long and too broad. And Andrea Sacchi, one of the greatest Italian painters, seems to have been of the same opinion, otherwise he would hardly (in a famous picture now in England) have given to his Apollo, crowning the musician Pasquilini, exactly the proportions of Antinous, seeing that in other respects it appears to be actually a copy of the Apollo. Although we frequently see in very great works some small part handled carelessly, this cannot be the case here. For in a beautiful statue correct proportion is one of the most essential beauties. We must conclude, therefore, that these limbs must have been purposely lengthened, otherwise it would have been easy to avoid it. If we therefore examine the beauties of this figure thoroughly, we shall with reason conclude that what we have

[193] 'how large a part of the *soul* '; Lessing's reference is to Pliny, x, section 51, p. 616.
[194] Lessing's reference is to Pliny, xxxiv, section 19, p. 651; Myron (fifth century BC), Greek sculptor, who worked mainly in bronze; Pythagoras Leontinus (fifth century BC), Greek sculptor of Rhegium.

hitherto considered indescribably excellent in its general aspect has proceeded from that which appeared to be a fault in one of its parts.
(Hogarth, *Analysis of Beauty*)[195]

All this is very illuminating, and I will add that in fact Homer has felt it and has pointed out that it gives a stately appearance, arising purely from this addition of size in the measurements of feet and legs. For when Antenor would compare the figure of Ulysses with that of Menelaus, he makes him say:

Στάντων μὲν Μενέλαος ὑπείρεχεν εὐρέας ὤμους,
Ἄμφω δ' ἑζομένω γεραρώτερος ἦεν Ὀδυσσεύς.[196]

('When both stood, then Menelaus stood the higher with his broad shoulders; but when both sat, Ulysses was the statelier.') As Ulysses therefore gained stateliness in sitting, which Menelaus in sitting lost, the proportion is easy to determine which the upper body had in each to feet and legs. Ulysses was the larger in the proportions of the former, Menelaus in the proportions of the latter.

XXIII

A single defective part can destroy the harmonious working of many parts towards beauty. Yet the object does not necessarily therefore become ugly. Even ugliness demands several defective parts which likewise must be seen at one view if we are to feel by it the contrary of that with which beauty inspires us.

Accordingly, ugliness also in its essential nature would not be a reproach to poetry; and yet Homer has depicted the extremest ugliness in Thersites, and depicted it, moreover, in its elements set side by side.[197] Why was that permitted to him with ugliness which in the case of beauty he renounced with so fine a discernment? Is the effect of ugliness not just as much hindered by the successive enumeration of its elements as the effect of beauty is nullified by the like enumeration of its elements? To be sure it is, but herein lies also Homer's justification. Just because ugliness becomes

---

[195] William Hogarth (1697-1764), painter and engraver, author of the *Analysis of Beauty* (1753, German translation, Berlin, 1754); Lessing's reference is to p. 47 of the German translation. The statue of 'Antinous' in the Vatican is now reckoned to be of Hermes.
[196] *Iliad*, III, 210 f.   [197] *Iliad*, II, 216–19.

in the poet's delineation a less repulsive vision of physical imperfection, and so far as effect is concerned ceases as it were to be ugliness, it becomes usable to the poet; and what he cannot use for its own sake, he uses as an ingredient in order to produce or intensify certain mixed states of feeling with which he must entertain us in default of feelings purely pleasurable.

These mixed feelings are awakened by the laughable and the terrible. Homer makes Thersites ugly in order to make him laughable. It is not, however, merely by his ugliness that he becomes so; for ugliness is imperfection and for the laughable a contrast is required of perfection and imperfection. This is the declaration of my friend Mendelssohn,[198] to which I should like to add that this contrast must not be too sharp or too glaring, that the *opposita* (to continue in painter's language) must be of the kind that can melt into each other. The wise and honest Aesop, even if one assigns him the ugliness of Thersites, does not thereby become laughable.[199] It was a ridiculous monastic whim to wish the γέλοιον[200] of his instructive tales transferred to his own person by the help of its deformity. For a misshapen body and a beautiful soul are like oil and vinegar, which, even when they are thoroughly mixed, still remain completely separated to the palate. They afford us no *tertium quid*; the body excites disgust, the soul satisfaction, each its own for itself. Only when the misshapen body is at the same time frail and sickly, when it hinders the soul in her operations, when it becomes the source of hurtful prepossessions against her – then indeed disgust and satisfaction mingle and flow together, but the new apparition arising therefrom is not laughter, but pity, and the object which we otherwise should merely have esteemed becomes interesting. The misshapen and sickly Pope must have been far more interesting to his friends than the sound and handsome Wycherley.[201] – But, however little would Thersites have been made laughable by mere ugliness, just as little would he have become laughable without it. The ugliness; the harmony of this ugliness with his character; the contradiction which both make to the idea he entertains of his own importance; the harmless effect of his malicious chatter, humiliating only to himself – all must work together to this end. The last-named particular is the οὐ φθαρτικόν[202] which Aristotle makes

---

[198] Moses Mendelssohn (1729–86), Jewish philosopher and close friend of Lessing.
[199] Aesop (sixth century BC), author of fables, who was reputedly extremely ugly; 'monastic whim' is an allusion to the commentaries of medieval scholastics.
[200] 'ridiculousness'.
[201] Alexander Pope; William Wycherley (*c.* 1640–1716), English Restoration dramatist.
[202] 'harmlessness'; Aristotle, *Poetics*, chapter 5.

indispensable to the laughable; just as also my friend makes it a necessary condition that such contrast must be of no moment and must interest us but little. For let us only suppose that Thersites' malicious belittling of Agamemnon had come to cost him dear, that instead of a couple of bloody weals he must pay for it with his life – then certainly we should cease to laugh at him. For this monster of a man is yet a man, whose destruction will always seem a greater evil than all his frailties and vices. This we can learn by experience if we read his end in Quintus Calaber.[203] Achilles laments having killed Penthesilea; the beautiful woman in her blood, so bravely poured out, commands the esteem and pity of the hero, and esteem and pity turn to love. But the slanderous Thersites makes that love a crime. He declaims against the lewdness that betrays even the worthiest man to folly:

> ... ἥτ' ἄφρονα φῶτα τίθησι
> Καὶ πινυτόν περ ἐόντα. . . .[204]

Achilles gets into a rage, and without replying a word strikes him so roughly between cheek and ear that teeth and blood and soul together gush from his throat. Horrible unspeakably! The passionate, murderous Achilles becomes more hateful to me than the spiteful, snarling Thersites; the jubilant cry which the Greeks raise over the deed offends me. I take part with Diomedes, who draws his sword forthwith to avenge his kinsman on the murderer: for I feel, too, that Thersites is my kinsman, a human being.

But grant only that Thersites' incitements had broken out in sedition, that the mutinous people had actually taken ship and traitorously forsaken their captains, that the captains had thus fallen into the hands of a revengeful enemy, and that a divine judgement had brought utter destruction to both fleet and people: in such a case how would the ugliness of Thersites appear? If harmless ugliness can be laughable, a mischievous ugliness is always terrible. I do not know how to illustrate this better than by a couple of excellent passages of Shakespeare. Edmund, the bastard son of the Earl of Gloucester in *King Lear*, is no less a villain than Richard, Duke of Gloucester, who paved his way by the most detestable crimes to the throne which he ascended under the name of Richard III. How comes it, then, that the former excites far less shuddering and horror than the latter? When I hear the Bastard say:

---

[203] See note 51 above.   [204] 'which makes even the wisest man foolish' (*Posthomerica*, I, 737).

> Thou, Nature, art my goddess, to thy law
> My services are bound; wherefore should I
> Stand in the plague of custom, and permit
> The curiosity of nations to deprive me,
> For that I am some twelve or fourteen moonshines
> Lag of a brother? Why bastard? Wherefore base?
> When my dimensions are as well compact,
> My mind as generous, and my shape as true
> As honest Madam's issue? Why brand they thus
> With base? with baseness? bastardy? base, base?
> Who in the lusty stealth of Nature take
> More composition and fierce quality
> Than doth, within a dull, stale, tired bed,
> Go to creating a whole tribe of fops
> Got 'tween asleep and wake? —[205]

in this I hear a devil, but I see him in the form of an angel of light. When, on the other hand, I hear the Duke of Gloucester say:

> But I, that am not shaped for sportive tricks
> Nor made to court an amorous looking-glass,
> I, that am rudely stamped and want Love's majesty,
> To strut before a wanton ambling nymph;
> I, that am curtailed of this fair proportion,
> Cheated of feature by dissembling Nature,
> Deformed, unfinished, sent before my time
> Into this breathing world scarce half made up,
> And that so lamely and unfashionably
> That dogs bark at me as I halt by them;
> Why, I (in this weak piping time of peace)
> Have no delight to pass away the time;
> Unless to spy my shadow in the sun
> And descant on mine own deformity.
> And therefore, since I cannot prove a lover
> To entertain these fair, well-spoken days,
> I am determined to prove a villain![206]

then I hear a devil and see a devil in a shape that only the Devil should have.

---

[205] *King Lear*, I, 2.   [206] *Richard III*, I, I.

XXIV

It is thus the poet uses the ugliness of forms; what use of them is permitted to the painter? Painting, as imitative dexterity, can express ugliness; but painting, as beautiful art, will not express it. To her, as the former, all visible objects belong; but, as the latter, she confines herself solely to those visible objects which awaken agreeable sensations.

But do not even the disagreeable sensations please in the imitation of them? Not all. A sagacious critic has already made the remark concerning the sensation of disgust. 'The representations of fear', he says,

> of sadness, of terror, of pity and so on, can only excite discomfort in so far as we take the evil to be actual. These, therefore, can be resolved into pleasant sensations by the recollection that it is but an artistic deceit. The unpleasant sensation of disgust, however, in virtue of the laws of the imagination, ensues on the mere representation in the mind whether the subject be considered as actual or not. Of what use is it, therefore, to the offended soul if Art betrays herself merely as imitation? Her discomfort arose not from the knowledge that the evil was actual but from the mere presentation of the same, and this *is* actual. The sensations of disgust are therefore always nature, never imitation.[207]

The same principle holds good of the ugliness of forms. This ugliness offends our sight, is repugnant to our taste for order and harmony, and awakens aversion without respect to the actual existence of the subject in which we perceive it. We do not want to see Thersites, either in Nature or in picture, and if in fact his picture displeases us less, this happens not for the reason that the ugliness of his form ceases in the imitation to be ugliness, but because we have the power of abstracting our attention from this ugliness and satisfying ourselves merely with the art of the painter. Yet even this satisfaction will every moment be interrupted by the reflection how ill the art has been bestowed, and this reflection will seldom fail to be accompanied by contempt for the artist.

Aristotle suggests another reason why things on which we look in Nature with repugnance do yet afford us pleasure even in the most faithful

---

[207] Lessing again quotes his friend Moses Mendelssohn (see note 198); the source is Letter 82 in the series *Letters concerning Recent Literature* (*Briefe, die neueste Literatur betreffend*, 1759–65), a collaborative and anonymous publication to which Lessing himself contributed.

copy – namely, the universal curiosity of mankind.[208] We are glad if we either can learn from the copy τί ἕκαστον, 'what anything is', or if we can conclude from it ὅτι οὗτος ἐκεῖνος, 'that it is this or that'. But even from this there follows no advantage to ugliness in imitation. The pleasure that arises from the satisfaction of our curiosity is momentary, and merely accidental to the subject from which it arises; the dissatisfaction, on the contrary, that accompanies the sight of ugliness is permanent, and essential to the subject that excites it. How, then, can the former balance the latter? Still less can the momentary agreeable amusement which the showing of a likeness gives us overcome the disagreeable effect of ugliness. The more closely I compare the ugly copy with the ugly original, the more do I expose myself to this effect, so that the pleasure of comparison vanishes very quickly, and there remains to me nothing more than the untoward impression of the twofold ugliness. To judge by the examples given by Aristotle, it appears as if he himself had been unwilling to reckon the ugliness of forms as amongst the unpleasing subjects which might yet please in imitation. These subjects are corpses and ravening beasts. Ravening wild beasts excite terror even though they are not ugly; and this terror, and not their ugliness, it is that is resolved into pleasant sensations by imitation. So, too, with corpses: the keener feeling of pity, the terrible reminder of our own annihilation makes a corpse in Nature a repulsive subject to us; in the imitation, however, that pity loses its sharper edge by the conviction of the illusion, and from the fatal reminder an alloy of flattering circumstances can either entirely divert us, or unite so inseparably with it that we seem to find in it more of the desirable than the terrible.

As, therefore, the ugliness of forms cannot by and for itself be a theme of painting as fine art, because the feeling which it excites, while unpleasing, is not of that sort of unpleasing sensations which may be transformed into pleasing ones by imitation; yet the question might still be asked whether it could not to painting as well as to poetry be useful as an ingredient, for the intensifying of other sensations. May painting, then, avail itself of ugly forms to evoke the laughable and the terrible?

I will not venture to give this question a point-blank negative. It is undeniable that harmless ugliness can even in painting be made laughable, especially when there is combined with it an affectation of charm and dignity. It is just as incontestable that mischievous ugliness does in

---

[208] Aristotle, *Poetics*, chapter 4.

painting, just as in Nature, excite horror, and that this laughable and this horrible element, which in themselves are mingled feelings, attain by imitation a new degree of attractiveness and pleasure.

I must at the same time point out that, nevertheless, painting is not here completely in the same case with poetry. In poetry, as I have already remarked, the ugliness of forms does by the transmutation of their coexisting parts into successive parts lose its unpleasant effect almost entirely; from this point of view it ceases, as it were, to be ugliness, and can therefore ally itself more intimately with other appearances in order to produce a new and distinct effect. In painting, on the contrary, the ugliness has all its forces at hand, and works almost as strongly as in Nature itself. Consequently, harmless ugliness cannot well remain laughable for long; the unpleasant sensation gains the upper hand, and what was farcical to begin with becomes later merely disgusting. Nor is it otherwise with mischievous ugliness; the terrible is gradually lost and the monstrous remains alone and unchangeable.

Keeping this in view, Count Caylus was perfectly right to leave the episode of Thersites out of the list of his Homeric pictures. But are we therefore right, too, in wishing them cut out of Homer's own work? I am sorry to find that a scholar of otherwise just and fine taste is of this opinion.[209] A fuller exposition of my own views on the matter I postpone to another opportunity.

XXV

The second distinction also, which the critic just quoted[210] draws between disgust and other unpleasant emotions of the soul, is concerned with the aversion awakened within us by the ugliness of physical forms.

'Other unpleasant emotions', he says,

> can often, not just in imitation but also in Nature itself, gratify the mind, inasmuch as they never excite unmixed aversion, but in every case mingle their bitterness with pleasure. Our fear is seldom denuded of all hope; terror animates all our powers to evade the danger; anger is bound up with the desire to avenge ourselves, as

---

[209] Christian Adolf Klotz (1738–71), philologist and Professor of Rhetoric at Halle, with whom Lessing, a few years later, had an acrimonious controversy which destroyed Klotz's reputation as a scholar. Lessing refers to Klotz's *Epistolae Homericae* (1764), pp. 33 ff.

[210] That is, Moses Mendelssohn (see note 207 above).

sadness is with the agreeable representation of the happiness that preceded it, whilst pity is inseparable from the tender feelings of love and affection. The soul is permitted to dwell now on the pleasurable, and now on the afflicting, parts of an emotion, and to make for itself a mixture of pleasure and its opposite which is more attractive than pleasure without admixture. Only a very little attention to what goes on within is needed to observe frequent instances of the kind; what else would account for the fact that to the angry man his anger, to the melancholy man his dejection, is dearer than any pleasing representations by which it is sought to quiet or cheer him? Quite otherwise is it in the case of disgust and the feelings associated with it. In that the soul recognizes no noticeable admixture of pleasure. Distaste gains the upper hand, and there is therefore no situation that we can imagine either in Nature or in imitation in which the mind would not recoil with repugnance from such representations.

Perfectly true! but as the critic himself recognizes yet other sensations akin to disgust which likewise produce nothing but aversion, what can be nearer akin to it than the feeling of the ugly in physical forms? This sensation also is, in Nature, without the slightest admixture of delight, and as it is just as little capable of it in imitation, so there is no situation in the latter in which the mind would not recoil with repugnance from the representation of it.

Indeed, this repugnance, if I have studied my feelings with sufficient care, is wholly of the nature of disgust. The sensation which accompanies ugliness of form is disgust, only somewhat fainter in degree. This conflicts, indeed, with another note of the critic, according to which he thinks that only the *blind* senses – taste, smell, and touch – are sensitive to disgust. 'The two former', he says, 'by an excessive sweetness and the third by an excessive softness of bodies that do not sufficiently resist the fibres that touch them. Such objects then become unendurable even to sight, but merely through the association of ideas that recall to us the repugnance to which they give rise in the taste, or smell, or touch. For, properly speaking, there are no objects of disgust for the vision.' Yet, in my opinion, things of the kind can be named. A scar in the face, a hare-lip, a flattened nose with prominent nostrils, an entire absence of eyebrows, are uglinesses which are not offensive either to smell, taste, or touch. At the same time it is certain that these things produce a sensation that certainly comes much nearer to disgust than what we feel at the sight of other deformities of body – a crooked foot, or a high shoulder; the more delicate our temperament, the more do they cause us those inward sensations that precede sickness. Only, these sensations very soon disappear, and actual sickness can scarcely result; the reason of which is certainly to be found in this fact, that they are objects of sight, which simultaneously perceives in them and with them a multitude of circumstances through the pleasant presentation of which those unpleasing things are so tempered and obscured that they can have no noticeable effect on the body. The blind senses, on the other hand – taste, smell, and touch – cannot, when they are affected by something unpleasant, likewise take cognisance of such other circumstances; the disagreeable, consequently, works by itself and in its whole energy, and cannot but be accompanied in the body by a far more violent shock.

Moreover, the disgusting is related to imitation in precisely the same way as the ugly. Indeed, as its unpleasant effect is more violent, it can even less than the ugly be made in and for itself a subject either of poetry or painting. Only because it also is greatly modified by verbal expression, I venture still to contend that the poet might be able to use at least some features of disgust as an ingredient for the mingled sensations of which we have spoken, which he intensifies so successfully by what is ugly.

The disgusting can add to the laughable; or representations of dignity and decorum, set in contrast with the disgusting, become laughable. Instances of this kind abound in Aristophanes. The weasel[211] occurs to me which interrupted the good Socrates in his astronomical observations:

> ΜΑΘ. Πρώην δέ γε γνώμην μεγάλην ἀφηρέθη
>   Ὑπ' ἀσκαλαβώτου. ΣΤ. Τίνα τρόπον; κάτειπέ μοι.
> ΜΑΘ. Ζητοῦντος αὐτοῦ τῆς σελήνης τὰς ὁδοὺς
>   Καὶ τὰς περιφοράς, εἶτ' ἄνω κεχηνότος
>   Ἀπὸ τῆς ὀροφῆς νύκτωρ γαλεώτης κατέχεσεν.
> ΣΤ. Ἥσθην γαλεώτῃ καταχέσαντι Σωκράτους.[212]

---

[211] In fact, a lizard.
[212] Aristophanes (*c.* 444–380 BC), comic dramatist; the quotation is from his *Clouds*, lines 169–74:

Student	And yet last night a mighty thought we lost
	Through a green lizard.
Strepsiades	Tell me, how was that?
Student	Why, as I himself, with eyes and mouth wide open,
	Mused on the moon, her paths and revolutions,
	A lizard from the roof squirted full on him.
Strepsiades	He, he, he, he. I like the lizard's spattering Socrates.

Suppose that not to be disgusting which falls into his open mouth, and the laughable vanishes. The drollest strokes of this kind occur in the Hottentot tale, Tquassouw and Knonmquaiha in the *Connoisseur*, an English weekly magazine full of humour, ascribed to Lord Chesterfield.[213] Everyone knows how filthy the Hottentots are and how many things they consider beautiful and elegant and sacred which with us awaken disgust and aversion. A flattened cartilage of a nose, flabby breasts hanging down to the navel, the whole body smeared with a cosmetic of goat's fat and soot gone rotten in the sun, the hair dripping with grease, arms and legs bound about with fresh entrails – let one think of this as the object of an ardent, reverent, tender love; let one hear this uttered in the exalted language of gravity and admiration and refrain from laughter!

With the terrible it seems possible for the disgusting to be still more intimately mingled. What we call the horrible is nothing but the disgusting and terrible in one. Longinus,[214] it is true, is displeased with the τῆς ἐκ μὲν ῥινῶν μύξαι ῥέον in Hesiod's description of melancholy;[215] but, in my opinion, not so much because it is a disgusting trait as because it is merely a disgusting trait contributing nothing to the terrible. For the long nails extending beyond the fingers (μακροὶ δ' ὄνυχες χείρεσσιν ὑπῆσαν) he does not appear to find fault with. Yet long nails are not less disgusting than a running nose. But the long nails are at the same time terrible, for it is they that lacerate the cheeks until the blood runs down upon the ground:

> ... Ἐκ δὲ παρειῶν
> Αἷμ' ἀπελείβετ' ἔραζε ... [216]

A running nose, on the contrary, is nothing more than a running nose, and I only advise Melancholy to keep her mouth closed. Let one read in Sophocles the description of the vacant, barren den of the unhappy Philoctetes. There is nothing to be seen of the necessaries or the conveniences of life beyond a trodden matting of withered leaves, a misshapen bowl of wood and a fireplace. The whole wealth of the sick, forsaken man! How does the poet complete the sad and fearful picture? With an addition

---

[213] Lessing's reference is to *The Connoisseur*, I, no. 21. His footnote quotes the original at length.
[214] Longinus: see note 109 above.
[215] Hesiod (*c.* 700 BC), among the earliest of the Greek poets; Lessing's reference is to *The Shield of Hercules* (a poem often ascribed to Hesiod), line 266: 'slime streamed from her nostrils'.
[216] 'blood flowed down her cheeks to the ground'.

of disgust. 'Ha!' exclaims Neoptolemus, recoiling – 'torn rags drying in the wind, full of blood and matter!'

NE. Ὁρῶ κενὴν οἴκησιν, ἀνθρώπων δίχα.
ΟΔ. Οὐδ' ἔνδον οἰκοποιός ἐστί τις τροφή;
NE. Στιπτή γε φυλλὰς ὡς ἐναυλίζοντί τῳ.
ΟΔ. Τὰ δ' ἄλλ' ἔρημα, κοὐδέν ἐσθ' ὑπόστεγον;
NE. Αὐτόξυλόν γ' ἔκπωμα, φλαυρουργοῦ τινὸς
   Τεχνήματ' ἀνδρός, καὶ πυρεῖ' ὁμοῦ τάδε.
ΟΔ. Κείνου τὸ θησαύρισμα σημαίνεις τόδε.
NE. Ἰοὺ ἰού. καὶ ταῦτά γ' ἄλλα θάλπεται
   Ῥάκη, βαρείας τοῦ νοσηλείας πλέα.²¹⁷

And, similarly, in Homer dead Hector, dragged along, his countenance disfigured with blood and dust and clotted hair:

Squalentem barbam et concretos sanguine crines²¹⁸

(as Virgil expresses it), a disgusting object, but all the more terrible on that account and all the more moving. Who can think of the torture of Marsyas in Ovid without a sensation of disgust?

Clamanti cutis est summos derepta per artus,
Nec quidquam nisi vulnus erat. Cruor undique manat,
Detectique patent nervi, trepidaeque sine ulla
Pelle micant venae: salientia viscera possis
Et perlucentes numerare in pectore fibras.²¹⁹

---

²¹⁷ Sophocles, *Philoctetes*, lines 31–9:

Neoptolemus	The chamber's empty; no man is within.
Odysseus	And no provision for a man's abode?
Neoptolemus	Litter of trodden leaves as for a couch.
Odysseus	And that is all – no other sign of life?
Neoptolemus	A cup of uncouth handiwork, rough hewn
	From out a log; some tinder, too, I see.
Odysseus	These are his household treasures.
Neoptolemus	Faugh! and here
	Spread in the sun to dry, are filthy rags
	Dank with the ooze of some malignant sore.

(Translated by F. Storr, Loeb Classical Library (London, 1913)).

²¹⁸ *Aeneid*, II, 277: 'his beard was ragged, his hair clotted with blood'.

²¹⁹ Ovid, *Metamorphoses*, VI, 387–91: 'Despite his cries, the skin was ripped from his whole body: it was all a single wound. Blood flowed everywhere, his nerves were exposed, his veins pulsed with no skin to cover them. One could count his throbbing entrails and the fibres shining through his breast.'

But who does not feel at the same time that the disgusting is here in place? It makes the terrible horrible; and the horrible itself in Nature, when our pity is engaged, is not wholly disagreeable; how much less in the imitation! I will not heap up instances. But one thing I must still note: that there is a variety of the terrible, the poet's way to which stands open simply and solely through the disgusting – this is the terrible of *hunger*. Even in common life it is impossible to express the extremity of hunger otherwise than by the narration of all the innutritious, unwholesome, and especially all the loathsome things, with which the appetite must be appeased. As the imitation can awaken in us nothing of the feeling of hunger itself, it resorts to another unpleasant feeling which in the case of the fiercest hunger we recognize as the smaller of two great evils. This feeling it seeks to excite within us in order that we may from the discomfort conclude how fearful must be that other discomfort under which this becomes of no account. Ovid says of the oread whom Ceres sent off to starve:

> Hanc (Famem) procul ut vidit...
> ... Refert mandata deae, paulumque morata,
> Quanquam aberat longe, quanquam modo venerat illuc,
> Visa tamen sensisse Famem ...[220]

An unnatural exaggeration! The sight of one who hungers, were it even Hunger herself, has not this infectious power; pity and horror and disgust it may make us feel, but not hunger. This horror Ovid has not spared us in his picture of famine, and in the hunger of Erysichthon, both in Ovid's description and that of Callimachus,[221] the loathsome features are the strongest. After Erysichthon had devoured everything, not sparing even the beast which his mother had reared to be a burnt-offering for Vesta, Callimachus makes him fall upon horses and cats, and beg upon the streets for the crusts and filthy fragments from strange tables:

> Καὶ τὰν βῶν ἔφαγεν, τὰν Ἑστίᾳ ἔτρεφε μάτηρ,
> Καὶ τὸν ἀεθλοφόρον καὶ τὸν πολεμήϊον ἵππον,

---

[220] Ovid, *Metamorphoses*, VIII, 809–12: 'When she saw her [Hunger]...she told her the instructions of the goddess, and after a short time, although she stood at a distance and had only just arrived, she seemed to feel hunger herself.'

[221] Callimachus (third century BC), Alexandrian poet and scholar; Lessing's reference is to his *Hymn to Ceres*, lines 111–16.

Καὶ τὰν αἴλουρον, τὰν ἔτρεμε θηρία μικκὰ –
Καὶ τόθ' ὁ τῶ βασιλῆος ἐνὶ τριόδοισι καθῆστο
Αἰτίζων ἀκόλως τε καὶ ἔκβολα λύματα δαιτός –[222]

And Ovid makes him finally put his teeth into his own limbs, to nourish his body with his own flesh:

Vis tamen illa mali postquam consumserat omnem
Materiam ...
Ipse suos artus lacero divellere morsu
Coepit, et infelix minuendo corpus alebat.[223]

For that very reason were the repulsive Harpies[224] made so noisome, so filthy, that the hunger which their snatching of the viands was to produce should be so much more terrible. Listen to the lament of Phineus in Apollonius:

Τυτθὸν δ' ἦν ἄρα δή ποτ' ἐδητύος ἄμμι λίπωσι,
Πνεῖ τόδε μυδαλέον τε καὶ οὐ τλητὸν μένος ὀδμῆς.
Οὔ κέ τις οὐδὲ μίνυνθα βροτῶν ἀνσχοιτο πελάσσας
Οὐδ' εἴ οἱ ἀδάμαντος ἐληλαμένον κέαρ εἴη.
Ἀλλά με πικρὴ δῆτά κε δαιτὸς ἐπίσχει ἀνάγκη
Μίμνειν, καὶ μίμνοντα κακῇ ἐν γαστέρι θέσθαι.[225]

I would from this point of view gladly excuse the loathsome introduction of the Harpies in Virgil;[226] but it is no actual present hunger which they cause, but only an impending one which they prophesy, and, furthermore, the whole prophecy is resolved in the end into a play upon words. Dante, too, prepares us not only for the story of the starvation of Ugolino by the most loathsome and horrible situation in which he places him in hell with

---

[222] *Hymn to Ceres*, lines 109–12 and 115 f.: 'And he devoured the cow which his mother had raised for Hestia [Vesta], as well as the racehorse and the martial steed; and then the cat, at which small animals had trembled. Then this son of a royal house sat down at the wayside and begged for crusts and the refuse of meals.'

[223] Ovid, *Metamorphoses*, VIII, 875–8: 'However, after the violence of his malady had consumed everything available, ... he began to tear pieces off his own limbs with his teeth, and fed his body by eating it away.'

[224] The Harpies, ravenous monsters with the bodies of birds and the heads of maidens, sent by the gods to torment the blind Phineas by stealing or defiling his food.

[225] *Argonautica* (see note 114 above), II, 228–33: 'And if they leave me any food at all it stinks of putrefaction, the smell is intolerable, and no one could bear to come near it, even for a moment, even if he had an adamantine will. Yet bitter necessity that cannot be gainsaid, not only keeps me there, but forces me to pamper my accursed belly' (translation by E. V. Rieu).

[226] *Aeneid*, III, 211 ff.

his aforetime persecutor;[227] but the starvation itself also is not without elements of disgust, which more particularly overcomes us at the point where the sons offer themselves as food to their father. There is in a drama of Beaumont and Fletcher a passage which I might cite here in place of all other examples were I not obliged to think it somewhat overdone.[228]

I turn to the question of disgusting subjects in painting. If it were quite incontestable that, properly speaking, there are no disgusting subjects whatever for sight, of which it might be assumed that painting, as fine art, would refuse them: all the same, she must avoid disgusting subjects in general, because the association of ideas makes them disgusting to sight also. Pordenone in a picture of Christ's burial makes one of the onlookers hold his nose.[229] Richardson condemns this on the ground that Christ was not yet so long dead that his body could have suffered corruption.[230] In the Resurrection of Lazarus, on the other hand, he thinks it might be permitted to the painter to show by such an indication what the story expressly asserts – that his body was already corrupt. In my view this representation is unendurable in this case also; for not only the actual stench, but the mere idea of it awakens disgust. We flee offensive places even if we actually have a cold. Yet painting accepts the disgusting not for disgust's sake: she accepts it, as poetry does, in order to intensify by it the laughable and the terrible. But at her own risk! What, however, I have in this case noted of the ugly holds yet more certainly of the disgusting. It loses in a *visible* imitation incomparably less of its effect than in an *audible* one; and therefore can mingle less intimately with the laughable and terrible elements in the former case than in the latter; as soon as the first surprise is past, as soon as the first eager glance is satisfied, it isolates itself in its turn completely and lies there in all its crudeness.[231]

---

[227] Dante, *Divine Comedy*, XXXII, 124–39.

[228] Francis Beaumont (1584–1616) and John Fletcher (1576–1625), English dramatists; Lessing's reference is to the starvation of the shipwrecked pirates in Act III, Scene 1 of *The Sea-Voyage*, which he quotes at length in his footnote.

[229] Giovanni Antonio de Sacchis Pordenone (1483–1539), Italian Mannerist painter.

[230] Lessing's reference is to the French translation of Richardson's *Theory of Painting* (see note 62 above), p. 74.

[231] The argument of Lessing's *Laocoön* ends at this point. The remaining four chapters, which are omitted here, are simply an appendix in which Lessing gives his initial reactions on the publication of Winckelmann's *History of the Art of Antiquity*: he defends his own dating of the Laocoön group against Winckelmann's contention that it dates from the age of Alexander the Great; he tries to prove (unsuccessfully, as it later emerged) that the statue of the so-called 'Borghese Gladiator' is in fact a representation of the Athenian general Chabrias; and he corrects various minor errors in Winckelmann's references to ancient literary sources.

KARL PHILLIPP MORITZ

From 'On the Artistic Imitation of the Beautiful' (1788)[1]

The difference between the Greek actor imitating Socrates on the stage in Aristophanes' comedy and the wise man imitating him in everyday life is that these two cannot be comprised under one and the same description; thus we say that the actor *parodies* Socrates, while the wise man *imitates* him.

The actor was clearly not concerned with imitating Socrates truly, but was rather concerned with *recreating* his *individual* way of walking, his composure, his posture and his comportment in a heightened way in order to make him seem laughable. Because he does this intentionally and in fun we say he parodies Socrates.

But if the actor before us were not an actor but rather someone of the people who feels an inner closeness to him and now also imitates him in all *seriousness*, in his external characteristic as well, that is, in his walk, his posture and his comportment, we would say of this fool that he *apes* Socrates; or, he is to Socrates like the ape's posture and comportment is to the human.

---

[1] Best known for his autobiographical novel *Anton Reiser* (1785–90), Moritz wrote two important essays on aesthetics, 'Attempt at a Unification of All the Fine Arts and Sciences under the Concept of That Which is Perfect Itself' (1785), and 'On the Artistic Imitation of the Beautiful' (1788). Only the first half of the latter essay is offered here. Although still burdened with mimetic and perfectionist notions, the essay continues the development of the conception of the artwork as autonomous and self-determining.

The actor thus excludes the wise man and only parodies Socrates; for wisdom cannot be parodied: the wise man excludes Socrates in his imitation, and imitates wisdom in the wise man; for Socrates' individuality can well be parodied and aped, but not imitated. The fool has no sense for the wisdom but is driven to a sort of imitation; he grabs hold of what is closest to him, he apes so as not to be permitted to imitate [*um nicht nachahmen zu dürfen*]; he transposes the whole surface of another human being onto his own person; the basis or sense of self for this is provided by his foolishness.

Thus we see, from its use in language, that *imitation* is used in the nobler moral sense and is almost synonymous with the concept of striving after and competing; this is the case because the virtue which I imitate, for example, in a particular role model has something universal, something which is above individuality, and which can be achieved by everyone who strives after it; it is thus achievable by me as well as by the role model I am competing against. But since I am lesser than this role model, and since a certain degree of noble sentiment and type of action would hardly [or not at all] have been possible without this role model, I call my striving for some communal good, which must, of course, also be achieved by my role model, the imitation of this role model.

I imitate my role model, I strive after him; I try to compete with him. – My role model has set my goal higher than if I had set it myself. I must thus strive, according to my powers, and in my way, to reach this goal; I may finally forget my role model and try to set my goal yet further, if this is possible.

Imitation only gains its true worth through this nobler moral sentiment. – The question is now: how might imitation in the moral sense be different from imitation in the beautiful arts, how might imitation of the good and noble be different from the imitation of the beautiful?

This question will answer itself as soon as we have differentiated between the concept of beauty and the concept of good, again according to the use of language: and it should not bother us that language users often confuse them, since our goal in reflecting upon them is merely to differentiate them; and it is necessary to draw certain fixed borders, just as are drawn on a globe but which do not occur in nature, if the concepts are not to lose themselves unnoticeably in one another, as the objects do. Although, in this case, objects might be faithful impressions of nature, genuine thinking, which simply must consist in differentiating, cannot continue [on this path].

Now, the good and the useful as well as the noble and the beautiful are naturally connected in language use; these four different terms describe such a fine gradation of concepts, and make for such a fine play of ideas, that it will be difficult for reflection to keep them apart and examine each individually and separately, since the terms constantly lose themselves in each other without our noticing it. So much clearly catches the eye, nonetheless: the useful is in greater opposition to the beautiful and the noble than is the good. This is because the transition of the useful to the beautiful and the noble is made through the good.

We might, for example, think of a useful man as someone who is noteworthy not in and of himself, but rather deserves our attention because of the relation he has to things outside of him. The good man, on the other hand, is someone who begins to draw our attention and love to himself in and of himself; for we think of him as someone who, according to his inner wealth of goodness, will never harm us through personal gain or selfishness, and will not bring dissonance into our relation with things, in short, he will not disturb our peace. – The noble man, however, attracts our whole attention and admiration simply through himself; this occurs without consideration for anything outside of him or of any advantage he might provide for our own self from his existence.

And since the noble human does not require physical beauty to be noble, the concepts of beauty and nobility may be divided into inner beauty of the soul and surface beauty. But insofar as outer beauty is a mark of the inner beauty of the soul, it already comprises the noble in it, and ought to always comprise it according to its own nature. Nonetheless, the distinction between beauty and nobility is not negated. For we imagine a noble posture to be, for example, a posture which at the same time reveals a certain inner dignity of the soul; but some passionate posture can nonetheless still be a beautiful posture, even if it does not explicitly express such a dignity of the soul, but it may never directly contradict such dignity; it may not be ignoble.

This, by the way, explains both the concept of the noble style in that artwork which is none other than that which is synonymous with the creative genius's inner dignity of soul. Although this noble style does not exclude the inferior types of beauty from the realm of beauty, it does cut off everything which directly opposes it; it excludes the ignoble.

Insofar as we can understand the noble, in opposition to outer beauty, as inner beauty of the soul, we can also imitate it *in* us, just like the good. – But, insofar as it distinguishes itself from the noble, which is only understood as outer in opposition to the inner, the beautiful cannot enter us through imitation –, it must, if it is to be imitated by us, necessarily be created *out of us*.

The creative artist, for example, can imitatively transfer into himself the inner beauty of the soul of a man, whom he takes as his role model in his changingness. If this artist feels compelled, however, to imitate the beauty of the soul of his role model, insofar as it is expressed in his facial characteristics, he must create his concept of it (by moving it from the inside to the outside), and thus try to depict it outside of himself. Thus he does not directly imitate the facial characteristics, but takes them only to aid him in depicting again the beauty of the soul he feels in the presence of another being outside of himself.

Genuine imitation of the beautiful distinguishes itself from the moral imitation of the good and the noble primarily because, according to its nature, it must strive not, as the other does, to create something within itself but must create out of itself.

Let us apply the concepts good, beautiful and noble to the concept of action. We think of an action as good if it can earn our attention and our applause not simply because of its consequences, but also because of its motivations. In judging a noble action we completely forget the consequences and the action seems worthy of our admiration for its motives alone, that is, for its own sake. If we consider the action according to its *surface*, which casts a gentle glow into our soul, or according to the pleasant sensations which mere observation of it awakens in us, we call it a *beautiful* action; but if we want to express its inner worth, we call it *noble*. Every beautiful *action* must necessarily also be noble; the noble is the basis of the wealth of beauty through which it shines forth. The concept of beauty is thus again pulled back into the realm of the moral and chained to it tightly by the mediating concept of the noble. In this way, the beautiful is at least given boundaries which it may not overstep.

Since we are necessitated to develop the concept of imitation of the genuinely beautiful, [which we do not have,] from the concept of the moral imitation of the good and noble, [which we do have,] and since we cannot think genuine imitation of the beautiful independently of the pleasure in the work itself, which arises from it, but in its difference to the mere moral imitation of the good and the noble, we must investigate the concepts of the useful, the good, the beautiful and the noble in even finer gradations.

For example, the fact that Mutius Scaevola's deed had the desired consequences did not make it any nobler than it already was;[2] and it would not have lost any of its intrinsic worth without its success; he did not need to be *useful* to be noble; it did not need success, for its inner worth rested in itself; and whence came this worth if not from it, through its origin, its being?

The great and noble quality of the action was precisely that the young hero, ready for *every* success, dared to do the utmost, placing his hand into the blazing flames without hesitation, even though he did not know how his enemy, in whose power he was, would punish him. – Only someone who undertakes a great deed, whose success is highly uncertain, and for whom it alone suffices that his great consciousness hold him innocent of any failed attempt, can do the act *for the sake of the deed itself*.

If, under different circumstances, Mutius had merely been the tool of another, whom he obeyed out of duty, for a similar deed, and had he, with the consent of his heart, executed the deed admirably and as he ought to have, he would not have acted nobly in a genuine sense, but would [merely] have acted very well; for though his action would have had great worth in itself, its goodness would still have been determined by its success.

Had this same Mutius conducted the attack on the enemy of his fatherland in treacherous fashion for private revenge and out of personal hatred, and had he not failed, he would have been useful to his fatherland without being good and noble, and still would have received a certain external worth *through his success*, without having the least inner worth.

The bad must have the same relationship to the ignoble as the good to the noble. The ignoble is the beginning of the bad, just as the good is the beginning of the beautiful and noble. And just as a merely good action is not necessarily a noble action, merely ignoble action is not necessarily a bad action. The useful is to the good as the useless is to the bad; the bad

---

[2] Gaius Mutius was a legendary Roman hero who, according to Livy, upon being captured by Etruscan King Porsena and threatened with being burnt alive, thrust his arm into the fire to show his contempt for bodily pain. His bravery led Porsena to make peace with Rome. Mutius thus earned the nickname Scaevolus (left-handed).

is the beginning of the useless, just as the useful is already the beginning of the good. Just as the merely useful is not necessarily good because of this, the bad is not necessarily useless.

The concepts ignoble, bad and useless are valued in descending order just as the concepts useful, good and beautiful are valued in ascending order. Of the ascending concepts, the noble and the beautiful are the highest, just as for the descending order the useless is the lowest. Of all these concepts, the beautiful and the useless seem the farthest apart and in greatest opposition to each other; since we just saw that the beautiful and the noble distinguish themselves from the good in that they need not be useful in order to be beautiful, we can conclude that the concept of beauty can stand in close proximity to the concept of the useless or the not useful.

Here we can see how a circle of concepts finally loses itself in itself again, because its extreme ends meet at the point at which, if they did not come in contact with each other, we would say that they were the furthest distance from each other.

For the concept of the useless, insofar as it has no end, no purpose outside of itself for which it exists, is the closest and most willing to connect up to the concept of the beautiful insofar as the beautiful does not *need* an end, a purpose for existing, except itself, but finds its whole worth, the end of its existence, within itself.

But insofar as the useless is not at the same time beautiful, it again becomes the most distant from the concept of the beautiful and falls down to the level of the bad, because it has a purpose for existing neither in itself nor outside itself and thus negates itself. But if the useless, or that which does not have the end for its existence outside of itself is also beautiful, it rises over the useful and the good to the highest level of concepts because it needs no end outside of itself, since it is perfect in itself, possessing its whole purpose for being in itself.

The three ascending concepts of useful, good and beautiful and the three descending concepts of ignoble, bad and useless form a circle for the reason that both of the outermost concepts, the useless and the beautiful, exclude each other least; and the concept of the useless at one end can be seen as the groove into which the concept at the other end, beauty, most easily fits, and in which it can lose itself unnoticed.

If we descend the ladder of concepts we see that beautiful and noble are compatible with useless, but not with bad and ignoble; good is compatible with ignoble, but not with bad or useless; useful with bad and ignoble, but not with useless; ignoble with good and useful, but not with beautiful; bad with useless but not with beautiful or good; useless with beautiful, but not with good and useful. – The concepts must rejoin one another where they seem to differ the most and appear to be departing from one another.

But we must only follow this play of ideas as long as it brings us closer to our end, to illuminate our representation of the imitation of the beautiful through the concept of the beautiful. Now, the representation of that which the beautiful *does not need to be* in order to be beautiful, and what is to be regarded as superfluous in it, can lead us to a not incorrect concept of the beautiful by abstracting everything which is not part of it and thus we can make out the true outline of the empty space, in which that which we are seeking would necessarily fit, if we could just think it positively.

Since the previous juxtaposition made clear that the concepts of the beautiful and the useless not only do not exclude each other, but willingly collapse into each other, we can conclude that the useful in the beautiful is clearly superfluous, and that if it is found in the beautiful, it may be regarded as contingent, as not belonging, because true beauty, just as nobleness in action, is neither increased through the presence of usefulness nor decreased through its absence.

We can recognize the beautiful in the universal by no other method than by distinguishing it as sharply as possible from the useful and by opposing it to the beautiful. A thing does not become beautiful merely because it is not useful, but only because it does not *need* to be useful. But to answer the question about how the thing must be composed so that it does not need to be useful, we must develop the concept of the useful still further.

For we think of the useful as the relation of a thing, seen as a part, to a connection of things, which we think of as a whole. And the relation must be of such a type that the connection of the whole steadily increases and is maintained; the more of these relations a thing has to the connection wherein it is found, the more useful it will be.

In this way each part of the whole must have a greater or lesser relation to the whole: the whole, seen as a whole, needs no further relations to anything outside of itself, however. Thus, every citizen must be in a certain relation to the state, or be useful to the state; but the state, insofar as it forms a whole, need not have any relation to things outside of it and thus need not be useful in a further way.

Thus we see that a thing necessarily must make up a whole existing in itself in order not to have to be useful, and the concept of a whole existing in itself is thus inseparably linked to the concept of the beautiful. – But we can see, this notwithstanding, that this is insufficient to form the concept of beauty because we would not apply the concept beautiful to the state, even if it exists completely in itself, for it does not appear to our outward senses, nor is captured by our imagination, *in its entirety*, but is merely thought by our understanding.

For the same reason we cannot attach the concept of beauty to the whole connection of things, all the more so because the connection, *in its entirety*, is given neither to our senses nor is grasped by our imagination, even if it can be thought by our understanding.

The concept of beauty, which for us has arisen from the fact that it need not be useful, thus requires not only that it exist as a self-contained whole, but that it be given as a self-contained whole *to our senses*, or can be *grasped as such by our imagination*.

And just as the useful has its degrees, the beautiful must have them too; for the more connection-enhancing relationships a useful thing has to the situation wherein it exists, the more useful it is; and the more such relationships the beautiful thing has from its parts to its nexus, that is, to itself, the more beautiful it is.

And just as the beautiful can be useful without losing any of its beauty, though it is not there to be useful; the useful can have a certain degree of beauty even though it is only there to be useful.

But the line may not be crossed even by a hair's breadth; as soon as the end of the useful thing, which is the purpose of its existence, suffers from the presumption of beauty, it becomes neither beautiful nor useful and sinks below itself, negates itself.

If the beautiful is found *in the useful,* it must subordinate itself to the useful – it is not there for its own sake – it serves to decorate the useful and thus descends to the useful and flows together with it. – It relinquishes its claim by giving up its name and steps into a bounded space, it becomes modest *decoration,* simple *elegance.*

The concept of the majestic arises out of the mixture of the beautiful and the noble, in which external beauty becomes the expression of inner honour and highness. If we imagine the majestic as lively, it must dominate the world, grasp the connection of things in itself, the whole world must bow to it.

If we *compare* the noble in action and thought with the ignoble, we call the noble great and the ignoble small. – And if we again measure the great, the noble and the beautiful according to the height at which it towers over us, almost eluding our powers of comprehension, the concept of beauty will transform itself into the concept of the *sublime*.

But insofar as the manifold relations of parts to the whole in a beautiful work are not, or not also, thought with our understanding, but rather are only given to our *external senses*, or must be grasped by our *imagination*, our *tools of perception*, they prescribe a *measure* for the beautiful.

For otherwise the whole connection of nature which comprises in itself the greatest and largest imaginable totality of relations, would also be the highest beauty for us, if it could be grasped even for a moment, by our imagination.

For this great interconnection of things is really the only, the true whole; because of the indissoluble concatenation of things every particular whole in it is merely *imagined* – but even this imagined whole, seen as a whole, must from itself be created by fixed rules according to which it supports itself on its centre from all sides and thus rests on its own existence, like that great whole in our representation.

Each beautiful whole coming from the hand of the artist is thus an impression in miniature of the highest beauty of the whole of nature; *mediated* through the hand of the artist, it recreates that which does not immediately belong to the great plan.

Whoever has been impressed by nature with a sense of the creative power in his whole being, and has received the impression of the *measure* of the beautiful in his eye and soul, cannot content himself merely to observe it; he must imitate it, strive after it, eavesdrop on nature in its secret workshop and make and create with blazing flames in his heart, as nature itself does: –

He does this by penetrating the inner being of nature, to the very spring of beauty itself and loosens the finest seams of nature with his glowing insight. He then rebuilds the seams even more beautifully on the surface, he impresses nature's noble traces in clay, in hard stone; or he separates out its form from the flat ground with a dividing point; by imitating mass itself with brave strokes of colour; and brings the surface closer to the eye by mixing light and shadow.

Reality must turn into appearance through the hand of the artist; his inner power of creativity [*Bildungskraft*] coming from the inside, though inhibited by matter, meets with his creating hand coming from the outside, on the surface of lifeless mass; and all that which is otherwise hidden from our eyes in the veil of *existence*, which itself weighs up every appearance, is transferred over onto this surface.

Thus from the real and complete beauty, that which can rarely develop itself immediately, nature created beings who could *mediately* reflect it and express nature so lifelike in the image that the image can again oppose itself to its own creation. – And thus, through its redoubled reflection of itself in itself, floating and fluttering above reality, nature has brought about an illusion which is even more attractive to the *mortal* eye than nature itself.

And although the human is as limited as is possible in his place in the series of things, so that as many different types of beings as possible may move about above and below him, nature did give him the power of creativity as well as pleasure, so that he could become as perfect as his kind allows; nature even allowed him to compete with it, and, so that no power should remain underdeveloped, even allowed him seemingly to surpass it.

But having a sense of the highest beauty in the harmonious structure of the whole, which the human power of representation does not comprise, lies in the *power to act* itself, which cannot rest before it has moved that which slumbers in it, towards at least one of the powers of representation. – It reaches into the nexus of things and, just like nature, wants to turn it into a *self-determining* whole which exists in itself. – The reality of things, whose essence and reality lie in this *particularity*, resists the power of action until it has dissolved the inner essence into appearance, and has made the thing its own, has created its own world wherein nothing particular can any longer take place but where every thing has, according to its type, become a whole, existing for itself.

Nature, however, could only plant the sense of the highest beauty in the power of action, and could only make the mediated impression of this highest beauty palpable in the imagination, visible to the eyes, audible to the ears, because the horizon of the power to act encompasses more than the outer senses, the imagination and the power of thought.

There are *always* so many occasions and beginnings of concepts in our power of action that the power of thought is not able to subsume them all, that the imagination is not able to *set them side by side*, and that the outer senses are even less capable of grasping the *reality* outside of themselves all at once.

In order to catch up *once* to the active power in its dark premonition, the power of thought must repeat itself until the whole reservoir of beginnings and occasions for concepts has been subdued and exhausted, and must thus begin the cycle anew. – The imagination must repeat itself even more often since it does not place the beginnings and occasions into each other but rather *next to each other*, and can thus grasp even less. – The outer sense is a constant repetition of itself because it can grasp only as much each time as is *really* present side by side in the horizon which opaquely surrounds it. The outer sense grasps so little that no lifetime is enough to catch up to the wealth of occasions for concepts which slumber in the power of action, and to bring all to intuition and reality; as long as we breathe, the eye will never be satisfied in looking nor the ear satisfied in hearing.

From the vivid and *dark premonition* of the reflection's power of action, through the *differentiating* power of thought, and the *depicting* power of imagination, to the *clairvoyant* eye and the distinctly hearing ear, the more complete and vivid the concepts become, in the lively process of mirroring, the more they also *eclipse* and *exclude* each other. – The place they exclude each other the least, and are *most* able to stand side by side, can only be where they are the most *incomplete*, where the mere beginnings and occasions come together, which, through their lack and incompleteness, produce the constant and irresistible stimulus which brings out their full effect.

The creative genius's horizon of active power must be *as extensive as nature itself*; that is, its organization must be spun so finely and must contain infinitely many *points of contact* to all-encompassing nature, that the farthest extremities of all relations to nature in general can stand next to each other in miniature, and will have enough space not to be allowed to eclipse each other.

If an organization of this fine fabric, in its fullest development, suddenly, in the active power of its dark premonition, grasps a *whole* which has entered neither the eye nor the ear, neither the power of the imagination nor the power of thought, there must ensue a restlessness, a misunderstanding between the contending powers until they again find their equilibrium.

In a soul whose mere active power already grasps the *noble*, the *very great* of nature in dark premonition, the distinctly cognitive power of thought and the even more lively depicting power of imagination, and the most brightly mirroring power of the outer senses, can no longer be satisfied with the consideration of the *singular* in the nexus of nature.

All those relationships of the great whole, merely felt in dark premonition, must necessarily be made visible in some way, audible or available to the power of the imagination; and for this the power of activity in which they slumber must *form itself, according to itself, out of itself.* – It must grasp all of those relationships of the great whole, and in them the highest beauty, like the tips of rays at one focal point. – Out of this focal point, and according to the eye's measure of distance, a delicate and yet faithful picture of the highest beauty must emerge, which can grasp the most complete relation of the great whole of nature in the same truth and correctness as it grasps its own small parameters.

But since this impression of the highest beauty must necessarily cling to something, the creative power selects, according to its *individuality*, something visible, audible or some object capable of being grasped by the imagination onto which it transfers the resplendence of the highest beauty on a scale which *rejuvenates*. – And this object in turn could not exist, if it *were really* what it depicted, that is, if it became a self-contained whole which, in relation to the connection to nature, could not tolerate a self-contained whole outside of itself; this brings us to a point which was made once before, namely that the inner being must turn itself into appearance before it can be turned through art into a whole existing for itself alone, and can thus reflect the relation of the great whole of nature *unhindered* in its full parameter.

But since those great relations in whose *complete parameter* beauty lies, do not fall into the field of the power of thought, the *living* concept of the creative imitation of nature can only take place in the feeling of active power, which evokes it in the first moment of its origination, where the work, already completed, through all degrees of its all-powerful becoming, steps all at once before the soul in dark premonition, and in this moment of the first generation it is also present in its *true* being. Through this the unnamable stimulus comes into existence which drives the creative Genius to continual creation.

Our consideration of the creative imitation of the beautiful, combined with the pure pleasure of the beautiful artwork itself, can, to be sure, create a lively concept in us which heightens the pleasure the artwork creates in us; – but since our highest pleasure in the beautiful still cannot grasp the *becoming of this beauty from its own power*, the single highest pleasure remains the creative genius himself who produces it. And the beautiful has therefore already reached its highest purpose in its generation, in its coming to be. Our *subsequent pleasure* in it is only the *consequence* of its being; and in the great plan of nature, the creative genius exists first *for his own sake* and only then for our sake; for there exist beings aside from him who do not themselves produce and create but who can comprehend the created thing with their imagination once it has been generated.

The nature of the beautiful consists precisely in the fact that its inner nature exists outside of the boundaries of the power of thought, in its generation, in its becoming. The beautiful is beautiful precisely because the power of thought can no longer ask why it is beautiful. – For the power of thought completely lacks a *point of comparison* from which to judge and consider the beautiful. What could present a point of comparison for the truly beautiful other than the essence of all harmonious relations of the great whole of nature which no power of thought can comprehend? Every instance of beauty strewn about in nature is beautiful only insofar as this essence of relations of the great whole is more or less revealed in it. – It can thus never serve as a point of comparison for the beautiful in the creative arts nor can it function as a model for the true imitation of the beautiful; this is so because the highest beauty of the particular in nature is still not beautiful enough to proudly imitate the noble and majestic relations of the great whole of nature. – The beautiful can thus not be recognized but must be brought out – or *felt*.

FRIEDRICH SCHILLER

'Kallias or Concerning Beauty: Letters to Gottfried Körner' (1793)

Jena, the 25 January [Friday] 1793

So far there has been no storm, although I have not been feeling too well and it is now six days past the time at which the paroxysm of last year overcame me. My concern came not from lack of courage, or from a mere hypochondriac fancy. I am prone to catarrhal illness which is exacerbated by winter – my two infectious fevers came from catarrhals. Equal causes give rise to equal effects. I must thus fear for my chest in winter as I fear my cramps in summer and spring. I am thus placed before miserable alternatives and every new animal sign brings a change in my suffering. And yet, the best I may hope for is to remain as I am, for any change in my condition would certainly be for the worse.

My projects have managed to sustain me, thank goodness. The investigation concerning the beautiful, which can hardly be separated from any part of aesthetics, has led me into a wide field where I may still come across strange lands. And yet I must become master of the whole realm if I am to produce any satisfying work. It is impossibly difficult to construct an objective concept of beauty and to legitimate it completely a priori out of the nature of rationality, in such a way that experience may confirm the concept, but that such confirmation from experience is not necessary for its validity. I have indeed attempted a deduction of my concept of the beautiful but was unable to do so without reference to experience. The problem remains that people will accept my explanation only because they find it to be in accordance with individual judgements of taste, and not (as it ought to be in an explanation of an objective principle) because they find that the judgement about the beautiful coincides with the explanation. You may say that this is to demand a lot, but as long as we have not succeeded here, taste will always remain empirical, just as Kant believed it must inevitably be. I cannot yet convince myself of the inevitability of the empirical, the impossibility of an objective principle of taste.

It is worth noting that my theory is a fourth possible way of explaining the beautiful. Either one declares it subjective or objective; and either subjective sensual (like Burke among others), subjective rational (like Kant) or rational objective (like Baumgarten, Mendelssohn and the whole crowd of men who esteem perfection), or, finally, sensuous objective: a term which will mean little to you at this point, save if you compare the other three forms with each other. Each of the preceding theories reflects a part of experience and clearly contains a part of the truth, and the error seems merely to be that one has taken the true part of the theory to coincide with beauty itself. The Burkian is completely justified in insisting on the unmediated quality, on the independence of beauty, against the Wolffian; but he is in the wrong against the Kantian to insist that beauty be posited as a mere affection of sensuousness. The fact that by far most experiences of beauty that come to mind are not completely free instances of beauty but logical beings which are subsumed under the concept of purpose such as all artworks and most beauties of nature – this fact seems to have led astray all those who have tried to situate beauty in intuitive perfection; for now the logically good was confused with the beautiful. Kant wanted to cut precisely this knot by assuming a *pulchritudo vaga* [free beauty] and *fixa* [fixed],[1] and by claiming, rather strangely, that every beautiful thing which is subsumed under the concept of a purpose is not a *pure* beautiful thing at all; that an arabesque or something similar, which is seen as beautiful, is seen as purer in its beauty than the highest beauty of humanity. I think that this observation may have the great advantage of being able to separate the logical from the aesthetic. Ultimately, however,

---

[1] In section 16 of the *Critique of Judgement* Kant distinguishes between free beauty which does not presuppose a concept of what the object is meant to be, and adherent beauty which does presuppose a concept of the object. In the following section, he urges that for an ideal of beauty we require that the beauty be fixed by a concept of objective purposiveness.

this observation seems to miss the concept of beauty completely. For beauty presents itself in its greatest splendour only once it has overcome the *logical* nature of its object, and how can this be done if there is no resistance? How can it provide a form for completely formless material? I am at least convinced that the beautiful is only the form of form and that that which we call its matter must be the at least formed matter. Perfection is the form of matter, beauty however, is the form of this perfection; it relates to beauty as matter does to form.

I have related my scattered thoughts to you and may raise the curtain again when I am in a talkative mood.

So long. A thousand greetings from all of us here to you and yours.

Your S.

Jena, Feb. 8 [Friday] 1793

From this letter you can see that the asphyxiating angel has passed over me so far. Three weeks have passed since the date at which I became ill last year, and four have passed since the day I became ill two years ago. I have great and relatively certain hopes that my nature will remain master over at least the winter. My affairs are running smoothly and this project keeps me afloat. Nothing will be finished for the Easter fair. This business must be thought through.

Your letter, which I received a few hours ago, pleased me greatly and put me in a mood in which I might succeed in giving you a short presentation of my idea about beauty. You will soon see just how close we are with respect to our ideas about beauty and perhaps you will find certain *inchoate* ideas of yours made clearer in *my* account. The terms you use: *life* in external objects, *dominating* power and *victory* of the dominating power, *heterogeneous* powers, *adverse* powers, and the like, are too ambiguous for you to ensure that they do not include anything arbitrary or contingent; they are more aesthetic than *clearly logical* and thus dangerous.

A Kantian will still be able to back you into a corner with a question about which principle of knowledge underlies taste. Your idea of the dominating power is based on the idea of the whole, on the concept of the unity of the connected parts, the manifold, but how can we recognize this unity? Apparently only through a concept; one must have a concept of the whole under which the manifold is united. Your *dominating power* and the *sensual perfection* of the Wolffian school are not so far apart since the process of judgement[2] is logical in both. Both assume that one must support the judgement with a concept. Now, Kant is certainly right in saying that the beautiful pleases *without* a concept. I can have found an object beautiful for quite a while before I am able to articulate the unity of its manifold, and to determine what power dominates it.

By the way, I am speaking here mostly as a Kantian, since it is possible that in the end my theory will not remain immune to this criticism either. In order to lead you to my theory, I must take a double path; one very entertaining and easy path, *through experience*, and a very dull one, through derivations from reason. Let me begin with the latter; once *it* has been completed, the *rest* will be all the more pleasant.

We behave towards *nature* (as appearance) either *passively* or *actively* or as *both* passive and active. *Passively* if we merely *experience* nature's effects; *actively*, if *we* determine its effects; *both at once*, if we *represent* nature to ourselves.

There are two ways of representing appearances. We are either intentionally directed towards their cognition; we *observe* [*beobachten*] them; or we allow things to invite us to represent them. We merely *watch* [*betrachten*] them.

When we *watch* appearances we are passive in that we receive impressions: *active*, in that we subject these impressions to our *forms of reason* (this is postulated from logic).

For appearances must appear to representation to accord with the formal conditions of representation (since it is this which makes them into *appearances*), they must come from us, the subject.

All representations are a manifold or matter; the way of connecting this manifold is its form. *Sense* [*Sinn*] provides the manifold; reason provides the connection (in the most extended sense), since reason is the power of connection.

If a manifold is given to the senses, reason attempts to give it its form, that is, to connect it according to laws.

The form of reason is the manner in which it manifests its connective power. There are two main manifestations of this connective power and as

---

[2] The German here is *Beurteilung*, which is sometimes translated as *estimation* in order to distinguish the kind of evaluative (aesthetic) judgement here at stake from cognitive judgement. While the difference is worth noting, since aesthetic judgement relates in dynamic ways to other kinds of judgement for Schiller and Kant, it seems appropriate to keep the word *judgement*.

many main forms of reason. Reason connects either representation with representation to gain knowledge (theoretical reason) or representation with the will in order to act (practical reason).

Just as there are two different forms of reason, there are two types of material for each of these forms. Theoretical reason applies its form to representations and these can be subdivided into immediate (intuitions) and mediated (concepts) types. The former are given through the senses, the latter are given by reason itself (although not without help from the senses). In the first, intuition, it is up to chance whether they agree with the form of reason; agreement is, however, necessary in concepts if they are not to negate [aufheben] each other. The latter therefore agree with their form, but the former are surprised if they find agreement.

The same goes for practical (acting) reason. It applies its form to action which can be subdivided into either free or unfree acts, acts either through or without reason. Practical reason demands from the first kind of acts the same thing theoretical reason demands from concepts. It is thus necessary that a free act agree with the form of practical reason; agreement of unfree action with this form is contingent.

One is thus correct in calling those representations which do not come from theoretical reason, and yet agree with its form, imitations of concepts. Acts which do not come from practical reason and still agree with its form are imitations of free actions; in short, one can call both types imitations (analoga) of reason.

A concept cannot be an imitation of reason, since it exists through reason and reason cannot imitate itself; it cannot be merely analogous to reason, it must be truly in accordance with reason. A willed act cannot be merely analogous to freedom, it must – or at least ought to – be truly free. A mechanical effect (any effect brought about by the laws of nature) on the other hand, can never be truly *free*, but can be judged to be merely analogous to freedom.

Let me allow you to rest for a moment, especially in order to draw your attention to the last paragraph, since I will probably be needing it to answer the objection I expect you will raise against my theory in what follows. I continue.

Theoretical reason aims at knowledge. By subsuming a given object under its form, it examines whether knowledge can be got from it, i.e., whether it can be connected with a representation we already have. The given representation is either a concept or an intuition. If it is a concept, it refers to reason already in its very origin, and the connection which already exists is merely expressed. A clock, for example, is such a representation. One evaluates it only according to the concept through which it has come about. Reason thus needs merely to discover that the given representation is a concept in order to decide whether it agrees with its form.

If the given representation is an intuition, however, and reason still wants to see the intuition agree with its form, then for the task to be accomplished, reason (regulative, not, as before, constitutive) must lend the given representation an origin in theoretical reason, in order to be able to judge it in terms of reason. Reason thus adduces an end of its own devising for the object and decides whether the object is adequate to that end. The former occurs in *teleological*, the latter in *logical* judgements of nature. The object of logical judgement is according to reason [*Vernunftmäßigkeit*]; the object of *teleological* judgement is similarity to reason [*Vernunftähnlichkeit*].

I imagine you *will be surprised* not to find the beautiful under the rubric of theoretical reason and that this will worry you a great deal. But I cannot help you, beauty can certainly not be found in theoretical reason since it is independent of concepts; and since beauty must still be counted in the *family of reason*, and practical reason is all there is besides theoretical reason, we will have to search and find beauty there. You will, I think, see from the following that this relationship will not cause you any problems.

Practical reason abstracts from all knowledge and has to do only with the determination of the will, with inner actions. Practical reason and determination of the will from mere reason, are one and the same. The *form* of practical reason is the immediate relation of the will to the representations of reason, that is, to the *exclusion of every external* principle of determination; for a will which is not determined purely by the form of practical reason is determined from outside, by what is material and heteronomous. To adapt or imitate the form of practical reason thus merely means not to be determined from the outside but from within, to be determined autonomously or to appear to be determined thus.

*Now, practical reason, just like theoretical reason, is capable of exerting its form on that which is through it (free actions), as well as on what is not through it (natural effects).

If practical reason applies its form to an act of will, it merely determines what it is; reason says whether the action is what it *wants* to be and *ought* to be. Every moral action is of this type. It is a product of pure will, that is, a will determined by mere form, and autonomously, and as soon as reason recognizes it as such, as soon as it knows that it is an action of a pure will, it becomes evident by itself that it accords with the form of practical reason, for it is fully identical with it.

If the object to which practical reason wishes to apply its form is not produced by the will or practical reason, practical reason acts just like theoretical reason acted with intuitions which appeared with similarity to reason. Reason lends the object (regulative and not, as with moral judgements, constitutive) a power to determine itself, a will, and then examines the object under the form of *that* will (not *its* will, since this would yield a moral judgement). Reason says of the object whether it is *what* it is, through *its pure will*, that is, through its self-determining power; for a pure *will* and the form of practical reason are one and the same.

Reason demands *imperatively* of acts of will, or moral acts, that they exist through the pure form of reason; reason can only wish (not demand) that natural effects be *through themselves*, that they show autonomy. (Let me here reiterate that practical reason absolutely cannot demand that the object be constituted through *it*, through practical reason; for then the object would not be constituted through *itself*, would not be autonomous but through something external, [since every determination of reason acts as external, as heteronomous to it] but through a foreign will.) *Pure self-determination* in general is the form of practical reason. When a rational being acts, it must act on the basis of *pure reason* if it is to show self-determination. If a mere natural being acts, it must act from *pure nature* if it is to show self-determination; for the self of the rational being is reason, while the self of the natural being is nature. If practical reason observes of a natural being that it determines itself, it ascribes to it (just as theoretical reason would, under similar circumstances, ascribe *similarity to the understanding [Vernunftfähigkeit]*) *similarity to freedom [Freiheitsähnlichkeit]* or just *freedom*. But since this freedom is merely lent to the object by reason, *since freedom as such can never be given to the senses and nothing can be free other than what is supra-sensible* – in short, it is all that matters here that the object *appears* as free not that it really is so; thus this analogy of the object with the form of practical reason is not freedom indeed but merely *freedom in appearance, autonomy in appearance.*

This gives rise to a fourfold of judgement and correspondingly a fourfold of classifications of represented appearances.

Judgement from concepts according to the form of knowledge is logical: judgement from intuitions according to this same form is teleological. A judgement of free effects (moral action) according to the form of a free will is moral; a judgement of unfree effects according to the form of the free will, is aesthetic. The *agreement* between a concept and a form of knowledge is in *accordance with the understanding* [*Vernunftmäßig*] (truth, purposiveness, perfection are merely terms for this), the analogy of an intuition with a form of knowledge is *similarity to the understanding* [*Vernunftfähigkeit*] (I would like to call them *Teleophanie, Logophanie*), the agreement of an action with the form of pure will is morality [*Sittlichkeit*]. The analogy of an appearance with the form of pure will or freedom is *beauty* (in its most general sense).

Beauty is thus nothing less than freedom in appearance.

Here I must stop since I wish you to receive this letter soon and eagerly await your answer. You will be able to surmise and extrapolate a great deal from what I have told you here. I will also be pleased if you hit upon a few results on your own. Please write me a prompt and elaborate response. I would happily give twenty Taler to speak with you for a few hours; surely our ideas would develop even better with a little friction. So long. My wife and sister-in-law send their greetings to you and yours. What do you say to these French events? I actually started a piece for the king, but I was not happy with it and so it just lies here. I haven't been able to read a French paper for 14 days, that's how much these lowlifes disgust me. So long.

Your S.

Jena, the 18. February [Monday] 1793

I see from your letter, which I have just received, that I have only to correct misunderstandings, but no actual misgivings, about my account of the beautiful and I will probably be able to clear up matters just by continuing my theory. Let me start by remarking only the following:

(1) My principle of beauty has, of course, been only subjective up to now since I have only been arguing from reason itself and have not discussed any objects yet. But it is no *more* subjective than all that can be got a priori out of reason. It goes without saying both that there must be something in the object itself which makes it possible to apply the principle to it, and that *I* have the obligation to show this. But that this something (the being-determined-through-itself of the thing) must be noticed by

reason, and is moreover noticed only by chance, this stems necessarily from the essence of reason, and to this extent, it can only be explained subjectively. I do, however, hope to show adequately that beauty is an objective quality.

(2) I must remark that *to give a concept of beauty* and *to be moved by beauty* are two completely different things. I would never think of denying that a concept of beauty could be given, since I myself am giving one, but with Kant, I deny that beauty pleases through a concept. To please through a concept presupposes the existence of the concept before the feeling of pleasure arises in the mind [*Gemüt*], just as is the case with perfection, truth and morality; although the presupposition of these three objects does not appear with the same level of clarity. The fact that our pleasure in beauty does not depend on a pre-existing concept is made clear by the fact that we are still searching for one.

(3) You say that beauty cannot be deduced from morality but that both must be deduced from a common, higher principle. I did not expect this objection after what I just said, since I am so far away from deducing beauty from morality that I almost consider the two incompatible. Morality is determination through pure reason, beauty, as a quality of *appearances*, is determination through pure nature. Determination through reason, perceived as an appearance, is rather the negation of beauty, since the determination by reason of a product that appears is true heteronomy.

The higher principle which you demand has been found and had been presented irrefutably. It subsumes beauty and morality under it, just as you require. This principle is none other than existence out of pure form. I cannot get bogged down in its explication at this point – it will become abundantly clear from my theory. Let me just note that you must free yourself from all lesser ideas with which the religiously oriented thinkers of moral philosophy or the poor amateurs, who meddle with the Kantian philosophy, try to disfigure the discussion of morality; only then will you recognize that all of your ideas, such as I have been able to gather from your previous remarks, are in even greater agreement with the Kantian principles of morality than you might have supposed. It is certain that *no* mortal has spoken a greater word than this Kantian word, which also encapsulates his whole philosophy: determine yourself from within yourself. The same goes for theoretical philosophy: nature stands under the laws of the understanding. This great idea of self-determination resonates back at us from certain appearances of nature, and we call it *beauty*. I will now rely on my good cause and continue with the already begun discussion, and I will be satisfied if you find it at least half as enjoyable to read as I find it enjoyable debating you.

Thus there is a view of nature, or of appearances, in which we demand nothing other than freedom from them and where our only concern is that they be what they are through themselves. This type of judgement is only important and possible through practical reason, since the concept of freedom cannot be found in theoretical reason and since autonomy is the overriding quality only of practical reason. Practical reason, applied to free action, demands that the action be performed only for the sake of the type of action (form) and that the action be influenced neither by matter nor end (which is always matter). If an object appears in the sense-world as determined only by itself, it will appear to the senses such that one cannot detect the influence of matter or purpose, it will thus be judged to be an *analogy* of the pure determination of the will (but not as a product of the will). Since only a will which can determine itself according to mere form can be called *free*, such a form in the sense-world which appears merely through itself, is an *exhibition of freedom*; and an exhibition of an idea is something which is connected with intuition in such a way that they share *one* rule of knowledge.

Freedom in appearance is thus nothing but the self-determination of a thing insofar as it is available to intuition. One sets it against every outside determination, just as one sets moral action against every determination of material reasons. An object seems less free, however, as soon as one *discovers* its determination in form which comes either from a physical power or from intelligible ends; for now the determination lies not in *the object* but outside of it, and it is no more *beautiful* than an *action with an end* is moral.

If the judgement of taste is to be absolutely pure, one must completely abstract from it the intrinsic (practical or theoretical) worth of the beautiful object, out of what matter it is formed and what purpose it might serve. May it be what it will! As soon as we make an aesthetic judgement of it, we only want to know if it is what it is through itself. We are so little concerned with its logical constitution that we even ascribe its 'independence from ends and rules as the highest attribute'. – Not as though purposefulness and regularity were incompatible with the beautiful in themselves; every beautiful object must subject itself to rules: but rather because the *visible* influences of the end and of a rule appear as constraints and bring along heteronomy in the object. The beautiful object may, and even must, be rule-governed, but it must *appear* as *free of rules.*

However, no object in nature and even less so in art is free of constraint and rules, *none is determined through itself*, as soon as we reflect on it [*nachdenken*]. Each exists through another, each exists for another, none has autonomy. The only existing thing which determines itself and exists for itself must be sought outside of appearances in the intelligible world. Beauty, however, resides only in the field of appearances and there can be no hope to find freedom in the sense-world either by theoretical reason or by contemplation [*nachdenken*].

But everything changes if one leaves theoretical investigation aside and takes the objects only *as they appear*. A rule or a purpose can never *appear* since they are concepts and not intuitions. The real ground [*Realgrund*] of the possibility of an object thus never lies in the field of the senses and is as good as absent 'as soon as the understanding is not incited to search it out'. Judging an object as free in appearance depends simply on completely abstracting it from its grounds of determination (since not-being-determined-from-the-outside is a negative representation of being-determined-through-oneself, which is its only possible representation, because one can only think freedom and not recognize it, and even the philosopher of morals must make do with this negative representation of freedom). Thus a form appears as free as soon as we are *neither able nor inclined* to search for its ground outside it. For if reason were compelled to look for the object's ground, it would *necessarily* have to find it outside of the thing; it is determined either by a *concept* or by an accidental determination, both of which are heteronomous for the object. It is thus a tenable principle that an object presents itself as free in appearance, if its form does not compel reflective understanding [*reflektierender Verstand*] to seek out a ground for it. A form is therefore beautiful only if it explains itself; explaining itself here means to explain itself without the help of a concept. A triangle explains itself but only through the mediation of a concept. A curving line explains itself without the mediation of a concept.

A form is beautiful, one might say, if it *demands no explanation*, or if it *explains itself without a concept.*

I imagine that some of your doubts will have been dispelled, at least you can see that the subjective principle can be led over into the objective. New light will be shed when we finally come to the field of experience, and only then will you rightly understand the autonomy of the sense-world. But let me continue:

Every form which we find possible only under the presupposition of a concept shows heteronomy in appearance. For every concept is something external to the object. Strict regularity is such a form (the highest manifestation of it being mathematical) because it *forces* upon us the concept from which it originates: strict purposefulness (especially *usefulness*, since it always refers to something else) is such a form because it recalls the purpose and use of the objects to us, thereby necessarily destroying the autonomy of appearance.

Supposing we undertake a moral project with an object – the form of the object will be determined by the idea of practical reason, not by itself, and will thus become heteronomous. This is why the moral purpose of a work of art or an action contributes so little to its beauty that these moral purposes are best hidden, and must appear to come from the nature of the thing completely freely and without force, if their beauty is not to be lost. Thus a poet may not excuse the lack of beauty in his work by its moral intentions. Beauty always refers to practical reason because freedom cannot be a concept of theoretical reason, since it refers merely to the *form* and not the material. A moral *end* belongs to either substance [*Materie*] or content, and not to mere form. To highlight this difference, which seems to have provoked your objection, I will add this: practical reason requires self-determination. Self-determination of the rational is pure determination of reason, morality; self-determination of the sense-world is pure determination of nature, beauty. When the form of the non-reasonable [*nicht-vernünftig*] is determined by reason (theoretical or practical, both are the same here), its natural determination is constrained and beauty cannot arise. In this case [the outcome] is a *product*, not an *analogy*, an effect not an imitation of reason, since the imitation of a thing requires that the imitator and the imitated have in common merely form but not content, not matter.

This is why moral conduct, if it is not at once related to taste, will always appear to be heteronomous exactly because it is a product of the autonomous will. Since *reason* and *sensibility* have different wills, the will of sensibility is broken when reason insists on its will. Unhappily, however, it is the will of sensibility which falls to the senses; just at the point that reason exercises its autonomy (which can never occur in appearance) its eye is insulted by heteronomy in appearance. But the concept of beauty is also wrongly applied to morality, for this application is here empty. *Moral beauty* is a concept to which something [must] correspond in experience even though beauty only exists in appearance. There is no better empirical proof of the truth of my theory of beauty than to show you that even the wrong use of this word only occurs in cases in which freedom shows itself in appearance. I will thus jump ahead to the empirical part of my theory, although this is contrary to my plans, and let you rest a little while I tell you a story.

'A man has happened upon some robbers who have undressed him and have thrown him out onto the street in the bitter cold.

'A traveller passes by to whom he complains of his lot and whom he begs for help. "I suffer with you", says the moved traveller, "and I will gladly give you what I have. I only request that you do not ask for any of my services, since your appearance revolts me. Here come some people, give them this purse and they will help you." – "That is well meant", said the wounded man, "but one must also be able to *see* the suffering if duty to humanity [*Menschenpflicht*] requires it. Reaching for your purse is not worth half as much as doing a little violence to your tender senses."'

What was this action? It was neither useful, morally generous nor beautiful. It was merely impulsive, kind-hearted out of affect.

'A second traveller appears and the wounded man renews his plea. This second man does not want to part with his money but still wants to fulfil his duty to humanity. "I will lose making a guilder if I spend time with you." he says. "If you will compensate me for the time I spend with you, I will load you onto my shoulders and carry you to a monastery which is only an hour away." – "That is a clever answer", the other says. "But one must say that readiness to help does not well become you. I see a courier over there who will give me the help for free that you wanted a guilder for."'

And what was this action? It was neither generous nor dutiful, neither magnanimous nor beautiful. It was merely useful.

'The third traveller stands silently as the wounded man repeats the story of his misfortune. After the story has been told the man stands there contemplatively and battling with himself. "It will be difficult for me", he says at last, "to separate myself from my coat, which is the only protection for my sick body, and to leave you my horse since my powers are at an end. But duty commands that I serve you. Get onto my horse and wrap yourself in my coat and I will lead you to a place where you will find help." – "I thank you, good man, for your honest opinion", the other replies, "but you shall not suffer on my behalf since you yourself are in need. Over there I see two strong men who will provide the help that you could not readily furnish."'

This action was *purely moral* (but also no more than that), because it occurred against the interests of the senses, out of pure respect for the law.

'Now the two men approach the wounded man and start asking him about his misfortune. No sooner has he opened his mouth than both shout with surprise: "It's him! It's the one we are looking for." The wounded man recognizes them and becomes afraid. It is revealed that both recognize in him a sworn enemy and the originator of their own misfortunes, and have travelled after him to revenge themselves on him violently. "So satisfy your hatred and take your revenge", the wounded man says, "I expect only death and not help from you." – "No", responds one of them, "so that you see who *we* are and who *you* are, take these clothes and cover yourself. We will pull you up between us and take you to a place where you will find help." – "Generous enemy", calls the wounded man full of remorse, "you shame me and disarm my hatred: come embrace me and complete your charity by forgiving me." – "Calm yourself, friend", the other responds frostily, "I help you not because I forgive you but because you are wretched." – "So take back your clothes", calls the unhappy man, as he throws them from himself. "May become of me what will. I would rather die a miserable death than to owe such an enemy my life."'

'As he gets up and tries to move away, he sees a fifth traveller who is carrying a heavy load approaching. "I have been deceived so many times", he thinks to himself, "and this one does not seem like someone who would help me. I will let him pass." As soon as the wanderer sees him, he lays down his load. "I see", he says of his own accord, "that you are wounded and tired. The next village is far and you will bleed to death ere you arrive there. Climb onto my back and I will take you there." – "But what will become of your load which you leave here on the open road?" – "That I don't know, and it concerns me little", says the carrier. "I do know, however, that you need help and that I am obliged to give it to you."'

Greetings from all of us here. In the meantime, think about why the action of the carrier was *beautiful*.

Your S.

the 19. February 1793

I can add a few more lines to yesterday's letter and do not want to owe you the *fabula docet* [the moral of the tale] of yesterday's story.

The beauty of the fifth action must lie in that characteristic which sets it apart from all the previous ones.

(1) All five wanted to help; (2) most of them chose an adequate means for the job; (3) several of them were willing to have it cost them something; (4) some overcome their own self-interest in order to help. One of them acted out of purest moral purpose. But only the fifth acted *without solicitation*, without considering the action, and disregarding the cost to himself. Only the fifth forgot himself in his action and 'fulfilled his duty with the ease of someone acting out of mere instinct'. – Thus, a moral action would be a beautiful action only if it appears as an immediate [*sich selbst ergebenden*] outcome of nature. In a word: a free action is a beautiful action, if the autonomy of the mind and autonomy of appearance coincide.

For this reason the highest perfection of character in a person is moral beauty brought about by the fact that *duty has become its nature*.

Clearly the violence against our drives which practical reason brings to bear on our moral determination of will appears as something insulting and embarrassing. We never want to see coercion, even if it is reason itself which exercises it; we want even nature's freedom to be respected because 'we regard every being in aesthetic judgement as an end in itself' and it disgusts (outrages) us, for whom freedom is the highest thing, that something should be sacrificed for something else, and used as a means. That is why a moral action can never be beautiful if we observe the operation through which it is won from the sensory-world. Our sensory nature must thus appear free, where morality is concerned, although it is really not free, and it must appear as if nature were merely fulfilling the commission of our drives by subjugating itself to the mastery of the pure will, at the expense of its own drives.

You can see from this little sample that my theory of beauty will hardly be threatened by experience. I challenge you to find a single theory among explanations of beauty, Kant's theory included, which resolves the problem of the wrong use of [the term] beauty as well as I hope to have done here.

Write to me again as soon as you can. In eight days I will let another such load loose on you.

Your S.

Jena, the 23. February [Sunday] 1793

The result of the previous demonstrations is this: there is a way of representing things which looks only for freedom and abstracts from all else, that is, whether the object appears as self-determined. This way of representation is necessary since it comes from the nature of reason, the practical use of which constantly demands autonomy in determination.

I have not yet shown that the quality of things which we call beauty is one and the same with this freedom in appearance; and this shall be my task from now on. I must show two things: *first*, that the objective fact about things which enables them to appear free is the very same which enables them, if it is present at all, to appear beautiful, and if it is not present, destroys their beauty; even if they posses no other advantageous qualities [*Vorzüge*] in the former case, and if they possess all other such qualities in the latter case. *Second*, I must show that freedom in appearance necessarily carries with it such an effect on our capacity for emotion which is the same as the emotions we feel when experiencing a representation of the beautiful. (Although it seems to be a hopeless project to prove the latter point a priori since only experience can teach us whether and how we should feel something during a given experience. For clearly the existence of such a feeling cannot analytically be got out of either the concept of freedom or the appearance of such a feeling, nor indeed can a synthesis a priori be derived thus; one is thus restricted to empirical proofs and I hope to accomplish whatever can be accomplished: namely to show by induction and by psychological means that a feeling of pleasure [*Wohlgefallen*] must flow from the combined concept of freedom and appearance, the harmony between reason and sense, which is the same as pleasure and which regularly accompanies the representation of beauty.) Let me note that I will not come to this latter part for a while, since the explication of the former should fill up several letters.

Freedom of appearance is one with beauty

I mentioned just recently that *freedom* does not really attach to any object in the sense-world, though it may appear to do so. But it may not even *appear* to be positively free since this is merely an idea of reason to which no intuition can be adequate. But how can we seek an objective ground of this representation in things, insofar as they appear, if they neither possess nor show freedom? The objective reason must be constituted such that its representation simply necessitates us to produce the idea of freedom from within ourselves, and to apply it to the object. This is what must be shown now.

It is the same thing to be free and to be determined through oneself and from within oneself. Every determination occurs either from the outside or not from the outside (from the inside) – that which is not determined from the outside and yet appears as determined must be represented as determined from the inside. '*But as soon as determination is thought*, not-being-determined-from-the-outside indirectly becomes the representation of being-determined-from-the-inside or of freedom.'

Now how is this not-being-determined-from-the-outside represented in turn? Everything depends on this: if this is not necessarily represented as pertaining to an object, then there is no reason to represent being-determined-from-the-inside or freedom. The representation of the latter must be *necessary* however, because our judgement of the beautiful contains necessity and *demands* everyone's agreement. It thus cannot be left to chance whether we take freedom into consideration in representing an object, but the representation of the object must necessarily include the representation of not-being-determined-from-the-outside.

This requires that the thing itself, in its objective constitution, invites us, or rather requires us to notice its quality of not-being-determined-from-the-outside; this is because a mere negation can only be recognized *if a need for its positive opposite is presupposed.*

A need for the representation of the being-determined-from-the-inside (ground of determination) can only come to be through the representation of *determination*. Though it is true that everything that we represent is determinate, not everything is represented as such and what is not represented scarcely exists for us at all. Since the object which says nothing is almost the same as nothing, something must lift the object out of the endless succession of non-saying and empty objects and pique our cognitive drive. It must show itself as something *determinate*, since it must lead us to something determining.

Since the understanding is the faculty which searches out the ground of an effect, the understanding must be put into play. The understanding must be spurred to reflect upon the form of the object: merely about the *form*, for understanding has only to do with form.

The object must possess and show a form which permits a rule to be applied to it; for the understanding can conduct its business only according to rules. It is, however, not necessary that the understanding *recognize* the rule (since recognizing the rule would destroy all semblance of freedom, as is indeed the case with every strict regularity), it is sufficient that the understanding be led to a rule – no matter which one. One need examine only a single leaf to be made instantly aware of the impossibility that the manifold can organize itself from nowhere and without rules, even if one abstracts from teleological judgement. Immediate reflection at its sight teaches us, without it even being necessary, to recognize this rule and to create a concept of its structure for oneself.

A form which points to a rule (which can be treated according to a rule) is art-like or *technical*. Only the technical form of an object compels the understanding to search out the ground of an effect and the relationship between determining and determined; and insofar as this form awakens a need to ask about the ground for determination, the negation of the *being-determined-from-the-outside* necessarily leads to the representation of *being-determined-from-the-inside* or freedom.

Just as freedom of will can only be thought with the help of causal and material determinations of will, freedom can only be exhibited sensuously with the help of technique. In other words: the negative concept of freedom is only conceivable through the positive concept of its opposite, and just as a representation of natural causality is necessary to lead us to a representation of freedom of will, a representation of technique is necessary to lift us from the realm of appearances to freedom.

Here we come to a second principle of beauty, without which the first would remain an empty concept. Freedom of appearance may be the ground of freedom, but *technique* is the necessary condition for our *representation* of freedom.

One could also express it in this way:
The ground of freedom is everywhere freedom in appearance.
The ground of our representation of beauty is technique in freedom.

If one unites both the foundations of beauty and the representation of beauty, this explanation arises:

Beauty is nature in artfulness [*Kunstmäßigkeit*].

Before I can make a secure and philosophical use of this explanation, I must determine the concept of *nature* and guard it from being misunderstood. I prefer the term *nature* to that of *freedom* because it connotes both the realm of the senses, to which beauty is limited, and the concept of *freedom* as well as its intimation in its sphere in the sense-world. Set against technique, *nature* is what is through itself and *art* is what is through a rule. *Nature in artfulness* is what gives itself the rule – what is through its own rule. (Freedom in the rule, the rule in freedom.)

When I say: *the nature of a thing: the thing follows its nature, it determines itself through its nature*, I am contrasting nature with all that is different from the object, what is regarded as merely coincidental and can be abstracted without negating its essence. It is as it were the person of the thing through which it is distinguished from other things which are not of its kind. That is why those qualities which an object shares with all other objects, even though it cannot do without these qualities without ceasing to exist, are not considered part of its nature. Only that which makes the determinate object become what it is, is designated by the term *nature*. For example, all objects are heavy, but we count only that heaviness to an object's nature which brings about the specificity of the object. As soon as gravity acts on an object in itself and independently of any specific constitution of the object, functioning rather as a *general force* of nature, gravity is seen as a foreign power and its effects are seen as heteronomous to the nature of the thing. An example will clarify this. A vase, considered as an object, is subject to gravity, but the effects of gravity must, if it is not to deny the *nature of the vase*, be modified, i.e. specifically determined and made necessary through its specific form. Every effect of gravity on the vase is contingent and can thus be abstracted from the vase without losing the essence of the form of the vase. Thus gravity functions outside of the economy, outside of the nature of the thing, and appears as an alien force. This occurs when the vase *ends* in a broad belly, because here it seems as if gravity had reduced the length of the vase and instead had given it breadth, in short, it seems as if gravity had prevailed over form and not form over gravity.

The same goes for movement. A movement belongs to the *nature* of the thing if it necessarily comes from the specific constitution or from the form of the thing. A movement, however, which is prescribed to the object, independently of its specific form, by the general rule of gravity, lies outside of its nature and consequently shows itself as heteronomy. Place a workhorse next to a light Spanish palfrey. The weight which the former has become accustomed to pulling has so robbed it of its natural movement that it trots just as tiredly and clumsily as if it were still pulling a wagon, even when it is not pulling one. Its movement no longer springs from its nature but rather reveals the pulled weight of the wagon. The light palfrey in contrast has never become accustomed to exerting greater effort than it feels like exerting in its most perfect freedom. Each of its movements is an effect of its nature that has been left to itself. This is why it moves over so lightly, as if it weighed nothing at all, the same area over which the workhorse moves as if it had feet of lead. 'The specific form of the horse has overcome the nature of bodies, which must follow the rules of gravity, to such an extent that one is not reminded that it is a *body* at all.' The clumsy movement of the workhorse, however, instantly conjures in us the representation of mass and the *particular* nature of the horse is dominated by the *general* nature of its body.

If one casts an eye onto the kingdom of animals one sees that the beauty of animals decreases with the degree to which they become more mass-like and seem only to serve gravity. The nature of an animal (in aesthetic terms) appears either in its movements or in its form, both of which are constrained by mass. If mass has influenced the form, we call it plump; if the mass has influenced movement, we call it awkward. Mass plays a visible role in the form as well as in the movement of the construction of the elephant, the bear, the bull, etc. Mass is at all times beholden to gravity which has an alien potential with respect to the organic body's *own* nature.

We perceive everything to be beautiful, however, in which *mass is completely dominated by form* (in the animal and plant kingdom) and by living forces (in the autonomy of the organic).

Clearly the mass of a horse is of unequal weight compared to the mass of a duck or a crab; nevertheless, the duck is heavy and the horse is light; this is simply because the living forces of each have different relationships to mass. In the former case, it is matter which dominates force; in the latter case, it is force which is the master of matter.

In the animal kingdom it is the birds which are the best proof of my claim. A bird in flight is the happiest depiction of matter dominated by form, of power overcoming weight. It is not unimportant to note that the ability to overcome heaviness is often used as the symbol of freedom. We express freedom of the imagination by giving it wings; when we want to describe Psyche's freedom from the bonds of matter, we let her soar above the world with the wings of a butterfly. Clearly gravity is the bond of every organic being and a victory over it is thus considered a good depiction of freedom. Now, there is no better depiction of something conquering gravity than a winged animal whose inner life (autonomy of the organic) determines itself by its opposition to gravity. The relationship of gravity to the living power of the bird is about the same as – in a pure determination of the will – inclination is related to law-giving reason.

I will resist the temptation to further illustrate the truth of my claims with reference to human beauty; this matter deserves its own letter. You can see from what I have said so far what I consider to be part of the concept of *nature* (in its aesthetic meaning) and what I consider to be outside of it.

The nature of a technical thing, insofar as we set it against the non-technical, is the technical form itself against which we consider as heteronomous and violent everything which does not belong to this technical economy, and which is external, and which has influence upon the thing: but this is not yet to say that a thing which is determined by its technique is purely technical; for this also goes for every strict mathematical figure which, nonetheless, may not be beautiful.

The technique itself must again appear as determined by the nature of the thing, which one can call the free consent of the thing to its technique. Here the nature of the thing is again distinguished from its technique, though it has just been declared identical to it. But this is only apparently a contradiction. The technical form of the thing behaves towards external determinations as nature; but it can behave as something external or foreign towards the inner essence of the thing in its technical form; for example, it is the nature of a circle that it is a line which, at each point, keeps the same distance from a given point. Now, if a gardener wants to cut a tree into a circular figure, the nature of the circle demands that the tree be cut completely round. As soon as a circular figure is *announced*, it must be completed, and it insults our eyes if the circle is not carried out perfectly. But the demands of the nature of circles and the nature of the tree are at odds with each other, and since we cannot help but respect the personality of the tree, we suffer at the violence inflicted upon it, and it pleases us when the external technique is destroyed by the tree's inner freedom. Technique is something foreign wherever it does not arise from the thing itself, is not one with the whole existence of the thing, does not come from it, but comes to it from the outside, is not necessary and innate in the thing, but is merely given or is accidental.

One more example will help us see eye to eye. The musical instrument a skilled craftsman makes may be purely technical but still may not lay claim to beauty. It is purely technical if everything is form, if it is everywhere the concept and not matter, or if it is a lack on the part of his art which determines the form. One might also say that this instrument has autonomy; one could say this as soon as one places the αυτον[3] into thought, which is completely and purely law-giving and which has dominated matter. But if one places the instrument's αυτον into what is its nature and that through which it exists, the judgement shifts. Its technique is recognized as something foreign, something independent of its *existence*, coincidental, and is thus regarded as outside violence. It becomes clear that this technical form is something external, that this technical form has been violently imposed by the artist's understanding. Although, as we have supposed, the technical form of the instrument *contains* and expresses pure autonomy, the form is itself still heteronomous towards the object in which it finds this autonomy. Although the form suffers *coercion* neither from the side of the material nor from the side of the artist, it nonetheless *exerts* coercion on the very nature of the thing as soon as we regard it as a natural thing which is compelled to serve a logical thing (a concept).

What would nature be in this sense? The inner principle of the existence of a thing, which can be at the same time seen as the ground of its form: *the inner necessity of form.* The form must, in the true sense of the word, be self-determining and self-determined; it needs not merely autonomy, but also heautonomy.[4] But, you will object, if form and the existence of the thing must be one in order to produce beauty, what becomes of beauty in art, which can never have this heautonomy? I will answer you only once we have arrived at a discussion of beauty in art, for this requires its own chapter. I can only tell you this much in advance, that art is not independent of these requirements, and that the forms of art and the existence of the formed object must become *one* if they are to lay claim to the highest beauty: and because they cannot in reality accomplish this,

---

[3] Schiller is probably here using the Greek root of autonomy to signify the independent idea of the instrument, hence its nature.

[4] In the *Critique of Judgement* Kant employs the concept of *heautonomy* in place of autonomy with respect to reflective judgement's adoption of a principle of reflection – that we assume that nature is coherently ordered through a hierarchical system of genus and species – which cannot be regarded as truly determinative of nature. Hence, heautonomy refers to a necessary self-determination of the power of judgement in its relation to nature which is nonetheless merely subjective since it is not legislative for nature. Schiller is using the term in an analogous way: nature's artfulness involves the necessary ascription of 'technique' (as the ground of form) to the object which does not belong in actuality to it. The heautonomy of the object is its appearing autonomy.

since the human form is always incidental to marble, this means that the artworks must at least appear to be one.

What then, is nature in artfulness? Autonomy in technique? It is the pure coincidence of the inner essence with form, *a rule, which is at once given and obeyed by the thing.* (The beautiful is merely a symbol of the completed and perfect, because it does not, as does the purposeful, require anything outside itself, but commands and obeys itself for the sake of its own law.) I hope that I have put you in a position to follow me without difficulty when I speak of nature, of self-determination, of autonomy and heautonomy, of freedom and of artfulness. I hope you will also agree with me that nature and heautonomy are objective characteristics of the objects which I have been describing, for they remain, even if they have been abstracted from by the thinking subject. The difference between two beings of nature where one of them is pure form and perfect domination of living power over mass and where the other is dominated by the mass, remains even after all judgement by the subject has been taken away. In this same way the difference between a technique through the understanding and technique through nature (as in everything organic) is completely independent of the existence of a rational subject. The difference is objective, and it is thus the concept of nature in technique which bases itself on this very difference.

Of course reason is necessary to make such use of the objective qualities of things as is necessary in the case of beauty. But the subjectivity of this use does not negate the objectivity of this ground, for even the perfect, the good and the useful are constituted such that their objectivity rests on much the same basis. 'Of course the concept of freedom itself or the *positive* aspect of reason are only placed into the object by considering the object under the form of the will, but reason does not give the *negative* aspect of the concept to the object since it finds it already present. The ground of the object's already granted freedom thus does lie in *it* itself, although *freedom* lies only in reason.'

Kant makes a claim in the *Critique of Judgement* (p. 177[5]) which is immensely fecund and which, I think, will find its full explanation only in my theory. Kant says that nature is beautiful when it looks like art; art is beautiful when it looks like nature. This claim turns technique

---

[5] *Critique of Judgement*, tr. Werner S. Pluhar (Indianapolis: Hackett Publishing Company, 1987), p. 306: 'Nature, we say, is beautiful [*schön*] if it also looks like art: and art can be called fine [*schön*] art only if we are conscious that it is art while yet it looks to us like nature.'

into an essential prerequisite of natural beauty and turns freedom into an essential prerequisite of artistic beauty. But since artistic beauty already includes the idea of technique and since natural beauty includes the idea of freedom, Kant himself must admit that beauty is nothing but nature in technique and freedom in artfulness [*Kuntsmässiigkeit*].

First of all, we must know that the beautiful thing is a natural object, that is, that it is through itself; *secondly*, it must seem to us as if it existed through a rule, since Kant says that it must look like art. The two claims: *it is through itself* and *it is through a rule* can only be combined in a single manner, namely if one says: *it is through a rule which it has given itself.* Autonomy in technique, freedom in artfulness.

From the previous discussion it might seem as if *freedom* and *artfulness* had the same claim in pleasing that beauty instils in us, as if technique and freedom stood on the same level – I would then be quite wrong in explaining beauty (autonomy in appearance) by concentrating on freedom alone, without reference to technique. But my definition is well balanced. Technique and freedom do not have the same relationship to beauty. *Freedom* alone is the ground of beauty, technique is merely the ground for the representation of freedom, the former is thus the immediate ground, the latter only the mediating condition of beauty. Technique contributes to beauty only insofar as it serves to stimulate the representation of freedom.

Perhaps I can explicate this sentence further, although it should be quite clear from what went before.

Where natural beauty is concerned, we can see with our own eyes that it stems from itself; understanding, not our senses, however, tells us that it comes from a rule. Now, the rule is towards nature as coercion is to freedom. But since we only *think* the rule but *see* nature, we think coercion and see freedom. The understanding expects and demands a rule, the senses teach us that the thing is through itself and not through any rule. If we were concerned with technique, its failure would disappoint our expectation, rather than give rise to pleasure. Therefore, we must be interested in freedom rather than in technique. We expected to find heteronomy in the logical form of the thing, but to our surprise found autonomy. The fact that we are pleased with this discovery and that our worry (which has its seat in our practical powers) is assuaged, proves that we do not gain as much through regularity as through freedom. It is merely a need of our theoretical reason to think of the form of the thing as dependent on rules; but that it is not through a rule, but through itself is a fact for our senses. How can we ascribe aesthetic value to technique and still derive pleasure from perceiving its opposite? The representation of technique, then, serves merely to recall the independence of the products from technique in our mind and to make freedom all the more attractive.

This leads me automatically to the difference between the beautiful and the perfect. Everything perfect, except the absolutely perfect, the moral, is contained under the concept of technique, since it is constituted by the accordance of the manifold and the one. Since technique contributes to beauty only through mediation, insofar as it draws attention to freedom, but the perfect is contained under the concept of technique, one can see right away that it is merely *freedom in technique* which distinguishes the beautiful from the perfect. The perfect can have autonomy insofar as its form is purely determined by its concept; but heautonomy is possible only in beauty, since only its form is determined by its inner essence.

When the perfect is shown with freedom it is instantly transformed into the beautiful. It is shown with freedom, if the nature of the thing appears as coinciding with its technique, if it appears as if technique flowed freely out of the thing itself. One might express what came before simply thus: an object is perfect if everything manifold in it coincides with the unity of its concept; it is beautiful when its perfection appears as nature. Beauty grows when perfection is assembled and nature does not suffer thereby; for the task of freedom becomes more difficult as the number of relations grow and hence its happy solution surprises all the more.

Purposefulness, order, proportion, perfection – all are qualities in which one thought one had found beauty – have nothing to do with it. But where order, proportion, etc. belong to the *nature* of the object, as is the case with everything organic, they are *eo ipso* untouchable, not for their own sake, but because they are inseparable from the nature of the thing. A crude injury of proportion is ugly, but not because observing proportion is beautiful. Not at all, but rather because it indicates an injury to nature, and thus heteronomy. I must note in general that the whole error of those who seek to derive beauty from proportion or perfection is due to this point; they found that injury to order or perfection makes the object ugly and concluded, against all logic, that beauty is contained in the close observation of these qualities. But all of these qualities are merely the *material* of beauty which can change in every object; they can belong to the truth which, however, is just the material of beauty. The form of beauty is a loose [*freier*] contract between truth, purposefulness and perfection.

We call a building perfect if all of its parts are purely determined according to its concept and the purpose of the whole, and when its *form* is determined by the idea. But we call it beautiful, if we do not need to be helped by the idea to see the form, if the form is free and purposeless and comes from itself, and all the parts seem to limit themselves from within themselves. This is why, by the way, a building can never be a completely free work of art, and can never achieve the ideal of beauty – it is completely impossible to regard a building that needs stairs, doors, chimneys, windows and stoves without making use of a concept and thus invoking heteronomy. Only artistic beauty, whose original can be found in nature, is completely pure.

A pot is beautiful if it resembles the free play of nature without contradicting its concept. The handle of a pot is caused merely by its use and thus its concept; if the pot is to be beautiful, its handle must spring from it so unforced and freely that one forgets its purpose [*Bestimmung*]. But if the body were suddenly to make a right angle and if the wide body were suddenly to turn into a narrow neck, and so forth, this abrupt change of direction would destroy all semblance of beauty and the autonomy of appearance would disappear.

When does one say that a person is well dressed? When freedom suffers neither through the clothes on the body nor the body through the clothes; if the clothes look like they have nothing in common with the body and still fulfil their purpose completely. Beauty, or rather taste, regards all things as *ends in themselves* and will not permit one to serve as the purpose of another, or to be under its control. Everyone is a free citizen and has the same rights as the most noble in the world of aesthetics, coercion may not take place even *for the sake of the whole* – everyone must *consent*. In this aesthetic world, which is quite different from the most perfect Platonic republic, even the gown I wear on my body demands respect for its freedom from me, much like a humble servant who demands that I never let on that he is *serving* me. In exchange, it promises to use its freedom in such a way that it will not curtail my own freedom; and if both keep their word, the world will say that I am well dressed. But if the gown *pulls*, both it and I lose some of our freedom. That is why both *very tight* and *very loose* clothes are not beautiful – for even leaving aside the point that both constrain movement, tight-fitting clothes show the body only at the expense of the clothes and loose clothes hide the shape of the body by blowing themselves up and reducing their master to a mere carrier.

A birch, a pine, a poplar are beautiful if they grow straight up, while an oak is beautiful if it bends; the reason for this is that the latter bends naturally if it is left to itself, while the former all grow straight up. If the oak grows straight up and the birch bends, neither are considered beautiful, since the direction they grow reveals foreign influence, heteronomy. Then again, we find the poplar bending in the wind beautiful because its swaying manner reveals its freedom.

Which tree will the artist seek out and most prefer to use in his landscapes? Surely the one which makes use of the freedom which is given to it despite the technique of its structure – the one which does not slavishly follow its neighbour's wishes but daringly searches something out, steps out of order, and turns this direction or that out of its own will, even if it leaves a gap here or there, or confuses things through its untamed entry. But the artist will pass up that tree in indifference which always remains turned in one direction, even if its species has granted it more freedom, whose branches remain in order as if they had been pulled thus by a string.

It is necessary for every great composition that the particular restrict itself to let the whole reach its effect. If this restriction by the particular is at once the effect of its freedom, that is, if it posits the whole itself, the composition is beautiful. Beauty is power limited through itself; restriction of power.

A landscape is beautifully composed if all of the particular parts out of which it is constituted play along together so well that they set their own limitations, and the whole becomes the result of the freedom of the particular parts. Everything in a landscape must refer to the whole and yet the particular should only be constrained by its own rule, should only seem to follow its own will. But it is impossible that the process of cohering to a whole should not require some sacrifices on the part of the particular, since a collision of freedoms is unavoidable. The mountain will want to cast a shadow on much that one would prefer to have illuminated. Buildings will limit natural freedom, they will obscure the view; branches will be bothersome neighbours; humans, animals, clouds will want to move since the freedom of living things expresses itself in action. The river does not want the shore to rule its direction, but wants to follow its own; in short: each particular wants to follow its own will. But what becomes of the harmony of the whole if each only looks out for itself? Freedom comes about because each restricts its inner freedom such as to allow every other to express *its* freedom. A tree in the foreground might cover a nice spot in the background; to *require* of the tree that it not do this would come too close to its freedom and would reveal dilettantism. What does the able artist do? He allows that branch of the tree which threatens to cover the background to sink down *under its own weight* and thus freely make place for the view behind it; thus the tree fulfils the will of the artist by following its own.

A versification is beautiful if each verse gives itself its length and shortness, its motion and its pause, if each rhyme comes from inner necessity and yet comes at just the right moment – in short, when no word or verse seems to take notice of the other, seems merely to be present for its own sake but comes as if on cue.

Why is the naïve beautiful? Because nature is in the right against artistic creating and representation. When Virgil wants to let us glance into Dido's heart to see how her love is progressing, he, as the narrator, could have done so quite well in his own name; but then this depiction would not have been beautiful. But if he chooses to allow us to make this same discovery through Dido herself, without her intending to be so open with us (see the conversation between Anna and Dido at the beginning of the fourth book), we call this truly beautiful; for it is nature itself which spills its secret.

The style of teaching wherein one progresses from the known to the unknown is good; it is beautiful if it progresses Socratically, that is, if the same truth is elicited from the head and the heart of the listener. In the former convictions are formally *demanded* by the understanding, while in the latter they are *elicited*.

Why is the curving line considered the most beautiful? I have tested my theory on this, the simplest of all aesthetic tasks and consider the trial to be decisive because there is no room for deception through auxiliary causes.

A follower of Baumgarten will say that the curving line is the most beautiful because it is the most perfect to the senses. It is a line which always changes direction (manifold) and always returns to the same direction (unity). But if it were beautiful for no other reason the following line would also have to be beautiful:

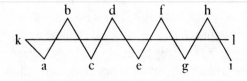

which is certainly not beautiful. Here too there is a change in direction; a manifold, namely a, b, c, d, e, f, g, h, i; there is also a unity of direction which reason adds to it and which is represented by the line k l. This line is not beautiful even though it is perfect to the senses.

The following line, however, is beautiful, or could be such if my pen were better.

Now, the whole difference between the second and the first line is that the former changes its direction *ex abrupto* while the latter does it unnoticed; the difference of their effects on the aesthetic feeling must be based on this single noticeable difference in quality. But what is a sudden change of direction if not a violent change? Nature does not love jumps. If we see it making one, it appears that it has suffered violence. A movement seems free, however, if one cannot name the particular point at which it changes its direction. This is the case with the curving line which is different from the line above only in its *freedom*.

I could pile up examples to show that everything which we call beautiful merits this predicate only by gaining freedom from its technique. But the proofs I have given will suffice for the moment. *Beauty* does not belong to material but exists only in its handling; but if everything which the senses represent to themselves appears as technical or non-technical, free or not free, it follows that the realm of beauty is vast indeed, since reason can and must ask about freedom in everything which the senses or the understanding immediately represent for it. That is why the realm of taste is the realm of freedom – the beautiful world of the senses is the happiest symbol, as the moral ought to be, and every object of natural beauty outside me carries a guarantee of happiness which calls to me: be free like me.

For this reason we are bothered by every sign of the despotic intrusion of the human hand into a natural realm, for this reason we are bothered by every dancing instructor's intrusion into positions, by every artifice in custom and manner, by every obtuseness in relations, by every insult to freedom of nature in constitutions, habits and laws.

It is striking how one can develop gentility (beauty in social relations) from my concept of beauty. The first law of gentility is: *have consideration for the freedom of others*. The second: *show your freedom*. The correct fulfilment of both is an infinitely difficult problem, but gentility always requires it relentlessly, and it alone makes the cosmopolitan man. I know of no more fitting an image for the ideal of beautiful relations than the well danced and arabesquely [*mit vielen verwickelten Touren*] composed English dance. The spectator in the gallery sees countless movements which cross each other colourfully and change their direction wilfully but *never collide*. Everything has been arranged such that the first has already made room for the second before he arrives, everything comes together so skilfully and yet so artlessly that both seem merely to be following their own mind and still never get in the way of the other. This is the most fitting picture of maintained personal freedom and the spared freedom of the other.

Everything one commonly calls *hardness* is nothing but the opposite of *freedom*. It is this hardness which often robs the greatness of the understanding, or even the moral of its *aesthetic* value. Gentility will not even excuse *brutality* in the highest accomplishment, and virtue itself only becomes beautiful through kindness. But a character, an action, is not beautiful if it shows the sensual nature of the person who is its recipient under the coercion of law, or constrains the senses of the viewer. In this case the actions will produce mere *respect*, not favour or a good disposition; mere respect humbles the person who receives it. This is why we like Caesar far better than Cato, Cimon better than Phocion, Thomas Jones far better than Grandison. We sometimes prefer *affected* actions to pure moral action, because they are voluntary, because they are accomplished not through commanding reason against the interests of nature (affect) – this may be the reason we prefer mild virtue to heroic action, the feminine to the masculine; for the female character, even the most perfect, cannot act but from inclination.

I will write you a separate letter about taste and its influence on the world, where I will develop all of this further. I think you will be satisfied with this missive for today. Now you have enough data to check my ideas thoroughly and I await your comments impatiently. Take care.

Your S.

Jena, the 28. Feb. [Thursday] 93

I shall surprise you with a new work by Kant in a few weeks, which will cause you much wonder. It is printed here and I have read the half that is so far finished. The title is: *Philosophische Religionslehre* [*Philosophy of Religion*][6] and the content – will you believe it? The shrewdest exegesis of the Christian concept of religion on philosophical grounds. As you have already noted several times, Kant loves to give writers a philosophical meaning. As becomes evident quickly, he is not so much concerned with supporting the authority of scripture as with connecting up the results of philosophical thinking with children's reasoning and at the same time to popularize it. He seems to be governed by a principle which *you* yourself are fond of; namely by this: not to throw out that which is present as long as a result can still be expected of it, but rather to ennoble it. I deeply respect this principle and you will see that Kant does it honour. But I sincerely doubt whether he should have taken up the task of giving the Christian religion philosophical foundations in the first place. All we can expect from the well-known quality of defenders of religion is that they will accept the support but will throw away the philosophical grounds, and so Kant will have done nothing more than to have patched up the decaying house of stupidity.

In any case, I am enthralled by the text and can hardly wait for the remaining sections. It is true, however, that one of his first principles gives rise to a feeling of indignation on my, and probably your, part. For he claims that the human heart has a propensity towards evil, which he calls radical evil, and which ought not be confused with the temptations of the senses. He presupposes it in the *person* of the human, as the seat of freedom. But you will read it yourself. One can find no objection against his proofs, as much as one would like to.

Let me also note in passing that he will not find much thanks among the theologians for he suspends all the authority of church doxa and makes rational faith the highest interpreter; he also quite clearly indicates that church doxa is merely subjectively valid and that it would be better if it could be done without. But since he is not convinced that we can do without it, nor will be able to do so in the near future, he makes it a duty of conscience to respect it. The logos, redemption (as philosophical myth), the representations of heaven and hell, the kingdom of God and all of these beliefs are most perfectly explained.

I don't know whether I have written to you already that I am considering a theodicy [*theodisee*]. If possible, it will happen this spring, in order to

---

[6] Schiller is almost certainly here referring to Kant's *Religion Within the Limits of Reason Alone.*

include it in my poems, which I will be publishing this summer in a very nice edition at Crusius. I am looking forward to the theodicy, especially since the new philosophy is a lot more poetic than Leibniz's and has far more character. Besides the theodicy I am still working on a poem with philosophical content from which I expect even more. But I cannot write you of this yet.

If my circumstances allow it, I will include it in my collection as well. If you can get *Jakob und sein Herr*[7] by Diderot, which Mylius has translated (it has not yet been published in French) by all means read it. Minna too will enjoy it very much. I have taken great pleasure in it.

This summer we will live out of town in a pleasant country house. My second sister will be with us and perhaps I will keep her indefinitely. If this happens I will have more of a family life and less noise about since I will then no longer take lodgers. Since my wife is often sickly, it will be a comfort for me to know that someone who is attached to me and healthy is about. Whether I will travel to my fatherland in the summer or fall will depend on my health which has not been the best since the arrival of spring three weeks ago.

We here recall the death of young Ludwig, who went to Kurland, and I really wish that nothing had happened to the poor devil. NB. I have just received word from Dorchen's letter of a funny misunderstanding.

Mainz still seems to be in quite a fix. The elector is at present in Erfurt where the coadjutor has also just arrived. The latter only receives half of his income and could not live on the whole income before. Heavens knows what will come of it.

If I find time, I will include the continuation of my theory. But it is also up to you to think about it. A thousand greetings to all of you.

Your S.

The news about Hubern has frightened me greatly. He is about to make a terrible decision from whichever side one looks at it. It can be predicted with certainty that both people will find each other insufferable within half a year. And to demand his resignation on top of it! Where will he go to find employment after he has severed his Mainz connections and has brought himself into disrepute by marrying F. Does he intend to live off his writing? He will have to take small bites. Ms Forster has nothing

---

[7] Presumably *Jacques The Fatalist*.

and wants him to support her and her child, although he cannot even support himself. I don't know what he means to do. Maybe he hopes to get an appointment at a university? But he will hardly better himself as an adjunct [*Extraordinarius*] and he cannot hope for professorship anywhere since he hasn't learned anything.

I will do my best to make him see this; but I fear that time has already run out. Do you know if he *had* to resign so as not to be sacked? Since one wants to make even *your* association with him a crime, one must think very badly of him indeed. But he must not rely on his parents. They are a mean pair who would rather have their son become desperate than pay a Heller on his behalf. I regard it as foolish, even from his point of view, for him to go to Dresden. For there he will surely find the most dreadful situation. Under no circumstances ought he come to you, but that will become clear to him, I think.

A letter addressed to him, which seems to be from his parents according to the address, arrived at my house along with yours. He probably had it sent to me himself. I am thus sure he will come.

What I am sending along was already finished before your letter arrived. I thus enclose it. I hope that my last package will answer the first part of your letter.

S.

Beauty in Art

There are two types: a) beauty of choice [*Wahl*] or of matter – imitation of natural beauty. b) beauty of depiction or form – imitation of nature. Without the latter there could be no artists. The unity of both makes the great artist.

Beauty of form or depiction is *specific* to art. 'The beauty of nature', Kant says quite rightly, 'is a beautiful thing; the beauty of art is a beautiful representation of a thing.' The ideal beauty, one might add, is a beautiful representation of a beautiful thing.

In beauty of choice one is concerned with *what* the artist depicts. In beauty of form (artistic beauty *stricte sic dicta*) one is merely concerned with *how* he depicts it. The first, one might say, is the free depiction of beauty, the second, the free depiction of truth.

Since the first limits itself to the conditions of natural beauty but the second deals with the specificity of art, I shall deal with the latter first;

for it must first be shown what the artist does in general before one can speak of the great artist.

A product of nature is beautiful if it appears free in its artfulness.
A product of art is beautiful if it depicts a product of nature as free.
Therefore the concept which we are dealing with here is freedom of depiction.

One *describes* an object if one makes its specific qualities explicit, turns them into concepts and places them into a unity of knowledge.

One *depicts it* if one displays the connected qualities immediately to intuition.

The faculty of intuition is the power of imagination. An object is said to be depicted if its representation is immediately brought before the power of imagination.

A thing is free which determines itself or appears to be doing so.

An object is said to be depicted freely if it is presented to the imagination as self-determining.

But how can it be presented to the imagination as appearing to be determined by itself, if the object is not even there, but is only imitated in something else and does not represent itself in person but in a representative?

For natural beauty it is not nature itself but its imitation in the *medium* which is completely different from the imitated material [*Materialiter*]. *Imitation* is the formal similarity of materially different things.

NB. Architecture, beautiful mechanisms, beautiful gardening [*Gartenkunst*], dancing and so on, may not serve as objections since these arts are also subject to this principle, as will be evident soon, even though they either do not imitate a product of nature or do not require a medium.

The nature of the object is not depicted in art in its personality or individuality, but through a medium which:

(a) has its own individuality and nature,
(b) depends on the artist, who must also be considered as a nature in his own right.

The object is thus placed in front of the imagination by a *third* party; but how is it possible that the nature of the object is still represented as pure and determined through itself, given that the material in which it is imitated and the artist who works on the material both possess their own natures, and act through them?

The object dispenses with its vitality and is not present itself, a completely foreign matter has taken over its cause, and it now depends on this foreign matter for how much of the object's individuality is saved or lost.

Now, the foreign nature of the matter steps *between* object and imitation and not only it, but also the equally foreign nature of the artist who must give the matter its form. And each of these things necessarily acts according to their nature.

Thus there are three natures which grapple with one another: the nature of the object to be depicted, the nature of the matter depicting the object and the nature of the artist which is supposed to bring the other two into harmony.

But it is merely the nature of the imitated object which we expect to find in the product of art; and this is the meaning of the phrase that it should be presented to the imagination as self-determining. But as soon as either the nature of the *material* or that of the *artist* enters, the depicted object is no longer determined through itself and instead there is heteronomy. The nature of the depicted thing suffers violence from the depicting matter as soon as the latter makes use of its nature in depicting the thing. An object may thus only be termed *freely depicted* if the nature of the depicted object has not suffered from the nature of the depicting matter.

The nature of the medium or the matter must thus be completely vanquished by the nature of the imitated [thing]. Now, it is merely the *form* of the imitated object which must be transferred; it is thus the form which must win over the matter in artistic depiction.

In an artwork, the *matter* (the nature of the imitating [object]) must lose itself in the *form* (the imitated [object]), the *body* in the *idea*, the *reality* in the *appearance*.

The body in the idea: for the nature of the imitated object is nothing bodily in the imitating material; it exists merely as an idea in the latter and everything which is bodily in the artwork belongs only to it and not to the imitated object.

Reality in appearance: reality here means the *real*, which, in an artwork, can only ever be the *material* and must be set against the *formal* or the *idea* which the artist must effect on the material. Form in an artwork is mere appearance, that is, marble *seems* to be a person, but remains, in reality, marble.

The depiction would thus be free if the nature of the medium were to appear as completely annihilated by the nature of the imitated object, if the *imitated* object could maintain its personality even in its representative, if the representative seems to have been completely replaced by shedding or by *denying* its own nature – in short, if nothing is through material and everything is through form.

If the carved column reveals its origin in stone even in a single mark, which originates not from the idea but from the nature of the material, its beauty suffers; for there is heteronomy. The nature of marble which is hard and brittle, must fully disappear into the nature of flesh which is flexible and soft and neither feeling nor the eye may be reminded of its disappearance. If a single stroke of the pen or the pencil, the paper or the copper plate, the brush reveals the hand which leads it, [the drawing] becomes *hard* or *heavy;* if it reveals the *specific taste* of the artist, the nature of the artist, it is *mannerly.* The depiction becomes ugly if the movement of the muscle (in a copper plate) suffers because of the hardness of the metal or the heavy hand of the artist, for here it is determined not by the idea but by the medium. If the specificity of the depicted object suffers because of the intellectual peculiarity of the artist, we say that the depiction is mannerly.

The opposite of this *manner* is *style*, which is none other than the highest degree of independence from all subjectively and objectively contingent determinations in depiction.

The essence of the good style is *pure objectivity:* the highest principle of the arts.

'Style is to manner as the type of action from formal principles is to action from empirical maxims (subjective principles). Style rises completely above the contingent to the universal and necessary.' (But this explanation of style already includes the *beauty of choice*, which we will leave for later.)

The great artist, one could say, shows the object (its depiction is purely objective), the mediocre artist shows himself (his depiction is subjective), and the bad artist shows his material (his depiction is determined by the nature of the medium and by the limitations of the artist). All of these three cases become clearer in the case of the actor.

1. When Ekhof or Schröder play Hamlet, their persons behave towards their *role* as matter to form, as the body to the idea, as reality to appearance. Ekhof was the marble out of which his genius formed Hamlet, and his (the actor's) person was completely submerged in the artistic person of Hamlet because only the *form* (the character Hamlet) and not the *matter* (nowhere

the real person of the actor) was noticeable – the fact that everything in him was pure form (only Hamlet) permits one to say that he acted beautifully. His depiction was full of style, *first* because it was completely objective and did not include any subjective elements; and *second* because it was objectively necessary, not merely contingent (more of this later).

2. When Madame Albrecht plays Ophelia one sees the nature of the matter (the person of the actress) and not the pure nature of what is to be depicted (the person Ophelia), but a wilful idea of the actress. For she has made it her subjective maxim to depict the pain, the madness and the nobleness of the character without concern for whether this depiction is objective or not. She has only shown *manner* and not *style*.

3. When Mr Brückl plays a king, one can see the nature of the medium dominate its form (the role of the king), for in every action the actor (the material) is apparent in all of his disgustingness and amateurishness. One sees the low effect of the *lack* of ability at once, for the artist (here the understanding of the actor) is unable to form the matter (the body of the actor) according to the idea. The performance is miserable because it makes both the nature of the material and the subjective limitations of the artist clearly visible.

In drawing and the plastic arts it is obvious enough how much the depicted nature suffers if the nature of the material is not fully dominated. But it might be more difficult to apply this principle to *poetic* depiction as well, which must be derived from it. I will try to give you an idea of this.

Here too, you must remember, we are speaking not of *beauty of choice* but merely of *beauty in depiction*.

It is presupposed that the poet already grasped the whole objectivity of his object in his imagination *truly*, *purely* and *completely* – the object stands before his soul *ideally* (that is, turned into pure form), and all that is now left to be done is for it to be *depicted outside of him*. This will require that the object in his mind does not suffer heteronomy from the nature of the medium which is to depict it.

The poet's medium is *words;* abstract signs [*Zeichen*] for types and species but never for individuals; and their relations are determined by *rules* of which *grammar* is the system. It does not present a problem that there is no *material* similarity (identity) between words and objects; for there is no similarity between a *carved pillar* and the *human being* depicted by it. But there is some difficulty in the mere *formal* similarity between words and things. The thing and its expression in words are connected only contingently and arbitrarily (a few cases notwithstanding), merely related by agreement. However, this would be of little importance since the concern is not what the word is in itself but what image it conjures up. If there were only words or phrases which represent to us the most individual character of things, their most individual relations, – in short their whole objective particularity, it would be of little importance whether this came about due to *conventions* or through inner necessity.

But just this is the problem. Words as well as the conditional and connecting laws are very general things which do not serve as signs to *one* but to an infinite number of individuals. This problem is compounded in the case of naming *relations*, which are constituted according to rules and which are applicable to countless and completely different cases at once, and which can only be fitted to an individual representation through the operations of the understanding. The object to be depicted must thus *take a very long detour* through the abstract realm of concepts in which it loses much of its vividness (sensuous power) before it can be brought before the imagination and can be turned into an intuition. The poet has no other means than the artistic *construction of the universal* to depict the particular. 'The lamp standing before me is falling over' is such an individual case, which expresses a relation through general signs.

The *nature* of the medium, which the poet helps himself to, is thus made up of 'the tendency to *universality*' and thus conflicts with the description (which is its task) of the individual. Language places everything before the *understanding* but the poet must place (depict) everything before the *imagination;* the art of the poet wants *intuition*, language provides only *concepts.*

Language thus robs the object, with whose depiction it has been entrusted, of its sensory nature, of its individuality, and imposes its own quality (universality) which is foreign to the object. To make use of terminology, it mixes the nature of the thing depicting, an abstraction, with the nature of the thing which is to be depicted, something sensuous, and thus brings heteronomy into the depiction. The object is thus not determined by itself for the imagination, but is moulded through the genius of language, or it is only brought before the understanding; and thus it is either not depicted as free or it is not depicted at all but merely described.

If the poetic depiction is to be free, the poet must '*overcome language's tendency to the universal by means of the highest art and vanquish matter* (words and their inflections and laws of construction) *through form* (namely its application)'. The nature of language (this is its tendency to the universal) must completely subjugate itself under the form, the body must lose itself in the idea, the sign in the term and reality in appearance. The object to be depicted must step forth freely and victoriously from the depicting object in spite of all the chains of language and stand before the imagination in its whole truth, liveliness and personality. In a word: the beauty of poetic depiction is: *'free self-activity of nature in the chains* of language'.

(The continuation will follow with the next mail.)

FRIEDRICH HÖLDERLIN

'Oldest Programme for a System of German Idealism' (1796)[1]

[...]

an ethics [Ethik]. Since in the future all of metaphysics will be part of *moral theory* (Kant, in his two practical postulates,[2] has only given an *example* of this, and has not exhausted the field), this ethics will be nothing less than a complete system of all ideas or, what come to the same, of all practical postulates. The first idea is, of course, the representation *of myself as* an absolutely free being. With this free, self-conscious being a whole *world* comes into existence – out of nothing – the only true and conceivable *creation from nothing*. – Here I will descend to the realm of physics; the question is this: How must a world be constituted for a moral being? I would like to give wings once again to our physics, which is otherwise sluggish and progresses laboriously via experiments.

This way – if philosophy furnishes the ideas, experience provides the data, we can get that grand physics which I expect will come in future ages. It does not appear that the current physics can satisfy the creative spirit, such as ours is or should be.

[1] The fragment was published and given its now standard title by Franz Rosenzweig in 1918. While the manuscript is in Hegel's handwriting, the ideas expressed in it are closer to those of Schelling and Hölderlin, especially Hölderlin's essay 'On Religion'. It is most plausible to regard the fragment as the result of an exchange of ideas amongst the three friends. The fragment is now dated between June and August 1796.

[2] The reference is to the postulates of the existence of God and the immortality of the soul which, in the *Critique of Practical Reason*, Kant argued were necessary for the possibility of morality.

From nature I proceed to *human works*. Before the idea of humanity, I will show, there is no idea of the *state*, since the state is something *mechanical*, just as there is no idea of a *machine*. Only what is an object for *freedom*, is called an *idea*. We must thus also progress beyond the state! – For every state must treat free humans as mechanical wheels; and it ought not do that; therefore it should *cease*. You see for yourselves that all ideas, of perpetual peace etc., are only ideas *subordinated* to a higher idea. At the same time, I want to set down the principles for a history of humanity and want to lay bare the completely wretched human production of state, constitution, government, legislation. Lastly the ideas of a moral world, divinity, immortality – the overturning of all superstition, persecution of the priesthood who have recently begun to feign obedience to reason, comes about through reason itself. – Absolute freedom of all spirits, who carry the intelligible world in themselves and may seek neither god nor immortality *outside of themselves*.

Finally, the idea which unites everyone, the idea of *beauty*, the word taken in the higher, platonic sense. I am now convinced that the highest act of reason, by encompassing all ideas, is an aesthetic act, and that *truth and goodness* are only siblings in *beauty*. The philosopher must possess as much aesthetic power as the poet. Those people without an aesthetic sense are our philosophers of literalness [*Buchstabenphilosophen*]. The philosophy of spirit is an aesthetic philosophy. One can be spiritually brilliant in nothing, one cannot even think about history – without an aesthetic sense. Here it should become apparent what those humans actually lack, who do not understand ideas – and are simple enough to admit that they are in the dark as soon as things go beyond tables and rosters.

Thus poetry gains a higher honour, it finally becomes what it was at its inception – *the teacher of humanity*; for there is no longer any philosophy, any history; the art of poetry alone will outlive all other sciences and arts.

At the same time we hear so often that the great masses must have a *sensuous* religion. Not only do the great masses have need of it, but also the philosopher. Monotheism of reason and of the heart, polytheism of the imagination and of the arts, that's what we need!

First I will speak here of an idea which, as far as I know, has not crossed anyone's mind – we must have a new mythology, but this mythology must be in the service of ideas, it must become a mythology of *reason*.

Until we make ideas aesthetic, that is, mythological, they are of no interest to the *people*, and vice versa: until mythology is rational, it will be an embarrassment to philosophy. Thus those who are enlightened and those who are not must finally make common cause, mythology must become philosophical, to make the people rational, and philosophy must become mythological, to make philosophy sensuous. Then eternal unity will reign among us. Never again the arrogant glance, never again the blind shuddering of the people before its wise men and priests. Only then will *equal* development of *all* of our powers await us, for the particular person as well as for all individuals. No power will again be suppressed, then general freedom and equality will reign among spirits! – A higher spirit, sent from heaven, must found this new religion among us, it will be the last, greatest task of humanity.

'Letter to Hegel, 26 January 1795'

Letter 94. To Hegel

Jena, the 26th January 95

Your letter was a cheerful greeting at my second entrance to Jena. I had left for Weimar at the end of December with the wife of Major von Kalb and my student, with whom I had spent two months alone here, without having expected such a quick return. The many sorrows which I suffered in my [student] subject through the particular circumstances of my duty in education, my poor health and my need to live for myself, at least for some time, which was further multiplied by my stay here, moved me to express to the wife of the Major my wish to leave my position, even before my departure to Jena. I allowed myself to be convinced by her and Schiller to make one last attempt, but could not endure this merriment for more than fourteen days since, among other things, it also cost me almost my whole nightly rest, and so, full of peace, I now return to Jena and enter into an independence which, truth be told, I now experience for the first time in my life and which I hope will not be fruitless. My productive energy is at present almost completely directed towards the transformation of the material from my novel. The fragment in the 'Thalia' is one of these raw materials. I plan to be finished with it by Easter, but let me be silent about it for now. I have put the transformed *Genius of Bravery*, which you may still remember, along with several other poems in the 'Thalia'. Schiller has taken a great interest in me and has encouraged me to contribute to his new journal the *Horen* as well as to his forthcoming *Musenalmanach*.[1]

I have spoken to Goethe, brother! He is the most beautiful genius of our time, to find so much humanity in such greatness. He entertained me so gently and kindly that my heart laughed and still laughs when I think of it. Herder was also friendly, shook my hand, but was more urbane; he often spoke allegorically, as you yourself know him to be; I will most likely visit him more often; the Major von Kalbs will probably stay in Weimar (which is also why the boy no longer needed me and my departure could be hastened), and my friendship, especially with the wife of the major, makes frequent visits in their house possible.

Fichte's speculative paper – the basis for the whole *Wissenschaftslehre* – as well as his published lecture about the vocation of the scholar, will be of great interest to you. At the beginning, I suspected him of dogmatism; he seemed, if I may hazard a guess, really to have stood, or still stands at the cross roads – he wanted to go beyond the fact of consciousness in the *Theory*,[2] this was evident from many of his remarks, and this is just as surely and even more obviously transcendent, than when earlier metaphysicians wanted to go beyond the being of the world – his absolute I (= Spinoza's substance) contains all reality; it is everything, and there is nothing outside it; there is thus no object for this absolute I, for otherwise all reality would not be in it; but a consciousness without object is unthinkable, and if I am myself this object, then I am as such necessarily limited, even if it is only in time, and thus not absolute; therefore, it is not possible to think consciousness in this absolute I; as absolute I, I have no consciousness and to the extent that I have no consciousness, to that extent I am (for myself) nothing, which means that the absolute I is (for me) nothing.

So I wrote down my thoughts while still in Waltershausen, as I read his first papers, immediately after reading Spinoza; Fichte assures me . . .

[. . .]

---

[1] The *Musenalmanach* was an eighteenth- and nineteenth-century almanac in which chiefly unpublished texts were published.

[2] Hölderlin is referring to Karl Leonard Reinhold's *Essay on a New Theory of the Human Power of Representation* (1789) which sought to reconstruct Kant's critical theory in a foundational manner using the human power of representation as his first principle. For a brief statement and evaluation of Reinhold's position see Paul Franks, 'All or Nothing; Systematicity and Nihilism in Jacobi, Reinhold, and Maimon', in Karl Ameriks (ed.), *The Cambridge Companion to German Idealism* (Cambridge: Cambridge University Press, 2000).

His engagement with the codetermination of the I and the not-I (according to his language) is certainly strange, the idea of *striving* as well etc. I must finish and must ask you to regard this as if it had not been written. It is probably good and important that you are applying yourself to concepts of religion. I assume that you treat the concept of providence entirely parallel to Kant's theology; the way in which he combines the mechanism of nature (and thus fate) with its purposefulness certainly seems to me to contain the entire spirit of the system; of course it is the same [purposefulness] with which he resolves all antinomies. With regard to the antinomies, Fichte has a very strange thought, about which I would, however, prefer to write you at another time. For a long time now I have been considering the idea of [writing a] public education [*Volkserziehung*], and since you yourself are currently dealing with a part of this, religion, I will choose your image and friendship as a conductor of [my] thoughts to the outside sensory world and will write, what I might have written later, *at the right time* to you in letters, which you must judge and correct...

'Being Judgement Possibility' (1795)[1]

Being –, expresses the combination of subject and object.

Where subject and object simply are, and not just partially, united, such that no separation can take place without injuring the nature of that which is to be divided, only there and nowhere else can there be talk of being as such, the same is the case in intellectual intuition.

But this being must not be confused with identity. When I say: I am I, then the subject (I) and the object (I) are not combined in such a way that no separation can take place without injuring the nature of what is to be separated; on the contrary, the I is only possible through the separation of the I from the I. How can I say: I! without self-consciousness? But how is self-consciousness possible? By setting myself in opposition to myself, by separating myself from myself but, the separation notwithstanding, by being able to recognize myself in what opposes me. But in what sense as the same? I can, must ask this; for in another respect it is opposed to itself. Therefore identity is not a unification of object and subject, which can take place absolutely, therefore identity is not = to absolute being.

Judgement – is in the highest and most strict sense the original [*ursprünglich*] separation of the most tight unity of object and subject in intellectual intuition, that separation which makes object and subject first

---

[1] Dieter Henrich, 'Hölderlin on Judgement and Being: A Study in the History of the Origins of Idealism', dates this text from the early days of April 1795. In making philosophically perspicuous the distinction between identity and unity, and so the limits of philosophy, Hölderlin lays the foundation for his theory of tragedy.

possible, the judgement [*Ur – theilung*, original – separation]. The concept of judgement already contains the concept of the reciprocal relation of object and subject to each other, as well as the necessary precondition of a whole of which object and subject are the parts. 'I am I' is the most fitting example of this concept of judgement [*Ur – theilen*], as a *theoretical* judgement [*Urtheilung*], for in the practical judgement it sets itself in opposition to the *not-I*, not in opposition to *itself*.

Actuality and possibility are differentiated, as mediate and unmediated consciousness. When I think of a thing [*Gegenstand*] as possible, I merely repeat the preceding consciousness through which it is actual. For us, there is no conceivable possibility which has not been actuality. For this reason the concept of possibility cannot be applied to objects of reason, for they never occur to consciousness as what they appear to be, but only [occur as] the concept of necessity. The concept of possibility belongs to the objects of the understanding, that of actuality [belongs to] objects of perception and intuition.

'The Significance of Tragedy' (1802)[1]

The significance of tragedy is most easily understood [*begriffen*] through paradox. Because all capability is divided justly and equally, everything that is original appears not in its original strength, not truly, but genuinely only in its weakness, so that in reality the light of life and appearance belong to the weakness of each whole. Now in the tragic, the sign is in itself meaningless, without power, but that which is original is straight out.[2] For really the original can only appear in its weakness, but insofar as the sign in itself is posited as meaningless = 0, the original too, the hidden ground of everything in nature can represent itself. If nature genuinely represents itself in its weakest gift [*Gabe*], then, when [nature] presents itself in its strongest gift, the sign = 0.

[1] Written about 1802 when Hölderlin was in the midst of composing his translations of Sophocles, this text proposes the death of the tragic hero (here the 'meaningless' sign '= 0') as the means for representing, or better indicating or testifying to, absolute being.

[2] In the sense of being openly revealed.

'Remarks on *Oedipus*' (1803)[1]

I

It would be good, here as well, if, in order to secure a civil existence for the poets, differences of time and situation notwithstanding, one elevated poetry to a craft [*mechane*], to the level of the ancients.

Other works of art too lack this reliability compared to the Greek works; they have, at least up to now, been judged more according to the impression they make, than according to the lawful calculation and other procedures through which beauty is brought out. Modern poetry especially lacks the schooling and dexterity which would allow it to be calculated and learned, and once learned, allow it to be reliably repeated in its practice. Among humans one must above all be concerned in each thing, that it is something, that is, that it be recognized in its way of appearance, that the way it is conditioned can be determined and taught. For this and higher reasons, poetry requires especially secure and characteristic principles and boundaries.

Lawful calculations are needed here as its first component.

---

[1] This and its companion piece, 'Remarks on *Antigone*,' were composed around 1803. In the text, Hölderlin quotes from his own, very distinctive, translation of *Oedipus*. I consulted David Grene's translation in his and Richmond Lattimore's (eds.) *Greek Tragedies*, 1 (Chicago: University of Chicago Press, 1992), but tried to make this translation, as far as was possible, accord with Hölderlin's German phrasing.

Then one ought to consider how the content differs from it, through which processes, and how, in the infinite but persistently determinate connection, the particular content relates to the general calculation; and how the course of events and that which is to be established, the living meaning which cannot be calculated, are brought into a relation with the calculable law.

The lawful calculus, the manner in which a system of sensibility, the whole human being develops under the influence of the elemental, and images [*Vorstellungen*] and sensations and reasons proceed in different orders, but always according to a certain rule – in the tragic [all this] is more in balance than in pure succession.

For the tragic *transport* is indeed properly empty and the utterly unbound.

In the rhythmic sequence of representations, in which the tragic transport exhibits itself, that which one calls the *caesura* in poetic metre, the pure word, the counter-rhythmic interruption, is necessary; precisely in order to counter the raging change of representations at its summit so that it is no longer the change of representations but the representation itself which appears.

The successions of calculation and rhythm are separated through this, and relate to each other, in their two halves, so that they appear as of equal weight.

Now if the rhythm of images is so constituted that, in its eccentric rapidity, the *first* are pulled along more by those *coming after*, then the caesura or the counter-rhythmic interruption must *lie at the front*, so that the first half is sheltered against the second and the balance is tilted more from the back towards the beginning, precisely because the second half is originally more rapid and seems to weigh more heavily because of the counter action of the caesura.

But if the rhythm of the images is constituted such that *those following* are more dense than those *at the beginning*, the caesura will lie more towards the end, because it is the end that therefore must be sheltered, and the balance will therefore tilt more towards the end, because the first half is more extended, and the balance must therefore occur later. So much for calculable laws.

The first of those tragic laws which have been indicated here is that of Oedipus.

Antigone follows that which has been mentioned second.

The caesura constitutes Teiresias' part in both plays.

He steps into the path of fate, as overseer over the power of nature, which tragically displaces human beings from their life-sphere, from the midpoint of their inner life into another world and jolts them into the eccentric sphere of the dead.

2

The *intelligibility* of the whole depends particularly on examining the scene in which Oedipus interprets the statement of the oracle towards infinity and is tempted to *nefas* [impiety].

> For the saying of the oracle is:
> King Phoebus in plain words commanded us,
> drive out the pollution of the land, nourished on this ground,
> do not nourish the unholy.

This could mean: generally create a strong and pure court and keep order among the citizens. But Oedipus responds to this in a priestly fashion:

> Through what kind of purification? Etc.
> [*Oed.* 98]

And becomes *specific*,

> Of which man does he pronounce this fate?
> [*Oed.* 101]

And thus turns Creon's *thoughts* to the terrible word:

> Oh King, before you piloted the state
> Laius was our lord in this land.
> [*Oed.* 102–3]

In this way the saying of the oracle and the story of Laius' death, which are not necessarily connected, are brought together. But in the immediately following scene the spirit of Oedipus, knowing all, expresses, in angry premonition, the *nefas* itself by interpreting the general command as pertaining to the particular and then applying it to the murderer of Laius, and then casting the sin as infinite:

Who so among you knows the murderer
by whose hand Laius, son of Labdacus,
died – I command him to tell everything
to me etc.

[*Oed.* 228–30]

I forbid that man, whoever he be, my land,
here where I hold sovereignty and throne;
and I forbid any to welcome him
or cry him greeting or make him a sharer
in sacrifice or offering to the gods,

[*Oed.* 240–5]

as the divine oracle,
of Pytho, prolaimed him now to me, etc.

[*Oed.* 247–8]

Thus, in the following conversation with Teiresias, the wondrous, furious curiosity arises, because knowledge, when it has broken though its barriers, as though drunk on its regal harmonic form, which can remain, at first is anxious to know more than it can bear or comprehend.

This later causes the suspicion in the scene with Creon: thought, unbridled and full of mournful secrets, becomes unsure and the faithful and sure spirit suffers in the angry excess, which, gleefully destructive, only follows the raging time.

Thus [occurs], in the middle of the piece, in the speeches with Jocasta, in the mournful calm, the stupor, the naïve error of the violent man, deserving of sympathy, where he tells Jocasta of his putative place of birth and of Polybos, whom he fears he might kill because he is his father, and of Merope, whom he wants to flee from in order not to marry her, who is his mother, according to the words of Teiresias, who, after all, has told him that he is Laius' murderer and that he [Laius] is his father. For Teiresias says, in the already touched on altercation between Oedipus and him:

this man,
whom you have long declared you are in search of,
indicting him in threatening proclamation as murderer of Laius
– he is here: in name he is a stranger living among us
but soon will be shown to be a native,

197

a Theban, and he'll have no joy
of the mishap.
[*Oed.* 455–60]

Yet he will be known, living with his children
as brother and as father, and of the woman
that gave him birth, a son and husband both;
in one bed with his father
that same father that he murdered.
[*Oed.* 463–6]

For this reason, then, the doubt-filled struggle to come to himself,
the humiliating and almost shameless striving to become master over
himself, the foolishly savage search for a consciousness, which occurs
in the beginning of the second half, in the scene with the Corinthian
messenger, in which he [Oedipus] is again tempted to life.

Jocasta:
For Oedipus bends his courage upwards,
in many-sided torture, not conjecturing,
like a man of sense, what will be from what was.
[*Oed.* 935–7]

Oedipus:
Dearest, you, of women, Jocasta captain,
why have you called me out my dwellings?
[*Oed.* 972–3]

Oedipus:
The old man seemed to die of sickness!
Messenger:
And measured well against all time.
[*Oed.* 984–5]

It is certainly remarkable how Oedipus' spirit lifts itself after this good
word; thus the following speeches can appear as the result of more noble
motives. Here he, who just then does not carry his regal worries with
Herculean shoulders, throws them off in supreme weakness, to gain control over himself:

Oedipus:
Well then. O dear wife, why should one
look to the Pythian hearth or
to the birds screaming overhead? They prophesied that
I should kill my father
who sleeps under the earth; but here
I am and my spear is clean –
unless perhaps he died in a dream of me,
and so I am his murderer. But they,
the oracles, as they stand – Polybus, he's taken them
away with him, and lies now in Hades,
worthless.

[*Oed.* 986–95]

In the end, the insane questioning after consciousness rules the speech
powerfully.

Messenger:
Well it's very plain child you don't know what you're doing
Oedipus:
What do you mean, old man? For God's sake, say something!

[*Oed.* 1032–3]

Oedipus:
What, was not Polybus my father?
Messenger:
No more than I but just so much.
Oedipus:
How so? A father who resembles no one?
Messenger:
Just a father, neither Polybus nor I.
Oedipus:
Why then did he call me son?

[*Oed.* 1041–5]

Messenger:
I loosed you;
The tendons of your feet were pierced and fettered, –
Oedipus:
My swaddling clothes brought me a rare disgrace.
Messenger:
So that from this you're called your present name.

199

Oedipus:
Was this my father's doing or my mother's?
For god's sake, tell me.

[*Oed.* 1058–61]

Jocasta:
By the gods – do not hunt this out – I beg you,
if you have any care for your own life.
What I am suffering is enough.
Oedipus:
Keep up
your heart. Though I'm proved a slave,
thrice slave, and though my mother is thrice slave,
you'll not be shown to be more lowly.

[*Oed.* 1084–7]

Oedipus:
Break out what will! I at least shall be
willing to see my ancestry, though humble.
Perhaps she is ashamed of my low birth,
for she has all a woman's high-flown pride.
But I account myself a child of Fortune,
beneficent Fortune, and I shall not be
dishonoured. She's the mother from whom I sprang,
and small and large the moons born with me surrounded me.
Such is my breeding,
and I shall never prove so false to it,
as not to find out entirely who I am.

[*Oed.* 1100–9]

Precisely this all-searching, all-interpreting is also [why] his spirit finally succumbs to the raw and simple language of his servant.

Because such people stand in violent relations, their language too speaks in violent connections, almost in the manner of the furies.

3

The presentation of the tragic rests preeminently upon this, that the monstrous – how god and man pair themselves, and the limitless power of nature and what is innermost in man becomes one in wrath – thereby grasping itself through a limitless becoming one with itself [that occurs] through a limitless division of itself that purifies.

της φυσεως γραμματευς ην τον καλαμον αποβρεξων ευνουν. [He (Aristotle) was nature's scribe, dipping the well-meaning quill.][2]

Hence, the constant antagonistic dialogue, hence the chorus as the opposition to it. Hence, the all too chaste, all too mechanical and factually ending interconnectedness between the different parts, in dialogue, and between the chorus and the dialogue and the great parts or actors, which are made up of chorus and dialogue. All is speech against speech which mutually negates itself.

Therefore, in the choruses of *Oedipus*, the plaintive and peaceful and religious, the pious lie [*If I am soothsayer*, etc. 1110] and sympathy until the total exhaustion [going] against the dialogue, which, in its angry sensitivity, wants to tear apart the soul of precisely these listeners; in the appearance of the terrible ceremonious forms, the drama imparts itself like an inquisition, like a language for a world of plague and confusion of the senses and in generally inflamed spirit of the soothsayer; so that in quiet times, in order that the course of the world will have no gaps and that *the memory of the heavenly ones will not cease*, God and man reveal themselves in the all-forgetting form of unfaithfulness, for divine unfaithfulness is what is best retained.

In such moments man forgets himself and the God, and turns around, to be sure in a sacred way, like a traitor. – For at the extreme limit of suffering nothing more exists than the conditions of time or space.

Here man forgets himself because he is wholly in the moment; the God, because he is nothing but time; and both are unfaithful, time, because, in such moments, it turns categorically so beginning and end simply cannot rhyme with one another in it; man, because in such moments he must follow this categorical reversal and can thus obviously no longer be identical to the beginning.

So stands Hermione in *Antigone*. So Oedipus himself stands in the middle of the tragedy of *Oedipus*.

---

[2] Hölderlin is here citing the tenth-century Byzantine lexicon, the *Suda*. The implication is that it is Sophocles rather than Aristotle who is truly nature's scribe.

NOVALIS

From *Miscellaneous Remarks* (1797)

1. We *look* everywhere for the Unconditional Absolute, and all we *find* are the conditions.[1]

6. We will never understand ourselves entirely, but we are capable of perceptions of ourselves which far surpass understanding.

8. The distinction between illusion and truth lies in the difference in their vital functions.

Illusion lives off truth – truth has its life within itself. We destroy illusion as we destroy diseases – and accordingly illusion is but an inflammation or an expiration of the intellect – the affliction of the fanatic or of the Philistine. The after-effect of the former is usually an *apparent failure of the power to think*, which can be remedied only by a diminishing series of incentives (coercive means). The latter often changes into a *deceptive animation*, the dangerous revolutionary symptoms of which can be dispelled only by an increasing sequence of violent measures.

Both conditions can be changed only by means of a thorough regimen strictly pursued.

---

[1] Richard Samuel draws attention to a passage in Schelling's treatise 'Vom Ich als Prinzip der Philosophie oder über das Unbedingte im Menschlichen Wissen' (1795), sections 2–3, which Novalis almost certainly had in mind.

9. Our entire perceptive faculty resembles the eye. The objects must pass through contrary media in order to appear correctly on the pupil.

10. Experience is the test of the rational – and the other way round.

The inadequacy of *mere* theory when it comes to application, so often remarked on by the practical man, has its counterpart in the rational application of *mere* experience. This is remarked distinctly enough by your true philosopher, but with the self-knowledge that this consequence is necessary. This is why the practical man rejects mere theory in its entirety, without any inkling of how fraught with problems the answer might be to the question: whether theory exists for the sake of practice, or practice for the sake of theory.

11. Death is an overcoming of the self, and like all self-conquest creates a new, and lighter, existence.

12. Perhaps we need to expend so much energy and effort on the common and ordinary because for the true human self there is nothing more uncommon, nothing more out of the ordinary, than the commonplace everyday?

The highest is the most comprehensible – the nearest, the most indispensable. Only if we have no acquaintance with ourselves, if we have lost the custom and habit of ourselves, something beyond comprehension will emerge which is itself incomprehensible.

14. Nature is the enemy of eternal possessions. According to strict laws she destroys all signs of property and obliterates all distinctive marks of its formation. The earth belongs to all the generations – each one has a rightful claim to everything. The earlier ones may not owe any advantage to this accident of primogeniture. The right of ownership lapses at certain times. The process of improvement and deterioration is determined by certain unchangeable conditions. But if my body is a possession by which I acquire only the rights of an active citizen of this earth, to lose this possession will not make me lose myself. I shall lose nothing but a place in this school for princes[2] – and I shall enter into a higher corporate state whither my dear fellow scholars will follow me.

[2] Cf. *Dialogue* 5.

15. Life is the beginning of death. Life exists for the sake of death. Death is at once end and beginning. At once separation and an even closer amalgam of the self. Death completes the process of reduction.

16. We are near to waking, when we dream we dream.

17. The imagination places the future world in relation to us either in the heights, or in the depths, or in the transmigration of souls. We dream of journeys through the universe – But is not the universe *within us*? We do not know the depths of our mind. Inward leads the mysterious path. Within us, or nowhere, lies eternity with its worlds – the past and future. The external world is the world of shadows – It casts its shadows into the realm of light. True, it all seems to be dark and lonely and formless within us now. But how different it will appear when this eclipse is over and the body casting its shadow has moved on. We will enjoy more fully than ever, for our spirit has abstained.

19. How can a man have a feeling for a thing, if he does not have the germ of it within himself? What I am to understand has to develop organically within me – and what I appear to be learning is only nourishment – a stimulus to the organism.

20. The seat of the soul is located at the meeting-place of the world within and the world without. Where they interpenetrate each other, there it is at every point of interpenetration.

21. The life of a truly canonical human being must be symbolic through and through. Given this assumption, would not every death be a death of expiation? More or less of course – and are there not several very remarkable inferences to be drawn from this?

22. He that seeks, doubts. But the genius can tell swiftly and surely what is taking place within him because he is not involved in his representation and consequently the representation is not embroiled in him, but his observation chimes in free accord with the thing observed, and they appear to unite freely to make one work. When we speak of the external world, when we describe real objects, then we proceed like the genius. So genius consists in the capacity to treat imaginary objects as if they were real, and real objects as if they were imagined. So the talent for representation, for exact observation, for the purposeful description of what has been

observed, is different from genius. Without this talent, one's vision is incomplete, one is but half a genius, one can have a disposition towards genius, but lacking that talent one will never develop into a genius. Without genius we would none of us exist at all. Genius is necessary to everything. But what we call genius – is the genius of genius.

23. It is the most arbitrary prejudice that man should be denied the power to be *beside himself*, to be conscious and at the same time beyond his senses. At every moment man has the capacity of an existence beyond his senses. Without this he would not be a citizen of the world – he would be a beast. True, in this state concentration, self-possession is very difficult, as it is constantly, necessarily bound up with our other states. But the more aware of this state we can become, the more vivid, powerful and satisfying is the conviction arising out of it – the belief in true revelations of the spirit. It is not a seeing, hearing, feeling – it is made up of all three – more than all three, it is a sense of immediate certainty – a prospect of my own, true, innermost life – thoughts are transformed into laws, wishes into their fulfilment. For the weak, *the fact of this moment is an article of faith*.

24. The phenomenon becomes particularly striking when we look at certain human figures and faces especially, at many eyes, expressions, gestures, as we hear certain words, read certain passages, view certain aspects of the world, life and destiny. Accidental things, a natural event, particularly the cycles of the day and the seasons, will very often yield such experiences. Certain moods are particularly favourable to these revelations. Most of them last but a moment, a few fleeting, fewest of all remaining. People are very various in this respect. The one is more capable of revelation than the other. The one has more feeling for it, the other more understanding. The latter will always dwell in its gentle light, and though the illuminations visiting the former may be but intermittent, yet they will be brighter and more various. This faculty is likewise potentially pathological when it is characterized either by too much feeling and too little understanding, or by too much understanding and too little feeling.

25. Modesty is very likely a feeling of profanation. Friendship, love and piety should be treated secretly. We should speak of them only in rare and intimate moments, and reach a silent understanding on them – there is

much which is too fragile to be thought, and still more too delicate for discussion.

26. Self-alienation is the source of all abasement, as well as being on the contrary the ground of all true elevation. The first step will be insight into ourselves – detaching contemplation of ourself – To stop here would be to go only half way. The second step must be the active glance outwards – the independent, steady observation of the outside world.

Man will never achieve any great representation, if he represents nothing further than his own experiences, his favourite themes and objects, if he cannot bring himself to study diligently an object which is quite alien and uninteresting to him. The artist who represents must have the ability and the will to represent everything. This is what gives rise to the grand style of representation, which we admire so much, and rightly so, in Goethe.

27. One remarkable characteristic of Goethe's is evident from the way he connects small insignificant incidents with more important events. He seems to have no other intention than to find a poetic way of engaging the imagination in a mysterious kind of play. Here too this rare man has caught the scent of Nature's way, and learned from her a pretty trick of art. Ordinary life is full of similar accidents. They constitute a kind of play, which like all play, ends in surprise and illusion.

Many common sayings depend on the observation of this topsy-turvy relationship – for example *bad dreams* mean good luck – news of a death means long life – a hare crossing your path bad luck. Almost all the common folk's store of superstition rests on interpretations of this seeming-arbitrary playfulness of Nature.

28. The highest task of education is – to seize the mastery of one's transcendental Self – to be at the same time the Self of one's Self.[3] Accordingly, our lack of full understanding and feeling for others is less strange. Without a complete understanding of ourselves, we will never truly come to understand others.

---

[3] This fragment was emended editorially by F. Schlegel. Samuel notes a similar turn of phrase in Schiller's 'On the Aesthetic Education of Man': 'Every individual man, one can say, carries, according to his natural tendency and destiny, a pure ideal man in himself; the greatest mission of his Being is to be in harmony with the inalterable unity of that ideal man in all his variations.' Schiller then refers to Fichte's publication, *Vorlesungen über die Bestimmung des Gelehrten*.

29. I cannot show that I have understood a writer until I am able to act in his spirit, until, without diminishing his individuality, I am able to translate, vary and change him.

30. Humour is a capriciously assumed style. This capriciousness gives it its piquancy. Humour is the result of a free combination of the Absolute and the Conditioned. Humour gives a general interest and an objective value to what is peculiar and conditioned. Where fantasy and judgement meet, we have wit – where reason and caprice come together, we have humour. Persiflage belongs to humour, but is a lesser thing. It is no longer artistic < and much more limited. Serene souls have no wit. Wit reveals a balance out of true – It is the consequence of a disturbance, and at the same time the means of restoring it. Passion has the strongest wit. Truly sociable wit has no violent resonance. There is a kind of wit which is the play of magical colours in the higher spheres. When all relationships are disintegrating, despair, spiritual death – these provide states of the most terrible wit.

Only wit can make the insignificant, the common, coarse, ugly, the immoral fit for society. They are there, as it might be, only for the sake of the witticism – their determining purpose is the joke. >[4]

32. We are on a *mission*. We are summoned to educate the earth. If a spirit were to appear to us, we would make ourselves master of our own spirituality at once – we would be inspired, both by ourselves and by the spirit. Without inspiration, no apparition. Inspiration is both appearance and appearance given in return, both appropriation and communication.

33. A Man's life and active impact survive only ideally, in the memory of his existence. For the present there is no other means of spiritual influence upon this world. We therefore have a duty to remember the dead. It is the only way of remaining in communion with them. This is the only way God himself acts as a moving spirit among us – through faith.

36. What Schlegel characterizes so sharply as Irony[5] is to my mind nothing other than the consequence, the character of presence of mind – of the true presence of the spirit. The spirit always appears in *strange and airy* form. To me, Schlegel's Irony seems to be genuine humour. One idea can usefully have several names.

[4] Lines enclosed in angled brackets were crossed out by Novalis while reworking the MS.
[5] *Lyceum* (that is, Critical) *Fragment* 108.

43. Among us humans, withdrawing into ourselves means abstracting ourselves from the external world. Among the spirits, earthly life is analogously called inward contemplation – an entering into oneself – an immanent activity. In this way earthly life arises out of an original reflection – a primordial withdrawal and concentration within the self, which is as free as our reflection. Contrariwise, spiritual life arises in this world out of an eruption in that primordial reflection – the spirit unfolds itself again – the spirit emerges forth to itself – partly suspends that reflection – and in this moment for the first time says – I. We can see here how relative is the emerging from and withdrawal into the Self. What we call withdrawing is actually emerging – a resumption of the original form.

45. Where a true disposition of mind towards reflection prevails, and not just an inclination towards thinking this or that thought – there you will find Progredibility [or the potentiality for progress].[6] Many scholars do not have this disposition. They have learned how to draw inferences and conclusions in the same way as a shoemaker has learned to make shoes, without ever coming upon the underlying design or troubling to discover the first principles behind the thought. Yet salvation is not to be found by any other route. In many thinkers, this disposition of mind only lasts a short time – it grows and declines – often as they grow older – often with the discovery of a System, which they have only sought in order to be relieved of the labour of any further reflection.

51. The interesting thing is what sets me in motion not for my own sake, but only as a means, as a member. *The Classical* does not disturb me at all – it affects me only indirectly through myself – It does not exist for me as classical, if I do not assume it to be the kind of thing that would affect me, if I did not for my part intend and encourage myself to produce it, if I did not tear off a part of myself and let this germinate and develop in its own way before my eyes – a development which often only requires a moment – and coincides with the sense-perception of the object – in such a way that I can behold an object before me in which the base object and the ideal, interpenetrating each other, form one single marvellous individual object.

58. Man appears at his most estimable when the first impression he gives is the impression of an absolutely witty idea, that is, of being spirit and a

---

[6] The German word is 'Progredibilitaet'.

certain individual at the same time. Each one of these excellent men must seem to be as it were permeated by an airy spirit, which acts as a kind of ideal parody of the visible phenomenon.

61. The best thing about the sciences is their philosophical ingredient – like life in a physical organism. If we dephilosophize the sciences – what is left – earth, air and water.

64. Courts of law, theatre, church, court, government, public assemblies, academies, colleges etc. are as it were the specialized inner organs of the mystical individual, the state.

65. All the actions of our life are materials of which we can make what we will – a great mind will make something great of his life – The great mind would make of every acquaintance, every incident, the first item in an infinite series – the beginning of a never-ending romance.

68. A translation is either grammatical, or transformatory, or mythical. Mythical translations are translations in the grand style. They present the pure and perfect character of the individual work of art. They do not give us the work of art in its reality, but in its ideal form. To the best of my belief, we do not yet have a perfect model of this kind, but we do encounter bright traces in the spirit of several descriptions and criticisms of works of art. It needs a mind in which the poetic spirit and the philosophical spirit have interpenetrated each other in all their fullness. Greek mythology is in some part a mythical translation of a national religion. The modern Madonna too is a myth of this kind.

Grammatical translations are translations in the ordinary sense. They require much scholarship, but only discursive talents.

Transformatory translations, if they are to be genuine, require the highest poetic spirit. They can come very close to travesty – like Bürger's Homer in iambics[7] – Pope's Homer – all the French translations. The true translator of this kind must indeed be an artist himself and be able to convey the idea of the whole in this way or that, as he pleases. He must be the poet's poet, and so enable him to speak according to the translator's and the poet's own idea *at the same time*. The genius of mankind stands in the same relationship to each individual.

[7] Gottfried August Bürger (1748–94), poet.

Not only books – everything can be translated in these three ways.

70. Our language is either – mechanical – atomistic – or dynamic. But true poetic language should be organic and alive. How often one feels the poverty of words to express several ideas at a blow.

73. Nothing is more indispensible to the truly religious temper of mind than an intermediary to unite us with the Divinity. Man simply cannot stand in an immediate relationship to the Godhead. His choice of this intermediary must be utterly free. The least compulsion in this respect will harm his religion. The choice is characteristic, and consequently men of cultivation will choose much the same intermediaries – on the other hand, the choice made by the uneducated is usually determined by accident. But since so few are capable of making a free choice, many intermediaries become more generally shared, whether by accident, by association, or by their special fitness. This is how national religions develop. The more independent man becomes, the more the number of the intermediaries diminishes, while their quality grows more refined – and his relationship to them becomes more various and more sophisticated – fetishes – stars – beasts – heroes – idols – gods – *One* Divine Man. We can quickly see how relative these choices are, and we will all unawares be drawn towards the idea – that the essence of the religion probably does not depend on the nature of the mediator, but consists simply of the view of it and of the relationships to it.

It is idolatry in the wider sense if in fact I regard this mediator as God himself. It is *irreligion* if I assume no mediator at all – and to that extent superstition, or idolatry – and unbelief – or theism, which can also be called the older Judaism – are both *irreligion*. On the other hand, atheism is the negation of all religion, and so has nothing to do with religion. True religion is one which takes its mediator to be mediator, regards him as it were as the organ of the Godhead, as its physical manifestation. In this respect the Jews at the time of the Babylonian Captivity had a true religious inclination – a religious hope – a faith in a future religion which they transformed fundamentally in so strange a way, and which they have maintained with remarkable persistence until the present day.

But observed more closely, true religion seems to be further divided into antinomies – into Pantheism and Entheism. I will allow myself some licence in using the term Pantheism in a different sense from the usual one – understanding by it the idea that every organ of the Godhead can be a mediator if I elevate it to make it so – just as by contrast the term Entheism designates the belief that there is only one organ of this kind in the world for us, which is the only one appropriate to the idea of mediator, and is the only one through which the voice of God is heard, and which I would compel myself to choose, for without this, Entheism would not be true religion.

However incompatible both may seem to be, their union can be brought about – if we make the entheistic mediator into the mediator of the pantheist's intermediary world and as it were its centre – so that each, though in different ways, is the necessary condition of the other.

Thus prayer, or religious thought, consists of a threefold ascending and indissoluble abstraction or assumption. To the religious mind, every object can be a temple, as the ancient Augurs intended. The spirit of this temple is the omni-present High Priest – the entheistic mediator – who alone stands in an immediate relationship to God, the Father of all things.

86. We usually understand the artificial better than the natural.

91. We are related to all parts of the universe – As we are to future and past. Which relation we develop fully, which is to be most important and effective for us depends only on the direction and duration of our attention. A true theory of this procedure would be nothing less than the long-desired art of invention. But it would be more than this. Man acts at all times according to its laws, and there is no doubt that by means of intense self-observation it is possible for the genius to discover them.

95. If the world is as it were a precipitate of human nature, then the divine world is its sublimate. Both take place *uno actu*. No precipitation without sublimation. What the former loses in agility is gained by the latter.

101. That which appears simply *still* is, in respect of the external world, that which is simply motionless. However variously it may change, its relation to the external world remains one of rest. This statement holds good for all self-modifications. That is why the Beautiful appears so still. Everything beautiful is a self-illuminated, perfect, individual object.

103. The more narrow-minded a system is, the more it will please the worldly-wise. That is why the Materialists' system, Helvetius' theory, and

even Locke have received most approval from this class. And Kant will still find more supporters than Fichte.

104. The art of writing books has not yet been invented. But it is on the point of being invented. Fragments of this kind are literary seed-houses. True, there may be many a barren grain among them. But meanwhile, if only a few germinate...

105. < Schlegel's writings are philosophy as lyric. His [essays on] Forster and Lessing are first-rate minor poetry, and resemble the Pindaric hymns. The lyrical prose writer will compose logical epigrams. If he is utterly intoxicated with life, they will be dithyrambs which the reader will of course have to enjoy and judge as dithyrambs. A work of art can be half-intoxicated – entirely intoxicated, the work of art melts into nothing – Man becomes an animal – The character of the animal is dithyrambic – The animal is an over-plus of life – the plant is a deficient life. Man is a *free* life. >

'Monologue'

Speaking and writing is a crazy state of affairs really; true conversation is just a game with words. It is amazing, the absurd error people make of imagining they are speaking for the sake of things; no one knows the essential thing about language, that it is concerned only with itself. That is why it is such a marvellous and fruitful mystery – for if someone merely speaks for the sake of speaking, he utters the most splendid, original truths. But if he wants to talk about something definite, the whims of language make him say the most ridiculous false stuff. Hence the hatred that so many serious people have for language. They notice its waywardness, but they do not notice that the babbling they scorn is the infinitely serious side of language. If it were only possible to make people understand that it is the same with language as it is with mathematical formulae – they constitute a world in itself – their play is self-sufficient, they express nothing but their own marvellous nature, and this is the very reason why they are so expressive, why they are the mirror to the strange play of relationships among things. Only their freedom makes them members of nature, only in their free movements does the world-soul express itself and make of them a delicate measure and a ground-plan of things. And so it is with language – the man who has a fine feeling for its tempo, its fingering, its musical spirit, who can hear with his inward ear the fine effects of its inner nature and raises his voice or hand accordingly, he shall surely be a prophet; on the other hand the man who knows how to write truths like this, but lacks a feeling and an ear for language, will find language making a game of him, and will become a mockery to men, as Cassandra was to the Trojans. And though I believe that with these words I have delineated the nature and office of poetry as clearly as I can, all the same I know that no one can understand it, and what I have said is quite foolish because I wanted to say it, and that is no way for poetry to come about. But what if I were compelled to speak? What if this urge to speak were the mark of the inspiration of language, the working of language within me? And my will only wanted to do what I had to do? Could this in the end, without my knowing or believing, be poetry? Could it make a mystery comprehensible to language? If so, would I be a writer by vocation, for after all, a writer is only someone inspired by language?

'Dialogues' (1798)

I

A. The new catalogue for the book fair?

B. Still wet from the printer's.

A. What a load of letters – what a monstrous waste of time!

B. You seem to belong to the Omarists[1] – if I may call you after the most thorough-going of your kind.

A. You don't intend to sing the praises of this book-making epidemic, do you?

B. Why praises? But I am certainly delighted at how the number of these articles of trade increases year by year. Their export brings only reputation, but their import brings solid profit. There are more honest and worthy ideas circulating among us than among all our neighbours put together. The middle of the present century saw the discovery of these great mines in Germany, richer than those of Potosi or Brazil, which will surely bring about a greater revolution, now and in the future, than the discovery of America. What advances we have since made

---

[1] 'Omarists': a reference to those who share the sentiments of the Caliph Omar, who, in the early stages of the Mohammedan expansion, ordered the burning of the books in the great library at Alexandria.

in the scientific extraction, treatment, and brilliant and useful process-
ing of their products! Every where we are bringing together the crude
ore or the beautiful moulds – we are melting down the ore, and have
the skills to imitate and surpass the moulds. And you want me to fill
all those mines in? And return to the rude poverty of our forefathers?
Are they not at least a spur to activity? And is not any activity worthy of
praise?

A. Put like that, there is nothing to object to. But let us take a closer look
at the fine art and the precious metal.

B. I shall not admit arguments against the whole enterprise which are
based on the frailty and inadequacy of the individual. This kind of thing
needs to be seen as a whole.

A. A whole which is made up of miserable parts is a miserable whole
itself – or rather, it is not a whole at all. Yes, if it were a progression
according to a plan, if every book filled a gap somewhere, and every book
fair were a kind of systematic link in the educational chain! Then each book
fair would mark a necessary period, and from these purposeful advances
there would finally emerge a perfect road to ideal culture – A systematic
catalogue of this kind – how much smaller in volume, and how much
greater in weight!

B. You, and many of your kind, are like the Jews. You are for ever hoping
for the Messiah, and he came long ago. Do you really believe that the
destiny of man, or, if you prefer, human nature, needs to frequent our
lecture-halls in order to learn what a system is? It seems to me that our
system-builders still have a lot to learn from them. The individual facts are
accidental – the arrangement, the conjunction of accidents is not accident,
it is law – the consequence of a wise and profound design. There is not
a book in the catalogue that has not borne its fruit, even if all it did was
fertilize the ground on which it grew. We think we have found many
redundancies [tautologies]. Where they occurred they gave life to this or
that idea. They are redundant only for the whole, for us; the worst novel
has at least given pleasure to the author's friends. Second-rate sermons
and books for our edification have their public, their devotees, and in the
armour of typography they make their effect tenfold upon their listeners
and readers – and that goes for the entire catalogue.

A. You seem to overlook entirely the harmful consequences of reading, to say nothing of the monstrous cost of these articles of modern luxury.

B. My dear friend, doesn't money exist to give life? Why shouldn't it serve this need of our nature, and rouse and satisfy our feeling for thought? As for the harmful consequences, do, I beg you, consider seriously for a moment, for a reproach of that kind from you almost makes me angry.

A. I know what you are aiming at, and I have no desire to take over the real Philistine's objections, but have you not yourself complained often enough about your reading? Have you not spoken often enough of our fatal habituation to a *printed* Nature?

B. It may be that these complaints of mine have given you cause for misunderstanding – but, considering that these are usually but the expressions of a moment's ill-humour, when we speak not in general truths but partially, as mood and passion do, I was complaining more at the inescapable weakness of our nature, its inclination towards custom and easy habit; it was not an objection in principle to the world of ciphers. It is not the ciphers' fault that we end up seeing nothing but books, no longer things[2] – nor that we have as good as lost our five bodily senses. Why do we cling so strangely, like thin and meagre moss, to the printer's vine?

A. But if things go on like this, in the end we will no longer be able to study a science in its entirety – the range of the literature grows so monstrously.

B. Don't believe it. Practice makes perfect, even in the reading of books. You will learn soon enough to be a good judge of your writers – Often you need only to have listened to barely two pages of an author, and you know who you have before you. The mere title is often a pretty readable profile. And the preface too is a subtle measure of the book. Which is why nowadays wiser writers usually omit that treacherous advertisement of its contents, and the easy-going ones usually leave it out because a good foreword is more difficult to write than the book itself – for, as Lessing put it in his younger, revolutionary days,[3] the foreword is at the same

---

[2] Cf. *Miscellaneous Remarks*, I, p. 203 above

[3] See *Critical Fragment* 8 and Friedrich Schlegel's article 'Über Lessing', where he refers to Lessing as one of the revolutionary spirits.

time the book's root and its square. And, I would add, it is also its best review.

And the older philologists' manner of filling their works with quotations and commentaries – what was it but the child of poverty? Born of lack of books and abundance of literary spirit.

A. But I don't know. As far as I am concerned, there are even too many *good* books. I spend so much time with a good book – or rather, every good book becomes the vehicle of a life-long interest, the object of never-ending enjoyment. And why do you limit yourself to the few good and intelligent writers? Is it not for the same reason? We are now so limited that there is very little we can enjoy wholly, and in the end is it not better to absorb and assimilate one beautiful object entirely than alight upon a hundred, tasting everything, and dulling our senses soon enough with often conflicting demipleasures, without having profited anything for eternity?

B. You speak like a man of religion – in me, unfortunately, you have met a Pantheist – for whom the vast, immeasurable world is just wide enough. I limit myself to the few good and intelligent people – because I must. What more could I want? And so it is with books. For me there could never be enough of the making of books. If I had the good fortune to be a father – I could never have enough children – not just ten or twelve – a hundred, at least.

A. And women too, my greedy friend?

B. No. Only one. Seriously.

A. What bizarre inconsistency.

B. Not bizarre. And not inconsistent either, for there is only one spirit within me, not a hundred. And just as my spirit can be transformed into a hundred or a million minds, my wife can be transformed into all the women there are. Every person is infinitely variable. I feel the same about children as I do about books. I would like to see before me as the work of my mind a whole collection of books from all the arts and sciences. I feel the same about everything. Wilhelm Meister's Years of Apprenticeship are all we have at the moment. We should have as many Years of Apprenticeship as possible, written in the same spirit – the collected Years of Apprenticeship of all the people who have ever lived!

A. Stop, stop. My head is in a whirl. More tomorrow. Then I will be in a fit state to drink a few glasses of your favourite wine with you.

2

A. Would you care to share your ideas further about writing and so on? I trust I can survive a lively paradoxical thrust – and if you set me going, I may give you some help. You know, once a slow mind is set in motion, its movements are all the bolder and more irresistible.

B. Of course. The more heavily a thing expresses force, the more force it can absorb – and with this remark, we have arrived at German literature, which is a striking confirmation of its truth. Its capacity is enormous. And I do not mean to offend tender sensibilities when I say that it is not easy to use it for filigree work. But that is not to deny that in the mass it resembles the ancient German warrior-troops, who would probably have vanquished ten Roman armies fighting man to man, but, I admit, were defeated in the mass by corporate discipline, rapid deployment and a general tactical view.

A. Do you think that its velocity and force are increasing, or are they still at least in a phase of equal acceleration?

B. Increasing, of course. And in such a way that the nucleus separates and refines more and more of the loose material surrounding it and hindering its motion. In the case of an entity such as literature, the force that gave the first impetus, the motive energy, increases in proportion to its acceleration, and thus enlarges its capacity. You see that this is a situation of infinite potential. There are two variables in a mutually increasing relationship, the product of which is in a state of hyperbolic progression. But to make the metaphor clearer, we have to do not with a quantity – motion and extension – but with a refining *variation* (distinction) of qualities, whose essence we call Nature. Let us call one of these variables the sense-faculty, the organibility, the faculty of animation – which then includes the idea of variability. Let us call the other the energy, order and variety of the moving powers. Think of the two in a mutually increasing relationship, and then deduce the series of their products. Richness increases with simplicity, fullness of tone with harmony, the individual and the perfection of the part with the perfection of the whole, inner union with outward separation.

A. However accurate and flattering a picture of our literary history this may be, it is a little too erudite. I can understand it only superficially – though that may be just as well – so I beg you, instead of giving an inexplicable explanation, come down from the eternal snows and talk to me as plainly as you can about certain phenomena below the tree-line, at the foot of the mountain, where you are not so close to the gods, and I do not have to fear your oracular speech.

3

[A.] Life is very short.

[B.] It seems very long to me.

[A.] It is short when it should be long, and long when it should be short.

[B.] Which of us is alive, then? Are you not the one who dwells on the disagreeable, and flees from the agreeable?

[A.] That is what is so bad: that in this respect I am as incapable of changing as you are. The agreeable stimulates one's energy, the disagreeable inhibits it.

[B.] Well . . . and you perceive an incompleteness here . . . ?

[A.] All too vividly, alas.

[B.] What is stopping you from pursuing this indication?

[A.] What indication?

[B.] That you should not expect what you desire, but should go in search of it. Don't you see that you are thrown onto your own resources?

[A.] To contain myself in patience? I've known that for a long time.

[B.] But not to help yourself too?

[A.] The sick man sends for the doctor because he cannot help himself.

[B.] But what if the doctor prescribes as medicine for his patient the exertion of his own intellect? The sick man who fails himself can only be cured by being prescribed – himself.

[A.] Don't forget that we started from the brevity and length of life.

[B.] Its application is as brief and easy as the gladness of pleasure, and as painfully slow as forebearance. The former I will give you, the latter is up to you. Moderate with reflection the current of energy flowing all too swiftly through your joy, hasten the slow progress – by regular activity.

[A.] Your prescription is not what I am looking for, after all: you are prescribing a mixture by *dilution*. I would accept half gratefully.

[B.] My dear friend, you are not a chymist, otherwise you would know that out of a true mixture, a third factor emerges which contains both elements at the same time, and is more than each separately.

4

[A.] You are right after all. Our conversation led me to a most interesting result –

[B.] Now it is my turn to be instructed – a turn-about which comes only from true friendship.

[A.] You cleared me a way right through my doubts at the value of pleasure. I understand now that our original existence, if I can express it like this, is pleasure. Time came into being with un-pleasure. That is why all un-pleasure is so long, and all pleasure so brief. Absolute pleasure is *eternal* – outside of all time. Relative pleasure more or less one integral moment.

[B.] You fill me with enthusiasm – only a few steps more, and we will be standing on the heights of the inner world.

[A.] I know what steps you mean. Like time, un-pleasure is finite. Everything finite arises from un-pleasure. Such as life.

[B.] I will take over from you – and continue. The Finite is finite – What remains? Absolute pleasure – eternity – absolute life. And what have we to do in time, whose purpose is the self-*consciousness* of infinity? Assuming that it has a purpose, for one could well ask whether purposelessness were not the very thing that characterizes illusion!

[A.] That too – meantime, what should we try to bring about? The transformation of un-pleasure into pleasure, and with it the transformation of time into eternity, by means of an independent abstraction and elation of spirit, consciousness and illusion, as such.

[B.] Yes, my dear friend. And here at the pillars of Hercules let us embrace, in our delight at the conviction that it is in our power to regard life as a beautiful, inspired illusion, and as a splendid spectacle, that in spirit we can even here be in a state of absolute pleasure and eternity, and that the old lament at the transience of things itself can, and shall, become the most joyful of our thoughts.

[A.] This view of life as a temporal illusion, as drama, might become second nature to us. How swiftly then would dark hours pass, and how enchanting transience would seem.

5

A. Dearest friend, give me a clear idea of the Prince, one that will stand the test of scrutiny. I have been brooding long on it, but these damned princes are not for me – they vanish in the light of my concentration. They cannot be fire-proof, or light-proof. Is the idea of the Prince rather like a frame around a picture of Egyptian darkness?

B. A fortunate genius has brought you to the very man, for a happy chance has revealed to me the following great mystery – although I admit, like every mystery, it sounds pretty paradoxical:

> Princes are zeroes – in themselves they are nought, but with numbers
> Which raise them at random beside them, they are worth a great deal.

A. But my good friend, what do these hypotheses amount to in the end? After all, one single fact truly observed is worth more than the most brilliant hypothesis. Hypothesizing is a risky pastime – in the end it turns into a passionate proneness to un-truth, and probably nothing has done more harm to the best minds and all the sciences than this extravagance of the fantasizing intelligence. This intellectual indecency wholly blunts our sense of the truth, and makes us lose the habit of strict observation, which is the only true foundation for extending and discovering new knowledge.

B.   Like nets are hypotheses – only the fisher who casts his net far
       Hauls in the catch. Was not America found by hypothesis?
       Praise to hypothesis, long may she live, for she only
       Stays ever-young, though oft she may be self-defeating.

And now the practical application in prose. The sceptic, my friend, has done little, and common empiricism even less, for the extension of science. All the sceptic does is to spoil things for the maker of hypotheses, and unsteady the ground beneath his feet. A strange way of advancing science. At the best a very indirect achievement. Your true maker of hypotheses is none other than the inventor himself, for the new-discovered land already hovers obscurely before his eyes before he has actually made his discovery. With this obscure image in mind, he hovers above observation and experience, and it is only after frequent and various contacts and frictions between his ideas and practical experience that he finally comes upon the idea which has a positive or negative relation to experience, such that both may then be linked for ever more, and a new, divine light may illumine the power that has come into the world.

6

[A.] Hark'ee, it is now fashionable to talk rationally about Nature – so we too must make our contribution. Well – what shall we do – come, answer me, do.

[B.] I have been trying for some time to think of a natural beginning for our conversation – I am pressing my natural intelligence into it, but it has dried up, and there is no more pith in it.

[A.] Perhaps some scholar has used it as a fine specimen to press between the leaves of his herbarium . . . ?

[B.] I would be curious to know how he has classified it.

[A.] Probably among the cryptogamia, for there is no trace of blossom or fruit.

[B.] You see, we are already inspired by Nature – we have slipped into Nature all unnoticed. You are one of the realists – or, in plain German, you are a bluff, coarse fellow.

[A.] That is a true word – a word of consecration. I am much disposed to become one of Nature's priests.

[B.] You mean because priests have a belly as great as yours, and Nature is in truth nothing more than a vast belly.

[A.] That is true too – but the true disposition lies in the coarseness. For see, Nature is tremendously coarse, and to know her aright, you have to grasp her coarsely. Coarse sand needs coarse sieve. This proverb was made for natural philosophy, for we are to grind it finer with our intellects. Our ancestors must have had a great insight into Nature, for only in Germany has true coarseness been discovered and cultivated.

[B.] It suits our soil very well – which is why things look so barren for us now, for we have neglected our national plant and been most careless of the wealth it has to offer. It flourishes now only among common men – and that is why Nature still grows green for them. She has long ago turned her back on the finer sort of people, and would be pleased to do so for ever.

[A.] Our conversation has given me a definition of Nature – she is the essence of all coarseness.

[B.] And all the laws of Nature can be deduced from that – she is constantly, unceasingly, coarse, she grows ever coarser, and no coarseness is the coarsest. *Lex continuitatis* [law of unbroken succession].

[A.] She likes going straight to the point without any ado. *Lex Parsimoniae* [law of parsimony].

[B.] Yes – and a number of unknown laws can be developed from this fruitful idea. But because we are philosophers, we do not have to bother about pursuing this in detail. We have the principle, and that is good enough – the rest we can leave to baser minds.

[A.] But tell me, how is it that Nature has become so damned rare now. Art is actually the usual thing.

[B.] Yes, she must be, for after all she makes herself comprehensible enough, and is always ready to burst forth in all her nature, so she ought to be much more widely understood.

[A.] The man who is so obsessed by the exaggerated artificiality of art will take her very coarseness to be art, and so she is misunderstood everywhere.

[B.] But we are also born to Nature, and all this comes naturally to the natural man – so what is there left to say about it? Merely talking about it shows you are a dull blunderer without pith or energy, for whereof one speaks, thereof one has nothing. That is an axiom.

[A.] Then let us stop talking about it, for otherwise our Nature will give us the slip.

[B.] You are right. And then fashion might almost have played us an underhand trick and falsely driven us from our nature. Let us go down to the cellar – Nature is at home there – so that we can restore our natural selves.

[A.] But take care not to talk about the wine – for whereof one speaks, thereof one has nothing.

[B.] True, that is why you are always talking about intelligence –

[A.] Only when you talk about short ears.

'On Goethe' (1798)

445. Goethe is a practical poet through and through. He is in his works –
what the English are in their wares – utterly simple, neat, convenient
and durable. He has done for German literature what Wedgwood did for
English art. Like the Englishman, he has a natural business sense and a
refined taste acquired by good sense. Both are wholly compatible with
each other, and are closely related, in the *chemical* sense. His studies in
physics make it quite clear that he is much more inclined to complete
something slight, and give it elegance and high finish, than tackle an
entire world, or take on something which one can be certain from the start
cannot be carried out perfectly, will surely remain awkward, and resists
the high polish of mastery. Even in this field he will choose a romantic
subject, or something similarly intricate. His observations on light and on
the metamorphoses of plants and insects[1] both confirm and demonstrate
most convincingly that the perfect style for instruction is also part of the
artist's range. There is a sense in which we might also, and rightly, declare
that Goethe is the foremost physicist of his time, and has in fact marked
an era in physics. It is not a question of the extent of his knowledge,
nor would we claim that discoveries determine the stature of a natural
scientist. It is rather a question of whether the scientist observes Nature
as an artist observes the ancient world – for Nature is something different

---

[1] Novalis refers to 'Beiträge zur Optik' (1791–4), 'Die Metamorphose der Pflanzen' (1790), and 'Die
Metamorphose der Insekten' (1796–8).

from living Antiquity. Nature and insight into Nature develop at the same time, as Antiquity and knowledge of Antiquity develop together. For it is a great mistake to believe that such things as ancient worlds really exist. It is only now that Antiquity is coming into existence. This is brought about by the artist's eyes and soul. The relics of the ancient world are only the particular stimulus to our creation of Antiquity. Antiquity was not built with hands. The mind produces it with the eye, and the hewn stone is but the body which acquires meaning only when imbued with the idea of Antiquity, and as its appearance. Goethe the poet has the same relationship to other poets as Goethe the physicist has to other physicists. Other poets may sometimes exceed him in range, variety or depth, but in the art that comes from cultivation, who would claim to be his equal? Where others only tend towards some end, he completes the deed. He really makes something, whereas others only make something possible – or necessary. We are all of us necessary or possible creators, but how few of us are real creators. A scholastic philosopher might call this active empiricism. We will content ourselves with observing Goethe's artistic talent and taking another look at the quality of his intellect. He casts new light for us on the gift of abstraction. He abstracts with a rare precision, but never without at the same time reconstructing the object which corresponds to the abstraction. This is nothing but applied philosophy – and so, to our astonishment, we finally discover a practical philosopher, applying his insights – which is after all what every true artist has always been. The *pure* philosopher too will be practical, although the applied philosopher does not need to devote himself to pure philosophy – for that is an art in itself. (Goethe's *Wilhelm Meister*.) True art is situated in the intellect, which creates according to a characteristic concept: only fantasy, wit and good judgement are required of it. Thus *Wilhelm Meister* is entirely a product of art, a work of the intellect. From this point of view, we see that many mediocre works of art are exhibited in the halls of art, while on the other hand many writings regarded as excellent are excluded. The Italians and the Spanish are far more talented in matters of art than we are. And even the French are not without gifts – the English have far fewer, and in this respect they resemble us, for we too rarely have a talent for art, although of all the nations we are most richly endowed with those capacities employed by the intelligence in its works. This abundance of the requirements needed for art is what makes the few artists amongst us so unique – so outstanding, and we can be assured that the greatest works of art will arise among us, for there is no nation to match us in energy and universality. If I have understood our modern lovers of ancient literature aright, their intention when they demand the imitation of classical writers is to educate our artists, and rouse in us a talent for art. No modern nation has possessed an artistic mentality to such a high degree as the ancients. Everything about them is art. But perhaps we would not be saying too much if we were to assume that they are, or could become, the supreme artists, only in our eyes. It is the same with classical literature as it is with ancient art: it is not a given, it is not there already, but it has first to be produced by us. We can bring a classical literature – which the ancients themselves did not possess – into existence only by keen and intelligent study of the ancients. The ancients would have to take on the opposite task – for the mere artist is a one-sided, limited being. Goethe may not be a match for the ancients in rigour, but he excels them in content – though that is not to his credit. His *Wilhelm Meister* approaches them pretty closely. It is the Absolute Novel, without qualification – and that is a great deal in our time.

Goethe will and must be surpassed – but only as the ancients can be surpassed – in content and energy, in variety and depth – not really as an artist – and even so, only by very little, for his rightness and rigour are perhaps more classic than they seem.

446. Consummate philosophers easily happen upon the principle: philosophy too is vanity – and this applies to all branches of learning.

447. *The art of living* – against *macrobiotics*.

448. the sensitive will/All stimuli *attract* – the *stimulation identifies*. Ego – Non-ego – product. All stimuli thought into one is Ego and Non-ego. Theory of magic./Individual definitions.

449. *Composition in speech*. musical treatment of writing.

450. The looser, the more *sensitive* – the denser, the more *capable of rousing sensitivity*.

[451.] All a prime minister, a prince, or any kind of director needs are *human beings* and *artists* – a *knowledge* of character and talent.

452. Truly universal thoughts are like the country parson in the second part of *Wilhelm Meister's Apprenticeship* – They seem so familiar because

they look like the general thoughts of mankind, and not like the thoughts of any Tom, Dick or Harry.[2]

453. World psychology. We cannot explain the organism without assuming *a world soul*, just as we cannot assume the universal plan without assuming a universal rational being.

The thinker who attempts to explain the organism without taking into consideration the *soul* and the mysterious bond between *soul and body*, will not get very far. Perhaps life is nothing but the result of this union, *the action of this contact.*

Light is produced by the friction of steel on stone, sound by the touch of bow on strings, spasmodic movement by the making and breaking of galvanic contact; it may be that life is likewise produced by the arousal (penetration) of organic matter.

Indirect construction. The right thing appears of its own accord, when the conditions for its appearance are present. The relationship of the *mechanical operation* to its higher *result* is absolutely the same as that of steel, stone and contact to the spark. (*Free collaboration*)

> Every dynamic effect is accompanied by a higher genius.
> The individual soul shall become congruent with the world soul.
> The world soul rules, and the individual soul rules jointly with it.

454. Of the many ways of making an *effect* or *stimulus* (by combination, impact, contact, indirect contact, mere presence, possible presence, etc.).

455. *Dramatic* narrative mode. Fairy-tale and *Wilhelm Meister*. Toujours en état de Poësie.

456. Great value of mathematics as an *active science*. Superior interest of *Mechanics*. (*The study of touch. Acoustics.*) The many kinds of touch – and tangents, active and passive tangents. Angles of contact. Rapidity of contact, or rhythmic units. Sequences and series of rhythmic units. Units of rhythmical pattern present in the line, the point, the surface, the mass. Persistent units of rhythm.

457. Foundations of geognosy and oryctognosy [that is, geology and mineralogy]. Critique of characteristic signs.

---

[2] Cf. Friedrich Schlegel's 'On Goethe's *Meister*', p. 270.

458. Theory of instruments – or *organology*.

459. Light is in any case action – Light is like life – dynamic action – a *phenomenon which reveals itself*, but only when the appropriate conditions conjoin. Light makes fire. Light is the genius of the combustion process. Like light, life is capable of intensification, fading, and gradual negation. Does it also break down, as light does into colours? The process of nutrition is not the cause, but only the consequence, of life.

460. All activity is *transition*. In chymistry, both elements transform each other in their combination. But not in what is called mechanical influence.

461. Signs of *disease* – of the instinct for self-destruction – This is so of everything imperfect – and so even of life – or rather, of organic matter. Cancellation of the distinction between life and death. Annihilation of death.

462. Might it not be so, that all the changes brought about by the mutual effect of bodies upon one another are merely changes of capacity and sensitivity, and that all chymical operations and influences have this *general unity*, in that they modify the sensitivity and capacity of every material? Thus, for example, oxygen acts in the process of combustion. All chymical elements are *indirectly congruent*. The characteristics and appearances of every substance depend on its sensitivity. All changes brought about by combination are connected with the capacity and sensitivity of the bodies. The bodies are distinguished by the variety of their sensitivity. Or could one say that bodies are most naturally classified as stimuli by the variety of their relations to *sensitivity*? All this agrees very well with Galvanism. Chymistry is already Galvanism – the Galvanism of inanimate Nature. Fire is only a *means* – a learned resource used by the Chymist. (Spontaneous combustion is Galvanization.) (Metallic calcides are still not sufficiently used in medicine.) Does heat have a chymical action? Strictly speaking, no – it only encourages galvanization.

463. Cold is an *indirect stimulation* – in healthy bodies it draws heat out. There is nothing that keeps a thoroughly healthy body so lively and active as an alternating deficiency and excess of stimulations – it is *stimulated* by the deficiency to find a *substitute* – excess moderates and inhibits its functioning, excess causes it to lower its *activity*.

The *deficiency* stimulates the healthy body to *activity*, and the *excess* to *rest*. Are not works of art the products of a healthy inactivity?

[464.] The drive to organization is the drive to turn everything into instrument and means.

465. Journals are actually the first books to be written *in common*. Writing in company is an interesting symptom giving us an inkling of a great development in authorship. Perhaps one day people will write, think and act as a mass. Entire communities, even nations, will undertake One Work.

466. Every person who consists of persons is a person *to a higher power*, a person *squared*. In this connection one might say that the Greeks never existed, only a Greek genius. A cultured Greek was only indirectly and only in very small part his own creator. This explains the great and pure individuality of Greek art and science, which is not to deny that on the fringes they succumbed to the modernizing influence of Egyptian and oriental mysticism. In Ionia we notice the relaxing effect of the warm Asian skies, whereas in the early Doric forms we are aware of the mysterious rigour and austerity of the Egyptian divinities. Later writers have often assumed this ancient style, out of a modern, romantic instinct, and filled these uncouth figures with a new spirit; they have set them among their contemporaries to bid them pause in the giddy course of civilization, and make them pay renewed attention to these long-abandoned sacred relics.

467. In early times only nations – or geniuses – really lived. / Genius to a higher power, squared. So the ancients must be regarded in the mass.

468. To inquire into the *basis*, the law of a phenomenon etc., is to put an abstract question, that is, one directed away from the object and towards the spirit. It aims at *appropriation*, assimilation of the object. Explanation makes the object no longer alien. The spirit aims at absorbing the stimulus. It is stimulated by what is alien. Hence, it is the unceasing occupation of the spirit to appropriate, to transform the alien into its own.

One day, there shall no longer be any stimulus nor anything alien; the spirit shall, or should deliberately be able, to make itself self-alienated and self-stimulating. Now, the spirit is spirit out of instinct – a Nature-Spirit – but reflection and *art* shall make him a Spirit of Reason.

(Nature shall become art, and art shall become second nature.)

469. The point of dispute between the pathologists who base their theories on the humours and those who base them on the nerves is a common point at issue between physicists.

This dispute touches on the most important problems in physics.

The pathologists of the humours have their equivalent in the physicists who multiply materials – the 'matter-seers'; the neural pathologists in the atomistic, mechanical 'form-seers'. The true *actionists*, such as Fichte, etc. combine both systems. These last could be called creative observers, *creators of modes of seeing*. The other two are the *directly* and *indirectly* Sluggish – the Fluid and the Rigid.

The concept of action can be analysed into the concept *Matter* and *Movement* (impact). Thus the actionist can be analysed into the *Humoralist* and the *Neurist*. They are his closest elements, his *most intimate* components.

470. Similarly between historical geognosy and oryctognosy on the one hand, and philology on the other.

471. Sciences can be analysed into sciences, senses into senses. The more limited and definite, the more practical. Of the inclination of scholars to universalize their science. Various objects come into being in this way. An object, [so] that various senses become one.

472. Presentation of an object in *series* – (series of variations, modifications, etc.) For example, as Goethe presents the persons of Wilhelm Meister, the beautiful soul, Nathalie. In self-reflection – in things at first, second and third hand, etc. An historical sequence is of this kind, a collection of engravings from the crudest beginnings of art to its perfection, and so on – of forms, from the frog to Apollo etc.

473. Religious, moral, spiritual, moral *crimes* etc. Poetry is the true and absolute reality. This is the heart of my philosophy. The more poetic, the more true. Is the beautiful neuter?/On general concepts. Are they neutra, combinations, or *quid*? Facility and popularity./Transforming the fiscal sciences into poetry./Critique of previous physicists./J. W. *Ritter*.[3] Concept of erudition./A *universal encyclopaedia* is the best handbook./

---

[3] J. W. Ritter (1776–1810), German physicist, who made discoveries in galvanism, electrochemical properties of elements, and the effects of light on chemical reactions.

What is more like life? Life-mass like Candlemass? A mass of life, like a mass of light?/Animals as attributes of the gods./The treatment of astrology by Theophrastus[4] and the astrologists./Murhard's History of Physics.[5] Reticulation./The mathematical nature of analogy./On the *surface*, as synthesis./On experiments/Time and space – treated with greater liveliness – /Nature – things born – Suggestion of procreation/Astronomical geognostic division of bodies into luminous and non-luminous./Electrometric electricity – absolute – relative./Essay on theorists and the *use* of speculative sciences.

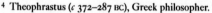

[4] Theophrastus (*c* 372–287 BC), Greek philosopher.
[5] F. W. A. Murhard, *Geschichte der Physik* (1798–9).

'Studies in the Visual Arts' (1799)

475. On the sensations of *thinking* in the *body*.

476. *Ancients*. The Madonna./Man is a self-endowed historical individual. Stages of mankind. When mankind has reached the highest stage, the higher will reveal and conceal itself spontaneously./Aspect of the history of mankind – the masses – nations – societies – individuals./Elevation of mechanics. Fichte's intellectual chemistry. Chemistry is the *passionate ground*. Chemistry is the crudest and first formation./*Descriptions of paintings etc.*/On *Landscape painting* – and painting against sculpture in general./*Everything must be amenable to being mathematically squared and resistant to being squared at the same time.* Use, practice is infinitely graded – so is measurement. Landscapes – *Surfaces* – *Structures* – *Architectonic*. Cavernous *Landscapes*. Atmospheres. Cloudlandscapes. The entire landscape should form *An Individual* – Vegetation and inorganic nature – Fluid Firm – *Masculine* – *Feminine*. geognostic Landscapes. Nature Variations./Must not sculpture and painting be symbolic. The picture gallery is a store-room for every kind of indirect stimulus for the poet./*Necessity* of all works of art./Every work of art has an Ideal a priori – has a necessity within itself to be there. Only this way is a true criticism of painters possible. Suite of madonnas. Suite of heroes. Suite of wise men. Suite of geniuses. Suite of gods. Suite of men. We are compelled by the ancients to treat them as holy relics. Particular kinds of *souls* and *spirits*. Who dwell in trees, landscapes, stones and paintings. A landscape

must be looked at as a dryad or an oread. A landscape must be felt like a body. Every landscape is an ideal body for a particular *kind of spirit.*/The Sonnet./The *Joke.*/Feeling for *Antiquity* – roused by the Ancients.

477. The poet borrows all his materials, except images./On Friedrich *Schlegel* – etc./Character, meaning.

478. Eternal virgins – born wives./Fichte's apotheosis of Kant's philosophy./*Thinking* about thinking certainly teaches one to get thinking in his power – because we learn thereby to think how and what we will./Innermost, furthestmost, infinite universe – Analogy with outside – light – gravity.

479. Do all humans have to be human beings? It is possible for beings quite other than human to exist in human form./Virtuousness in the educator is the indirectly positive principle in education./*Universal writer's dexterity.*/On the wide thinkers – and the deep thinkers – e.g. [Friedrich] Schlegel and Fichte./Trivializing the divine, apotheosizing the base./We are past the time of generally valid *forms* –/Influence of the sculptural material upon the figure – and its *effect.*/Might not the stronger and more attractive effect of rarer and more delicate materials be *galvanic? Compulsion* is a stimulus for the mind – compulsion has something absolutely stimulating for the mind./Medicinal application of happiness and unhappiness./On neutralization – complicated diseases – local pain – reproductive system./All doubt, all need for *truth* – dissolution – Knowledge is the consequence of *crudity* and *over-education* – Symptom of an imperfect constitution. Hence all scientific *education* aims at dexterity – practice – All scientific *healing* aims at the *restitution* of health where there are no scientific needs.

480. Revolutionizing and adaptation of mathematics./Letter on art and antiquity to Schlegel[1] sen. *Gedichte*/Letter to F[riedrich] S[chlegel]./Fichte's synthesis – true chemical compound. In suspension./Individuality and generality of humans and diseases./On necessary *self-limitation* – infinite versatility of the cultivated mind – it is possible to draw oneself out of everything, twist and turn everything at will./The *powerful geniuses.*/Headings of the main masses in letters etc./On the *inks* – and

[1] Cf. Novalis to Caroline Schlegel, 9 September 1798: 'The letter about antiquity is completely altered.'

the *tone* – analogously moral./On the right condition of dialogue. On the experimental genius./The essential businessman has less need of knowledge and skill than of historical spirit and culture./Spiritual metre./On mechanics./Learned conferences – their purpose./Marriages are mostly divorces./Mimicry in musical *notation*./Wit in the great./Experimental religion and philosophy./What effect on one has ordinary intercourse in Brown's sense.[2]/Stimulus *becomes* capable of stimulation – etc. Physiology./Concept of neutralization. Is the Neutrum the highest – negative neutrum positive neutrum and synthesis./On the transformation of history into tradition. The latter is the higher.

481. Everything visible cleaves to the Invisible – the Audible to the Inaudible – the Palpable to the Impalpable. Perhaps the Thinkable to the Unthinkable –. The *telescope* is an *artificial, invisible organ./Vessel./*The imagination is the marvellous sense which can *replace* all senses for us – and which is so much ours to command. If the outward senses seem to be ruled entirely by mechanical laws – the imagination is obviously not bound to the present and to contact with external stimuli.

482. Herder's *Plastik* p. 7.[3] They taught the man who was born blind and who recovered his sight to recognize his touch with his eyes. He often forgot the meanings of the symbols for his tactile feeling until his eye grew practised in regarding figures in space and coloured images as the letters of previous physical sensations; it became accustomed to associating the one rapidly with the other and reading the objects around him.

483. The unity of the picture, the form, the graphic composition rests upon firm proportions, like the unity of musical harmony./Harmony and melody./

484.

Space	Visual arts	Sight	Surface	
Time	Music	Hearing	Sound	
Energy	Poesy	Feeling	Body	Herder[4]

485. Our *body* is *part* of the *world* – or better, a member: it already expresses

---

[2] Probably a reference to John Brown (1735–88), medical doctor of Edinburgh and author of *Elementa Medicinae* (1780), in which Brown describes the concept of excitability and stimulation.

[3] J. G. Herder, *Plastik. Einige Wahrnehmungen über Form und Gestalt aus Pygmalions bildendem Traum* (Riga, 1779; Suphan edn, VIII, 1–87).

[4] *Ibid.*, VIII, 15f.

the *independence*, the analogy with the whole – in short the concept of the microcosm. This member must correspond to the whole. So many senses, so many modi of the universe – the universe entirely an analogy of the human being in body, soul and spirit. The former the abbreviated form, the latter the extended form of the same substance.

I should not and will not on the whole act arbitrarily upon the world– that is why I have a body. By modifying my body, I modify *my* world. By not acting upon the *vessel of my existence*, I likewise indirectly shape my world.

486. The tree can turn for me into a flame burgeoning – man into a flame speaking – beast into a flame walking.

487. Everything perceived is perceived in proportion to its repulsive power. Explanation of the Visible and the Illuminated – by analogy to sensible warmth. Likewise with sounds. Perhaps also with thoughts.

FRIEDRICH SCHLEGEL

From 'Critical Fragments' (1797)

4. There is so much poetry and yet there is nothing more rare than a poem! This is due to the vast quantity of poetical sketches, studies, fragments, tendencies, ruins and raw materials.

8. A good preface must be at once the square root and the square of its book.

9. Wit is absolute social feeling, or fragmentary genius.

14. In poetry too every whole can be a part and every part really a whole.

16. Though genius isn't something that can be produced arbitrarily, it is freely willed – like wit, love and faith, which one day will have to become arts and sciences. You should demand genius from everyone, but not expect it. A Kantian would call this the categorical imperative of genius.

20. A classical text must never be entirely comprehensible. But those who are cultivated and who cultivate themselves must always want to learn more from it.

21. Just as a child is only a thing which wants to become a human being, so a poem is only a product of nature which wants to become a work of art.

22. The flame of the most brilliantly witty idea should radiate warmth only after it has given off light; it can be quenched suddenly by a single analytic word, even when it is meant as praise.

239

23. Every good poem must be wholly intentional and wholly instinctive. That is how it becomes ideal.

25. The two main principles of the so-called historical criticism are the Postulate of Vulgarity and the Axiom of the Average. The Postulate of Vulgarity: everything great, good and beautiful is improbable because it is extraordinary and, at the very least, suspicious. The Axiom of the Average: as we and our surroundings are, so must it have been always and everywhere, because that, after all, is so very natural.

26. Novels are the Socratic dialogues of our time. And this free form has become the refuge of common sense in its flight from pedantry.

27. The critic is a reader who ruminates. Therefore he ought to have more than one stomach.

28. Feeling (for a particular art, science, person, etc.) is divided spirit, is self-restriction: hence a result of self-creation and self-destruction.

29. Gracefulness is life lived correctly, is sensuality contemplating and shaping itself.

33. The overriding disposition of every writer is almost always to lean in one of two directions: either not to say a number of things that absolutely need saying, or else to say a great many things that absolutely ought to be left unsaid. The former is the original sin of synthetic, the latter of analytic minds.

37. In order to write well about something, one shouldn't be interested in it any longer. To express an idea with due circumspection, one must have relegated it wholly to one's past; one must no longer be preoccupied with it. As long as the artist is in the process of discovery and inspiration, he is in a state which, as far as communication is concerned, is at the very least intolerant. He wants to blurt out everything, which is a fault of young geniuses or a legitimate prejudice of old bunglers. And so he fails to recognize the value and the dignity of self-restriction, which is after all, for the artist as well as the man, the first and the last, the most necessary and the highest duty. Most necessary because wherever one does not restrict oneself, one is restricted by the world; and that makes one a slave. The highest because one can only restrict oneself at those points and places where one possesses infinite power, self-creation and

self-destruction. Even a friendly conversation which cannot be broken off at any moment, completely arbitrarily, has something intolerant about it. But a writer who can and does talk himself out, who keeps nothing back for himself, and likes to tell everything he knows, is to be pitied. There are only three mistakes to guard against. First: What appears to be unlimited free will, and consequently seems and should seem to be irrational or supra-rational, nonetheless must still at bottom be simply necessary and rational; otherwise the whim becomes wilful, becomes intolerant, and self-restriction turns into self-destruction. Second: Don't be in too much of a hurry for self-restriction, but first give rein to self-creation, invention and inspiration, until you're ready. Third: Don't exaggerate self-restriction.

42. Philosophy is the real homeland of irony, which one would like to define as logical beauty: for wherever philosophy appears in oral or written dialogues – and is not simply confined into rigid systems – there irony should be asked for and provided. And even the Stoics considered urbanity a virtue. Of course, there is also a rhetorical species of irony which, sparingly used, has an excellent effect, especially in polemics; but compared to the sublime urbanity of the Socratic muse, it is like the pomp of the most splendid oration set over against the noble style of an ancient tragedy. Only poetry can also reach the heights of philosophy in this way, and only poetry does not restrict itself to isolated ironical passages, as rhetoric does. There are ancient and modern poems that are pervaded by the divine breath of irony throughout and informed by a truly transcendental buffoonery. Internally: the mood that surveys everything and rises infinitely above all limitations, even above its own art, virtue or genius; externally, in its execution: the mimic style of an averagely gifted Italian *buffo*.

44. You should never appeal to the spirit of the ancients as if to an authority. It's a peculiar thing with spirits: they don't let themselves be grabbed by the hand and shown to others. Spirits reveal themselves only to spirits. Probably here too the best and shortest way would be to prove one's possession of the only true belief by doing good works.

48. Irony is the form of paradox. Paradox is everything simultaneously good and great.

51. To use wit as an instrument for revenge is as shameful as using art as a means for titillating the senses.

55. A really free and cultivated person ought to be able to attune himself at will to being philosophical or philological, critical or poetical, historical or rhetorical, ancient or modern: quite arbitrarily, just as one tunes an instrument, at any time and to any degree.

56. Wit is logical sociability.

57. If some mystical art lovers who think of every criticism as a dissection and every dissection as a destruction of pleasure were to think logically, then 'wow' would be the best criticism of the greatest work of art. To be sure, there are critiques which say nothing more, but only take much longer to say it.

62. We already have so many theories about poetic genres. Why have we no concept of poetic genre? Perhaps then we would have to make do with a single theory of poetical genres.

65. Poetry is republican speech: a speech which is its own law and end unto itself, and in which all the parts are free citizens and have the right to vote.

70. People who write books and imagine that their readers are the public and that they must educate it soon arrive at the point not only of despising their so-called public but of hating it. Which leads absolutely nowhere.

73. What is lost in average, good or even first-rate translations is precisely the best part.

78. Many of the very best novels are compendia, encyclopedias of the whole spiritual life of a brilliant individual. Works which have this quality, even if they are cast in a completely different mould – like *Nathan*[1] – thereby take on a novelistic hue. And every human being who is cultivated and who cultivates himself contains a novel within himself. But it isn't necessary for him to express it and write it out.

84. From what the moderns aim at, we learn what poetry should become; from what the ancients have done, what it has to be.

85. Every honest author writes for nobody or everybody. Whoever writes for some particular group does not deserve to be read.

[1] *Nathan der Weise* (1779), by Gotthold Ephraim Lessing.

86. The function of criticism, people say, is to educate one's readers! Whoever wants to be educated, let him educate himself. This is rude: but it can't be helped.

88. Nothing is more piquant than a brilliant man who has manners or mannerisms. That is, if he has them: but not at all, if they have him. That leads to spiritual petrification.

89. Isn't it unnecessary to write more than one novel, unless the artist has become a new man? It's obvious that frequently all the novels of a particular author belong together and in a sense make up only one novel.

96. A good riddle should be witty; otherwise nothing remains once the answer has been found. And there's a charm in having a witty idea which is enigmatic to the point of needing to be solved: only its meaning should be immediately and completely clear as soon as it's been hit upon.

100. The poetry of one writer is termed philosophical, of another philological, of a third, rhetorical, etc. But what then is poetical poetry?

101. Affectation doesn't arise so much out of a striving to be new as out of a fear of being old.

102. To want to judge everything is a great fallacy, or a venial sin.

104. What's commonly called reason is only a subspecies of it: namely, the thin and watery sort. There's also a thick, fiery kind that actually makes wit witty, and gives an elasticity and electricity to a solid style.

108. Socratic irony is the only involuntary and yet completely deliberate dissimulation. It is equally impossible to feign it or divulge it. To a person who hasn't got it, it will remain a riddle even after it is openly confessed. It is meant to deceive no one except those who consider it a deception and who either take pleasure in the delightful roguery of making fools of the whole world or else become angry when they get an inkling they themselves might be included. In this sort of irony, everything should be playful and serious, guilelessly open and deeply hidden. It originates in the union of *savoir vivre* and scientific spirit, in the conjunction of a perfectly instinctive and a perfectly conscious philosophy. It contains and arouses a feeling of indissoluble antagonism between the absolute and the relative, between the impossibility and the necessity of complete communication.

It is the freest of all licences, for by its means one transcends oneself; and yet it is also the most lawful, for it is absolutely necessary. It is a very good sign when the harmonious bores are at a loss about how they should react to this continuous self-parody, when they fluctuate endlessly between belief and disbelief until they get dizzy and take what is meant as a joke seriously and what is meant seriously as a joke. For Lessing irony is instinct; for Hemsterhuis[2] it is classical study; for Hülsen[3] it arises out of the philosophy of philosophy and surpasses these others by far.

109. Gentle wit, or wit without a barb, is a privilege of poetry which prose can't encroach upon: for only by means of the sharpest focus on a single point can the individual idea gain a kind of wholeness.

112. The analytic writer observes the reader as he is; and accordingly he makes his calculations and sets up his machines in order to make the proper impression on him. The synthetic writer constructs and creates a reader as he should be; he doesn't imagine him calm and dead, but alive and critical. He allows whatever he has created to take shape gradually before the reader's eyes, or else he tempts him to discover it himself. He doesn't try to make any particular impression on him, but enters with him into the sacred relationship of deepest symphilosophy or sympoetry.

114. There are so many critical journals of varying sorts and differing intentions! If only a society might be formed sometime with the sole purpose of gradually making criticism – since criticism is, after all, necessary – a real thing.

115. The whole history of modern poetry is a running commentary on the following brief philosophical text: all art should become science and all science art; poetry and philosophy should be made one.

117. Poetry can be criticized only by way of poetry. A critical judgement of an artistic production has no civil rights in the realm of art if it isn't itself a work of art, either in its substance, as a representation of a necessary impression in the state of becoming, or in the beauty of its form and open tone, like that of the old Roman satires.

---

[2] François Hemsterhuis (1721–90), Dutch aesthetician and moral philosopher influenced by the Neoplatonic tradition.
[3] August Ludwig Hülsen (1765–1810), German philosopher and educator, friend of Fichte and the Schlegels.

120. Whoever could manage to interpret Goethe's *Meister* properly would have expressed what is now happening in literature. He could, so far as literary criticism is concerned, retire forever.

121. The simplest and most immediate questions, like Should we criticize Shakespeare's works as art or as nature? and Are epic and tragedy essentially different or not? and Should art deceive or merely seem to do so? are all questions that can't be answered without the deepest consideration and the most erudite history of art.

123. It is thoughtless and immodest presumption to want to learn something about art from philosophy. There are many who start out that way as if they hope to find something new there, since philosophy, after all, can't and shouldn't be able to do more than order the given artistic experiences and existing artistic principles into a science, and raise the appreciation of art, and create here as well that logical mood which unites absolute tolerance with absolute rigour.

126. The Romans knew that wit is a prophetic faculty; they called it nose.

From '*Athenaeum* Fragments' (1798)

1. Nothing is more rarely the subject of philosophy than philosophy itself.

24. Many of the works of the ancients have become fragments. Many modern works are fragments as soon as they are written.

27. Most people are, like Leibniz's possible worlds, only equally rightful pretenders to existence. Few exist.

32. One should have wit, but not want to have it. Otherwise, you get persiflage, the Alexandrian style of wit.

35. A *cynic* should really have no possessions whatever: for a man's possessions, in a certain sense, actually possess him. The solution to this problem is to own possessions as if one didn't own them. But it's even more artistic and cynical not to own possessions as if one owned them.[1]

37. Many witty ideas are like the sudden meeting of two friendly thoughts after a long separation.

39. Most thoughts are only the profiles of thoughts. They have to be turned around and synthesized with their antipodes. This is how many philosophical works acquire a considerable interest they would otherwise have lacked.

[1] The last two sentences of this fragment are by Schleiermacher.

41. Those people who have made a profession of explaining Kant to us were either of the sort that lacked the capacity to gain an understanding for themselves of the subjects about which Kant has written; or else such people as had only the slight misfortune of understanding no one except themselves; or such as expressed themselves even more confusedly than he did.

43. Philosophy is still moving too much in a straight line; it's not yet cyclical enough.

44. Every philosophical review should simultaneously be a philosophy of reviews.

46. According to the way many philosophers think, a regiment of soldiers on parade is a system.

51. Naïve is what is or seems to be natural, individual, or classical to the point of irony, or else to the point of continuously fluctuating between self-creation and self-destruction. If it's simply instinctive, then it's childlike, childish, or silly; if it's merely intentional, then it gives rise to affectation. The beautiful, poetical, ideal naïve must combine intention and instinct. The essence of intention in this sense is freedom, though intention isn't consciousness by a long shot. There is a certain kind of self-infatuated contemplation of one's own naturalness or silliness that is itself unspeakably silly. Intention doesn't exactly require any deep calculation or plan. Even Homeric naïveté isn't simply instinctive; there is at least as much intention in it as there is in the grace of lovely children or innocent girls. And even if Homer himself had no intentions, his poetry and the real author of that poetry, Nature, certainly did.

53. It's equally fatal for the mind to have a system and to have none. It will simply have to decide to combine the two.

54. One can only become a philosopher, not be one. As soon as one thinks one is a philosopher, one stops becoming one.

63. Every uncultivated person is a caricature of himself.

64. The demand for moderation is the spirit of castrated intolerance.

66. When an author doesn't know anymore what sort of answer to make to a critic, then he usually says: But you can't do it any better. That's like

a dogmatic philosopher accusing the sceptic of not being able to create a system.

71. People always talk about how an analysis of the beauty of a work of art supposedly disturbs the pleasure of the art lover. Well, the real lover just won't let himself be disturbed!

76. An intellectual point of view is the categorical imperative of any theory.[2]

77. A dialogue is a chain or garland of fragments. An exchange of letters is a dialogue on a larger scale, and memoirs constitute a system of fragments. But as yet no genre exists that is fragmentary both in form and in content, simultaneously completely subjective and individual, and completely objective and like a necessary part in a system of all the sciences.

78. Usually incomprehension doesn't derive from a lack of intelligence, but from a lack of sense.

96. Whoever doesn't pursue philosophy for its own sake, but uses it as a means to an end, is a sophist.

99. At the words 'his philosophy, my philosophy', one is always reminded of that line in *Nathan*:[3] 'Who owns God? What kind of God is that who belongs to a man?'

104. The world considers anyone a Kantian who is interested in the latest German philosophical writings. According to the school definition, a Kantian is only someone who believes that Kant is the truth, and who, if the mail coach from Königsberg[4] were ever to have an accident, might very well have to go without the truth for some weeks. According to the outmoded Socratic concept of disciples being those who have independently made the spirit of the great master their own spirit, have adapted themselves to it, and, as his spiritual sons, have been named after him, there are probably only a very few Kantians.

111. The teachings that a novel hopes to instil must be of the sort that can be communicated only as wholes, not demonstrated singly, and not

[2] On the importance of the 'intellectual point of view' see 'On Goethe's *Meister*', pp. 273–7.
[3] Lessing's play, *Nathan der Weise* (1779).
[4] Birthplace and residence of Kant throughout his life.

248

subject to exhaustive analysis. Otherwise the rhetorical form would be infinitely preferable.

114. A definition of poetry can only determine what poetry should be, not what it really was and is; otherwise the shortest definition would be that poetry is whatever has at any time and at any place been called poetry.

116. Romantic poetry[5] is a progressive, universal poetry. Its aim isn't merely to reunite all the separate species of poetry and put poetry in touch with philosophy and rhetoric. It tries to and should mix and fuse poetry and prose, inspiration and criticism, the poetry of art and the poetry of nature; and make poetry lively and sociable, and life and society poetical; poeticize wit and fill and saturate the forms of art with every kind of good, solid matter for instruction, and animate them with the pulsations of humour. It embraces everything that is purely poetic, from the greatest systems of art, containing within themselves still further systems, to the sigh, the kiss that the poetizing child breathes forth in artless song. It can so lose itself in what it describes that one might believe it exists only to characterize poetical individuals of all sorts; and yet there still is no form so fit for expressing the entire spirit of an author: so that many artists who started out to write only a novel ended up by providing us with a portrait of themselves. It alone can become, like the epic, a mirror of the whole circumambient world, an image of the age. And it can also – more than any other form - hover at the midpoint between the portrayed and the portrayer, free of all real and ideal self-interest, on the wings of poetic reflection, and can raise that reflection again and again to a higher power, can multiply it in an endless succession of mirrors. It is capable of the highest and most variegated refinement, not only from within outwards, but also from without inwards; capable in that it organizes – for everything that seeks a wholeness in its effects – the parts along similar lines, so that it opens up a perspective upon an infinitely increasing classicism. Romantic poetry is in the arts what wit is in philosophy, and what society and sociability, friendship and love are in life. Other kinds of poetry are finished and are now capable of being fully analysed. The romantic kind of poetry is still in the state of becoming; that, in fact, is its real essence: that it should forever be becoming and never be perfected. It can be exhausted by no theory and only a divinatory criticism would dare try to characterize its

[5] This is probably the most famous, most frequently quoted of all Schlegel's fragments.

ideal. It alone is infinite, just as it alone is free; and it recognizes as its first commandment that the will of the poet can tolerate no law above itself. The romantic kind of poetry is the only one that is more than a kind, that is, as it were, poetry itself: for in a certain sense all poetry is or should be romantic.

120. They have so little regard for wit because its expressions aren't long and wide enough, since their sensitivity is only a darkly imagined mathematics; and because wit makes them laugh, which would be disrespectful if wit had real dignity. Wit is like someone who is supposed to behave in a manner representative of his station, but instead simply *does* something.

149. The systematic Winckelmann[6] who read all the ancients as if they were a single author, who saw everything as a whole and concentrated all his powers on the Greeks, provided the first basis for a material knowledge of the ancients through his perception of the absolute difference between ancient and modern. Only when the perspective and the conditions of the absolute identity of ancient and modern in the past, present and future have been discovered will one be able to say that at least the contours of classical study have been laid bare and one can now proceed to methodical investigation.

162. In investigating ancient Greek mythology, hasn't too little attention been paid to the human instinct for making analogies and antitheses? The Homeric world of gods is a simple variation of the Homeric world of men, while the Hesiodic world, lacking the principle of heroic contrast, splits up into several opposing races of gods. In that old remark of Aristotle that one gets to know people through their gods, one finds not only the self-illuminating subjectivity of all theology, but also the more incomprehensible innate spiritual dualism of man.

164. The mistakes of the Greek sophists were errors more of excess than omission. Even the confidence and arrogance with which they presumed and pretended to know everything has something quite philosophical about it: not intentionally but instinctively. For surely the philosopher has only the choice of knowing either everything or nothing. And certainly no philosophy worthy of the name tries to teach only some particular thing or some melange of things.

---

[6] Johann Joachim Winckelmann (1717–68), German aesthetician and archaeologist, famous for his work, *Die Geschichte der Kunst im Altertum* (1762), which had a profound impact upon the development of aesthetics in Germany over the next several decades.

165. In Plato we find unmixed all the pure types of Greek prose in their classic individuality, and often incongruously juxtaposed: the logical, the physical, the mimical, the panegyrical and the mythical. The mimical style is the foundation and general component of all the rest; the others often occur only episodically. And then he has a further type of prose that is particularly characteristic of him and makes him most Platonic: the dithyrambical. It might be called a mixture of the mythical and panegyrical if it didn't also have something of the conciseness and simple dignity of the physical.

167. Almost all criticisms of art are too general or too specific. The critics should look for the golden mean here, in their own productions, and not in the works of the poets.

168. Cicero ranks philosophies according to their usefulness to the orator; similarly, one might ask what philosophy is fittest for the poet. Certainly no system at variance with one's feelings or common sense; or one that transforms the real into the illusory; or abstains from all decisions; or inhibits a leap into the suprasensory regions; or achieves humanity only by adding up all the externals. This excludes eudaemonism, fatalism, idealism, scepticism, materialism or empiricism. Then what philosophy is left for the poet? The creative philosophy that originates in freedom and belief in freedom, and shows how the human spirit impresses its law on all things and how the world is its work of art.

206. A fragment, like a miniature work of art, has to be entirely isolated from the surrounding world and be complete in itself like a porcupine.

216. The French Revolution, Fichte's philosophy and Goethe's *Meister* are the greatest tendencies of the age. Whoever is offended by this juxtaposition, whoever cannot take any revolution seriously that isn't noisy and materialistic, hasn't yet achieved a lofty, broad perspective on the history of mankind. Even in our shabby histories of civilization, which usually resemble a collection of variants accompanied by a running commentary for which the original classical text has been lost; even there many a little book, almost unnoticed by the noisy rabble at the time, plays a greater role than anything they did.[7]

---

[7] See 'On Incomprehensibility' for a discussion of this fragment.

220. If wit in all its manifestations is the principle and the organ of universal philosophy, and if all philosophy is nothing but the spirit of universality, the science of all the eternally uniting and dividing sciences, a logical chemistry: then the value and importance of that absolute, enthusiastic, thoroughly material wit is infinite, that wit wherein Bacon and Leibniz, the chief representatives of scholastic prose, were masters, the former among the first, chronologically speaking, the latter among the greatest. The most important scientific discoveries are bons mots of this sort – are so because of the surprising contingency of their origin, the unifying force of their thought, and the baroqueness of their casual expression. But they are, of course, in respect to content, much more than the unsatisfied and evanescent expectation of purely poetical wit. The best ones are *echappées de vue* into the infinite. Leibniz's whole philosophy consists of a few fragments and projects that are witty in this sense. It may be that Kant – the Copernicus of philosophy – has even more natural syncretistic spirit and critical wit than Leibniz, but his situation and his education aren't as witty; and furthermore the same thing has happened to his ideas that happens to popular songs: the Kantians have sung them to death. Therefore it's quite easy to be unfair to him and think him less witty than he really is. Of course, philosophy will only be healthy when it no longer expects and counts on getting brilliant ideas, when it's able to make continuous progress, relying, naturally, on enthusiastic energy and brilliant art, but also on a sure method. But are we to despise the few still extant products of synthesizing genius because no unifying art and science exists as yet? And how could they exist as long as we still simply spell out most sciences like schoolchildren and imagine that we've achieved our object when we can decline and conjugate one of the many dialects of philosophy but have no notion of syntax and can't construct even the shortest periodic sentence?

234. It's only prejudice and presumption that maintain there is only a single mediator between God and man. For the perfect Christian – whom in this respect Spinoza probably resembles most – everything would really have to be a mediator.[8]

238. There is a kind of poetry whose essence lies in the relation between ideal and real, and which therefore, by analogy to philosophical jargon,

---

[8] See Novalis, *Miscellaneous Remarks*, 73 on the idea of the mediator.

should be called transcendental poetry. It begins as satire in the absolute difference of ideal and real, hovers in between as elegy, and ends as idyll with the absolute identity of the two. But just as we wouldn't think much of an uncritical transcendental philosophy that doesn't represent the producer along with the product and contain at the same time within the system of transcendental thoughts a description of transcendental thinking: so too this sort of poetry should unite the transcendental raw materials and preliminaries of a theory of poetic creativity – often met with in modern poets – with the artistic reflection and beautiful self-mirroring that is present in Pindar, in the lyric fragments of the Greeks, in the classical elegy, and, among the moderns, in Goethe. In all its descriptions, this poetry should describe itself, and always be simultaneously poetry and the poetry of poetry.

247. Dante's prophetic poem is the only system of transcendental poetry, and is still the greatest of its kind. Shakespeare's universality is like the centre of romantic art. Goethe's purely poetical poetry is the most complete poetry of poetry. This is the great triple chord of modern poetry, the inmost and holiest circle among all the broad and narrow spheres of a critical anthology of the classics of modern poetry.

249. The poetizing philosopher, the philosophizing poet, is a prophet. A didactic poem should be and tends to become prophetic.

250. Whoever has imagination, or pathos, or a gift for mimicry ought to be able to learn poetry like any other mechanical art. Imagination consists of both enthusiasm and invention; pathos, of soul and passion; and mimicry, of penetration and expression.

252. A real aesthetic theory of poetry would begin with the absolute antithesis of the eternally unbridgeable gulf between art and raw beauty. It would describe their struggle and conclude with the perfect harmony of artistic and natural poetry. This is to be found only among the ancients and would in itself constitute nothing but a more elevated history of the spirit of classical poetry. But a philosophy of poetry as such would begin with the independence of beauty, with the proposition that beauty is and should be distinct from truth and morality, and that it has the same rights as these: something that – for those who are able to understand it at all – follows from the proposition $I = I$. It would waver between the union and the division of philosophy and poetry, between poetry and practice, poetry

as such and the genres and kinds of poetry; and it would conclude with their complete union. Its beginning would provide the principles of pure poetics; its middle the theory of the particular, characteristically modern types of poetry: the didactic, the musical, the rhetorical in a higher sense, etc. The keystone would be a philosophy of the novel, the rough outlines of which are contained in Plato's political theory. Of course, to the ephemeral, unenthusiastic dilettantes, who are ignorant of the best poets of all types, this kind of poetics would seem very much like a book of trigonometry to a child who just wants to draw pictures. Only a man who knows or possesses a subject can make use of the philosophy of that subject; only he will be able to understand what that philosophy means and what it's attempting to do. But philosophy can't inoculate someone with experience and sense, or pull them out of a hat – and it shouldn't want to do so. To those who knew it already, philosophy of course brings nothing new; but only through it does it become knowledge and thereby assume a new form.

253. In the nobler and more original sense of the word correct – meaning a conscious main and subordinate development of the inmost and most minute aspects of a work in line with the spirit of the whole – there probably is no modern poet more correct than Shakespeare. Similarly, he is also systematic as no other poet is: sometimes because of those antitheses that bring into picturesque contrast individuals, masses, even worlds; sometimes through musical symmetry on the same great scale, through gigantic repetitions and refrains; often by a parody of the letter and an irony on the spirit of romantic drama; and always through the most sublime and complete individuality and the most variegated portrayal of that individuality, uniting all the degrees of poetry, from the most carnal imitation to the most spiritual characterization.

255. The more poetry becomes science, the more it also becomes art. If poetry is to become art, if the artist is to have a thorough understanding and knowledge of his ends and means, his difficulties and his subjects, then the poet will have to philosophize about his art. If he is to be more than a mere contriver and artisan, if he is to be an expert in his field and understand his fellow citizens in the kingdom of art, then he will have to become a philologist as well.

256. The basic error of sophistic aesthetics is to consider beauty merely as something given, as a psychological phenomenon. Of course, beauty

isn't simply the empty thought of something that should be created, but at the same time the thing itself, one of the human spirit's original ways of acting: not simply a necessary fiction, but also a fact, that is, an eternally transcendental one.

258. All poetry that wants to produce an effect, and all music that tries to imitate the comic or tragic excesses and exaggerations of eccentric poetry for the sake of exhibiting itself or of making an impression, is rhetorical.

262. Every good human being is always progressively becoming God. To become God, to be human, to cultivate oneself are all expressions that mean the same thing.

263. True mysticism is morality at its most exalted.

267. The more one knows, the more one still has to learn. Ignorance increases in the same proportion as knowledge – or rather, not ignorance, but the knowledge of ignorance.

270. As is well known, Leibniz went to Spinoza to have his glasses made; and that's the only contact he had with him or his philosophy. If only he had also ordered his eyes there, so that he might have gazed at least from a distance into that continent of philosophy that was unknown to him and where Spinoza has his home.

274. Every philosophy of philosophy that excludes Spinoza must be spurious.

275. People are always complaining that German authors write for such a small circle, and even sometimes just for themselves. That's how it should be. This is how German literature will gain more and more spirit and character. And perhaps in the meantime an audience will spring into being.

278. Much seeming stupidity is really folly, which is more common than one might think. Folly is an absolute wrongness of tendency, a complete lack of historical spirit.

281. Fichte's theory of knowledge is a philosophy about the subject matter of Kant's philosophy. He doesn't say much about form because he is a master of it, but if the essence of the critical method is that the theory of the determining ability and the system of determined affective impressions

should be intimately united in it, like object and idea, in a pre-stabilized harmony, then it might very well be that even formally he is a Kant raised to the second power, and the theory of knowledge much more critical than it seems to be. Especially the new version of the theory of knowledge is always simultaneously philosophy and philosophy of philosophy. There may be valid meanings of the word critical that don't apply to every work of Fichte's, but in Fichte one has to look as he does – without paying attention to anything else – only at the whole and at the one thing that really matters. Only in this way can one see and understand the identity of his philosophy with Kant's. And besides, one can never be too critical.

298. In vain do the orthodox Kantians seek the principle of their philosophy in Kant. It's to be found in Bürger's[9] poems, and reads: 'The words of the Emperor shouldn't be twisted and turned.'

301. Philosophers still admire only Spinoza's consistency, just as the English praise only Shakespeare's truth.

302. Jumbled ideas should be the rough drafts of philosophy. It's no secret how highly these are valued by connoisseurs of painting. For a man who can't draw philosophical worlds with a crayon and characterize every thought that has a physiognomy with a few strokes of the pen, philosophy will never be an art and consequently never a science. For in philosophy the way to science lies only through art, just as the poet, on the other hand, finds his art only through science.

304. Philosophy too is the result of two conflicting forces – of poetry and practice. Where these interpenetrate completely and fuse into one, there philosophy comes into being; and when philosophy disintegrates, it becomes mythology or else returns to life. The wisdom of the Greeks was created out of poetry and law. The most sublime philosophy, some few surmise, may once again turn to poetry; and it is in fact a common occurrence that ordinary people only begin to philosophize according to their own lights after they've stopped living. It seems to me that Schelling's real vocation is to describe better this chemical process of philosophizing, to isolate, wherever possible, its dynamic laws and to separate philosophy – which always must organize and disorganize itself anew – into its living, fundamental forces, and trace these back to their origins. On the other

---

[9] Gottfried August Bürger (1748–94), poet of ballads, the most famous of which was 'Lenore'.

hand, his polemics, particularly his literary critique of philosophy, seem to me to represent a false tendency; and his gift for universality is probably still not sufficiently developed to be able to discover in the philosophy of physics what it seeks.

305. Intention taken to the point of irony and accompanied by the arbitrary illusion of its self-destruction is quite as naïve as instinct taken to the point of irony. Just as the naïve plays with the contradictions between theory and practice, so the grotesque plays with the wonderful permutations of form and matter, loves the illusion of the random and the strange and, as it were, coquettes with infinite arbitrariness. Humour deals with being and nonbeing, and its true essence is reflection. Hence its closeness to the elegy and to everything transcendental; and hence its arrogance and its bent for the mysticism of wit. Just as genius is necessary to naïveté, so too an earnest, pure beauty is a requisite of humour. Most of all humour likes to hover about the gently and clearly flowing rhapsodies of philosophy or poetry, and abhors cumbersome masses and disconnected parts.

393. In order to translate perfectly from the classics into a modern language, the translator would have to be so expert in his language that, if need be, he could make everything modern; but at the same time he would have to understand antiquity so well that he would be able not just to imitate it but, if necessary, recreate it.

395. In true prose, everything has to be underlined.

402. In trying to see if it's possible to translate the classical poets, the important thing is to decide whether or not even the most faithful German translation isn't still Greek. To judge by the reaction of the most sensitive and intelligent laymen, there are valid grounds for such a suspicion.

418. Even by the most ordinary standards, a novel deserves to become famous when it portrays and develops a thoroughly new character interestingly. *Wilhelm Lovell*[10] undeniably does this, and the fact that all the rest of its staging and scenery is either commonplace or a failure, just like the great stage manager behind it all, and the further fact that what's extraordinary about it is only the ordinary turned inside out would probably

---

[10] *Wilhelm Lovell* (1793–6), and *Franz Sternbalds Wanderungen* (1798), novels by Ludwig Tieck. *Herzensergiessungen eines kunstliebenden Klosterbruder* (1797) was written with Wilhelm Wackenroder, as a mixed genre of the historical, religious and aesthetic.

not have done the book a great deal of damage, except that unfortunately the character was poetical. Lovell, like his insufficiently differentiated alter ego, Balder, is a complete phantast in every good and every bad, every beautiful and every ugly sense of the word. The whole book is a struggle between prose and poetry, in which prose is trodden underfoot and poetry stumbles and breaks its neck. Besides, it suffers from the fault of many first productions: it wavers between instinct and intention because it doesn't have enough of either. Hence the repetitions whereby the description of sublime boredom at times shifts into a communication of the thing itself. This is the reason why the absolute imaginativeness of this novel could have been misunderstood even by the initiates of poetry and disdained as mere sentimentalism. And this is the reason too why the reasonable reader, who likes to be moderately moved in return for his money, didn't like at all – in fact thought quite mad – the sentimentality of the novel. Tieck has perhaps never again portrayed a character so profoundly and thoroughly. But *Sternbald* combines the seriousness and vitality of *Lovell* with the artificial religiosity of the *Klosterbruder* and with everything that, taken as a whole, is most beautiful in those poetical arabesques he fabricated out of old fairy tales: namely their fantastic richness and facility, their sense of irony, and particularly their intentional variety and uniformity of coloration. Here too everything is clear and transparent, and the romantic spirit seems to be daydreaming pleasantly about itself.

421. Perhaps the great mass likes Friedrich Richter's novels only because of their apparent adventurousness. All in all he is probably interesting in the greatest variety of ways and for the most contradictory reasons. Although the educated businessman sheds quantities of noble tears while reading him, and the exacting artist hates him as the bloody symbol of the triumphant unpoetry of his nation and his age, the man of universal tendency can idolize his arbitrariness or else find great pleasure in those grotesque porcelain figures that his pictorial wit drums together like imperial soldiers. Richter is a unique phenomenon: an author who hasn't mastered the first principles of his art, who can't express a bon mot properly and can't tell a story in a better than average way, and yet someone who – if only because of a humorous dithyramb like the mulish, pithy, tense and magnificent Leibgeber's letter to Adam[11] – cannot justly be denied the name of a great poet. Even if his works don't have a great deal of

[11] Leibgaber was a character in Jean Paul's novel *Siebenkäs.*

cultivation, they are nonetheless cultivated. The whole is like the part, and vice versa; in short, he is accomplished. It is a great advantage of *Siebenkäs* that its execution and descriptions are even better than those of his other works; and it has the far greater advantage of having so few Englishmen in it. To be sure, his Englishmen are ultimately Germans too, but in idyllic surroundings and with sentimental names; still, they always have a strong resemblance to Louvet's Poles and so belong with those false tendencies he is so given to. In the same category is also where his women, philosophy, the Virgin Mary, delicacy, ideal visions and self-criticism belong. His women have red eyes and are paragons, puppets who serve as occasions for psycho-moralistic reflections on womanhood or infatuation. In fact, he almost never comes down to the level of portraying his characters; it is enough for him to have thought of them, and now and then to say something striking about them. And so he sides with the passive humorists, the people who are actually nothing more than humorous objects; the active ones seem more self-sufficient, but they share too much of a family likeness amongst themselves and with the author to make us think of their self-sufficiency as a merit. His decor consists of leaden arabesques in the Nuremberg style. It is here that the monotony of his imagination and intelligence – bordering almost on destitution – becomes most noticeable; but here too do we find that charming dullness of his, and that piquant tastelessness which we can censure only on the grounds that he doesn't seem to be aware of it. His Madonna is a sentimental sexton's wife, and his Christ is cast in the role of an enlightened student of divinity. The more moral his poetical Rembrandts are, the more common and ordinary they become; the funnier, the closer to the good; the more dithyrambical and provincial, the more divine: for he conceives of the village primarily as the City of God. His humorous poetry is separating itself more and more from his sentimental prose; often it appears, like interpolated songs, as an episode, or else it destroys the book in the shape of an appendix. But at times large masses of it still escape from him into the universal chaos.

431. To sacrifice to the Graces means, when said to a philosopher, as much as: create irony and aspire to urbanity.

438. Urbanity is wit of harmonious universality, and that is the beginning and the end of historical philosophy and Plato's most sublime music. The humanities are the gymnastics of this art and science.

446. Consistent empiricism ends in contributions toward settling misunderstandings, or in a subscription to truth.

450. Rousseau's polemic against poetry is really only a bad imitation of Plato. Plato is more against poets than he is against poetry; he thought of philosophy as the most daring dithyramb and the monodic music. Epicurus is the real enemy of art, for he wants to root out imagination and retain sense only. Spinoza might be viewed as the enemy of poetry in quite a different way: because he demonstrates how far one can get with philosophy and morality unaided by poetry, and because it is very much in the spirit of his system not to isolate poetry.

From 'Ideas' (1800)

5. The mind understands something only in so far as it absorbs it like a seed into itself, nurtures it and lets it grow into blossom and fruit. Therefore scatter holy seed into the soil of the spirit, without any affectation and any added superfluities.

8. The mind, says the author of the *Talks on Religion*,[1] can understand only the universe. Let imagination take over and you will have a God. Quite right: for the imagination is man's faculty for perceiving divinity. ✓

11. Only through religion does logic become philosophy; only from it comes everything that makes philosophy greater than science. And instead of an eternally rich, infinite poetry, the lack of religion gives us only novels or the triviality that now is called art. ✓   *religion = way of looking at infinity*

13. Only someone who has his own religion, his own original way of looking at infinity, can be an artist.

15. Every particular conception of God is mere gossip. But the idea of God is the Idea of ideas. ⋆

16. The priest as such exists only in the invisible world. In what guise is it possible for him to appear among men? His only purpose on earth will

---

[1] Friedrich Schleiermacher's *Reden über Religion* (1799).

be to transform the finite into the infinite; hence he must be and continue to be, no matter what the name of his profession, an artist. ~~priest~~

19. To have genius is the natural state of humanity. Nature endowed even humanity with health, and since love is for women what genius is for men, we must conceive of the golden age as a time when love and genius were universal.

20. Everyone is an artist whose central purpose in life is to educate his intellect.

21. The need to raise itself above humanity is humanity's prime characteristic.

24. The symmetry and organization of history teach us that mankind, for as long as it existed and developed, has really always been and has always become an individual, a person. In the great person of mankind, God became a man.

26. Wit is the appearance, the outward lightning bolt of the imagination. Hence the divinity and witty appearance of mysticism.

27. Plato's philosophy is a worthy preface to the religion of the future.

28. Man is Nature creatively looking back at itself.

33. The morality of a work is to be found not in its subject or in the relation of the speaker to his audience, but in the spirit of its execution. If this is infused with the whole wealth of humanity, then the work is moral. If it is only the product of a particular ability or art, then it is not.

34. Whoever has religion will speak in poetry. But to seek and find religion, you need the instrument of philosophy.

36. Every complete human being has some sort of genius. True virtue is genius.

37. Culture is the greatest good and it alone is useful.

39. The Kantians' conception of duty relates to the commandment of honour, the voice of God and of one's calling in us, as the dried plant to the fresh flower on the living stem.

40. A definite relationship to God must seem as intolerable to the mystic as a particular conception or notion of God.

42. If one is to believe the philosophers, then what we call religion is simply intentionally popular or instinctively artless philosophy. The poets, however, seem to prefer to think of it as a variety of poetry which, unsure of its own lovely playfulness, takes itself too seriously and too one-sidedly. Still, philosophy already admits and begins to recognize that it must start with religion and achieve perfection in religion, and poetry strives only for the infinite and despises wordly practicality and culture as the real opposites of religion. Hence eternal peace among artists is no longer a distant prospect.

43. What men are among the other creatures of the earth, artists are among men.

45. An artist is someone who carries his centre within himself. Whoever lacks such a centre has to choose some particular leader and mediator outside of himself, not, to be sure, forever, but only to begin with. For a man cannot live without a vital centre, and if he does not yet have one within himself, then he can only seek it in another man, and only a man and a man's centre can stimulate and awaken his own.

46. Poetry and philosophy are, depending on one's point of view, different spheres, different forms, or simply the component parts of religion. For only try really to combine the two and you will find yourself with nothing but religion.

47. God is everything that is purely original and sublime, consequently the individual himself taken to the highest power. But aren't nature and the world also individuals?

48. Where philosophy stops, poetry has to begin. An ordinary point of view, a way of thinking, natural only in opposition to art and culture, a mere existing: all these are wrong; that is, there should be no kingdom of barbarity beyond the boundaries of culture. Every thinking part of an organization should not feel its limits without at the same time feeling its unity in relation to the whole.

54. The artist should have as little desire to rule as to serve. He can only create, do nothing but create, and so help the state only by making rulers and servants, and by exalting politicians and economists into artists.

55. Versatility consists not just in a comprehensive system but also in a feeling for the chaos outside that system, like man's feeling for something beyond man.

60. Individuality is precisely what is original and eternal in man; personality doesn't matter so much. To pursue the cultivation and development of this individuality as one's highest calling would be a godlike egoism.

63. The really central insight of Christianity is sin.

64. Artists make mankind an individual by connecting the past with the future in the present. Artists are the higher organ of the soul where the vital spirits of all external humanity join together, and where inner humanity has its primary sphere of action.

65. Only by being cultivated does a human being, who is wholly that, become altogether human and permeated by humanity.

69. Irony is the clear consciousness of eternal agility, of an infinitely teeming chaos.

73. There is no dualism without primacy; and therefore morality is not equal to religion, but subordinate to it.

74. Join the extremes and you will find the true middle.

79. There is only a single sense incorporating all the others. The most spiritual sense is the most original; all others derive from it.

83. Only through love and the consciousness of love does man become man.

85. The kernel, the centre of poetry, is to be found in mythology and the mysteries of antiquity. Satiate the feeling of life with the idea of infinity, and you will understand both the ancients and poetry.

86. Beautiful is what reminds us of nature and thereby stimulates a sense of the infinite fullness of life. Nature is organic, and whatever is most sublimely beautiful is therefore always vegetal, and the same is true of morality and love.

87. A true human being is one who has penetrated to the centre of humanity.

92. The only significant opposition to the religion of man and artist now springing up everywhere is to be expected from the few remaining real Christians. But they too, when the sun really begins to dawn, will fall down and worship.

95. The new, eternal gospel that Lessing prophesied will appear as a bible: but not as a single book in the usual sense. Even what we now call the Bible is actually a system of books. And that is, I might add, no mere arbitrary turn of phrase! Or is there some other word to differentiate the idea of an infinite book from an ordinary one, than Bible, the book per se, the absolute book? And surely there is an eternally essential and even practical difference if a book is merely a means to an end, or an independent work, an individual, a personified idea. It cannot be this without divine inspiration, and here the esoteric concept is itself in agreement with the exoteric one; and, moreover, no idea is isolated, but is what it is only in combination with all other ideas. An example will explain this. All the classical poems of the ancients are coherent, inseparable; they form an organic whole, they constitute, properly viewed, only a single poem, the only one in which poetry itself appears in perfection. In a similar way, in a perfect literature all books should be only a single book, and in such an eternally developing book, the gospel of humanity and culture will be revealed.

96. All philosophy is idealism, and there exists no true realism except that of poetry. But poetry and philosophy are only extremes. If one were to say that some people are pure idealists and others very definitely realists, then that remark would be quite true. Stated differently, it means that there as yet exist no wholly cultivated human beings, that there still is no religion.

105. So Fichte is supposed to have attacked religion? If an interest in the world beyond the senses is the essence of religion, then his whole doctrine is religion in the form of philosophy.

108. Whatever can be done while poetry and philosophy are separated has been done and accomplished. So the time has come to unite the two.

109. Imagination and wit are everything to you! Explain a beautiful illusion and take playfulness seriously, and you will apprehend what is at the centre and rediscover your revered art in a more sublime light.

110. The difference between religion and morality is to be found quite simply in the old classification of all things into divine and human, if only it were understood properly.

115. If you want to achieve great things, then inspire and educate women and young men. Here, if anywhere, fresh strength and health are still to be found, and this is the way that the most important reformations have been accomplished.

118. What blindness to talk of atheism! Are there any theists? Did any human mind ever encompass the idea of divinity?

127. Women have less need for the poetry of poets because their very essence is poetry.

129. You're not really supposed to understand me, but I want very much for you to listen to me.[2]

131. The hidden meaning of sacrifice is the annihilation of the finite because it is finite. In order to demonstrate that this is its only justification, one must choose to sacrifice whatever is most noble and most beautiful: but particularly man, the flower of the earth. Human sacrifices are the most natural sacrifices. But man is more than the flower of the earth; he is reasonable, and reason is free and in itself nothing but an eternal self-destination into the infinite. Hence man can only sacrifice himself, and he does so in an omnipresent sanctity the mob knows nothing of. All artists are Decians,[3] and to become an artist means nothing but consecrating oneself to the gods of the underworld. In the enthusiasm of annihilation, the meaning of the divine creation is revealed for the first time. Only in the midst of death does the lightning bolt of eternal life explode.

133. To begin with, I speak only to those who are already facing the Orient.

134. You suspect something greater even in me and ask why I keep silent precisely at the threshold? It's because it's still so early in the day.

137. The piety of philosophers is theory, pure contemplation of the divinity, calm and gay in silent solitude. Spinoza is the ideal of the species. The religious state of the poet is more passionate and more communicative. At

---

[2] This fragment, from the manuscript of the *Ideas*, was not printed in the *Athenaeum*.
[3] Decii, a Roman family noted for sacrificing their lives for the sake of Rome's glory.

the root of things lies enthusiasm, and at the end there remains mythology. Whatever stays at the midpoint possesses the character of life to the point of sexual differentiation. Mysteries are, as I said before, female; and orgies seek, in the happy exuberance of their male strength, to overcome everything around them or fertilize it.

139. There is no self-knowledge except historical self-knowledge. No one knows what he is if he doesn't know what his contemporaries are, particularly the greatest contemporary of the brotherhood, the master of masters, the genius of the age.

141. Oh, how wretched are your conceptions of genius (I mean the best among you). Where you see genius, I often see a wealth of false tendencies, the very centre of incompetence. A little talent and a lot of humbug are things everyone praises, and which even lead everyone to proclaim that genius is incorrect, must be incorrect. So, this idea is gone too? Isn't the thoughtful man the one who is fittest to perceive the language of the spirit? Only the spiritual man has a spirit, a genius, and every genius is universal. Whoever is merely representative, merely has talent.

146. Even in their outward behaviour, the lives of artists should differ completely from the lives of other men. They are Brahmins, a higher caste: ennobled not by birth, but by free self-consecration.

148. Who unlocks the magic book of art and frees the imprisoned holy spirit? Only a kindred spirit.

149. Without poetry, religion becomes murky, false, and evil; without philosophy, extravagant in its lewdness and lustful to the point of self-emasculation.

150. You can neither explain nor understand the universe, but only contemplate and reveal it. Only stop calling the system of empiricism the universe, and if you haven't yet understood Spinoza, discover for the present the true religious conception of the universe in the *Talks on Religion*.[4]

153. All self-sufficiency is radical, is original, and all originality is moral, is originality of the whole man. Without originality, there is no energy of reason and no beauty of disposition.

[4] See *Ideas* 8 above, and note 1.

155. I have expressed a few ideas pointing toward the heart of things, and have greeted the dawn in my own way, from my own point of view. Let anyone who knows the road do likewise in his own way, from his own point of view.

156. *To Novalis:* You don't stay at the threshold of things. On the contrary, your spirit is deeply suffused with poetry and philosophy. It was closest to me in these images of uncomprehended truth. What you've thought I think; what I've thought you will think or have already thought. There are misunderstandings that serve only to confirm the greatest shared understanding. Every doctrine of the eternal Orient belongs to all artists. I name you instead of all the others.

'On Goethe's *Meister*' (1798)

With no presumption, no sound and fury, like the quiet unfolding of an aspiring spirit, like the new-created world rising gently from within, the lucid tale begins. There is nothing extraordinary about what happens or what is said in it; the figures who appear first of all are neither great nor marvellous: a shrewd old woman who always has an eye to her own advantage and supports the wealthier suitor; a girl who escapes the snare of this dangerous schemer in order to give herself passionately to her lover; a pure youth who devotes the sweet ardour of his first love to an actress. Moreover, it is all there right before our eyes, appealing and alluring. The outlines are light and general, but they are sharp, precise and sure. The smallest trait is meaningful, every touch a gentle hint; and everything is enhanced by clear and lively contrasts. There is nothing here to enflame the passions, nothing at the outset to make violent claims upon our sympathies. But of their own accord the sprightly tableaux remain fixed in a mind cheerfully disposed to quiet enjoyment, just as we might retain the strangely clear and ineradicable memory of a landscape of simple and modest charm, which for a moment appears new and unique, suffused in a rare and beautiful illumination, or tempered by a marvellous mood of our feelings. The feelings are gently touched by the cheerful story, sweetly stirred in many ways. Without being entirely familiar with them, the reader already feels as if he has met these people, before he ever knows or even asks how it was he made their acquaintance. The reader feels the same about them as the company of actors did towards the Stranger

269

on their gay excursion on the river. He thinks he must have met them already, because they look like real human beings, not like any mere Tom, Dick or Harry. They do not owe this appearance to their nature or their education: for only in one or two cases do these approach the general level, and even then in different ways and to a different extent. It is rather the manner of the representation, which endows even the most circumscribed character with the appearance of a unique, autonomous individual, while yet possessing another aspect, another variation of that general human nature which is constant in all its transformations, so that each variation is a small part of the infinite world. That is the great thing about this novel: every cultured reader believes he recognizes only himself in it, whereas he is raised far beyond himself; which is only as it should be, and yet far more than one might expect.

Benevolently, the delighted reader follows Wilhelm's tender memories of the puppet plays that filled the inquisitive boy with greater happiness than any other delicacy, at a time when he still drank in at random every spectacle and pictures of all kinds, with the same pure thirst with which the new-born child takes the sweet nourishment from his fond mother's breast. Wilhelm's credulity makes the good-natured children's stories of that time important, indeed sacred to him, for then he would yearn passionately to see everything that was new and unfamiliar to him, and promptly try to imitate what he had just seen. Now his affection paints them in the most charming colours, and his hope lends them the most flattering significance. It is these attractive characteristics that make up the fabric of his dearest ambition: to use the theatre to elevate, enlighten and ennoble mankind and to become the creator of a new and greater age in the history of his country's stage. His childish inclination burns ardently for this idea, intensified by his virtue and redoubled by his love. Though our response to such feelings and desires cannot be wholly without misgivings, still it is absorbing and delightful to read how for the first time Wilhelm is sent by the two fathers on a short journey, how he encounters an adventure that begins seriously and develops amusingly, and in which he glimpses the image of his own enterprise – not, it is true, reflected very flatteringly, but that cannot make him untrue to his enthusiasm. Meanwhile, all unnoticed, the tale has become more vivid and passionate. In the balmy night when Wilhelm, believing he is close to an eternal union with his Mariane, lingers lovingly and ecstatically about her house, the ardent yearning that seems to lose itself in itself, soothed and revived in the enjoyment of its own sounds, rises to a climax until Wilhelm's passion is suddenly extinguished by sad certainty and Norberg's base letter: the entire dream-world of the young man in love is destroyed at a blow.

The first book closes with this harsh dissonance. The end resembles a music of the spirit, in which the most various voices change rapidly and vehemently, like so many inviting sounds from a new world whose wonders are to unfold before us. And the sharp contrast can season and salve with a dash of impatience that tension roused first a little and then more than we expected, without ever disturbing the most even-tempered enjoyment of what is going on, or removing the most delicate features from the secondary development nor the slightest hints from our perception of the work, desiring as we do to understand every glance and changing expression of the poetic spirit made visible in the work.

But in order that our feelings should not strive merely in an empty infinity, but rather that the eye might estimate the distance according to some higher point of view and set some bounds to the vast prospect, the Stranger is there – so rightly called the Stranger. Alone and incomprehensible, like a manifestation from another, nobler world, as different from the real world surrounding Wilhelm as *it* is from the possible world of his dreams, the Stranger acts as a measure of the heights to which the work has yet to rise, where art will become a science, and life an art.

The mature intelligence of this cultivated man is separated by an abyss from the flourishing imagination of the young man in love. But the transition from Wilhelm's serenade to Norberg's letter is not a gentle one, and the contrast between his poetry and Mariane's prosaic, nay, low surroundings, is stark. Introductory to the whole work, the first book is a series of varied situations and picturesque contrasts, each casting a new and brighter light on Wilhelm's character from a different, noteworthy perspective; and each of the smaller, clearly distinct chapters and blocks of narrative forms in itself more or less a picturesque whole. Wilhelm has already won the reader's complete good-will, to whom he utters (as much as to himself) the noblest sentiments in the most splendid words. His entire nature consists of feeling, willing, aspiring; and although we can foresee that he will come to act as a mature man only very late (or perhaps never), his easy adaptability is a sure promise that men and women will make his education their business and their pleasure. Perhaps without knowing or even wishing it, they will thereby stimulate in numerous ways that gentle, many-sided receptivity which gives his mind such great appeal; and they will develop his dim, early awareness of the whole world into a beautiful form. He will have to be able to learn wherever he goes, and he will not be without his trials and temptations. But if a kindly destiny or a friend with a wide scope of experience supports him with good will, guiding him with warnings and promises, then his years of apprenticeship cannot but end happily.

The second book begins with a musical recapitulation of what has happened up to the end of the first book, concentrating the issues into a few focal points, and pushing them to the farthest possible extent. At first, the gradual but complete destruction of the poetry of Wilhelm's childish dreams and his first love is examined with a sparing generality of representation. The reader's mind, having sunk to these depths in sympathy with Wilhelm and become as inactive as he, is reenlivened and roused into pulling itself out of this vacancy by the most passionate recollections of Mariane and by the young man's inspired praise of poetry, transposing us into the ominous past of ancient heroes and the still innocent world of poetry.

Then follows his entry into the world, made neither formally, nor tumultuously, but as sweetly and gently as the wanderings of someone caught between melancholy and expectation, or wavering between bitter-sweet memories and desires heavy with presentiments. A new scene opens, a new world stretches out beckoning to us. Here everything is strange, significant, marvellous, enveloped by a mysterious enchantment. Events and characters move more rapidly, and each character is like a new act. Even events not in themselves unusual appear surprising. But these events are only the natural element of the characters, in whom the spirit of this entire massive system is most clearly revealed. They too express a fresh sense of the present, a magic hovering between forwards and backwards. Philine is the seductive symbol of easy sensuality; likewise, the volatile Laertes lives only for the moment, and to complete the merry company, the fair-haired Friedrich represents a hale and hearty loutishness. The old Harper breathes and laments all that is touching of memory and melancholy and remorse, out of fathomless depths of grief, seizing our hearts with a sudden sadness. The holy child Mignon excites an even sweeter spasm, a delicious shudder, and with her appearance the innermost spring of this strange work is released. Now and again Mariane's image appears like a dream of great import; suddenly the mysterious Stranger enters the scene and then vanishes like lightning. The Melinas too reappear, but changed, in their true colours. The clumsy vanity of Madame Melina's excessive sensibility makes a pretty contrast with the lightness of the dainty sinner Philine. The reading of the drama of chivalry offers over-all a profound glance behind the scenes of theatrical enchantment, as if into a comic world in the background. Humour, feeling, mystery, allure are all marvellously interwoven in the Finale, and the conflicting voices clash harshly with one another. This harmony of dissonance is even more beautiful than the music with which the First Book ended. It is more de-lightful, and yet it cuts deeper; it is more overwhelming, and yet it leaves us more composed.

It is a beautiful and indeed necessary experience when reading a poetic work to give ourselves up entirely to its influence, to let the writer do with us what he will; perhaps only in matters of detail is it necessary to pause and confirm our emotional response with a moment's reflection, raise it into a thought, and where there is room for doubt or dispute, decide and amplify the matter. This is the prime, the most essential response. But it is no less necessary to be able to abstract from all the details, to have a loose general concept of the work, survey it en bloc, and grasp it as a whole, perceive even its most hidden parts and make connections between the most remote corners. We must rise above our own affection for the work, and in our thoughts be able to destroy what we adore; otherwise, whatever our talents, we would lack a sense of the whole. Why should we not both breathe in the perfume of a flower and at the same time, entirely absorbed in the observation, contemplate in its infinite ramifications the vein-system of a single leaf? The whole man who feels and thinks in universal terms is interested not only in the brilliant outward covering, the bright garment of this beautiful earth; he also likes to investigate the layering and the composition of the strata far within; he would wish to delve deeper and deeper, even to the very centre, if possible, and would want to know the construction of the whole. So we gladly tear ourselves away from the poet's spell, after we have willingly let him cast his enchantment upon us; what we love most is to seek out what he has hidden from our gaze or was reluctant to reveal at first, what it is that most makes him an artist: the hidden intentions he pursues in secret. In a genius whose instinct has become will, there are many more intentions than we can take for granted.

Both the larger and the smaller masses reveal the innate impulse of this work, so organized and organizing down to its finest detail to form a whole. No break is accidental or insignificant; and in this novel, where

Friedrich Schlegel

everything is at the same time both means and end, it would not be wrong to regard the first part, irrespective of its relationship to the whole, as a novel in itself. If we look at the preferred topics of conversation, at all the incidental developments, at the preferred relationships between all the incidents, characters and their surroundings, we are struck by the fact that everything is concerned with spectacle, drama, representation, art and poetry. It was so much the poet's intention to set up a comprehensive theory of art or rather to represent one in living examples and aspects, that this purpose can divert him into introducing events which are really only episodes, such as the comedy presented by the factory-workers, or the play put on by the miners. It is possible, indeed, to find a system in the author's presentation of this physics of poetry – not by any means the dead framework of a didactic structure, but stage after stage of every natural history and educational theory in living progression. For example, in this period of his apprenticeship, Wilhelm is concerned with the first, most elementary beginnings of the art of living. Hence this is where the simplest ideas about art are also presented, the most basic facts and the crudest efforts – in short, the rudiments of poetry: the puppet plays, the early childhood years of poetic instinct common to all people of sensibility, even those without any particular talent. Then there are the observations about how the learner should practise his art and make his judgements, and about the impressions made by the miners and by the tight-rope walkers; there are the poetic passages on the Golden Age of early poetry, and on the acrobat's art, and there is the improvised comedy during the excursion on the river. But this natural history of the fine arts is not restricted only to the actors' skills and related arts. The romantic songs of Mignon and the Harper also reveal poetry as the natural language and natural music of beautiful souls.

With this intention, the actor's world was bound to become both the setting and the foundation of the whole work, because his art is not only the most versatile, but also the most sociable of all the arts, and because it makes the perfect meeting-place for poetry and life, for the world and the times; whereas the solitary studio of the painter or sculptor does not offer so much material, and poets only live as poets within themselves, no longer forming a separate social guild of artists.

This might suggest that the novel is as much an historical philosophy of art as a true work of art, and that everything which the poet so lovingly presents as his true aim and end is ultimately only means. But that is not

274

so: it is all poetry – high, pure poetry. Everything has been thought and uttered as though by one who is both a divine poet and a perfect artist; and even the most delicate secondary features seem to exist in their own right and to rejoice in their own independent life, even against the laws of petty, inauthentic probability. What is lacking in the paeans of praise that Werner and Wilhelm raise to Trade and to Poetry but the metre, for everyone to acknowledge them as high poetry? Every page offers us golden fruits upon silver platters. This marvellous prose is prose, and yet it is poetry. Its richness is graceful, its simplicity significant and profound, and its noble and delicate development is without stubborn rigour. Though the main threads of this style are on the whole drawn from the cultivated speech of social life, it also takes pleasure in rare and strange metaphors which aim at establishing a resemblance between the highest and the purest on the one hand, and some aspect peculiar to this or that everyday trade or skill on the other, or such similar spheres which, according to public commonplace, are utterly remote from poetry.

But we should not be deceived into thinking that the poet is not utterly serious about his masterpiece, even though he himself seems to take the characters and incidents so lightly and playfully, never mentioning his hero except with some irony and seeming to smile down from the heights of his intellect upon his work. We should think of this work in connection with the very highest ideas, and not read it as it is usually taken on the social level: as a novel in which the persons and incidents are the ultimate end and aim. For this book is absolutely new and unique. We can learn to understand it only on its own terms. To judge it according to an idea of genre drawn from custom and belief, accidental experiences and arbitrary demands, is as if a child tried to clutch the stars and the moon in his hand and pack them in his satchel.

Our feelings too protest against an orthodox academic judgement of this divine organism. Who would review a feast of the finest and choicest wit with all the usual fuss and formalities? An academic review of *Wilhelm Meister* would look like the young man who went walking in the woods with a book under his arm and drove away Philine as well as the cuckoo.

Perhaps then we should judge it, and at the same time refrain from judging it; which does not seem to be at all an easy task. Fortunately it turns out to be one of those books which carries its own judgement within it, and spares the critic his labour. Indeed, not only does it judge itself; it also describes itself. A mere description of the impression it makes, quite apart from being superfluous, would be bound to come off badly, even if it were not the worst of its kind. It would lose out not only to the poet, but also to the thoughts of the kind of reader who knows the highest when he sees it and has the capacity to worship, a reader who can tell at once without art or science what he should worship, and who responds to the real, right thing as though struck by lightning.

Our usual expectations of unity and coherence are disappointed by this novel as often as they are fulfilled. But the reader who possesses a true instinct for system, who has a sense of totality or that anticipation of the world in its entirety which makes Wilhelm so interesting, will be aware throughout the work of what we might call its personality and living individuality. And the more deeply he probes, the more inner connections and relations and the greater intellectual coherence he will discover in it. If there is any book with an indwelling genius, it is this. And if this genius could characterize itself in detail and as a whole, then there would be no need for anyone else to say what it is all about, or how it should be taken. A little elaboration is possible here, and some explanation need not seem unnecessary or superfluous, for despite this feeling of its wholeness, the beginning and the end of the work, as well as one or two parts in the middle, are generally felt to be superfluous and unrelated. Even the reader who is able to recognize the divine nature of its cultivated randomness, and do it honour, has a sense of something isolated at the beginning and the end as if despite the most beautiful coherence and innermost unity of the work, it lacked the ultimate interdependence of thoughts and feelings. Many readers, to whom one cannot deny this sense, are uneasy about several parts of the work, for in such developing natures, idea and feeling are mutually extended, sharpened and formed by one another.

The differing nature of the individual sections should be able to throw a great deal of light on the organization of the whole. But in progressing appropriately from the parts to the whole, observation and analysis must not get lost in over-minute detail. Rather analysis must pause, as if the detail were merely a matter of simple parts, at those major sections whose independence is also maintained by their free treatment, and by their shaping and transformation of what they have taken over from the previous section; and whose inner, unintentional homogeneity and original unity the poet himself has acknowledged in using the most various, though always poetic, means, in a deliberate effort to shape them into a rounded whole. The development within the individual sections ensures the overall coherence, and in pulling them together, the poet confirms their variety. And in this way each essential part of the single and indivisible novel becomes a system in itself. The means of connection and progression are more or less the same in all sections. In the second volume, Jarno and the appearance of the Amazons raise our expectations in the same way as the Stranger and Mignon had done in the first; and they likewise rouse our interest in the far distance and point forward to heights of education not yet visible. Here too, every book opens with a new scene and a new world; here too the old figures reappear with youth renewed; here too every book contains the germ of the next, and with vital energy absorbs into its own being what the previous book has yielded. And the third book, distinguished by the freshest and happiest colouring, is beautifully framed, as if by the blossoms of youth still burgeoning but already mature, first by Mignon's song 'Kennst du das Land . . .' and at the end by Wilhelm's and the Countess's first kiss. Where there is so much to be noticed, there would be little point in drawing attention to something that has been there already, or recurs again and again with a few changes. Only what is quite new and individual requires commentary – but of the sort which should by no means make everything clear for everybody. It deserves the name of excellence only when the reader who understands *Wilhelm Meister* completely finds it utterly familiar and when the reader who does not understand it at all finds it as stupid and empty as the work it is supposed to elucidate. On the other hand, the reader who only half-understands the work would find such a commentary only half-comprehensible; it would enlighten him in some respects, but perhaps only confuse him the more in others – so that out of this disturbance and doubt, knowledge might emerge, or the reader might at least become aware of his incompleteness. The second volume in particular has least need of explanations. It is the fullest, but also the most charming. It is full of keen understanding, but still very understandable.

In the sequence of grades of these apprentice years in the art of living, this volume represents for Wilhelm the higher degree in temptations, and the time of errors and instructive but dearly purchased experiences. It is true that his principles and his actions run, as ever, side by side like parallel lines, without ever crossing or touching. But in the meantime he does finally reach the stage whereby he has gradually raised himself out of that baseness which originally adheres even to the noblest natures or accidentally forms their environment – or at least he has seriously endeavoured to rise above it. At first, Wilhelm's infinite impulse towards education only lived and moved within him, even to the point of bringing about the self-destruction of his first love, and of his aspirations as an artist. Then, after it had led him to venture out into the world, it was natural that his aspirations should carry him to the very heights, even though it were only the heights of an ordinary theatre stage; it was natural that his highest aim should become all that was noble and distinguished, even if that were only the representative mode of existence of a not very cultivated nobility. This is probably the only way such an aspiration, in its origins so worthy of our respect, could have worked out successfully, for Wilhelm was still so innocent and so young. That is why the Third Book was bound to come so close to comedy, all the more so as its intention was to shed the fullest light on Wilhelm's unworldliness, and on the contrast between the magic of the play, and the common, ordinary life of the players. In the earlier sections, only individual traits were distinctly comic – perhaps a few figures in the foreground, or an indefinite one in the distance. But here the entire Book, the setting and the action are themselves comic. Indeed, we might call it a comic world, for in fact it contains infinite cause for amusement. The nobility and the actors form two quite separate bodies, neither of whom yield the prize for absurdity to the other, and who manoeuvre against each other in the most amusing way. The elements in this comedy are not at all dainty or delicate or noble. Rather, much of it is the kind of thing we are all accustomed to laughing at heartily, such as the contrast between high expectations and bad management. The contrasts between hope and success, and between imagination and reality, play a great part throughout: the claims of reality are asserted with cruel severity, and the pedant even gets knocked about because he is also an idealist. In sheer infatuation, his fellow, the Count, is pleased to acknowledge him across the enormous gulf of their different social positions. For sheer intellectual silliness, the Baron yields pride of place to no one, nor the Baroness for moral turpitude. The Countess herself is at best a charming excuse for a beautiful justification of adornment. And apart from their social class, the only superiority these nobles show over the actors is that they are more thoroughly common. But these people, whom we should call figures rather than people, are sketched with the light touch and delicate brush we might imagine in the daintiest caricatures of the finest painting. It is foolishness shaped into transparency. This freshness of colour, this child-like variety, this love of trimmings and trappings, the wit, the lightness of heart, the fleeting high spirits are characterized by something we might call an ethereal merriment, whose impression is too fine and delicate for the mere letter of commentary to be able to reflect and reproduce. Only reading it aloud with total understanding can convey to those with a feeling for it the irony which hovers over the entire work, but becomes beautifully clear here. This illusion of dignity and importance, mocking itself gently, in the periodic style, this apparent negligence, these seeming tautologies, determine the work so perfectly, that they themselves become subject to its conditions, together with everything else in the world of the novel. This style enables the narrator to say or to seem to want to say everything or nothing; this highly prosaic tone in the midst of the poetic mood of the subject presented or turned into comedy, this delicate breath of poetic pedantry on the most prosaic occasions – often it all depends upon a single word, or indeed on the merest matter of emphasis.

Perhaps there is no section of the work as free and independent of the whole as this third book. But not everything in it is playful, or intended for the pleasure of the moment. Jarno makes to Wilhelm and the reader a powerful affirmation of his faith in a grand and dignified reality and in serious endeavour in the world and his works. His dry and simple common sense is the perfect antithesis to Aurelia's sophistical sensibility, which is half natural and half affected. She is actress through and through, even in her own character; all she can do, all she wants to do, is represent and perform, best of all herself; she puts everything on display, even her femininity and her love. Both figures are distinguished only by common sense. For the poet gives Aurelia a good measure of shrewdness. But she lacks judgement and a sense of propriety, as much as Jarno lacks imagination. They are excellent persons, but thoroughly limited, and certainly not great, and the book's distinct pointers towards this limitation are proof that it is far less of a eulogy of common sense than might first appear. Each acts as a foil to the other, as the deeply feeling Mariane does to the light and promiscuous Philine; and like them, they both stand out more strongly than would be necessary merely to furnish the theories of art under discussion with examples, or provide the complications of the plot as a whole with characters. They are major figures, and each of them in its substantiality sets the tone. They earn their places because they too want to shape Wilhelm's mind; they too have his education at heart. Despite the honest concern of so many pedagogues in his personal and moral education, their pupil, it is true, seems to have acquired little more than the external graces, which he imagines he has learned from the great variety of his social acquaintance, and from his practice in dancing and fencing. However, it seems he does make great advances in art, at least, more as a natural development of his own mind than because others have urged him towards it. And he now makes the acquaintance of real experts, and their conversations about art – quite apart from the fact that they lack the heavy splendour of what is known as concentrated brevity – are real conversations, with many voices engaging with one another, not mere one-sided sham conversations. Serlo is in a certain sense a generally representative human being, and even the story of his youth is appropriate to one with such a distinct talent and an equally distinct absence of any sense of higher things. In this respect he resembles Jarno: in the last resort, both are masters only of the mechanical aspects of their craft. There is an immeasurably wide gulf between the first apprehensions and elements of poetry with which the first volume concerned Wilhelm and the reader, and the point where man becomes capable of grasping both the highest and the most profound. And if the passage from the one to the other, which always has to be a leap, were brought about by the mediation of a great model, as is only fitting, what poet could perform this function more appropriately than the one who deserves so eminently to be called unlimited? This is the view of Shakespeare which Wilhelm seizes upon first of all, and since the greatness of his nature is less important to this theory than his profound artistry and purposefulness, the choice was bound to fall on *Hamlet*, for there is probably no other play that offers the occasion for such varied and interesting debate on what the secret intention of the artist might be, or what the accidental flaws in the work are. This drama also plays its part beautifully in the theatrical plot and setting of the novel, and almost of its own accord it raises the question of how far it is possible to alter a finished masterpiece or perform it unchanged on the stage. With its retarding action, which is also the very essence of the novel, *Hamlet* can seem so closely related to *Wilhelm Meister* as to be mistaken for it. Also, the spirit of contemplation and withdrawal into the self, of which the novel is so full, is a characteristic common to all intellectual poetry, so much so that even this terrible tragedy which represents the visible earth as a rank garden of luxurious sin, and its hollow depths as the seat of punishment and pain, and which is founded on the harshest ideas of honour and duty, even this drama can in one characteristic at least tend towards the happy prentice years of a young artist.

The view of *Hamlet* to be found scattered partly here and partly in the next volume is not so much criticism as high poetry. What else but a poem can come into being when a poet in full possession of his powers contemplates a work of art and represents it in his own? This is not because his view makes suppositions and assertions which go beyond the visible work. All criticism has to do that, because every great work, of whatever kind, knows more than it says, and aspires to more than it knows. It is because the aims and approach of poetic criticism are something completely different. Poetic criticism does not act as a mere inscription, and merely say what the thing is, and where it stands and should stand in the world. For that, all that is required is a whole and undivided human being who has made the work the centre of his attention for as long as necessary. If he takes pleasure in communication, by word of mouth or in writing, he will enjoy developing and elaborating an insight which is fundamentally single and indivisible. That is how a critical characterization of a work actually comes into being. The poet and artist on the other hand will want to represent the representation anew, and form once more what has already been formed; he will add to the work, restore it, shape it afresh. He will only divide the whole into articulated parts and masses, not break it down into its original constituents, which in respect of the work are dead things, because their elements are no longer of the same nature as the whole; however, in respect of the universe they are certainly living, and could be articulated parts or masses there. The ordinary critic relates the object of his art to these, and so he is inevitably bound to destroy his living unity, sometimes breaking it down into its elements, sometimes regarding it as an atom itself within a greater mass.

The fifth book moves from theory to practice, considered and proceeding according to certain principles. And the crudeness and selfishness of Serlo and the others, Philine's frivolity, Aurelia's extravagance, the old man's melancholy and Mignon's longing also pass over into action. Hence the not infrequent approach to madness, which seems to be a preferred tone and relationship in this Book. Mignon as Fury is a brilliant blaze of light – but there are many. On the whole, however, the work seems to lapse somewhat from the heights of the second volume. It seems to be already preparing itself to plunge into the furthermost depths within man, from thence to climb to even greater heights – indeed the greatest, where it is able to remain. In general, the work appears to be at a crossroads, and caught up in an important crisis. The complication and confusion reaches a climax, as does the tense expectation, about the outcome of so many interesting riddles and enjoyable marvels. Also, the false direction Wilhelm has taken assumes the form of maxims. But the strange warning admonishes the reader too not to believe too credulously that Wilhelm has reached his goal, or is even on the right way to it. None of the parts seems so dependent on the whole, or to serve merely as a means, as this one. It even indulges in merely theoretical afterthoughts and interpolations, such as the ideal of the prompter, the sketch of the connoisseur of acting, or the theoretical basis for the distinction between novel and drama.

By contrast, the 'Confessions of a Beautiful Soul' come as a surprise in their unaffected singularity, their apparent isolation from the whole, and the arbitrariness of their involvement in it, or rather their absorption into it, which has no precedent in the earlier parts of the novel. But on closer reflection, Wilhelm probably ought not to be without any relationship to his aunt before his marriage, just as her Confessions should have some connection with the novel as a whole. After all, these are also years of apprenticeship when nothing else than how to exist is learnt, to live according to his particular principles or his unalterable nature. And if Wilhelm continues to interest us only by virtue of his own capacity to be interested in everything, the way in which his aunt is interested in herself gives her the right to communicate her feelings. Fundamentally she too lives a theatrical life, only with this difference: that she combines all the roles which in the Count's residence had been distributed among many figures who all acted and performed to one another; moreover her heart is the stage on which she is at the same time actor and spectator and mistress of the intrigues behind the scenes. She constantly stands before the mirror of her conscience, prinking and preening her feelings. In this figure the highest degree of inwardness is reached – which was bound to happen, for the work has from the start displayed a decided inclination towards distinguishing sharply between the inner and the outer life, and to contrasting them. In this section, the inner life has as it were undermined itself. It is the very peak of consciously articulated one–sidedness, to which is contrasted the image of the mature generality of a great purpose. For the uncle is present in the background of this picture, like a mighty building in the grand old style devoted to the art of living, with proportions of noble simplicity, in the purest, finest marble. His appearance comes as something quite new in this sequence of educative examples. Writing confessions would surely not have been his favourite pastime; and since he was self-taught, he cannot have had any years of apprenticeship, like Wilhelm. But with the energy of maturity he shaped the natural world around him into a classical world which circled about his independent spirit as if he were its centre.

It is wholly in accord with the artistic spirit of the whole work that religion too should be presented here as an inborn pastime which creates its own room to develop and grows stage by stage into perfect art. And this is only the most striking example to show how the spirit of the work would like to treat everything thus, and see it treated so. The uncle's forbearance towards the aunt is the strongest symbolization of how incredibly tolerant those great men were, in whom the universal spirit of the work is most immediately manifest. The presentation of a nature constantly gazing upon itself as though into infinity was the finest proof an artist could give of the unfathomable depths of his range. He painted even external objects with the light and shade and colour with which this spirit, seeing everything in its own reflected light, must inevitably have mirrored and represented itself. But it could not be his intention to present this with any greater depth and fullness than would be right and necessary for the intention of the whole; still less his duty to resemble a definite reality. In general the characters in this novel resemble the portrait in the way they are presented, but they are more or less general and allegorical by nature. For that reason they provide an excellent collection of examples and inexhaustible material for moral and social enquiry. For this purpose, the conversations in *Wilhelm Meister* about the characters can be most interesting, although for the understanding of the work itself they can only have an episodic effect. But conversations they had to be, for this form removes any one-sidedness. For if one single figure were to discuss each of these persons solely from his individual point of view, and give his own moral testimonial to them, it would be the most fruitless way possible of regarding *Wilhelm Meister*. And in the end it would tell us no more than that the speaker's opinions on these matters were as stated.

With the fourth volume, the work comes of mature and marriageable age, as you might say. It has now become clear that the work is intended to embrace not only what we call theatre or poetry, but the great spectacle of humanity itself, and the art of all arts, the art of living. We also perceive that Wilhelm is the last person these years of apprenticeship would and could turn into a fit and able artist and man. The intention is not to educate this or that human being, but to represent Nature, Education itself in all the variety of these examples, and concentrated into single principles. The 'Confessions of a Beautiful Soul' made us believe that we were suddenly translated from the world of poetry into the world of morality; similarly we are presented with the sound results of a philosophy founded on the higher spirit and feeling, which aspires with equal ardour towards both the strict separation and the noble universality of all human arts and faculties. Wilhelm himself will probably be taken care of at the end, but he has become the butt of the novel, perhaps more than is either fair or mannerly. He is even educated by little Felix, who shames him into an awareness of how little he knows. After a few less than tragic attacks of fear, defiance and remorse, his independence vanishes from the society of the living. He resigns all claim to a will of his own. And now his years of apprenticeship are really completed, and Nathalie becomes the 'Supplement', as she puts it (Book 8, chapter 7), to the novel. She is the most beautiful embodiment of kindness and womanliness, and this makes her an agreeable contrast to the rather practical Therese. Nathalie makes her benevolent influence felt by her mere presence in society; Therese creates a similar world about herself, as the uncle did. They furnish examples and instances for a theory of womanly virtue which has an essential place in the grand theory of the art of life. The sociability of good manners and morals, and domestic activity, each embodied in a romantically beautiful figure, are the two archetypes, or the two halves of one archetype, which are put forward for this part of humankind.

How disappointed the reader of this novel might be by the end, for nothing comes of all these educational arrangements but an unassuming charm; and behind all those amazing chance occurrences, prophetic hints and mysterious appearances, there is nothing but the most lucid poetry; the final threads of the entire action are guided merely by the whim of a mind cultivated to perfection. And indeed, quite deliberately it seems, this controlling mind allows itself almost any liberty, with a particular fondness for the most far-fetched connections. Barbara's speeches possess the tremendous power, the dignity and the grandeur of ancient tragedy; of one of the most interesting figures in the entire book we learn nothing more circumstantial than his affair with a smallholder's daughter; immediately after the fall of Mariane, who interests us not as Mariane, but as the epitome of deserted, distracted womanhood, we are promptly entertained by the sight of Laertes counting out the ducats; and even the most important minor figures, such as the surgeon, are deliberately presented

as odd and eccentric. The true centre of this waywardness is the secret
society of pure intellect, which makes a mock of both Wilhelm and itself,
and finally turns out to be right and just and useful and economical. But
on the other hand, Chance itself is here a cultivated man, and since the
presentation gives and takes everything else on a large scale, why should
it not make use of traditional poetic licence on a large scale too? It goes
without saying that treatment of this kind and in this spirit will not spin
out all the threads slowly and long. Nevertheless, the end of the fourth
volume, coming as it does so swiftly and then unexpectedly so long drawn
out like Wilhelm's allegorical dream at the beginning, does remind us of
many of the most interesting figures and themes in the novel as a whole.
Among others, there are the Count and his blessing, a pregnant Philine
in front of the mirror as a warning and an example of comic nemesis; and
the boy thought to be dying who demands a piece of bread and butter, the
burlesque height of comic absurdity.

The first volume of this novel is distinguished by its modest charm; the
second by its brilliance and beauty; the third by the depth of its artistry
and purposefulness. And the true character of the fourth volume – and
of the entire work – lies in its grandeur. Even the articulation of the parts
is nobler, the light and colouring brighter and more intense; everything
is as well-made as it is captivating, and the surprises come thick and fast.
But not only are the dimensions enlarged; the characters too appear on a
grander scale. Lothario, the Abbé, and the Uncle each in his own way to a
certain extent represent the genius of the book itself; the others are only its
creatures. This is why they withdraw modestly into the background, like
an old master by his painting, although from this point of view they are
really the main characters. The Uncle has a great heart, the Abbé a great
intellect, and he moves over the whole work like the spirit of God. Since
he enjoys playing the role of fate, that is the part he has to take over in this
book. Lothario is a great man. There is something heavy and sprawling
about the Uncle, something meagre about the Abbé, but Lothario is entire.
His appearance is simple, his mind constantly moving forward; he has
no flaws, except the original flaw of all great men: he is also capable of
destruction. He is the dome rising to heaven, they are the mighty pillars on
which it rests. These architectonic natures encompass, bear and support
the whole. The others, presented so amply that we could take them to
be the most important, are only the minor pictures and decorations in
the temple. They are infinitely interesting to the mind and a constant

stimulus to discussion about whether we should or could respect them or love them, but to our hearts they are still only marionettes, allegorical playthings. This does not apply to Mignon, Sperata and Augustino, the holy family of natural poetry, who fill the whole work with music and romantic enchantment. It is as if their sorrow would tear our hearts in two, but this sorrow has the form, the tone of some lamenting dignity, and its voice swells upon waves of melody like the devotions of great choirs.

It is as if everything that had gone before were only a witty, interesting game, and now the novel were to become serious. The fourth volume is really the work itself; the previous parts are only preparation. This is where the curtain of the holy of holies is drawn back, and we suddenly find ourselves upon a height where everything is godlike and serene and pure, and in which Mignon's exequies appear as important and significant as the necessary coming of her end.

'Letter about the Novel' (1799)

[In this extract, Antonio, one of the main interlocutors of the *Dialogue*, speaks to Amalia. The context becomes clear below.]

I must retract, my dear lady, what I seemed to say yesterday in your defence, and say that you are almost completely wrong. You yourself admitted as much at the end of the argument, having become involved so deeply, because it is against female dignity to come down in tone, as you so aptly put it, from the innate element of gay jest and eternal poetry to the thorough or heavy-handed earnestness of the men. I agree with you against yourself that you are wrong. Indeed, I maintain that it is not enough to recognize the wrong; one must make amends for it and, as it seems to me, proper amends for having degraded yourself with your criticism would now be that you force yourself to the necessary patience and read this critical epistle about the subject of yesterday's conversation.

What I want to say I could have said yesterday; or rather I could not have because of my mood and the circumstances. What kind of opponent are you dealing with, Amalia? Certainly he understands quite well what it is all about, as it could not otherwise be with a clever virtuoso. He could have talked about it as well as anyone else, provided he could talk at all. This the gods have denied him; he is, as I have already said, a virtuoso and that's it; the Graces, unfortunately, stayed away. Since he was not quite certain what you meant in the deepest sense, and externally the right was so completely on your side, I made it my business to argue for you with all my might, to prevent the convivial balance from being destroyed. And besides, it is more natural for men, if it really has to be done, to give written instructions rather than oral which I feel violate the dignity of conversation.

Our conversation began when you asserted that Friedrich Richter's[1] novels are not novels but a colourful hodgepodge of sickly wit; that the meagre story is too badly presented to be considered a story; one simply had to guess it. If, however, one wanted to put it all together and just tell it, it would at best amount to a confession. The individuality of the man is much too visible, and such a personality at that.

I disregard this last point because it is only a question of individuality. I admit the colourful hodgepodge of sickly wit; but I shall defend it and emphatically maintain that such grotesques and confessions are the only romantic productions of our unromantic age.

On this occasion let me get something off my mind that I have been thinking about for a long time.

With astonishment and inner anger, I have often seen your servant carry piles of volumes in to you. How can you touch with your hands those dirty volumes? And how can you allow the confused and crude phrases to enter through your eye to the sanctuary of your soul? To yield your imagination for hours to people with whom, face to face, you would be ashamed to exchange even a few words? It serves no purpose but to kill time and to spoil your imagination. You have read almost all the bad books from Fielding to La Fontaine.[2] Ask yourself what you profited by it. Your memory scorns this vulgar stuff which has become a necessity through an unfortunate habit of your youth; what has to be acquired so laboriously, is entirely forgotten.

But then perhaps you remember that there was a time when you loved Sterne and enjoyed assuming his manner, partially to imitate, partially to ridicule him. I still have a few jocular letters of this kind from you which I will carefully save. Sterne's humour did make a definite impression on you. Even though it was no ideally perfect form, yet it was a form and a witty one which captivated your imagination. And an impression that is so definite that we make use of it and cultivate it in seriousness and jest is not lost. And what can have a more fundamental value than those things which in some way stimulate or nourish the play of our inner makeup.

---

[1] Friedrich Richter is Jean Paul.
[2] Jean de la Fontaine (1621–95), French author famous for his *Fables*.

You feel yourself that your delight in Sterne's humour was pure and of an entirely different nature than the suspense which can be often forced upon us by a thoroughly bad book, at the very time that we find it bad. Now ask yourself if your enjoyment was not related to what we often experience while viewing the witty paintings called arabesques. In case you cannot deny some sympathy with Sterne's sensibility, I am sending you a book, but I have to warn you about it so that you will be careful with regard to strangers, for it has the fortune or misfortune to be somewhat notorious. It is Diderot's[3] *The Fatalist*. I think you will like it and will find in it an abundance of wit, quite free of sentimental admixtures. It is designed with understanding and executed with a firm hand. Without exaggerating, I can call it a work of art. To be sure, it is not a work of high rank, but only an arabesque. But for that reason it has in my eyes no small merit; for I consider the arabesque a very definite and essential form or mode of expression of poetry.

This is how I think of the matter. Poetry is so deeply rooted in man that at times, even under the most unfavourable circumstances, it grows without cultivation. Just as we find in almost every nation songs and stories in circulation and, even though crude, some kind of plays in use, so in our unfantastic age, in the actual estate of prose, and I mean the so-called educated and cultured people, we will find a few individuals who, sensing in themselves a certain originality of the imagination, express it, even though they are still far removed from true art. The humour of a Swift, a Sterne is, I believe, natural poetry of the higher classes of our age.

I am far from putting them next to the great ones; but you will admit that whoever has a sense for these, for Diderot, has a better start on the way to learning to appreciate the divine wit, the imagination of an Ariosto, Cervantes, Shakespeare, than one who did not even rise to that point. We simply must not make exaggerated demands on the people of our times; what has grown in such a sickly environment naturally cannot be anything else but sickly. I consider this circumstance, however, rather an advantage, as long as the arabesque is not a work of art but a natural product, and therefore place Richter over Sterne because his imagination is far more sickly, therefore far more eccentric and fantastic. Just go ahead

---

[3] Denis Diderot (1713–84), author of *Jacques le Fataliste*, French philosopher, novelist and critic, whose novels and *Encyclopédie* brought him international repute.

and read Sterne again. It has been a long time since you read him and I think you will find him different. Then compare our German with him. He really does have more wit, at least for one who takes him wittily, for he could easily put himself in the wrong. And this excellence raises his sentimentality in appearance over the sphere of English sensibility.

There is another external reason why we should cultivate in ourselves this sense for the grotesque and remain in this mood. It is impossible in this age of books not to have to leaf through very many bad books, indeed, read them. Some of them always – one can depend on it – are fortunately of a silly kind, and thus it is really up to us to find them entertaining by looking at them as witty products of nature. Laputa is everywhere or nowhere, my dear friend; without an act of our freedom and imagination we are in the midst of it. When stupidity reaches a certain height, which we often see now when everything is more severely differentiated, stupidity equals foolishness even in the external appearance. And foolishness, you will admit, is the loveliest thing that man can imagine, and the actual and ultimate principle of all amusement. In such a mood I can often break out in almost incessant laughter over books which seem in no way meant to provoke it. And it is only fair that nature gave me this substitute, since I cannot laugh at all at many a thing nowadays called anecdote and satire. For me, on the other hand, learned journals, for example, become a farce, and the one called *Die Allgemeine Zeitung* I subscribe to very obstinately, as the Viennese keep their Jack Pudding.[4] Seen from my point of view, it is not only the most versatile of them all but in every way the most incomparable: having sunk from nullity to a certain triviality and from there to a kind of stupidity, now by way of stupidity it has finally fallen into that foolish silliness.

This in general is too learned a pleasure for you. If, however, you were to carry on what unfortunately you cannot stop doing, then I will no longer scorn your servant when he brings you the stacks of books from the loan library. Indeed, I offer myself as your porter for this purpose and promise to send you any number of the most beautiful comedies from all areas of literature.

---

[4] *Die Allgemeine Zeitung*, a contemporary newspaper published by Cotta. 'Jack Pudding' – a literal rendering of the German 'Hanswurst', the traditional name for the clown in comedy. The clown was formally banished from the German stage of Leipzig in the 1730s by Gottsched, in an attempt to raise the tone of the drama; the Viennese, on the other hand, obstinately clung to the Hanswurst right into the following century.

I now take up the thread again: for I am determined to spare you nothing but to follow up your statements step by step.

You also criticized Jean Paul, in an almost cavalier manner, for being sentimental.

May the gods grant it was in the sense in which I understand the word and as I feel I must understand it according to its origin and nature. For according to my point of view and my usage, that is romantic which presents a sentimental theme in a fantastic form.

Forget for a moment the usual notorious meaning of the sentimental, by which one understands almost everything which, in a shallow way, is maudlin and lachrymose and full of those familiar noble feelings whose awareness makes people without character feel so unspeakably happy and great.

Think rather of Petrarch or Tasso, whose poetry in comparison to the more fantastic Romanzo of Ariosto can well be called sentimental; I cannot recall offhand an example where the contrast is so clear and the superiority so decisive as here.

Tasso is more musical, and the picturesque in Ariosto is certainly not the worst. Painting is no longer as fantastic, if I can trust my feeling, as it was prior to its best period: in numerous masters of the Venetian school, also in Correggio, and perhaps not only in the arabesque of Raphael. Modern music, on the other hand, as far as the ruling power of man in it is concerned, has remained true on the whole to its character, so that I would dare to call it without reservation a sentimental art.

What then is this sentimental? It is that which appeals to us, where feeling prevails, and to be sure not a sensual but a spiritual feeling. The source and soul of all these emotions is love, and the spirit of love must hover everywhere invisibly visible in romantic poetry. This is what is meant by this definition. As Diderot so comically explains in *The Fatalist*, the gallant passions which one cannot escape in the works of the moderns from the epigram to tragedy are the least essential, or more, they are not even the external letter of that spirit; on occasion they are simply nothing or something very unlovely and loveless. No, it is the sacred breath which, in the tones of music, moves us. It cannot be grasped forcibly and comprehended mechanically, but it can be amiably lured by mortal beauty and veiled in it. The magic words of poetry can be infused with and inspired by its power. But in the poem in which it is not everywhere present nor could be everywhere, it certainly does not exist at all. It is an infinite being and by no means does it cling and attach its interest only to persons, events, situations and individual inclinations; for the true poet all this – no matter how intensely it embraces his soul – is only a hint at something higher, the infinite, a hieroglyph of the one eternal love and the sacred fullness of life of creative nature.

Only the imagination can grasp the mystery of this love and present it as a mystery; and this mysterious quality is the source of the fantastic in the form of all poetic representation. The imagination strives with all its might to express itself, but the divine can communicate and express itself only indirectly in the sphere of nature. Therefore, of that which originally was imagination there remains in the world of appearances only what we call wit.

One more thing resides in the meaning of the sentimental which concerns precisely the peculiar tendency of romantic poetry in contrast with ancient. No consideration is taken in it of the difference between appearance and truth, play and seriousness. Therein resides the great difference. Ancient poetry adheres throughout to mythology and avoids the specifically historical themes. Even ancient tragedy is play, and the poet who presented a true event of serious concern for the entire nation was punished. Romantic poetry, on the other hand, is based entirely on a historical foundation, far more than we know and believe. Any play you might see, any story you read – if it has a witty plot – you can be almost sure has a true story at its source, even if variously reshaped. Boccaccio is almost entirely true history, just as all the other sources are from which all Romantic ideas originate.

I have set up a definite characteristic of the contrast between the antique and the Romantic. Meanwhile, please do not immediately assume that the Romantic and the Modern are entirely identical for me. I consider them approximately as different as the paintings of Raphael and Correggio are from the etchings which are fashionable now. If you wish to realize the difference clearly, read just *Emilia Galotti*,[5] which is so extremely modern and yet not in the least Romantic, and then think of Shakespeare, in whom I would like to fix the actual centre, the core of the Romantic imagination. This is where I look for and find the Romantic – in the older moderns, in Shakespeare, Cervantes, in Italian poetry, in that age of knights, love and fairytales in which the thing itself and the word for it originated. This, up

---

[5] *Emilia Galotti*, a tragedy by Lessing.

to now, is the only thing which can be considered as a worthy contrast to the classical productions of antiquity; only these eternally fresh flowers of the imagination are worthy of adorning the images of the ancient gods. Certainly all that is best in modern poetry tends toward antiquity in spirit and even in kind, as if there were to be a return to it. Just as our literature began with the novel, so the Greek began with the epic and dissolved in it.

The difference is, however, that the Romantic is not so much a literary genre as an element of poetry which may be more or less dominant or recessive, but never entirely absent. It must be clear to you why, according to my views, I postulate that all poetry should be Romantic and why I detest the novel as far as it wants to be a separate genre.

Yesterday when the argument became most heated, you demanded a definition of the novel; you said it as if you already knew that you would not receive a satisfactory answer. I do not consider this problem insolvable. A novel is a romantic book. You will pass that off as a meaningless tautology. But I want to draw your attention to the fact that when one thinks of a book, one thinks of a work, an existing whole. There is then a very important contrast to drama, which is meant to be viewed; the novel, on the other hand, was from the oldest times for reading, and from this fact we can deduce almost all the differences in the manner of presentation of both forms. The drama should also be romantic, like all literature; but a novel is that only under certain limitations, an applied novel. On the contrary, the dramatic context of the story does not make the novel a whole, a work, if the whole composition is not related to a higher unity than that of the letter which it often does and should disregard; but it becomes a work through the bond of ideas, through a spiritual central point.

Having made this allowance, there is otherwise so little contrast between the drama and the novel that it is rather the drama, treated thoroughly and historically, as for instance by Shakespeare, which is the true foundation of the novel. You claimed, to be sure, that the novel is most closely related to the narrative, the epic genre. On the other hand, I want to admonish you that a song can as well be romantic as a story. Indeed, I can scarcely visualize a novel but as a mixture of storytelling, song and other forms. Cervantes always composed in this manner and even the otherwise so prosaic Boccaccio adorns his collections of stories by framing them with songs. If there is a novel in which this does not or cannot occur, it is only due to the individuality of the work and not the character of the genre; on the contrary, it is already an exception. But this is only by the way.

My actual objection is as follows. Nothing is more contrary to the epic style than when the influence of the subjective mood becomes in the least visible; not to speak of one's ability to give himself up to his humour and play with it, as it often happens in the most excellent novels.

Afterwards you forgot your thesis or gave it up, and decided to claim that all those divisions lead to nothing; that there is *one* poetry, and what counts is whether something is beautiful, and only a pedant would bother with titles and headings. You know what I think of the classifications in current use. And yet I realize that it is quite necessary for each virtuoso to limit himself to a well-defined goal. In my historical research I came upon several fundamental forms which are not further reducible. Thus, in the sphere of Romantic poetry, for instance, novellas and fairy tales seem to me, if I may say so, infinitely contrasted. I only wish that an artist would rejuvenate each of these genres by restoring them to their original character.

If such examples became known, then I would have the courage for a *theory of the novel* which would be a theory in the original sense of the word; a spiritual viewing of the subject with calm and serene feeling, as it is proper to view in solemn joy the meaningful play of divine images. Such a theory of the novel would have to be itself a novel which would reflect imaginatively every eternal tone of the imagination and would again confound the chaos of the world of the knights. The things of the past would live in it in new forms; Dante's sacred shadow would arise from the lower world, Laura would hover heavenly before us, Shakespeare would converse intimately with Cervantes, and there Sancho would jest with Don Quixote again.

These would be true arabesques which, together with confessions, as I claimed at the outset of my letter, are the only romantic products of nature in our age.

It will no longer appear strange to you that I include confessions here, when you have admitted that true story is the foundation of all romantic poetry; and you will – if you wish to reflect on it – easily remember and be convinced that what is best in the best of novels is nothing but a more or less veiled confession of the author, the profit of his experience, the quintessence of his originality.

Yet I appreciate all the so-called novels to which my idea of romantic form is altogether inapplicable, according to the amount of self-reflection and represented life they contain. And in this respect even the followers of Richardson, however much they are on the wrong track, are welcome. From a novel like *Cecilia Beverley*,[6] we at least learn how they lived there in London in boredom, since it was the fashion, and also how a British lady for all her daintiness finally tumbles to the ground and knocks herself bloody. The cursing, the squires and the like in Fielding are as if stolen from life, and *Wakefield*[7] grants us a deep insight into the world view of a country preacher; yes, this novel would perhaps – if Olivia regained her lost innocence at the end – be the best among all the English novels.

But how sparingly and only drop by drop even the small amount of the real in all those books is handed out. Which travelogue, which collection of letters, which autobiography would not be a better novel for one who reads them in the romantic sense than the best of these?

Confessions, especially, mainly by way of the naïve, develop of themselves into arabesques. But at best those novels rise to the arabesque only at the end, when the bankrupt merchants regain their money and credit, all the poor devils get to eat, the likeable scoundrels become honest, and the fallen women become virtuous again.

The *Confessions* of Rousseau is in my opinion a most excellent novel, *Héloïse* only a very mediocre one.

I will send you the autobiography of a famous man which, as far as I know, you are not acquainted with: Gibbon's *Memoirs*. It is an infinitely civilized and infinitely funny book. It will meet you half way, and really the comic novel contained in it is almost complete. You will see before your eyes, as clearly as you could wish, the Englishman, the gentleman, the virtuoso, the scholar, the bachelor, the well-bred dandy in all his affected absurdity, through the dignity of the historic periods. One can go through many bad books and many insignificant men before finding so much to laugh about gathered in one place.

After Antonio had read this epistle, Camilla began to praise the goodness and forbearance of women: that Amalia did not object to receiving such an amount of instruction and, that in general, women were a model of modesty since they remained patient in the face of men's seriousness and, what

---

[6] *Cecilia Beverley*, a novel by Fanny Burney, Mme d'Arblay (1752–1840).
[7] Oliver Goldsmith's sentimental novel, written in 1766.

is more, remained serious and even expressed a certain belief in the art of men. If by modesty you mean this belief, added Lothario, this premise of an excellence which we do not yet possess, but whose existence and dignity we begin to realize; then it would be the firmest basis of a noble education for excellent women. Camilla asked if pride and self-complacency had this function for men, since every one of them considered himself the more unique the more incapable he was of understanding what the other wanted. Antonio interrupted her by remarking that he hoped for the sake of mankind that that belief was not as necessary as Lothario thought, for it was a rare quality. Women, he said, as far as he could observe, think of art, antiquity, philosophy and such as of unfathomed traditions, prejudices with which men impress each other in order to pass the time.

'On Incomprehensibility' (1800)

Because of something either in them or in us, some subjects of human thought stimulate us to ever deeper thought, and the more we are stimulated and lose ourselves in these subjects, the more do they become a Single Subject, which, depending on whether we seek and find it in ourselves or outside of ourselves, we designate the Nature of Things or the Destiny of Man. Other subjects perhaps would never be able to attract our attention if we were to withdraw into holy seclusion and focus our minds exclusively on this subject of subjects, and if we did not have to be together with people and hence busy our minds with real and hypothetical human relationships which, when considered more carefully, always become more numerous and complex and thereby make us diverge into directions contrary to this single subject.

Of all things that have to do with communicating ideas, what could be more fascinating than the question of whether such communication is actually possible? And where could one find a better opportunity for carrying out a variety of experiments to test this possibility or impossibility than in either writing a journal like the *Athenaeum* oneself or else taking part in it as a reader?

Common sense which is so fond of navigating by the compass of etymologies – so long as they are very close by – probably did not have a difficult time in arriving at the conclusion that the basis of the incomprehensible is to be found in incomprehension. Now, it is a peculiarity of mine that I absolutely detest incomprehension, not only the incomprehension

of the uncomprehending but even more the incomprehension of the com-
prehending. For this reason, I made a resolution quite some time ago to
have a talk about this matter with my reader, and then create before his
eyes – in spite of him as it were – another new reader to my own liking:
yes, even to deduce him if need be. I meant it quite seriously and not
without some of my old bent for mysticism. I wanted for once to be really thorough and go through the whole series of my essays, admit their
frequent lack of success with complete frankness, and so gradually lead
the reader to being similarly frank and straightforward with himself. I
wanted to prove that all incomprehension is relative, and show how incomprehensible Garve,[1] for example, is to me. I wanted to demonstrate
that words often understand themselves better than do those who use
them, wanted to point out that there must be a connection of some secret
brotherhood among philosophical words that, like a host of spirits too
soon aroused, bring everything into confusion in their writings and exert
the invisible power of the World Spirit on even those who try to deny
it. I wanted to show that the purest and most genuine incomprehension
emanates precisely from science and the arts – which by their very nature
aim at comprehension and at making comprehensible – and from philosophy and philology; and so that the whole business shouldn't turn around
in too palpable a circle I had made a firm resolve really to be comprehensible, at least this time. I wanted to focus attention on what the greatest
thinkers of every age have divined (only very darkly, to be sure) until
Kant discovered the table of categories[2] and there was light in the spirit
of man: I mean by this a real language, so that we can stop rummaging
about for words and pay attention to the power and source of all activity.
The great frenzy of such a Cabala where one would be taught the way
the human spirit can transform itself and thereby perhaps at last bind its
transforming and ever transformed opponent in chains – I simply could
not portray a mystery like this as naïvely and nakedly as, when with the
thoughtlessness of youth, I made *Lucinde* reveal the nature of love in an
eternal hieroglyph. Consequently I had to think of some popular medium
to bond chemically the holy, delicate, fleeting, airy, fragrant, and, as it
were, imponderable thought. Otherwise, how badly might it have been

[1] Christian Garve (1742–98), German popularizer of philosophy.
[2] Immanuel Kant (1724–68); the 'table of categories' refers to section 3, chapter 1 of Book 1 of the
'Transcendental Analytic' under the first main section, 'Transcendental Doctrine of Elements'
(p. 113 of Kemp-Smith's translation).

misunderstood, since only through its well-considered employment was an end finally to be made of all understandable misunderstandings? At the same time, I noted with sincere pleasure the progress of our country – not to speak of our age! The same age in which we too have the honour to live; the age that, to wrap it all up in a word, deserves the humble but highly suggestive name of the Critical Age,[3] so that soon now everything is going to be criticized, except the age itself, and everything is going to become more and more critical, and artists can already begin to cherish the just hope that humanity will at last rise up in a mass and learn to read.

Only a very short while ago this thought of a real language occurred to me again and a glorious prospect opened up before my mind's eye. In the nineteenth century, so Girtanner[4] assures us, in the nineteenth century man will be able to make gold; and isn't it now more than mere conjecture that the nineteenth century is shortly going to begin? With laudable confidence and some huffing and puffing, the worthy man says: 'Every chemist, every artist will make gold; the kitchen utensils are going to be made of silver, of gold.' How gladly all artists will now resolve to go on being hungry for the slight, insignificant remainder of the eighteenth century, and in future no longer fulfil this sacred duty with an aggrieved heart; for they know that in part they themselves, and in part also (and all the more certainly) their descendants will shortly be able to make gold. That he should specify precisely kitchen utensils is due to the fact that what this ingenious prophet finds really beautiful and great in this catastrophe is that we won't be swallowing so much vile vinegary wine out of ordinary, ignoble, base metals like lead, copper, iron and suchlike.

I saw the whole thing from another point of view. I had often secretly admired the objectivity of gold, I might say even worshipped it. Among the Chinese, I thought, among the English, the Russians, in the island of Japan, among the natives of Fez and Morocco, even among the Cossacks, Cheremis, Bashkirs and Mulattoes, in short, wherever there is even a little enlightenment and education, silver and gold are comprehensible and through them everything else. When it comes to pass that every artist possesses these materials in sufficient quantity, then he will be allowed only to write his works in bas-relief, with gold letters on silver tablets.

---

[3] 'Critical Age', parodying the name given to Kant's Critical Philosophy.
[4] Christoph Girtanner (1760–1800), German physician whose publications included research into medicine and chemistry.

Who would want to reject so beautifully printed a book with the vulgar remark that it doesn't make any sense?

But all these things are merely chimeras or ideals: for Girtanner is dead and consequently for the moment so far removed from being able to make gold that one might extract with all possible artistry only so much iron out of him as might be necessary to immortalize his memory by way of a little medallion.

Furthermore, the complaints of incomprehensibility have been directed so exclusively and so frequently and variously at the *Athenaeum* that my deduction might start off most appropriately right at the spot where the shoe actually hurts.

A penetrating critic in the *Berliner Archiv der Zeit* has already been good enough to defend the *Athenaeum* against these attacks and in so doing has used as an example the notorious fragment about the three tendencies. What a marvellous idea! This is just the way one should attack the problem. I am going to follow the same procedure, and so as to let the reader perceive all the more readily that I really think the fragment good, I shall print it once more in these pages:

> The French Revolution, Fichte's philosophy, and Goethe's *Meister* are the greatest tendencies of the age. Whoever is offended by this juxtaposition, whoever cannot take any revolution seriously that isn't noisy and materialistic, hasn't yet achieved a lofty, broad perspective on the history of mankind. Even in our shabby histories of civilization, which usually resemble a collection of variants accompanied by a running commentary for which the original classical text has been lost; even there many a little book, almost unnoticed by the noisy rabble at the time, plays a greater role than anything they did.[5]

I wrote this fragment with the most honourable intentions and almost without any irony at all. The way that it has been misunderstood has caused me unspeakable surprise because I expected the misunderstanding to come from quite another quarter. That I consider art to be the heart of humanity and the French Revolution a marvellous allegory about the system of transcendental idealism is, to be sure, only one of my most extremely subjective opinions. But I have let this opinion be known so often and in so many different ways that I really might have hoped the

[5] This is Fragment 216 of the *Athenaeum* collection.

reader would have gotten used to it by now. All the rest is mere cryptology. Whoever can't find Goethe's whole spirit in *Wilhelm Meister* won't be able to find it anywhere else. Poetry and idealism are the focal points of German art and culture; everybody knows that. All the greatest truths of every sort are completely trivial and hence nothing is more important than to express them forever in a new way and, wherever possible, forever more paradoxically, so that we won't forget they still exist and that they can never be expressed in their entirety.

Up to this point I have not been ironical and by all rights I ought not to be misunderstood; and yet it has happened, to the extent in fact of having the well-known Jacobin, Magister Dyk of Leipzig,[6] even find democratic leanings in it.

To be sure, there is something else in the fragment that might in fact be misunderstood. This lies in the word *tendencies* and this is where the irony begins. For this word can be understood to mean that I consider the *Theory of Knowledge*, for example, to be merely a tendency, a temporary venture like Kant's *Critique of Pure Reason* which I myself might perhaps have a mind to continue (only rather better) and then bring to completion; or else that I wish to use the jargon that is most usual and appropriate to this kind of conception, to place myself on Fichte's shoulders, just as he placed himself on Reinhold's[7] shoulders, Reinhold on Kant's shoulders, Kant on Leibniz's and so on infinitely back to the prime shoulder. I was perfectly aware of this, but I thought I would like to try and see if anyone would accuse me of having had so bad an intention. No one seems to have noticed it. Why should I provide misunderstandings when no one wants to take them up? And so I now let irony go to the winds and declare point-blank that in the dialect of the *Fragments* the word means that everything now is only a tendency, that the age is the Age of Tendencies. As to whether or not I am of the opinion that all these tendencies are going to be corrected and resolved by me, or maybe by my brother or by Tieck, or by someone else from our group, or only some son of ours, or grandson, great-grandson, grandson twenty-seven times removed, or only at the last judgement, or never: that I leave to the wisdom of the reader, to whom this question really belongs.

---

[6] Johann Dyk (1750–1813), Leipzig bookseller and translator of French popular comedies.
[7] Karl Leonard Reinhold (1758–1823), German philosopher and follower of Kant. See *Critical Fragment* 66 on Reinhold.

Goethe and Fichte: that is still the easiest and fittest phrase for all the offence the *Athenaeum* has given, and for all the incomprehension it has provoked. Here too probably the best thing would be to aggravate it even more: when this vexation reaches its highest point, then it will burst and disappear, and then the process of understanding can set to work immediately. We haven't gotten far enough in giving offence; but what is not yet may still come to be. Yes, even those names are going to have to be named again – more than once. Just today my brother wrote a sonnet which I can't resist passing along to the reader because of the charming puns which he (the reader) loves almost more than he loves irony:

Go, admire idols[8] that are finely made
And leave us Goethe to be master, guide and friend:
When his spirit's rosy dawns do fade
Apollo's golden day no joy will send.

He lures no new spring green from barren trunks,
But cuts them down to give us warmth and fire.
And so the time will come when all the Muse's clunks
Will curse themselves to stone and stiffened mire.

Not to know Goethe means to be a Goth.
Fools are first blinded by every new, bright flame,
Then too much light kills them, like the moth.

Goethe, you who by the mercy of the gods came
To us, an angel from the stars: we are not loth
To call you godly in form, look, heart, and name.

A great part of the incomprehensibility of the *Athenaeum* is unquestionably due to the *irony* that to a greater or lesser extent is to be found everywhere in it. Here too I will begin with a text from the *Lyceum* [*Critical*] *Fragments*:

Socratic irony is the only involuntary and yet completely deliberate dissimulation. It is equally impossible to feign it or divulge it. To a person who hasn't got it, it will remain a riddle even after it is openly confessed. It is meant to deceive no one except those who consider it a deception and who either take pleasure in the delightful roguery of making fools of the whole world or else become angry when they

---

[8] 'Götzen' in the German, probably referring to Goethe's play *Götz von Berlichingen*.

get an inkling they themselves might be included. In this sort of irony, everything should be playful and serious, guilelessly open and deeply hidden. It originates in the union of *savoir vivre* and scientific spirit, in the conjunction of a perfectly instinctive and a perfectly conscious philosophy. It contains and arouses a feeling of indissoluble antagonism between the absolute and the relative, between the impossibility and the necessity of complete communication. It is the freest of all licenses, for by its means one transcends oneself; and yet it is also the most lawful, for it is absolutely necessary. It is a very good sign when the harmonious bores are at a loss about how they should react to this continuous self-parody, when they fluctuate endlessly between belief and disbelief until they get dizzy and take what is meant as a joke seriously and what is meant seriously as a joke. For Lessing irony is instinct; for Hemsterhuis it is classical study; for Hülsen it arises out of the philosophy of philosophy and surpasses these others by far.[9]

Another one of these fragments recommends itself even more by its brevity: Irony is the form of paradox. Paradox is everything which is simultaneously good and great.[10]

Won't every reader who is used to the *Athenaeum* fragments find all this simply trifling – yes, even trivial? And yet at the time it seemed incomprehensible to many people because of its relative novelty. For only since then has irony become daily fare, only since the dawn of the new century has such a quantity of great and small ironies of different sorts sprung up, so that I will soon be able to say, like Boufflers,[11] of the various species of the human heart:

> J'ai vu des coeurs de toutes formes,
> Grands, petits, minces, gros, médiocres, énormes.

In order to facilitate a survey of the whole system of irony, we would like to mention here a few of the choicest kinds. The first and most distinguished of all is coarse irony. It is to be found in the real nature of things and is one of the most widespread of substances; it is properly at home in the history of mankind. Next there is fine or delicate irony; then extra-fine. Scaramouche employs the last type when he seems to be talking amicably and earnestly with someone when really he is only waiting for the chance

---

[9] *Critical Fragment* 108.   [10] *Critical Fragment* 48.
[11] Stanislas, Chevalier de Boufflers (1738–1815), French poet.

to give him – while preserving the social amenities – a kick in the behind. This kind of irony is also to be found in poets, as well as straightforward irony, a type that flourishes most purely and originally in old gardens where wonderfully lovely grottoes lure the sensitive friend of nature into their cool wombs only to be-splash him plentifully from all sides with water and thereby wipe him clean of delicacy. Further, dramatic irony; that is, when an author has written three acts, then unexpectedly turns into another man and now has to write the last two acts. Double irony, when two lines of irony run parallel side-by-side without disturbing each other: one for the gallery, the other for the boxes, though a few little sparks may also manage to get behind the scenes. Finally, there is the irony of irony. Generally speaking, the most fundamental irony of irony probably is that even it becomes tiresome if we are always being confronted with it. But what we want this irony to mean in the first place is something that happens in more ways than one. For example, if one speaks of irony without using it, as I have just done; if one speaks of irony ironically without in the process being aware of having fallen into a far more noticeable irony; if one can't disentangle oneself from irony anymore, as seems to be happening in this essay on incomprehensibility; if irony turns into a mannerism and becomes, as it were, ironical about the author; if one has promised to be ironical for some useless book without first having checked one's supply and then having to produce it against one's will, like an actor full of aches and pains; and if irony runs wild and can't be controlled any longer.

What gods will rescue us from all these ironies? The only solution is to find an irony that might be able to swallow up all these big and little ironies and leave no trace of them at all. I must confess that at precisely this moment I feel that mine has a real urge to do just that. But even this would only be a short-term solution. I fear that if I understand correctly what destiny seems to be hinting at, then soon there will arise a new generation of little ironies: for truly the stars augur the fantastic. And even if it should happen that everything were to be peaceful for a long period of time, one still would not be able to put any faith in this seeming calm. Irony is something one simply cannot play games with. It can have incredibly long-lasting after effects. I have a suspicion that some of the most conscious artists of earlier times are still carrying on ironically, hundreds of years after their deaths, with their most faithful followers and admirers. Shakespeare has so infinitely many depths, subterfuges and intentions. Shouldn't he also, then, have had the intention of concealing insidious traps in his works to catch the cleverest artists of posterity, to deceive them and make them believe before they realize what they're doing that they are somewhat like Shakespeare themselves? Surely, he must be in this respect as in so many others much more full of intentions than people usually think.

I've already been forced to admit indirectly that the *Athenaeum* is incomprehensible, and because it happened in the heat of irony, I can hardly take it back without in the process doing violence to that irony.

But is incomprehensibility really something so unmitigatedly contemptible and evil? Methinks the salvation of families and nations rests upon it. If I am not wholly deceived, then states and systems, the most artificial products of man, are often so artificial that one simply can't admire the wisdom of their creator enough. Only an incredibly minute quantity of it suffices: as long as its truth and purity remain inviolate and no blasphemous rationality dares approach its sacred confines. Yes, even man's most precious possession, his own inner happiness, depends in the last analysis, as anybody can easily verify, on some such point of strength that must be left in the dark, but that nonetheless shores up and supports the whole burden and would crumble the moment one subjected it to rational analysis. Verily, it would fare badly with you if, as you demand, the whole world were ever to become wholly comprehensible in earnest. And isn't this entire, unending world constructed by the understanding out of incomprehensibility or chaos?

Another consolation for the acknowledged incomprehensibility of the *Athenaeum* lies in the very fact of this acknowledgement, because precisely this has taught us that the evil was a passing one. The new age reveals itself as a nimble and quick-footed one. The dawn has donned seven-league boots. For a long time now there has been lightning on the horizon of poetry; the whole thunderous power of the heavens had gathered together in a mighty cloud; at one moment, it thundered loudly, at another the cloud seemed to move away and discharge its lightning bolts in the distance, only to return again in an even more terrible aspect. But soon it won't be simply a matter of one thunderstorm, the whole sky will burn with a single flame, and then all your little lightning rods won't help you. Then the nineteenth century will indeed make a beginning of it and then the little riddle of the incomprehensibility of the *Athenaeum* will also be solved. What a catastrophe! Then there will be readers who will know how to read. In the nineteenth century everyone will be able to savour the fragments with much gratification and pleasure in the after-dinner hours and not need a nutcracker for even the hardest and most indigestible ones. In the nineteenth century every human being, every reader will find *Lucinde* innocent, *Genoveva*[12] Protestant, and A. W. Schlegel's didactic *Elegies*[13] almost too simple and transparent. And then too what I prophetically set forth as a maxim in the first fragments will hold true:

> A classical text must never be entirely comprehensible. But those who are cultivated and who cultivate themselves must always want to learn more from it.[14]

The great schism between understanding and not understanding will grow more and more widespread, intense and distinct. Much hidden incomprehension will still erupt. But understanding too will reveal its omnipotence: understanding that ennobles disposition into character, elevates talent into genius, purifies one's feelings and artistic perceptions. Understanding itself will be understood, and people will at last see and admit that everyone can achieve the highest degree and that up to now humanity has been neither malicious nor stupid but simply clumsy and new.

I break off at this point so as not to profane prematurely the worship of the highest divinity. But the great principles, the convictions on which this worship depends may be revealed without profanation; and I have attempted to express the essentials by adding on something myself, by way of what the Spanish call a gloss, to one of the profound and admirable verses of the poet. And now all I have left to wish for is that one of our excellent composers will find my lines worthy of being set to music. There is nothing more beautiful on earth than poetry and music mingled in sweet compliance for the greater ennoblement of mankind.[15]

> The rights of Jove are not for all.
> Don't go too far,
> Stay where you are,
> Look how you stand, or else you'll fall.

---

[12] *Genoveva*: Tieck's play, *Leben und Tod der Heiligen Genoveva* (1799), based on a medieval legend.
[13] A. W. Schlegel's didactic 'Elegies' in *Sämtliche Werke* (1846–7), I–II.
[14] *Critical Fragment* 20.
[15] Schlegel's gloss takes off from the last stanza of Goethe's poem 'Beherzigung'.

One man is very humble,
Another's cheeks swell up with pride;
This one's brains are all a jumble,
Another's still less well supplied.
I love a fool, his hair and hide,
I love it when he roars and rants,
And love his languid, flowery dance.
Forever will I now recall
What in the master's heart I spied:
The rights of Jove are not for all.

To keep the mighty pyre burning
A host of tender souls must be
Who fresh to every labour turning
Will make the heathen light to see.
Now let the din grow loud and louder:
Watch where you bite,
Watch what you write,
For when the fools with gun and powder
Crawl from their lairs, think who they are:
Don't go too far.

Some few have caught and kept the spark
That we have lighted.
The masses still are in the dark:
The dolts remain united.
Lack of understanding understood
Confers a lasting gloom
On all that issues from the womb.
The latest word brings lust for blood,
The wasps fly in from near and far:
Stay where you are.
Let them talk from now till doomsday
They never will understand.
Some are born to go astray,
Artists buried in the sand. –
There are sparrows every season
Exulting in their song:
Does this seem wrong?
Let them live by their own reason,
Just make sure you're big and tall:
Look how you stand, or else you'll fall.

Index

Cambridge texts in the history of philosophy

Titles published in the series thus far

Aristotle *Nicomachean Ethics* (edited by Roger Crisp)

Arnauld and Nicole *Logic or the Art of Thinking* (edited by Jill Vance Buroker)

Bacon *The New Organon* (edited by Lisa Jardine and Michael Silverthorne)

Boyle *A Free Enquiry into the Vulgarly Received Notion of Nature* (edited by Edward B. Davis and Michael Hunter)

Bruno *Cause, Principle and Unity* and *Essays on Magic* (edited by Richard Blackwell and Robert de Lucca with an introduction by Alfonso Ingegno)

Cavendish *Observations upon Experimental Philosophy* (edited by Eileen O'Neill)

Cicero *On Moral Ends* (edited by Julia Annas, translated by Raphael Woolf)

Clarke *A Demonstration of the Being and Attributes of God and Other Writings* (edited by Ezio Vailati)

Classic and Romantic German Aesthetics (edited by J. M. Bernstein)

Condillac *Essay on the Origin of Human Knowledge* (edited by Hans Aarsleff)

Conway *The Principles of the Most Ancient and Modern Philosophy* (edited by Allison P. Coudert and Taylor Corse)

Cudworth *A Treatise Concerning Eternal and Immutable Morality* with *A Treatise of Freewill* (edited by Sarah Hutton)

Descartes *Meditations on First Philosophy*, with selections from the *Objections and Replies* (edited by John Cottingham)

Descartes *The World and Other Writings* (edited by Stephen Gaukroger)

Fichte *Foundations of Natural Right* (edited by Frederick Neuhouser, translated by Michael Baur)

Hobbes and Bramhall on Liberty and Necessity (edited by Vere Chappell)

Humboldt *On Language* (edited by Michael Losonsky, translated by Peter Heath)

Kant *Critique of Practical Reason* (edited by Mary Gregor with an introduction by Andrews Reath)

Kant *Groundwork of the Metaphysics of Morals* (edited by Mary Gregor with an introduction by Christine M. Korsgaard)

Kant *The Metaphysics of Morals* (edited by Mary Gregor with an introduction by Roger Sullivan)

Kant *Prolegomena to any Future Metaphysics* (edited by Gary Hatfield)

Kant *Religion within the Boundaries of Mere Reason and Other Writings* (edited by Allen Wood and George di Giovanni with an introduction by Robert Merrihew Adams)

La Mettrie *Machine Man and Other Writings* (edited by Ann Thomson)

CPSIA information can be obtained at www.ICGtesting.com
Printed in the USA
LVOW122204200313

325267LV00002B/170/P